Impact of Artificial Intelligence on Organizational Transformation

Scrivener Publishing
100 Cummings Center, Suite 541J
Beverly, MA 01915-6106

Artificial Intelligence and Soft Computing for Industrial Transformation

Series Editor: Dr S. Balamurugan (sbnbala@gmail.com)

Scope: Artificial Intelligence and Soft Computing Techniques play an impeccable role in industrial transformation. The topics to be covered in this book series include Artificial Intelligence, Machine Learning, Deep Learning, Neural Networks, Fuzzy Logic, Genetic Algorithms, Particle Swarm Optimization, Evolutionary Algorithms, Nature Inspired Algorithms, Simulated Annealing, Metaheuristics, Cuckoo Search, Firefly Optimization, Bio-inspired Algorithms, Ant Colony Optimization, Heuristic Search Techniques, Reinforcement Learning, Inductive Learning, Statistical Learning, Supervised and Unsupervised Learning, Association Learning and Clustering, Reasoning, Support Vector Machine, Differential Evolution Algorithms, Expert Systems, Neuro Fuzzy Hybrid Systems, Genetic Neuro Hybrid Systems, Genetic Fuzzy Hybrid Systems and other Hybridized Soft Computing Techniques and their applications for Industrial Transformation. The book series is aimed to provide comprehensive handbooks and reference books for the benefit of scientists, research scholars, students and industry professional working towards next generation industrial transformation.

Publishers at Scrivener
Martin Scrivener (martin@scrivenerpublishing.com)
Phillip Carmical (pcarmical@scrivenerpublishing.com)

Impact of Artificial Intelligence on Organizational Transformation

Edited by

S. Balamurugan
Sonal Pathak
Anupriya Jain
Sachin Gupta
Sachin Sharma
and
Sonia Duggal

Scrivener
Publishing

WILEY

Wiley Global Headquarters
111 River Street, Hoboken, NJ 07030, USA

For details of our global editorial offices, customer services, and more information about Wiley products visit us at www.wiley.com.

Limit of Liability/Disclaimer of Warranty
While the publisher and authors have used their best efforts in preparing this work, they make no representations or warranties with respect to the accuracy or completeness of the contents of this work and specifically disclaim all warranties, including without limitation any implied warranties of merchantability or fitness for a particular purpose. No warranty may be created or extended by sales representatives, written sales materials, or promotional statements for this work. The fact that an organization, website, or product is referred to in this work as a citation and/or potential source of further information does not mean that the publisher and authors endorse the information or services the organization, website, or product may provide or recommendations it may make. This work is sold with the understanding that the publisher is not engaged in rendering professional services. The advice and strategies contained herein may not be suitable for your situation. You should consult with a specialist where appropriate. Neither the publisher nor authors shall be liable for any loss of profit or any other commercial damages, including but not limited to special, incidental, consequential, or other damages. Further, readers should be aware that websites listed in this work may have changed or disappeared between when this work was written and when it is read.

Library of Congress Cataloging-in-Publication Data

ISBN 978-1-119-71017-2

Cover image: Pixabay.Com
Cover design by Russell Richardson

Set in size of 11pt and Minion Pro by Manila Typesetting Company, Makati, Philippines

10 9 8 7 6 5 4 3 2 1

Contents

Foreword

It gives me immense pleasure to write the foreword to this book. In choosing the impact of artificial intelligence on organizational transformation as their subject, the editors have selected a subject that has great contemporary relevance. Artificial intelligence is here to stay and will continue to flourish. It has come a long way since it was conceived a few decades back. Previously, its application was confined to automation in manufacturing only, but with the passage of time has expanded to cover almost every sphere of human activity.

Organizational transformation does not happen overnight. One has to steadily and meticulously strive and work hard to achieve it. Artificial intelligence is definitely contributing in a big way towards the organizational transformation of both the manufacturing and service sectors. Against this backdrop, I am optimistic that the book will make for interesting reading. I extend my best wishes to the entire editorial team for this sterling academic endeavor.

Prof. (Dr.) Karunesh Saxena
Vice Chancellor
Sangam University Bhilwara, Rajasthan, India
October 2021

Preface

The idea of a book on the impact of artificial intelligence (AI) on organizational transformation occurred to us almost simultaneously. Even though we realized putting together an edited volume on such an ever-evolving topic would not be an easy task, the capacity that AI has to significantly transform organizations is too important to ignore. Therefore, we started deliberating as to how to include scholarly research articles written by eminent academicians on the topic. The outcome of our deliberations can be seen in the quality of the chapters included in this book, which highlight the applications and interlinkages of artificial intelligence with HR function, and its application in the banking and finance sector, along with many other diverse sectors such as energy and sports. One of the chapters even discusses how AI is revolutionizing India byte by byte.

All of us are highly grateful to the authors for taking time to contribute to this book despite the tense situation caused by the lockdown due to the COVID-19 pandemic.

The Editors
October 2021

1

Artificial Intelligence Disruption on the Brink of Revolutionizing HR and Marketing Functions

Akansha Mer[1]* and Amarpreet Singh Virdi[2]†

¹Department of Commerce and Management, Banasthali Vidyapith, Rajasthan, India
²Department of Management Studies, Kumaun University, Bhimtal Campus, Uttarakhand, India

Abstract

Artificial Intelligence (AI) disruption is rapidly revolutionizing the various functions of HR, marketing, finance, etc. Before the advent of AI, several biases occurred on part of humans in terms of hiring, promotion, performance appraisal, compensation, etc. Similarly, in marketing, the customers' needs and wants are of immense importance for marketers. Traditional marketing generally used feedback from consumers and also the managers had to rely on the market research to interpret the market trends, customers' needs, tastes, and preferences. But now AI disruption has addressed the HR issues and made substantial improvements in the prediction of precise trends, customer purchase intention, and consumer behavior.

Thus, the paper attempts to unravel how AI is revolutionizing the various functions of HR and marketing. The study elucidates that AI has revolutionized the functions of HR by removing biases in recruitment and performance appraisal and is assisting the organizations in employee engagement and retention. It has made the orientation and onboarding process easy. AI has widely reduced the cost of the organizations with respect to hiring, training, etc. Similarly, in the field of marketing, the study also elucidates that with the advent of technological advancement during recent times (AI), a wealth of information about the consumers, their

*Corresponding author: akanshamer3@gmail.com
†Corresponding author: virdi_amar@rediffmail.com

S. Balamurugan, Sonal Pathak, Anupriya Jain, Sachin Gupta, Sachin Sharma, Sonia Duggal (eds.)
Impact of Artificial Intelligence on Organizational Transformation, (1–20) © 2022 Scrivener Publishing LLC

consumption patterns, and purchase behavior can be traced to a large extent. AI has opened an opportunity for marketers to enhance the effectiveness of the marketing campaigns which can be measured as a return on investment (ROI). AI is enhancing the marketing strategies for businesses. AI disruption is helping in quick and effective decisions. AI is optimizing the advertising and customer segmentation and is also helping companies with better product design to the delight of the customers.

Thus, the managers should look to AI as a tool for empowering and supporting their employees rather than replacing them. Since AI automates various process-oriented and administrative tasks, therefore managers should adopt AI so that they may shift their focus from administrative tasks to cross-functional reasoning tasks. Such a human-machine association will generate various new jobs and will pave way for innovation.

Keywords: Artificial intelligence, disruption, HR, marketing, chatbots, algorithms, machine learning

1.1   Introduction

Artificial Intelligence (AI) that was coined by McCarthy [3] is a branch of computer science encompassing areas such as machine learning (ML) and cognitive computing. AI can also be divided into the categories as strong AI, weak AI, and super intelligent AI. The strong AI or Artificial General Intelligence (AGI) refers to a system with logic, sensory and cognitive abilities that rely on the association of data to produce human brain-like decisions. The weak AI or Artificial Narrow Intelligence (ANI) is the system that focuses on a single task and work in a particular domain [34]. Super intelligent AI is a futuristic system that shall surpass the cognitive abilities and intelligence of human beings.

The study by Carbonell *et al.* has mentioned that ML is a basic requirement for the generation and development of AI [8]. The prominent ML tools are as follows:

  a) Neural Network or Artificial Neural Network (ANN): It comprises of many interconnected nodes (like neurons in the brain) and works on the rules that define what kind of output to be generated based on input.
  b) Support Vector Machine (SVM): It is used for predicting time series predictions.
  c) Natural Language Processing (NLP): It consists of a) Natural Language Understanding (NLU) and b) Natural Language

Generation (NLG). NLU converts the natural language into computer language; therefore, it is termed as Speech Recognition or speech to text conversion. It uses Hidden Markov Model (HMM).

According to Merriam Webster.com, "Artificial Intelligence is a branch of computer science dealing with the simulation of intelligent behavior in computers."

According to John McCarthy, AI is "the science and engineering of making intelligent machines, especially intelligent computer programs" [22]. AI simulates intelligent behavior in computers. In ML, the machine learns on its own based on patterns and training data sets. It enables machines to process like the human brain.

It is revolutionizing various industries. The study conducted by Xaxis [35] concluded that AI will be the next industrial revolution. The economic impact of AI is estimated to reach 13 trillion dollars by 2030 [7].

A survey conducted by Deloitte on 250 executives on the benefits endowed by AI revealed that 51% of the executives were of the view that AI enhances the features, functions, and performance of the product, 36% of the employees were of the view that AI optimizes internal business operations, 36% of employees indicated that AI frees up the workforce to be more creative by automating tasks, 35% indicated that AI assists in making better decisions, 32% of the employees revealed that AI helps in creating new products, 30% of employees suggested that AI helps in optimizing external processes like marketing and sales, 25% of employees were of the view that AI helps in pursuing new markets, 25% revealed that AI helps in capturing and applying scarce knowledge where needed, whereas only 22% of employees indicated that AI reduced headcount through automation [9]. Figure 1.1 depicts the benefits endowed by AI on organizations. Thus, it can be seen that no aspect of management has been left untouched by AI. AI is gaining prominence in various managerial functions like HR, finance, and marketing. AI brings with it personalized experience.

A study carried by Oracle and human resources advisory and research firm, Future Workplace revealed that 80% of Asia Pacific (APAC) countries surveyed indicated that 50% of their employees are currently availing AI in some or the other form in their organization. The results also indicate that 77% of employees in China and 78% of employees in India have adopted AI which is more than double the 32% in France and 38% in the United Kingdom [23].

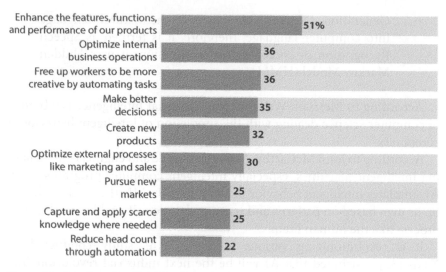

Figure 1.1 Benefits of Artificial Intelligence. Source: Deloitte 2017.

1.2 Research Methodology

The study is exploratory in nature. The researchers have explored various studies on the role of AI in the various functions of HR and marketing.

1.2.1 Research Objectives

1. To explore how AI disruption is revolutionizing HR functions.
2. To explore how AI disruption is revolutionizing marketing functions.

1.2.2 Data Collection

The study is based on secondary data, sourced from various databases like Ebsco, Google Scholar, and ProQuest.

1.3 Artificial Intelligence in HRM

Research suggests that biasness creeps in when humans are assigned the task of hiring, promotion, performance appraisal, compensation, etc.

For instance, racial discrimination occurs when humans are assigned the task of hiring [29]. Another study conducted by Mckinsey and LeanIn revealed that entry-level women faced discrimination during the promotion as against their male counterparts [20]. Employees also face discrimination during performance appraisal on grounds of their age [33]. Research also suggests that women face discrimination while receiving compensation and promotion [18]. AI helps in overcoming such biasness. AI is used in all the aspects of HRM like recruitment, engaging the applicants and the employees, orientation, onboarding, performance evaluation, training, compensation, and employee retention. These aspects are discussed below in detail.

1.3.1 Recruitment

As against the traditional recruitment process, recruiters are now using chatbots that are powered by AI (ML) [10]. Chatbots use natural language processing to facilitate real-time interaction with the applicants through skype, email, social media, etc. They are useful in gathering a pool of information from the applicants regarding their competencies, qualification, and experience and can even generate their profile, based on the information gathered. They are programmed in such a way that they can comprehend written and oral communication and can address routine queries of the applicants appropriately. Furthermore, these chatbots are efficient enough to even prescreen potential job applicants by matching their competencies, traits, experience, culture fit, etc., with the open positions and can schedule an interview for the applicants. With the advent of AI in recruitment, the hiring process has become faster as it can auto-screen thousands of resumes in a minute which are free from biases. Examples of various chatbots used by organizations are a) IBM Watson Recruitment, b) Jobs Intelligence Maestro of DBS Bank, which has successfully decreased the time involved in screening per candidate from 32 minutes to 8 minutes [26], and c) Mya, which provides 24/7 support.

1.3.2 Engaging the Applicants and Employees

Earlier, when AI was not introduced in HR, engaging the employees was time-consuming. Now, various software backed by AI like chatbots and Applicant Tracking System can engage the applicants by addressing their routine queries on a real-time basis and update them regarding their current status. The striking feature of these chatbots is that they become robust and smarter with every interaction. Example of engaging the applicants:

IBM uses Watson Candidate Assistant (WCA) to engage its applicants in personalized conversation and also suggests the job positions that resonate with their competencies and experiences in which they can excel. Such engagement is a win-win situation for both the applicants and the organization. The applicants feel delighted and the organizations also become free from committing costly hiring mistakes.

Example of engaging the employees: AI-backed Amber chatbot, which is used by Oyo, Marico Ltd., and many more, is instrumental in identifying disengaged workforce in the organization. Thus, the organizations can take measures to engage the disengaged workforce.

1.3.3 Orientation and Onboarding

Organizations organize orientation programs for acquainting the new joiners regarding the organizational culture, rules and regulations, employee benefits, etc. According to Miller, nearly 90% of the new joiners tend to miss some or the other details during the orientation program [27]. The organizations can overcome this problem by using chatbots that can answer all the queries of new joiners which they might miss during the orientation program.

The AI-backed programs are enhancing onboarding programs as well. With the help of chatbots, the newly joined employees can get all the information regarding whom to report, their team members, what work is assigned to them, etc. Example: Amber is a chatbot that is used by Oyo, Marico Ltd., and many more. Mr. Amit Prakash, Chief HR Officer of Marico Ltd., emphasized the importance of Amber in the onboarding process in Marico Ltd. He said, "When employees join us at different locations, the supervision for onboarding employees has to be better. On the day of joining, the new members are taken out for lunch with the supervisor. For me to get into that detail is difficult. Amber helps to manage this information with little effort" [1].

1.3.4 Performance Appraisal

Performance appraisal deals with gathering, analyzing, and assigning numerical values and grades to the performance of the employees. The numerical values and scores assigned by human beings for evaluating the performance may not be precise. To overcome this issue, the fuzzy logic approach is used for evaluating the performance of the employees. A study which employed hierarchical fuzzy influence approach, indicated that reasoning based on fuzzy models are more accurate in evaluating the performance of employees [4]. Studies suggest that performance appraisal based on fuzzy logic helps in drawing definite results from ambiguous information [25].

Furthermore, various chatbots are used in the process of performance appraisal. Example: Engazify is used for performance appraisal as it gives real-time feedback and appreciation to its workforce [2]. Besides, data analytics and big data are also used to evaluate the performance of the employees, wherein the grades and the ratings are assigned on a scientific basis. The process begins by feeding the integrated performance metrics into the analytics software to determine the ranks of the employees. Such automated performance appraisal is free from biases that may occur by human beings while assigning grades or while ranking and brings transparency in the appraisal system.

1.3.5   Training

In this era of disruptions, the concept of one size fits all (same course content) for the learners cannot be applicable. Through AI, the learning material can be personalized in accordance with the learner's requirements (skill gaps). With the help of AI, suitable content can be recommended to the learners, based on their past behavior. Besides, several content creation algorithms can be used to auto-generate content. AI gives the flexibility to the employees to learn at their own pace. Studies indicate that the robot training instructor can track the daily learning status of the learners and can even compute the average value of the learners' attention [17]. Based on the learning objectives entered by the employees, the robot training instructor can automatically complete the course. Thus, AI facilitates personalized learning.

Furthermore, a qualitative study conducted by IBM Smarter Workforce Institute on senior HR executives of IBM revealed that their organization is enhancing skills inference technology internally. Consequently, employees of IBM have access to their real-time skill insights through an expertise management interface, which is more accurate. AI skill inference technology also helps IBM to analyze the skills of its employees relative to business needs and can also compare the skill profile of its employees with its competitors. This helps IBM to bridge the skill gaps of its employees [15]. Another example of an AI system as used in the military is intelligent tutoring systems [21, 30].

1.3.6   Compensation

Some of the prominent organizations like Google and Tesla use techniques like big data, predictive analytics, and ML techniques to monitor the talent of their employees, and thus, based on their performance, they remunerate their employees. These companies are following the recommendations of the AI-backed software and thus ensure that their employees are not under or overpaid. Example: IBM uses an AI-powered decision support system which helps in the compensation planning of front-line employees and thereby overcomes the issue of underweighting or overweighting the critical data points [15].

1.3.7 Employee Retention

AI helps in employee retention by satisfying the employees through ensuring unbiased performance appraisal. Algorithms can predict as to which employee is likely to leave the organization. AI software can predict the likelihood of employee turnover by tracking their browsing history and emails. Organizations are also using AI-based mood meters which help in tracking the sentiments of their employees and assist the organization in identifying the causes of employee turnover. The organizations are also using predictive statistical models that help in forecasting the employees' intention to quit the organization and thus help in preventing employee turnover [13].

1.4   Artificial Intelligence in Marketing

The marketing concept comprises of 4Ps, namely, Product, Price, Place, and Promotion. This concept is all about making customer the king, i.e., satisfying the needs, wants, and desires of the customers. The customer satisfaction, over the period, graduated to customer delight. The organizations can delight the customers only when the tastes, preferences, and behavioral aspects regarding their purchase can be traced or known. With the advent of technological advancement during recent times (AI), a wealth of information about the consumers, their consumption patterns, and purchase behavior can be traced to a large extent. The database can be created for the information collected about consumers. The pattern analysis using data mining techniques can reveal homogeneity and heterogeneity. This shall reveal the basis for segmenting the markets into a precise group of consumers/customers. The latest technological innovations especially AI have opened an opportunity for the marketers to enhance the effectiveness of marketing campaigns which can be measured as a return on investment (ROI). The application of AI in marketing and sales has the highest potential value, with estimates up to 2.6 trillion dollars [7]. Earlier marketing was a one-way communication or push the product to inform, persuade, and remind with catchy slogans/jingles. With the advent of AI, consumers can buy/sell anything from any part of the planet anytime. The studies show that "consumers today search much less on brand names than they did 10 years ago. If someone wants to buy shoes on Amazon, they are five to six times more likely to search by category name than by brand name and follow the recommendations suggested by the Amazon algorithms" [32]. The industries where the customers are large in numbers and need to interact frequently with customers have a high potential for using AI. Since the interaction between the two generates a huge amount of data [10], customers perceive AI at a very high level [12]. Potential message from an AI application is convincing when it pertains to the usage of the product or service, instead of why that product or service should be used [19].

AI algorithms can perform pre-defined tasks, for example, automated email replies, blocking of debit/credit cards, etc., and also these AI algorithms can analyze the customer data which can be in various forms, *viz.*, text, voice, and facial expression.

Marketing has become a two-way communication which means consumer searches/transacts with the seller. Some of the ways in which AI can be used for marketing are as follows.

1.4.1   Creation of Customer Profiles/Market Segmentation

The customers' needs and wants are of immense importance for marketers. Traditional marketing generally used the feedback from consumers' and also the marketers had to rely on the data provided by the market research firms. With the advent of AI and more people inclined to use the digital platform to search for their requirements, the marketers can now precisely segregate the customers for their product/service requirements. The technological advancement has let the marketers collect the customer's data such as customer's name, mobile, email, gender, search pattern, and so on. With this data, marketers can create customer profiles. Therefore, the customers can be segmented and targeted for personalized promotions. It can also help in retaining the customers. Studies indicate that VPSAs (Virtual Personal Shopping Assistants) can predict and optimize the tastes and needs of customers [11]. Lucy: it is created by Equals3 and is named after the granddaughter of IBM's founder Thomas Watson. It can analyze structured and unstructured data. It helps in segmentation, planning, and

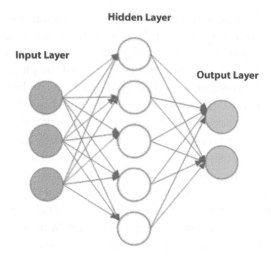

Figure 1.2 ANN for market segmentation.

interaction with humans in an easy way. SOFMs (self-organizing feature maps) are used for market segmentation, i.e., portioning of a large market into small homogeneous groups of consumers.

The market segmentation for an organization provides translate the opportunity for not only optimally utilizing the resources but also, at the same time, ensuring high profitability. But it remains a big challenge to translate the market's needs in a precise manner. The ANN provides the solution with several methods developed over a period of time. The SOM (self-organized feature maps), GKA (genetic K-means algorithm), and ART (adaptive resonance theory) are some of the methods used for clustering/segmentation.

An ANN can be constructed for segmenting the market, suppose the parameters for the customer are socio-economic factors, demographic factors, and so on (input layer). The organization aims to segment the market to two segments (output layer). The hidden layer contains the algorithms that result in an outcome. The same can be demonstrated as in Figure 1.2 [39].

1.4.2   Cognizance of Consumers Purchase Behavior/Intention

AI is helpful in comprehending the behavioral aspects of the customers. AI not only helps in understanding customer loyalty but also customer engagement. AI precisely predicts the CLV, i.e., customer lifetime value. This enables the organizations to maintain a better and attractive customer relationship with high valued customers. AI and ML can provide accurate recommendations to organizations on product features and display by pattern analysis of the behaviors of customers purchasing. This helps to improve the customer's experience. AI is now able to analyze and understand human emotions such as delight, sadness, and anger. Ampsy uses hyper-local geo wall/fence to store publically shared content. This content is analyzed to understand consumer's intention toward purchase. For example, Alibaba, the world's largest e-commerce provider company uses AI to predict the pattern of customer purchase. Also, Alibaba is a solution provider to traffic maintenance with the help of AI [24].

1.4.3   Pricing

AI can help increase the sales of an organization by precisely the dynamic pricing. AI recommends the prices for the product and service by analyzing the demand/supply data. An app or website bot which keeps track of the history of sites and cookies can be used for the predictive analysis, thereby enabling the customer to enjoy real-time pricing. For example, during the lean season, the hotel room's occupancy reduces, and AI can recommend dynamic pricing/real-time competitive pricing. AI helps to provide dynamic pricing by analyzing the historical transactions, competitor's pricing, customer's preview/reaction on social platforms, etc. There are several AI platforms, for example, Wise Athena recommends pricing and advertising decisions. Navetti Price Point uses ML to recommend pricing. Perfect Price empowered by AI provides dynamic pricing for auto rentals [5].

1.4.4   Content/Product/Service Recommendations/ Search Optimization

According to lexico.com, content marketing is "a type of marketing that involves the creation and sharing of online material (such as videos, blogs, and social media posts) that does not explicitly promote a brand but is intended to stimulate interest in its products or services." In recent times, the marketers are using AI tools to write content/recommendations to the target audience based on their likes and dislikes. Some of the AI tools are Wordsmith, WordAi, Rocco, etc.; these tools help the marketers by creating the content which is known as Content Curation and Content Automation. The rationale of these tools is to provide organized and customized content to the target audience for better customer engagement. The recommender systems developed with AI can enrich the shopping experience of customers. For example, personalized recommendations suggested by Netflix and Spotify.

1.4.5   Sales Prediction Based on Consumer's Demographics

Based on the analysis of data, AI can predict and prioritize sales leads. AI can estimate the probability of a purchase by a customer. AI and ML analyze the data from the emails and phone calls that are with the company. This analysis can predict the present and future sales trends. Pointillist's Behavioral Marketing Platform discovers and analyzes the path and patterns of behavior of the consumer to predict sales. Dominos uses AI tool called Dom Pizza Tracker. According to its website, in-store cameras "use advanced machine learning, artificial intelligence, and sensor technology to identify pizza type, even topping distribution and correct toppings".

1.4.6   Virtual Assistants/Real-Time Conversations

AIs, known as chatbots like Alexa, Google Assistant, and Siri, are voice recognition technology that can understand and recognize speech or spoken words and execute the command from the internet through an AI drive assistant. For example, Indian Railways use chatbots as ask Deesha, etc. These chatbots simulate the natural language simulation and usually are prepared to answer the FAQs. This can reduce human intervention and reduce response time. Google is incorporating and innovating the use of AI and ML. Google's division Waymo is working on AI for self-driving technology for automobiles. While Google Duplex has introduced the voice interface with the help of AI to automate phone calls. Amazon has introduced the AI-based voice assistant, Alexa. Also, Amazon is using AI to beforehand predict the products required by the customers. Microsoft is using AI in developing intelligent capabilities in its products and services, such as Cortana, Skype, and Bing [24].

1.4.7   Visual Searching

ML and AI provide the platform to the customers to search for the product with the help of a picture. It is far advanced from text-based searches. Pinterest CEO, Ben Silbermann predicts, "The future of search will be about pictures rather than keywords" [38]. For example, ZALORA online fashion retailer has a catalog of 3,000+ brands on their website. By implementing Search by Image (Visual Searching) and Visually Similar Product Recommendations, Zalora enabled a better search experience for its customers. Facebook uses Deep Text, an AI-based application to interpret the content of the posts, which can be in any language. Another application DeepFace is used to recognize the face of a person in a photo. Apple uses AI and ML in its products, for example, iPhone has the feature of face recognition, voice assistant Siri, etc.

1.4.8   CRM

AI is changing the scenario toward the customer relationship with the organizations. AI helps decode and provide insights into the customer behavior, patterns of purchase by analyzing the emails, telephonic conversations, chatbots, etc. Cogito provides the analysis of telephonic conversations and provides the customer's emotional state. AI is also capable of detecting anomalies and duplicacy in CRM data. Amplero, a platform based on ML, works for the customer relationship management (CRM) domain. Salesforce Einstein is the AI platform for CRM, which provides solutions for the prediction of customer behavior and purchase patterns. It is used for data mining, deep learning, and NLP.

1.5   Discussion and Findings

The study attempted to unravel how AI disruption is revolutionizing HR and marketing. Our contribution is an exploration of various studies on the role of AI in the various functions of HR and marketing. The study revealed that AI in the field of HR has facilitated quality hiring [17, 30], personalized training [17, 31], ensured transparency in compensation management [17], and performance management [14, 17]. AI is also helping in removing biasness in recruitment and performance appraisal and is assisting the organizations in employee retention. Furthermore, both the candidates and the employees feel engaged. Besides, AI has widely reduced the cost of the organizations with respect to hiring, orientation, onboarding, training, etc.

As regards marketing, AI has transformed the way marketing was done traditionally. AI has facilitated the marketers to satiate the ever-demanding customers and steep rise in competition. These findings suggest that substantial improvement in the prediction of precise trends, customer purchase intention, and consumer behavior has become possible with AI and ML and therefore has improved the ROI for the organizations. The AI has reduced the time and the efforts, which were earlier used to collect the data and analyze the data and further processing [16]. From the consumer's point of view, AI has offered several advantages as convenient shopping and after-sales service. Further, AI has improved the marketing mix as the development of the new product, automatic recommendations, dynamic pricing, and availability of product/service at any place and at any time (mostly, 24/7), creation of personalized advertisement communication and other personalized promotional offers. The results of this study have provided strong evidence in support of AI and ML can enhance the marketing results. The study "Lessons of 21st-Century Brands Modern Brands & AI Report (17 pp., PDF, free, opt-in)" concluded, "AI enables marketers to increase sales (52%), increase in customer retention (51%), and succeed at new product launches (49%). AI is making solid contributions to improving lead quality, persona development, segmentation, pricing, and service." Internet marketers can now focus on heavy internet users for the products and services offered on e-commerce sites. The AI and ML should be used in marketing analytics to achieve better ROI [37].

1.6   Implication for Managers

AI is influencing various functions of management. The AI can help managers especially in human resource management and marketing management. Earlier, the HR managers had to spend a lot of time in screening various candidates manually. Similarly, biasness prevailed in recruitment, performance appraisal process, etc. Now, the managers can use AI to overcome issues of biasness. With the advent of AI in HR, the recruitment and hiring process has become faster as AI can auto screen thousands of resumes in a minute which are free from biasness. Besides, the managers can also use AI for engaging its workforce and employee retention. The orientation and onboarding processes have become easy.

In marketing management, earlier, the managers had to rely on the market research, data mining to interpret the market trends, customer's needs, taste, and preferences. The AI has made possible the above interpretations in the real-time scenario. As it can precisely estimate the probability of a customer making a purchase and also can predict the customer value [36]. The benefits of using AI and ML in marketing is improved efficiency and optimal utilization of marketing efforts and resources, time-saving, creation of better customer profiles, and transforming customer satisfaction into customer delight [28].

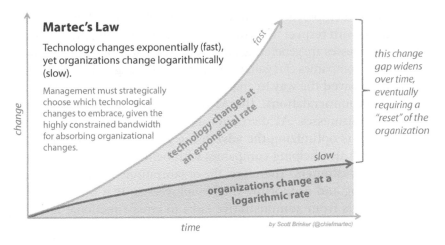

Figure 1.3 Martec's Law.

AI offers quality and quick decision-making to the managers. The managers should look to AI as a tool for empowering and supporting them rather than replacing them. Thus, the managers should adopt AI in various aspects of management like HR, marketing, finance, etc. Since AI automates various process-oriented task administration tasks, therefore managers should adopt AI so that they may shift their focus from administrative tasks to cross-functional reasoning tasks. Such a human-machine association will generate various new jobs and will pave way for innovation.

But technology is changing at a fast pace. Since the concept of AI implementation is a capital-intensive activity and continuous up-gradation is required. According to Martec's Law, "technology changes exponentially, organizations change logarithmically" [6], as depicted in Figure 1.3. This becomes a challenge for organizations from developing countries. Thus, managers in developing countries should try to keep pace with technological advances.

1.7   Conclusion

Thus, it can be concluded that AI disruption is rapidly revolutionizing the various functions of HR, marketing, finance, etc. AI in the field of HR has facilitated quality hiring and ensured transparency in compensation management and performance management. AI is also helping in removing biasness in recruitment and performance appraisal and is assisting the organizations in employee retention. AI has widely reduced the cost of the organizations with respect to hiring, training, and engaging the employees.

Today, businesses are generating huge data, especially from the e-commerce segment. The companies can gain a competitive advantage with this data. AI and ML have paved the way to analyze, scrutinize, and draw precise inferences and recommendations. The AI is enhancing the marketing strategies for the businesses. AI disruption is helping in quick and effective decisions. ML is optimizing the advertising and customer segmentation. AI and ML are also helping companies with better product design to the delight of the customers. Therefore, the organizations should embrace AI for empowering and supporting their employees so that the focus of the employees shifts from administrative tasks to cross-functional reasoning tasks.

References

1. Ahuja, A., Heave a sigh of relief HR, Amber's here to help. *[Online] Livemint*. Retrieved from https://www.livemint.com/Leisure/G5Dnhxq3i9jt78gDoCgn7K/Heave-a-sigh-of-relief-HR-Ambers-here-to-help.html, 2018.
2. Amla, M. and Malhotra, P.M., Digital Transformation in HR. *Int. J. Interdiscip. Multidiscip. Stud. (IJIMS)*, 4, 3, 536–544, 2017, Retrieved from http://www.ijims.com.
3. McCarthy, J., Programs with Common Sense at the Wayback Machine (archived October 4, 2013), in: *Proceedings of the Teddington Conference on the Mechanization of Thought Processes*, Her Majesty's Stationery Office, London, pp. 756–91, 1959.
4. Arbaiy, N. and Suradi, Z., Staff performance appraisal using fuzzy evaluation, in: *IFIP International Conference on Artificial Intelligence Applications and Innovations*, 2007, September, Springer, Boston, MA, pp. 195–203.
5. de Jesus, A., AI for Pricing–Comparing 5 Current Applications. Emerj. Retrieved from https://emerj.com/ai-sector-overviews/ai-for-pricing-comparing-5-current-applications/2019.
6. Brinker, S., Martec's Law: the greatest management challenge of the 21st century. *[Online] Chiefmartec.com*. Retrieved from https://chiefmartec.com/2016/11/martecs-law-great-management-challenge-21stcentury/., 2016.
7. Bughin, J., Seong, J., Manyika, J., Chui, M., Joshi, R., Notes from the AI frontier: Modeling the global economic impact of AI, *McKinsey Global Institute, 2018*,

Retrieved from https://www.mckinsey.com/featured-insights/artificial-intelligence/notes-from-the-ai-frontiermodeling-the-impact-of-ai-on-the-world-economy.

8. Carbonell, J.G., Learning by analogy: Formulating and generalizing plans from past experience, in: *Machine learning*, pp. 137–161, Springer, Berlin, Heidelberg, 1983.

9. Davenport, T.H., Loucks, J., Schatsky, D., Bullish on the business value of cognitive: Leaders in cognitive and AI weigh in on what's working and what's next. *Deloitte state of cognitive survey*. Retrieved from https://www2.deloitte.com/content/dam/Deloitte/us/Documents/deloitte-analytics/us-da-2017-deloitte-state-of-cognitive-survey.pdf, 2017.

10. Eubanks, B., *Artificial intelligence for HR: use AI to support and develop a successful workforce*, Kogan Page Limited, United Kingdom, 2018.

11. Forrest, E. and Hoanca, B., Artificial intelligence: Marketing's game changer, in: *Trends and innovations in marketing information systems*, pp. 45–64, IGI Global, US, 2015.

12. Gray, K., *AI can be a troublesome teammate*, Harvard Business Review, Boston, 2017, July 20, Retrieved from https://hbr.org/2017/07/ai-can-be-a-troublesome-teammate, February 11, 2019.

13. Grillo, M., *What types of predictive analytics are being used in talent management organizations?*, Cornell University, ILR School, New York, 2015.

14. George, G. and Thomas, M.R., Integration of Artificial Intelligence in Human Resource. *Int. J. Innov. Technol. Exploring Eng. (IJITEE)*, 9, 2, 5069–5073, 2019, Blue Eyes Intelligence Engineering & Sciences.

15. Guenole, N. and Feinzig, S., *The Business Case for AI in HR. With Insights and Tips on Getting Started*, IBM Smarter Workforce Institute, IBM Corporation. [Google Scholar], Armonk, 2018.

16. Jarek, K. and Mazurek, G., Marketing and Artificial Intelligence. *Cent. Eur. Bus. Rev.*, 8, 2, 46–55, 2019.

17. Jia, Q., Guo, Y., Li, R., Li, Y., Chen, Y., A conceptual artificial intelligence application framework in human resource management, in: *Proceedings of the International Conference on Electronic Business*, pp.106–114, 2018.

18. Joshi, A., Son, J., Roh, H., When can women close the gap? A meta-analytic test of sex differences in performance and rewards. *Acad. Manage. J.*, 58, 5, 1516–1545, 2015.

19. Kim, T. and Duhachek, A., The impact of artificial agents on persuasion: A construal level account, in: *ACR Asia-Pacific Advances*, 2018.

20. Krivkovich, A., Robinson, K., Starikova, I., Valentino, R., Yee, L., Women in the Workplace 2017, *LearnIn. org*, Retrieved from https://www.mckinsey.com/featuredinsights/gender-equality/women-in-theworkplace-2017.

21. Lesgold, A., Lajoie, S., Bunzo, M., Eggan., G., *SHERLOCK: A Coached Practice Environment for an Electronics Troubleshooting Job*, Pittsburgh University, Learning Research and Development Center, 1988.

22. McCarthy, J. What is artificial intelligence. Technical report, Stanford University, http://www-formal.stanford.edu/jmc/whatisai.html, 2004.

23.   Maraziti, P., 2020. Tomorrow's Workpplace: Humans And AI Co-existing As Colleagues. *[Online] Business World.* Retrieved from http://bwpeople.business world.in/article/Tomorrow-s-Workplace-Humans-And-AI-Co-existing-As-Colleagues/25-01-2020- 182461/.

24.   Marr, B., The 10 Best Examples Of How Companies Use Artificial Intelligence In Practice. *[online] Forbes.* Retrieved from https://www.forbes.com/sites/bernardmarr/2019/12/09/the-10-best-examples-of-how-companies-use-artificial-intelligence-in-practice/, 2019.

25.   Macwan, N. and Sajja, D.P.S., Performance appraisal using fuzzy evaluation methodology. *Int. J. Eng. Innov. Technol.*, 3, 3, 324–329, 2013.

26.   Meister, J., Ten HR Trends In The Age Of Artificial Intelligence, *[online] Forbes.* Retrieved from https:// www.forbes.com/sites/jeannemeister/2019/01/08/ten-hr-trends-in-the- age-of-artificial-intelligence/#5bb4b6363219, 2019.

27.   Miller-Merrell, J., 9 Ways to Use Artificial Intelligence in Recruiting and HR. *Workology.* Retrieved from https://workology.com/artificial-intelligence-recruiting-humanresources/, 2016.

28.   Shahid, M.Z. and Li, G., Impact of Artificial Intelligence in Marketing: A Perspective of Marketing Professionals of Pakistan. *Global J. Manage. Bus. Res.*, 19, 2, 26–33, 2019.

29.   Quillian, L., Pager, D., Hexel, O., Midtbøen, A.H., Meta-analysis of field experiments shows no change in racial discrimination in hiring over time. *Proc. Natl. Acad. Sci.*, 114, 41, 10870–10875, 2017, applicants with identical resumes.

30.   Rathi, R.A., Artificial intelligence and the future of hr practices. *IJAR*, 4, 6,113–116, 2018.

31.   Upadhyay, A.K. and Khandelwal, K., Artificial intelligence-based training learning from application. *Dev. Learn. Org.: Int. J.*, 3, 2, 20–33, 2019.

32.   Van Belleghem, S., *Customers the day after tomorrow: How to attract customers in a world of AI, bots and automation*, Lannoo Meulenhoff-Belgium, 2017.

33.   Waldman, D.A. and Avolio, B.J., A meta-analysis of age differences in job performance. *J. Appl. Psychol.*, 71, 1, 33, 1986.

34.   Walch, K., 2019, Rethinking weak-vs-strong-AI. *[online] Forbes.* https://www.forbes.com/sites/cognitiveworld/2019/10/04/rethinking-weak-vs-strong-ai/137808f86da3 accessed on 20 Jan, 2020.

35.   Xaxis, ARTIFICIAL INTELLIGENCE Myth versus reality in the digital advertising world. Retrieved from https://www.xaxis.com/wp-content/ uploads/2018/07/IAB-EU_XAXIS-AI-REPORT_2018- 07-.pdf, 2018.

36.   Kietzmann, J.H., Paschen, J., Treen, E., Artificial intelligence in advertising: How marketers can leverage artificial intelligence along the consumer journey. *J. Advert. Res.*, 58, 3, 263e267, 2018.

37.   https://www.lexico.com/definition/content_marketing, accessed on 20 Jan 2020.

38. https://www.cnbc.com/2017/04/03/pinterest-ceo-future-of-search.html. Accessed on 20 Jan 2020.
39. http://www.ecommerce-digest.com/neural-networks.html. Accessed on 20 Jan 2020.

2

Ring Trading to Algo Trading—A Paradigm Shift Made Possible by Artificial Intelligence

Aditi R. Khandelwal

IIS Deemed to be University, Jaipur, India

Abstract

This chapter explains a framework which shows the transformations which took place in Indian stock markets and their working. Several year's back the stock exchanges were physical places bussing with people and where everything used to happen manually by humans. The trades were executed by a process referred to as open outcry. Clients had to wait till the next day to see the high low prices of shares in the newspaper. The participation in stock market was low and selective.

Then came the time when a boom in stock market came and people at large started investing with the coming up of brokers cum investor like Harshad Mehta but sadly now we remember him as a fraud. The stock market also saw a change in the working of exchanges. Systems started becoming computerized and one fine day everything shifted to internet-computer based systems called online trading. The latest scenario is where highly sophisticated computer based programmes called as Algorithmic trades came into force. These are trades which are totally human less and thus help in normalizing the trading, too high or too low is detected and stopped by auto cut off modes.

Keywords: Stock market, ring trading, open outcry, settlement cycle, depository, algorithmic trade, stock exchange

Email: Aditig.1986@gmail.com; aditir.khandelwal@iisuniv.ac.in

S. Balamurugan, Sonal Pathak, Anupriya Jain, Sachin Gupta, Sachin Sharma, Sonia Duggal (eds.)
Impact of Artificial Intelligence on Organizational Transformation, (21–32) © 2022 Scrivener Publishing LLC

2.1   Introduction

Stock markets are the nerves of an economy and industry of any country. They are the intermediaries who move the savings from households into the main stream industry on one hand and on the other makes a common man part owner of big companies of the country and the world. Since the inception of stock markets which dates back to 1875 when "Native Share and Stock Broker's Association", India's first share trading association was formed which later came to be known as Bombay Stock Exchange (BSE). It was created with just 318 members. Since then, stock exchanges and trading have gone through a lot of changes. If we see the broadest bifurcation of stock market generations, then it can be broken down into three major generations. The first was the era of ring trading, followed by the transformation period from ring trading to online trading based on sentiments and run by major few, and the latest which is even more neutral and runs on artificial intelligence (AI) algorithms.

2.2   Ring Trading

Traditionally, rather I should say historically trading in the stock market used to happen in the *trading ring* which was physical areas in stock exchanges where the stock brokers used to stand and trade stock by *open outcry*. To understand it better, a ring is a location on the floor of a stock exchange where trades were executed in old times before internet came in our lives. Few renowned brokers used to enter the ring and shout out the orders placed by their clients; these were then sent to the record keeper of trades who would also keep a track of lowest and highest prices of each stock. Since the whole process used to be done manually, there was less efficiency and a lot of confusion as well [1].

2.3   Features of Generation 1: Ring Trading

1. *Complete Human Interaction*: Back in the days of ring trading, no technology was used and the whole system worked manually. There were no computers to store the data, no internet to circulate the information to the places, so everything was managed by a few people who were closely associated with the stock markets of that time.

2. *Low Volume*: Since a lot of information flow and also awareness about the businesses and their stock was not there, so stock trading did not used to happen at grass root level. It was only limited to a few people who knew big business houses or their associates or the ones who had good financial background who were approached by the brokers.

3. *Less Transparency*: Since there was no centralization and everything used to happen with hand by a few people, also with less information flow, the mechanism was not very transparent [4]. Clients had to trust the brokers for information and also regarding the prices of the shares they traded in.

4. *No Authenticated Trade Verification*: If we compare it with current times when at the end of every day broker has to confirm the trade personally to the client and which is also intimated to him by SEBI and his DP at the times of ring trading, then no such authentication used to take place at broker and client end which at many times resulted in defaults.

5. *Physical Exchange of Share Certificates and Money*: Share certificates existed in physical form in hard copy, had to be sealed with company stamp, and had to be posted from one owner to another in case of a trade. Same was the case with money; it actually changed hands between clients, brokers, stock exchanges, etc. [2]. So, the whole process was very lengthy and time taking which also resulted in loss and theft of share certificates and money.

6. *Localized Functioning of Exchanges*: There were a lot of stock exchanges; literally, at all centers of trade, otherwise people of that city could not trade efficiently. Companies had to be listed on each stock exchange to create volume and presence at all places. It all gave rise to complexities and also gave way for scams and frauds.

7. *No Participation of Tiers II & III and Rural India*: Since information flow was very less, so people in smaller cities and towns had no idea about the working of stock exchanges. They either thought of it as a place of making big money or a hoax to lose money. So, the actual participation was not there by the people of smaller places.

8. *Long Trading Cycles*: Today, a trade squares up in T+2 days that means that with 3 working days after a trade has been executed, the seller gets the money in his account and shares

from his DP are transferred to the buyers account, and at buyers end, he gets the shares in his DP and money from his account gets deducted. This all happens in 2 days, but back in ring trading days, all took T+5 days at least, actual receiving of share certificates may have taken even longer than that.

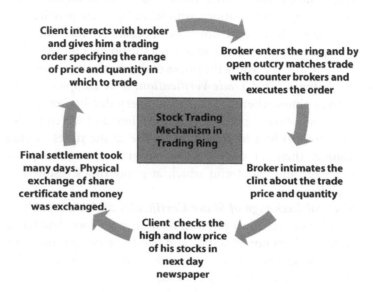

2.4   Generation 2: Shifting to Online Platform

This was the era of big transformation in stock broking. All the systems which used to happen manually were shifted to computers and online trading was started [3]. Online trading replaced ring-based trading and made physical stock exchanges less important in stock trading since it made share trading possible from any place anywhere. Online share trading was initiated in India in the year 2000 by NSE (National Stock Exchange) after getting the sanction from regulatory authority the Securities and Exchange Board of India (SEBI). Online trading was proposed in a committee set up by SEBI on Internet Trading and services and was approved in January 2000. This transformation from manual to computer-based trading gave way for more transparent execution of working of stock exchanges [5]. It also augmented the speed at which trades were executed and completed. It also induced convenience and security in share trading for investors. This

simplicity and a sense of security made more and more people to participate in stock broking which led to a tremendous growth in retail participation [6]. There were few major changes that appeared in this age which
are as follows:

1. ***Only Two Stock Exchanges Prevailed:*** We discussed earlier
   that almost every major city of India had a stock exchange
   of its own and companies were listed on them. By 1990s,
   there were 24 stock exchanges in India in all major cities.
   But when everything shifted online the physical exchanges
   became just buildings as the broking was consolidated
   and all the companies listed themselves only on two major
   exchanges, namely, BSE and NSE. The sensitivity index on
   stock markets is the barometer of the stocks, low and high
   cumulative of major stocks listed on that exchanges. BSE has
   SENSEX with 30 stocks and NSE has NIFTY with 50 stocks.
   It was in January 1986 that BSE's sensitivity index SENSEX
   was launched. It was the first stock market index which came
   into being. Its base year was set as 1978–1979. The underlying principle for selecting companies that would go in
   SENSEX or NIFTY are trading frequency, market capitalization, trading history, listing history, and industry representation. In March 1995, BSE ended its 120 years history of
   floor trading and shifted to computerized trading operations
   and then began the screen-based trading system nationwide.
   NSE came into force in November 1992. It was set up to
   accommodate to medium sized companies. In June 1994,
   NSE commenced operation in wholesale debt market segment. In November 1994, NSE shifted to screen-based trading format for the first time in India. Sensitivity index of
   NSE, NIFTY, was created in April 1996. It consists of top
   50 scripts with highest market capitalization and it is an
   indicator of all the major companies in the NSE. NSE also
   has NIBIS (NSE's Internet-Based Information System) for
   online real-time diffusion of trading related information on
   the Internet.
2. ***Online Trading Software:*** The biggest challenge in online
   trading was to make it error free, transparent, and easily
   accessible. For this purpose, NSE was the primary stock
   exchange in India which started providing pan India

screen-based, order-driven, trading system. The trading system at NSE is known as the National Exchange for Automated Trading (NEAT) system. It is an online, fully computerized, nameless, order-driven system with nation-wide presence. Another package offered by NSE is "NEAT Plus". Neat Plus provides a novel service to the subscribers which makes them trade in more than one stock exchange simultaneously. To ensure that that the system does not collapse due to over burden, NSE undertakes periodic testing and capacity enhancements as soon as its users and trading volume increases. NEAT also provides real-time data sharing on trading volumes and thus traders and investors can factor in the second to second changes in their Trades. BSE also has a system just like NEAT which is called as BOLT. BSE Online Trading (BOLT) is also a computerized, screen-based trading platform which can be used to punch in orders from anywhere, anytime during trading hours. It has a turnover capacity of 8 million orders each day. The BSE has also pioneered a nation-alized exchange-based internet order punching system, to facilitate investors from all over the world to trade in scripts listed on BSE.

3. **Depositories**: Two major depositories were made to keep a record of stock holdings and their owners and also to keep a track of buying and selling activities by these depository account holders. NSDL (National Securities Depositories Ltd.) and CDSL (Central Depositories Services Ltd.) were the two biggest depositories which hold the maximum accounts of the nation [7].

4. **T + 2 Rolling Day Settlement**: [8] Rolling settlement is a settlement process where a trade executed in the stock market is settled in trading day plus 2 more working days. In the ring trading system, this process used to take days at minimum 5–6 days, but in online trading with the help of [9] depositories and back accounts and their sync with the stock exchanges, the time to complete the process of trans-ferring shares from the account of seller to buyer and also monetary transaction of money from seller to buy's account took only 2 days after the day of trading. This increased

liquidity to a large extent as the money exchanged hands quickly.

5. *Investor Registration Norms*: The two major parties in stock broking are the investors and the brokers. The registration norms for both parties were made stricter. Brokers could not be registered unless they passed exams from NCFM to show that they have required knowledge of stock broking and its process. The clients could not trade unless they presented documents of their address, identity, and financial standing. These strict norms were not there earlier. These helped in making the stock broking forgery free.

6. *Order Verification by SEBI*: In this stage, a very elaborative order verification system was put in place. The brokers were directed very strictly that they need to get the order slips signed by the clients on a daily basis, and also after the end of each day, they were required to make a call to the clients and tell them the exact order which was executed on behalf of him. Stock exchanges and DPs were also advised to keep sending the order details and statements on a regular basis. All this helped in making the system very transparent and full proof where investors do not feel cheated. This all led to more satisfaction in the clients/investors [10].

7. *Strict Regulation of Brokers*: Brokers were very strictly monitored by the regulatory authority SEBI [11]. Regular audits were conducted by SEBI to see that all norms were followed by the broking firms and also the companies. SEBI also issued regular guidelines for the brokers laying out very clearly the process to be followed by the brokers for client registration and executing their trades and also communication with them. These norms were also updated from time to time if technology or economy changed.

8. *Investor Protection*: [12] determined that norms for investor protection lead to investor confidence and thus helped in boosting investor morale and increase in their participation. Participation over a period of time happened in two ways: direct and indirect mode. Directly was when investors participated in buying and selling from your own account and indirectly was when they invested in mutual funds and other such instruments. Investor protection was taken very

seriously by regulators and new act was passed with strict adherence norms to be followed by each and every broker and intermediary.

9. **Operators/Punters**: Though the online system of stock trading is totally nameless, but still there were ways in which stocks could be maneuvered to an extent with lot of money and connections. Operators driven scripts are the type of scripts which are controlled by the people who maneuver the stock price according to their will. These stocks could be found even in the index companies. This was one of the hind sides of this system. It was believed that when stocks do not follow the fundamental analysis, it might be moved by an operator.

2.5   Generation 3: Algo Trading

Today is the age of AI which has made its way in every aspect of our lives whether shopping or investing. So, stock markets globally are no different. AI has taken over all the aspects of trading in stock broking and investment including surveillance, monitoring, compliance, and controlling price and volume of stocks. AI has been a major tool to predict trends and also in managing investment portfolios and selecting good return generating stocks. While large companies have been making use of AI for years to mine huge amounts of data together with not only stock performance but also corporate commentary, social media trends, consumer behavior, credit card trends, etc., the advent and rise of AI-based technology have set international stock markets in a new age.

Until recent times, stock market data and price movements were analyzed via quantitative analysis was but it was time-consuming and only a few could do it and extract meaningful information, so it was used only by a few major players like Goldman Sachs and J.P Morgan, which managed nearly 20% of its portfolios with AI. Now that AI is nearly everywhere and the barriers to entry have decreased, small-time brokers and startups have started looking to leverage this tech into building a new model for investors to pick stocks.

Let us create an understanding as to what exactly is AI and how it is being used in trading and analyzing stocks, and some controversy surrounding AI's mass acceptance.

2.6   Artificial Intelligence

The simplest definition of AI was given by famous professor McCarthy (1950), dating back to the 1950s by Dartmouth professor Joseph McCarthy, which is a process of using software to mimic aspects of learning and decision-making so that a machine can be made to simulate it. Since the starting of AI, its applications have modified and process has scaled to accommodate growing technology. At present, modern world has stuck to the concept, AI is being used nearly everywhere:

- Google's Map application uses AI to predict traffic patterns to offer the quickest route and also tells about the precise amount of traffic and congestion one would find after an hour or two on any required route.
- Online shopping at retailers like Amazon use AI to make price changes and product recommendations to meet customer's demands.
- Uber and Lyft use AI to determine fair pricing based on peak usage.
- Banks use AI as part of their fraud protection and prevent identity theft.
- Credit card companies use AI to determine whether a customer is eligible for a credit increase.
- Every flight in the world uses AI-powered autopilot to steer the vehicle (humans only account for ~7 minutes of control, reserved for take-offs and landings).
- Spam filters on your email sort out behavior patterns of junk mail and scammer tactics.
- Plagiarism checks in professional and academic settings can quickly analyze papers for stolen or redundant content.

The list goes on. So, if you think that AI is something new and has come up in recent years, then it is important that you know that it is an old concept which was there for many decades though not in the same shape as it has evolved over years. Aspects of AI have been refined in recent years which have made it smarter to the current status, with machine learning and deep learning being popular buzzwords.

Machine Learning means training a machine to perform a particular action by programming algorithms set by a programmer. This includes things like recognizing a particular any patter of expenditure made by a person by her credit card and then indentifying any inconsistency to trace fraud. As more algorithms are added and data accumulated, the AI becomes more precise and capable of processing data to make better-informed decisions.

Deep Learning, which is almost like machine learning, is a process of training a machine to perform actions and become more precise over time. However, deep learning goes further, involving an approach that involves artificial neural networks—similar to how human brains learn patterns of behavior (for example, someone falls and you automatically extend your hand to help without any conscious thought). With researchers making new breakthrough in this concept every year, deep learning becomes a type of responsive intelligence that learns as it goes. Usually, deep learning enhances machine learning by being able to adapt to new data by itself, changing algorithms to create more favorable output. Of course, this requires considerable amounts of computing power and it has not been until recent years where humans have closed the gap to creating amore sophisticated and developed form of AI.

2.7   AI Stock Trading

So, let us make an effort to understand how does AI apply to the stock markets and stock trading? For a technology which specializes into number crunching and analyze that data to predict the future, AI is a natural fit for the world of finance. In stock market every day, a lot of data is generated regarding lows, highs, volume of trade, etc., which is used by the analysts to predict the future movements of stocks. A combination of deep learning along with machine learning allows financial firms to analyze not only stock price fluctuations but also unstructured data that reveals patterns of behavior that may have not been perceptible by a human [13]. This paves way for a new level of accuracy in trading decisions that goes beyond traditional investing strategies. Of course, these are just some of the known usages of AI. Stock markets around the world have realized the application of AI and begun to shift their focus toward bringing in AI experts from Information Technology sector to the world of hard core finance and investment. This competitive uproar has led to companies to move forward and apply this technology in relation to real-world investing applications.

2.8   Algorithmic (Algo Trading) Trading

Algorithmic Trading or Algo Trading refers to triggering trades on stock exchanges based on predefined criteria and without any human interference using computer programs and software [14]. Algorithmic Trading is normally defined as the use of computer algorithms to mechanically make certain orders, trading decisions, and manage those orders after compliance. While being a division of algorithmic trading, high-frequency trading involves buying and selling oodles of shares in a very small period of time like fractions of seconds. After so many frauds and downturns in stock market, the common agreement is that algorithmic trading is an unavoidable evolution of the trading process and markets all over the world have implemented various measures to provide a unhampered experience to investors. In the United States and other such developed stock markets, High-Frequency Algorithmic trading accounts for about 70% of trades in equities segment. In India, this percentage of trades done with the help of algorithmic trading to the total turnover has moved up to as much as 49.8%.

In India, Algo Trading was introduced on April 3, 2008, when DMA (Direct Market Access) facility was made available to institutional clients by SEBI (Securities and Exchange Board of India). DMA facility was a platform which allowed brokers to provide their set up to clients and gave them direct right to use to the exchange trading system without any participation of a broker. To start with retail, clients were not given this facility; thus, only institutional clients could avail this service. But later, it was also given to retail-individual traders. It brought down the costs of trading for the institutional investors and also helped in improved execution by reducing the time spent in steering the order to the broker and issuing the necessary commands. But DMA had a negative effect on the brokerage business of stock brokers as investors both institutional and retail clients start accessing DMA services. To sustain the times, they started providing computerized software to the clients.

2.9   Conclusion

Since 1800s, Indian stock markets have come a long way from trading in the ring to complete computer-based trading to algorithmic trading. These have been years of complete change and cumulative improvement. Programs which were used by select few are now approachable to people at large creating more volumes in the exchanges every day. Markets have given confidence to the retail traders with safety measures and transparency. The future defiantly lies in more sophisticated research tools on computers more advanced and AI featured.

References

1. Strasburg, J. and Bray, C., Six charged in vast insider-trading ring. *Wall St. J.*, A1, 2009.
2. Khandelwal, A., Data Compliance in Stock Broking–Boon or Bane. *Int. J. Res. Eng., IT Soc. Sci.*, VI, Issue IV, 28–33, 2015.
3. Hendershott, T., Electronic trading in financial markets. *IT Prof.*, 4, 10–14, 2003.
4. Jennings, M., The Lessons from Galleon Hedge Fund and the Insider Trading Ring. *Corp. Finance Rev.*, 14, 5, 43, 2010.
5. Rahim, A., Problems and prospects of online share trading practices in India. *Int. J. Marketing Financ. Serv. Manage. Res.*, 2, 4, 150–155, 2013.
6. Rajendran, R. and Palanisamy, S., The History and Evolution of Indian Online Share Trading as a Technological Tool for Sustainable Wealth Creation for Individual Investors. *Presented at International Conference on Innovations in Engineering and Technology for Sustainable Development*, Bannari Amman Institute of Technology, 2012.
7. Khandelwal, A., E-Accounting as a Way to Maintain Financial Data with Special Reference to Indian Stock Market. Available at SSRN 2859616, *Economic Challenger*, 73, 77–80, 2016.
8. Kyriacou, K. and Mase, B., Rolling settlement and market liquidity. *Appl. Econ.*, 32, 8, 1029–1036, 2000.
9. J. Morik, C.V. Austin, E. Lunceford, B. Blank, U.S. Patent Application No. 13/894,991, 2013.
10. Amsaveni, R. and Gomathi, S., A study on satisfaction of online share traders with special reference to Coimbatore district of Tamil Nadu in India. *Asia-Pac. J. Manage. Res. Innov.*, 8, 2, 145–153, 2012.
11. Stout, L.A., The investor confidence game. *Brook. L. Rev.*, 68, 407, 2002.
12. Srivastava, S., Impact of internet growth on the online stock trading in India. Available at SSRN 1964838, 2011.
13. Barclay, M.J. and Hendershott, T., Price discovery and after trading hours. *Rev. Financ. Stud.*, 16, 1041–1073, 2003.
14. Hendershott, T., Jones, C.M., Menkveld, A.J., Does algorithmic trading improve liquidity? *J. Finance*, 66, 1, 1–33, 2011.

3

AI in HR a *Fairy Tale* of Combining People, Process, and Technology in Managing the Human Resource

Jyoti Jain[1] and Sachin Gupta[2*]

[1]*Department of Management, JECRC University, Jaipur, (Rajasthan), India*
[2]*Department of Business Administration, Mohanlal Sukhadia University, Udaipur (Rajasthan), India*

Abstract

It is the world of magical performance with unseen possibilities. It is the time of working smart rather than working hard. It is the time when machines in collaboration with the human are working hand to hand to ease the work and hence to increase the productivity. Use of machines with human help is not a new idea or a thought, way back with the use of simple computer till Hi-Fi gadgets like laptops, and employees are rather habitual of working with machines.

The use of Artificial Intelligence is not limited to the Information Technology sector only but has laid its different wings toward the medical, education, business, automotive vehicles, etc. AI in HR has also enabled the managers to work efficiently starting from the smart people analytics to the team training and hiring; the AI in HR is also dealing with the data transactions and limiting the repetitive work and low value task.

The present chapter focuses on the use of AI in HR as AI and HR are now going together to manage the human as the resource and are enabling the organizations to help out in reducing the carbon footprint.

Keywords: Artificial intelligence, Human resource and AI, Artificial intelligence and recruitment, SMART HR, smart people analytics, machine learning

Corresponding author: sachinguptabusadm@gmail.com

S. Balamurugan, Sonal Pathak, Anupriya Jain, Sachin Gupta, Sachin Sharma, Sonia Duggal (eds.)
Impact of Artificial Intelligence on Organizational Transformation, (33–56) © 2022 Scrivener Publishing LLC

"The science and engineering of making intelligent machines, especially intelligent computer programs"—According to the father of
Artificial Intelligence, John McCarthy [1]

3.1   Introduction

It seems like the world of fairy tales where the works are done with a whirl
of wand or rather via click on fairies like smart machines. It is the world
of magical performance with unseen possibilities. It is the time of working
smart rather than working hard. It is the time when machines in collaboration with the human are working hand to hand to ease the work and
hence to increase the productivity. Use of machines with human help is
not a new idea or a thought, way back with the use of simple computer till
Hi-Fi gadgets like laptops, and employees are rather habitual of working
with machines. But as a limit, machines can only provide the clerical assistance or do the work related with documentation, writing or securing the
data. To make even this possible and to prove that sky is not the limit, the
concept of AI is slowly creeping in to HR.

In the midst of the upcoming technologies, Artificial Intelligence (AI) is
the new dimension which could be better defined as the Processing Human
Intelligence by Advanced Machines. In the age of new advanced computers, the world has changed drastically. Now, it is not only the money and
the management required to run the organization successfully, but the
combination of people, process, and performance with the use of technology has become the essential ingredients of successful business recipe.

The use of AI is not limited to the Information Technology sector only
but has laid its different wings toward the medical, education, business,
automotive vehicles, etc. Customer is the king always, and keeping that fact
in mind, the AI has also helped the businesses to enrich its CRM to serve
the customer better by going through its past shopping history and serving
the best at its end. It has also enabled the HR to reduce its task repetition
and by saving the data on the cloud for the future use and security.

AI in HR has also enabled the managers to work efficiently by starting
from the smart people analytics to the team training and hiring, the AI in
HR also dealing with the data transactions and limiting the repetitive work
and low value task.

Present chapter focuses on the use of AI in HR as AI and HR are now
going together to manage the human as the resource and are enabling the
organizations to help out in reducing the carbon footprint.

People and learning machines are working each other to deliver enriched
experience for the working platform. The use of computer-based logical

and algorithm is proposing better experience to the HR managers to perform the task more effectively and efficiently. The accomplishment of any link lies upon how adequately it links people, process, and technology to execute the HR work at advance level.

AI innovations have significantly changed the HR working; it has not only enhanced the working but also made the recruitment, selection, training, retaining, and developing of the employees more easy and advanced. As righty said by Tata 2018, the ability of the AI lies in providing a "novel cognitive respective" that may be fruitfully used in managing the challenges in satisfying the stakeholders and shareholder and keeping both of them happy together. It is the time humanity focusing upon reaching at the Zenith of efficacy and efficiency of doing the business in better way. It is the time where the focus is upon reducing the human interface and depending upon the machines for more structured way of working.

HRs do believe that combining AI into HR organization would improve the performance and productivity of the organization. It would also give greater edge, extra time, and payments plan and gradually exact data for more accurate decisions.

3.2   Problem Recognition

- 52% of the HR hunters accept that most typical part of the recruitment is accessing the worth of the right applicant for the right job from the pool of the applicants.
- Finding the right candidate from the pool of resumes for the particular position is another tough job of avoiding the fitting of square into hole.
- Once the employees are on the board, the next hard task is to let them fit in the profile with the adequate training and instructions.
- To lead the employee throughout his career is also another difficult task, as a star employee may become the NPA without any obvious reason or may quit the organization without any specification. So, the retention also becomes the reclusive task.
- Succession planning or the promotion may also become imperative for the right candidate, and HR sometimes may not judge the right talent and may lose the right talent by misfit promotion or posting.
- Survey done by the Delottie (Figure 3.1) [2] found that most of the HR and employees waste their time in the different office

| 82% | 79% | 78% | 69% | 65% |
| Paperwork | Scheduling | Timesheets | Accounting | Personal expenses |

| 60% | 60% | 49% | 37% |
| HR functions, like benefits | Email management | Proposal writing | HR management |

Figure 3.1 The wastage of time in the duplication of work.
Note: It is showing the percentage of time wastage in the duplication of work. Source: Image courtesy of PWC Consumer Intelligence.

> activities like 82% of the time in paperwork, 79% in scheduling, 78% in timesheets, 69% in keeping the accounts of different activities, 60% in performing other HR functions, and 60% in emails.

The study shows that such wastage of time in repetitive tasks can be eliminated and the saved time can be further invested in self-development and learning. The Figure 3.1 shows the findings of the research and the wastage of the time in the duplication of the low volume task and work.

3.3   Journey of AI in HR "From Where Till What"

Advent of electronic computers in 1941 opened the successful use of machine in humans' day-to-day activity. The early research in 1949 showed the possibility of using the stored data in Machines, and by the late 1950, the link between the Human intelligence and stored information was established. By the initiation of Norbert Wiener, it was found that showing intelligence was the outcome of the mechanism of feedback system that was easy to read by the smart Machines. In 1955, Newell and Simon created "The Logic Theorist" which was the first of its kind AI program. Later, John McCarthy coined the term AI. Slowly and steadily, it creeps into the professional world and became a part and parcel of day-to-day life. As per the survey done by various firms, it is found that AI in HR is gaining tremendous growth, and organizations are adopting it.

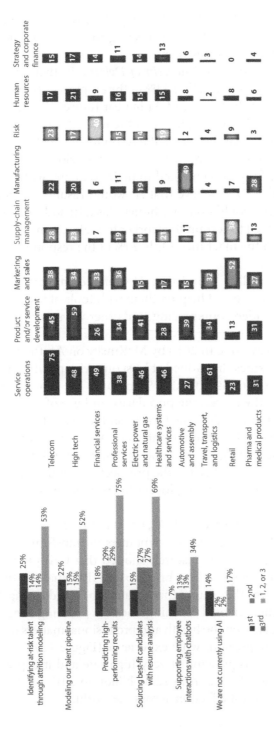

Figure 3.2 Use of AI in HR. Oracle AI usage in different business functions, showing the % of respondents. Source: McKinsey.

According to the Ji-A Min [3], today, 38% of the organizations are already using the AI and 62% are expecting to start using the AI for day-to-day work by the end of this year.

Another survey done by *Johbersin of Delottie* in their survey Delottie Human Capital trends found that 33% of the employees hope that their job would become better by the use of AI in near future. The study shows that AI and robotics are in flowing faster in the lives of the humans as before. The research was carried out on 10,400 respondents of 104 companies and 38% of the employees believe that AI with the help of robotics and animation would be fully implemented in their company within 5 years. The research found that 77% believe that AI would result in better job, while 33% expect that AI would do more human task. In addition, 50% thought that they would need to retrain the worker to make them able to work side by side along with the machines. Only 20% of the respondents took it as a threat on their job.

Survey by the Gallup found that 31% of the employees are working remotely without office and helping them with tools of team management, live chat through video conferencing, and other ways to coach and engage the people.

As per the survey done in 2018 by McKinsey on AI, the report showed that 47% of the business has added at least one AI capability in the process of the business in contrast to only 2% in 2017. The growth of more than the double shows the increasing popularity and use of AI in business.

Another research was done by Oracle on the uses of advance analytics in HR department to find the utilization of AI in various field of Human Resource, and the finding showed that the use of AI in HR would help the organization to create a dataset of the prospective candidates, past employees for rehiring, and current employees to create a mix of the fertile environment (Figure 3.2).

As per the survey done by the IBM, 6,000 HR professionals admitted the importance of AI-added cognitive computers in transforming the HR and employees experience. Their research showed that CHROs and CEOs are recognizing the advantages AI can bring to the HR domain by the help of the cognitive computers. They found that it can help in addressing the new talent, on board hiring, personal coaching, vacation planning, meeting reviews, and personal guidance on the health and professional matters judging on the temperaments from previous work experience (Figure 3.3).

Investment in AI is growing at very high rate and it is predicated that percentage of AI would rise from 12.5$ billion in 2017 to 46%$ billion by 2020. It will have a great effect on across the world.

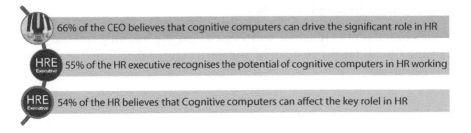

Figure 3.3 Need of AI in HR. https://www.aihr.com/blog/ai-in-hr-impact-adoption-automation

3.4   Work Methodology of AI in HR

The AI plays a very crucial HR by transforming the way it used to work earlier. Using various algorithms, based on the machine learning and NLP and the chatbots, the AI in HR is creeping slowly to strengthen its roots. The various branches in HR are discussed below which helps the HR persons in performing the task differently.

3.5   Branches of AI in HR

3.5.1   Machine Learning

It is the branch of AI that helps or makes the machines able to study the data and makes future forecast based on the collected data. The source of machine learning lies in the pattern and appraising the data based on the algorithm. According to Davenport and Ravenki [5], machine learning possesses the ability of identifying probable matches based on the most similar data and can also be associated with the same person and the beauty lies in the fact that the data may appear in slightly different formats across databases. Machine learning helps in following areas in HR context.

3.5.1.1   Variance Detection

Variance detection identifies the items, events, or observation which shows some deviation from the expected pattern or the routine task in the database. The said algorithm can be used tom study the constant behavior of the employee behavior and the deviation from the same can be used to study the reason behind so.

3.5.1.2   Background Verification

Models based on the machine learning can get the meaning and blow the warning signals for the structured and unstructured data from the resume of the applicant.

3.5.1.3   Employees Abrasion/Attrition

It helps the employer to recognize the employee who is at the border of abrasion and makes the HR manager to involve actively with this employee and try all the remedies to hold them.

3.5.1.4   Personalized Content

It provides a more tailored made employee engagement by using the predictive analytics to endorse career goals based on professional growth programs or to enhance the career based on data of the prior action of the applicants collected from different sites.

3.5.2   Deep Learning

Deep learning is a division or branch of machine learning that prepares a technical device like computer or laptop to learn and comprehended from great amounts of data through neural network construction. As it is the more developed stream of the machine learning, it divides the data into layers of impression. Deep learning makes the computers able to set up primary basics about the data and trains them to learn and execute by its own by recognizing the patterns using multiple neural network layers for working.

Deep learning algorithms can start working after sufficient training; Deep learning can instigate to make forecasts or elucidations of very complex data.

3.5.2.1   Important Use of Deep Learning in HR Context

3.5.2.1.1   Recognition of Video and Image

Deep learning assists in classification of objects and identification and classification of the candidates based on the objective data. So, it helps to read the image and identify the video and get the deep learning based on the expression tones and features. Figure 3.4 shows different branches of AI and its uses in various function of HR. Researchers' own conception.

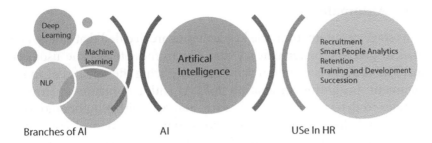

Figure 3.4 Branches of AI in HR and its uses. Source: Mckinsey Global Institute for HR.

3.5.2.1.2   Speech Recognition

By understanding the human voice, pitch, accent, and voice input, the machine can respond accordingly and select the candidates as per the requirement.

3.5.3   Natural Language Processing

The work of understanding human nature, language, tone, and context is done with the help of natural language processing (NLP) trains chatbots. NLP enables the AI system as the capable capacity builder for the organizations to continue to automate HR service delivery with chatbots.

3.5.4   Recommendation Engines

Digital learning capabilities mostly encompass tailored learning recommendations correlated to level of skills and the professional interests. By the use of Big Data and the Deep learning, learning experience stages can recognize learning pathways that might interest individual employees.

3.6   Implication Stages of AI in HR

In the consumer survey done by PWC of its consumer Intelligence series, they propose the following implication stages of AI in HR.

The image above shows the vital variables that are needed to build an AI tactic for HR and workforce. The creator of the model shows to how the begin the implication AI in automation, work force, key job roles, and work processes.

3.6.1   Automate

At this stage of automation, the key activities are decided that can be automated to give the better efficacy and effectiveness to get the usual task done. The process is center around computerizing the updates of routine assignment. Insightful automation links AI with automation to empower machines to detect, comprehend, learn, and act—either autonomously or with human help. Intelligent automation can perform manual assignments and can also decide as human would. AI capacities can empower machines to understand process and its variations. Intelligent mechanization can be used do monotonous manual procedures to help proficiency and profitability and drive advancement.

3.6.2   Augment

The process of augment decides the way the value that can be developed by using human analytics to recognize the upcoming opportunities for better strategic adaptation.

3.6.3   Amplify

It decides the work procedures and flow of the work that could be modified by AI skills to enhance the growth. Figure 3.5 is showing the various of implication of AI in HR at short term, medium term and long term. Source: Image courtesy of PWC Consumer Intelligence Series.

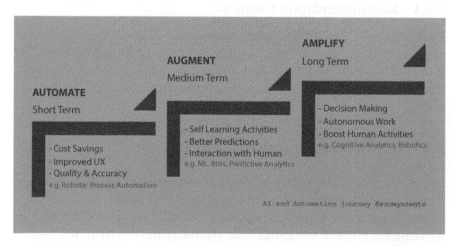

Figure 3.5 Implication stages of AI in HR. Source: https://www.cmswire.com/digital-workplace/7-ways-artificial-intelligence-is-reinventing-human-resources.

3.7   Process Model of AI in HR

The process of the use of AI in HR flows from left the right. The NLP software comes with the Natural Language Generation (NLG) software has the skills to change the data from the automated collected data and draws an insight from it. It reduces the bottle neck of human bias, faulty selection, and mismatch of the employee profile and reaches to the decision based on the algorithms.

The exhibit shows that HR teams collect the data from the various resources. Sometimes, it collects the data from the social sites, companies' record, candidates' activities from the social sites, etc.

The AI helps to extract the insight from the data and analysis the data through pre-defined algorithm as stated above by combining and systematically analyzing statement of the people, attitude, and intents on social media.

Analysis of the data is done with the auto med work which is done with the help of NLP, deep learning, and machine learning.

For example, the movement of the muscles can be great describer of the employee's behavior or attitude toward work, for example, interviewee frown while describing his previous boss or job experience, AI can judge the attitude and can relate. By recording the voice tone, the machine can Judge or interpret whether the respondents are enthusiastic or depressed while describing the past and her career goals. Likewise, the smart people analytics helps innovative approach to collect, manage, analyze, and protect the data in regard to human resource. The help of AI would help to gain the deeper insight in the sub conscious mind of the applicant, which would result in tracking the people with high IQ and EQ and would overrule the interview bias. Figure 3.6 is showing the entire process as model of AI in HR and how it helps in decision making.

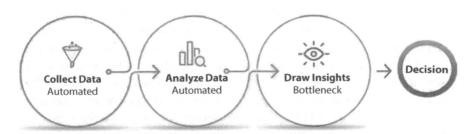

Figure 3.6 Process model of AI in HR. https://www.aihr.com/blog/ai-in-hr-impact-adoption-automation.

3.8   Key Roles of AI in HRM

Organizations now are facing complex workforce challenges at higher rates. Expectations of the employer combined with the visualization of the workforce, which is equipped with the novel skill set, technology driven, and uniqueness of one to perfectly fit in the job, is increasing. The HR plays a crucial role in addressing these challenges. The upcoming technologies or the updation in the earlier one are becoming the savior of the HR to take the challenges of fitting in the employers expectations. With the advancement of the cloud computing, data decision matrix, and Internet of the Things, the life of a HR became so easy and another savior in the pipe line is the cognitive computing, emerging to help the business outcomes by expanding the expertise of the human and improving its decision-making. The digital age is bringing the opportunity, challenges, and trends to impact the HR functions of the organizations across the globe (see Figure 3.7).

Quickly changing requirements for novel ranges of abilities signal a requirement for adapting a recruitment-selection program that scour new talent pools. The present employee must have the option to explore the advanced world, which incorporates getting in to and drawing lots of knowledge from volumes of new information. As the work environment is becoming more competitive, the need of adapting the virtual scenario is growing worldwide. Also, eventually, there has been a significant move in the desires for the workforce; employees request work assignment that are close to home, connecting with and legal. Expanding on existing HR interests in innovation and procedure, including center HR platforms, cognitive arrangements give a chance to improve the general worker experience, reduce expenses, and increment the precision and nature of HR administrations. Cognitive solutions constantly collect information, understand natural language and use reasons to assess multiple data of information very quickly. By consolidating these, three significant characteristic—comprehension, assessment, and extracting meaning, cognitive computing enables the quick decision-making based on gathered insight and support the quick and error-free decision-making. The one of a kind capacities of cognitive computing frameworks make the way for a totally different way to deal with HR, one that addresses the difficulties of the present workforce, profiting both the association and its representatives. As CHROs center around changing the worker experience, subjective arrangements can expand on existing HR innovation ventures to improve the representative experience, help diminish operational expenses, and empower the revelation of new workforce bits of knowledge.

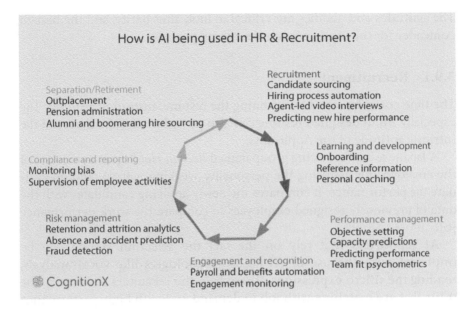

How is AI being used in HR & Recruitment?

Separation/Retirement
Outplacement
Pension administration
Alumni and boomerang hire sourcing

Recruitment
Candidate sourcing
Hiring process automation
Agent-led video interviews
Predicting new hire performance

Compliance and reporting
Monitoring bias
Supervision of employee activities

Learning and development
Onboarding
Reference information
Personal coaching

Risk management
Retention and attrition analytics
Absence and accident prediction
Fraud detection

Performance management
Objective setting
Capacity predictions
Predicting performance
Team fit psychometrics

Engagement and recognition
Payroll and benefits automation
Engagement monitoring

CognitionX

Figure 3.7 Use of AI in HR.
Note: It is showing various uses of AI in different function of HR and it helps to make a
HR system more efficient. Source: CognitionX.

3.9   Broad Area of Uses of AI in HR

Innovations that build up the applicant understanding and meet possibilities will assist with recognizing organizations from all the others. Deep digital business acumen would help the business to gain the heights. The advance technology would bring the business out of the "Sub conscious mind" of information and would help in getting more precious decision. The human behavior could be predicted well in advance with the help of self-ruling learning machines. These machines pre-read the mood of the candidate by the statements, comments, and post on the social media, and through other open data sources, this makes it logical to endorse the specialist experience. HR does the execution and advancement on the information that is tested and verified. That gives another measurement to key workforce trying to lessen the productivity gaps. It is a helpful tool to find the right mix of man and machine in the workplace, which would help to keep the balance between the technology and human working.

By solving and separating the individuals' speech, mindset, and expectations via social media, alongside other public data sources, human behavior can be recreated via self-sufficiently learning machines. This makes it conceivable to approve the worker experience on an everyday premise.

The aptitudes and abilities are critical to look after parity, and the best-fit contender for the inside or outer recruiting process.

3.9.1   Recruitment

The time could be saved by scanning the resume, instead of reading. The especially fill in designed resume can also posted on the site that read the intrinsic aptitude of the Applicants.

A Japanese staff servicing group named *Recruit Holdings* uses the data of the employee for assessing the personality, working pattern, and do evaluate the performance. It compares the newly applying candidates with the data of previously resigned employees to compare the work performance [6].

AI supporters that rely on the fact the selection system can be improved with the use of AI-based technologies like vocal analysis, reading the micro expressions. These help the recruiters to identify the traits that are matching with job in demand and with high-performance employees [7].

3.9.2   Interviews

The interviewer can take the unbiased Interviews based on the Psychographic-Based Questionnaire. Here, the AI judges the candidate irrespective of its demographic profile. It also helps to read the right candidates based on the following:

- **Muscular moment:** The moment of the muscles can be great describer of the employee's behavior or attitude toward work, e.g., interviewee frown while describing his previous boss or job experience, AI can judge the attitude and can relate.
- **Voice Tone:** Whether the respondents enthusiastic or depressed while describing the past and her career goals.

3.9.3   Reduction in the Human Biases

People may have inalienably inclination toward any. In any event, when taking an attempt at comprehensiveness, HR experts may subconsciously lean toward a specific applicant because of any reason. By using AI, calculations can be intended to assist managers with recognizing and evacuate these predispositions. That possibly means better employing interchanges and attracting a divers gathering of the applicants those equivalent calculations can likewise discover up-and-comers who may have been screened out because of human inclination. AL permits the process to go beyond the human feelings and relish upon the machine intelligence.

3.9.4   Retention

A few organizations are utilizing AI to single out employees that might be setting out toward the exit doorway. These track the PC movement, messages, keystrokes, web surfing, etc., and store it. At that point, AI reads the routine pattern of the working of an employee and reports the deviation, if remains continuous. Computer-based intelligence is additionally being utilized to identify variations in the general attitude of employees' communications to forecast when employees might be thinking of leaving the organizations.

3.9.5   AI in Learning and Advancement

Execution surveys additionally provide with the prospect to figure out the skills that should be polished and which new skill or the new aptitudes the employee should learn to confirm the enhancement at their specific work place. With the help of cutting edge technology, it is now feasible to personalize the employee's experiential learning. Today, skills have a less timeframe than ever before. AI can facilitate the structure to differentiate which member of staff need to polish their abilities a lot before they become out of date or show signs of improvement advancements.

3.9.6   Diminish Gender Bias Equality

In a period where old prejudices are being challenged and individuals are entreating for equity all over the world in term of gender. AI is reducing the bias of gender-based selection by eliminating the personal interaction while interview. AL may also help in reducing the "glass ceiling effect" in terms of promotion of women after a certain designation.

While numerous organizations are taking the activities to connect this gap, it is difficult to change cultural beliefs in terms of gender imparity.

AI is not worried about the gender of people with regard to measuring execution, experience or compensation. Consequently, it will be a lot simpler to lessen this gender orientation gap and offer equivalent chance to everybody in the working environment. Aside from gender orientation, the equivalent can be said for race, ethnicity or nationality.

3.9.7   Candidate Engagement

Not all organization has the setup of reciting the correct any employees with right tools to engage the talent as often they should be. Al could potentially do the task of matching the skills with the tolls needed.

Use of AI can be done to robotize for writing mails, sending messages, keeping the tracked on the ongoing and incoming calls; these all can track the employees' behavior and can help in enhancing the applicant experience.

3.9.8   Prediction

Machine Learning and AL makes it easy to read the past data and make prediction based on it for the evaluation and forecasting of the future turnover. Keeping the track of the workers' commitment needs assessment, and keeping the track of workflow pattern is a very hard task; however, it is regular work of the HR manager. The AI can help in predicting the future trend and can ease the work of the HR.

3.9.9   Smart People Analytics

Smart people analytics deals with the analysis of the people for acquiring the top talent and to gain insight the deeper insight of the human behavior to predict the future skills. The smart people analytics is an innovative approach to collect, manage, analyze, and protect the data in regard to human resource. The help of AI would help to gain the deeper insight in the sub conscious mind of the applicant, which would result in tracking the people with high IQ and EQ and would overrule the interview bias. It would also help in analyzing the behaviors of the human resources by analyzing the mood, behavior, and intention and people as statement at work and on the social media. By simulating the human behavior by autonomously learning machines, the HR manager could analysis the employee experience, performance and succession also.

3.9.10   Employee Experience

One of the challenging tasks for the organizations is the employee experience and the future of HR is focused on the worker experience and initialing engagement. Amid the wake of digitization when personnel have smart assistants at home and recommendation engines for shopping assistance, they also ask for the personalized experience when they come to work. Organizational leaders and HR executives have confidence that developing

AI into HR functions like hiring and administration of benefits can and will improve the overall employee experience.

The software which there currently being used by the HR professionals are as follows: The HR nowadays are using Textron for the sourcing. The software enables the companies to architect and amplified writing. *Textio* helps ideas to transform instantly into powerful language with a single key-stroke. It builds the owed typed by the professional and provides a data fueled predictive engine generator.

Software: *These are the few software being used in HR based on the AI automation algorithm.*

Myinterview: It is cloud-based interview platform for the interview that brings the candidates and the employees together. The prescreening of the candidates is done by one way interview. It has different features which include customized questions, managing candidate applications, and reviewing and providing a comment upon them. It helps to make the recruitment process more effective affordable and efficient. It brings the personality of the candidates in the forefront of the employer and ensures a best fit to the company.

Talla: Talla is an AI auto med platform to help the customer support. It automates the answering of the queries, provides the reports when needed, and maintains the accuracy of the report.

Saberr: The creator believes that development of the technology should promote and automate a meaning full relationship between people and technology. AI should help the human rather than replace them. The software helps the team member and candidate to receive an individual report which shows the value based on the values and personality based on Schwartz and Big 5 personality. The report helps to increase the self-awareness and helps the teams to understand about type values and personality and tells that how the act at work.

Hemingway App: This app uses a primitive AI that recognizes writing by NLP and polishes the writing structure. It helps in saving the time and increases the readability.

Skype Translator: It reduces the language barrier as it works on eight languages and the text translator helps in more than 500 languages for prompt messaging.

Clarke AI: It is an AI bot that helps in dialing the conference calls and does the entire noting for the entire conference, and after the completion of the calls, the notes are emailed directly to the email box.

Google smart reply: It uses the machine learning to analyze the emails and suggests a quick response the person wants to send. It helps the employee to save the time in deciding the response for the mail and keeps the mails updated and well answered.

Paradox: With the help of AI assistant, it focuses on the entire candidate Management. With the help of VCV it helps to search the candidates: it calls them with the questions by using the voice recognition and invites them for the video interview.

So, it can be said that AI can be effectively intertwined into the complete life cycle of the employee; it starts with *recruitment and selection,* to HR service delivery and career designing, along with the personalized experience, and ends with the succession planning. HR agility has emerged as a critical theme for organizations in the war for talent.

3.10   Dark Side of AI

"Bad implementation of AI is a bias itself"

"You can have data scientists, but the ability to translate that to actual AI has become a struggle in HR."

–Sonny Tambe [8]

Like a fairy tale dream, the life is always not a fancy land where all wishes comes true with a spiral of magic band. There always lies a bad in between the good and an evil between the boons, so is the case of AI in HR. As it is said that all the coins have two sides, so the AI is likewise among perusing resumes to grab best applicants more accurately by using the data to have a detailed discussion with the applicant. These are the positivity of the Big Data and AI technology in the HR department. But as the coin has two sides, so is the AI.

Between good and bad, there is a managerial conflict going on in totally believing a machine for "devolving" people management tasks as an HR function or to took up a strategic challenge by totally believing upon it [9]. However, it is debatable issue that can be argued over time (e.g., Wood [10]) that AI proposes a real opportunity for HR to make its mark.

Use of AI in HR is just like embracing algorithm to decide the fate of the organization and employees, which is also like a Disney cartoon with an evil always prowling in background to find its own way to bring harm to otherwise all good.

In terms of ethics of organization, the point arises in terms of permission in regard to the use of AI in organizations. The question pertains in terms of the use of machines in selecting the future success of any organizations. The issue of the trust rises. It is also difficult to judge the ill effects of AI in terms of errors, as in contrast to a human being, so to use the AI, new methodology ought to be determined for AI.

From an organizational psychology viewpoint, there are lots of issues to be handled before implementing the AI in HR In particular, the loss or the gain has to be carefully calculated before the inclusion. Researchers are expecting that, in the next 10–20 years, around 40%–50% of jobs in Germany could be computerized and round 12 % of all the employees will be substituted by means of machines technology like AI, where selection of the employees would also be greatly affected. It would certainly cause fear of job security result in lack of task interest under performance. It would also result in mental stress and negative fitness and poor outcome for the organizations.

In addition, from an economic point of view, AI calls for a big deal of training and skill updating before using it have to be taken care of, and lots of cost involve in regard to most of the companies having a big population of employee.

It would additionally result in mainstream bias via incorrect training. There are various threats, and significant changes also would not take place and loop holes in the transparency can also become a disadvantage. After all, at some factors, the companies may not recognize how constantly and continuously self-schooling AI makes its selections or recommendations.

3.10.1 Technical Requirements and Acceptance

Currently, there also are various questions in regard to technical competency. The quality and advancement of the machine may give varied results in interpretation of data. For example, the speech conception tool of AI may give wrong result based on the poor quality of the machine or poor algorithm. The technological structure and the essential resource needs also are still unclear at this time.

Applicants face the threat of being misjudged by the use of AI, in which it can bring the image of the company down in the eyes of the other applicants. Furthermore, because of the specialized process of application, the handling of AI can be in particular intricate for managers.

Technology can help in providing effective data in regard to the employees' performance, but still, it lacks how effectively the Machine Feedback can bring the change in behavior and performance of an employee [11].

Finally, the legal component is likewise imperative. Some of the dark side of AI in HR is as follows:

> *"There is a central idea in machine learning: the data you use to teach a machine learning algorithm can significantly influence its behavior."*
>
> – *Pinar Yardage, Manuel Cambrian, and Iyad Rahwan, MIT*

3.10.2   Cost Involvement

As per the comments from the several HR professionals, HR is still considered as the traditional department and the backbone of any organization; hence, it is necessary to update the work methodology of the HR with the new technology. But in order to gain the initiative, cost is implied and so in the case of AI. As per the report of TATA [12], implementing AI in HR involves two types of cost: fixed cost and variable cost. Fixed cost deals with the machinery purchase, software automation, and the software implementation, while variable cost deals with training of the employees in reference to AI in terms of adoptability and functioning. It may be a huge investment for an organization in comparison to the traditional method of HR. So, most of the organization may retain itself from it.

3.10.3   Machine Biases

It is found that danger from the bias of the machine is also possible as in case of Amazon in 2015. It found the favorable sum for the male by their new recruitment engine, at the time of new recruitment of the software developer for the AI team. It showed biases against women. As per the professionals, the AI may found difficulties in understanding the cultural barriers as the terminologies differ between cultures to culture. So, training the employees in right direction becomes the most primary care of using AI in recruitment as how to provide the training to the men who trains machines in order to avoid biases.

3.10.4   Job Losses

The biggest fear among the employee or rather in between the HR mangers is the loss of their job or an impact of the use of software on the importance of their workability. The fears are largely confined to the concern in regard to losing their job and the changes to change of their work through new automation capabilities. AI is causing damage to employees' experience as an introduction of elimination of human labor, like the use of Uber's self-driving cars results in the loss to taxi drivers.

3.10.5   Emotional Turmoil

The AI like other disruptive change agents on the workplace can create an emotional turmoil, resulting in intensified level of anxiety and fear. As per the Mewald C [13], people tend to fear or do not accept the ill-defined factors or unknown impact creating a negative impact of their jobs. The feeling of being judge by the machines creates a pressure and results in emotional ups and downs in mood based on the uncertainty of the results. As most of the leaders still doubt on the *AI as* these machines do not have feelings (except automated to display them) and they possess "no moral code" [14].

Another problem is the risk of machine learning repeating the prejudices; another is that AI may fail to imitate human instinct since machines do not understand how human consciousness works [15].

3.10.6   Fake Identity

It is believed that uses of AI can also be done in making the fake identity to impress the organization. Like *Nvidia*, a computer chip maker, is reportedly invested in high involving AI, creating very realistic fake celebrity photos. Researcher has recently reported that machine can help in creating a new real-time photos based on recognized common patterns. This fake photo may hamper the results of the company while selecting and recruiting process and so on.

According to McKinsey [16], comments that most of the most of the HR divisions or vertical departments of today's era have changed into process-driven "machines" that manage people like assets, instead of treating them as exclusive human beings that encompass personalized attention. HR departments run top-down process systems to employees' large number of resources, manage payroll, prepare annual appraisals, send instantaneous batches of employees to training, etc. It leaves no room for personalization, flexibility, and creativity.

3.10.7   Having an Audit Trail

The challenges with the machine learning are divided between the learning and outcomes, and all outcomes are based on what the machine has learned and on what basis it has come to its conclusions. The basis and the reasons of working are based on the written down rules and algorithms, which rules the entire human on the same ground. As it hard to decide on "what is always going on under the Bonnet", so generating an audit troll of how the system makes a decision could be a tough task. The decision and processing based on these machines can raise challenge on selection and recruitment based on AI. The decision taken by the AI can be challenged under the General Data Protection Regulation (GDPR). The leading expert on AI [17] doubts on the success of AI on the understanding of machine in comparison to humans and also doubts on the decision-making power of AI by surpassing the explanatory power of human language and reasons.

3.10.8   Question on Decisions

No one can be judged by type of machines that could not understand the emotions rather work on the intelligence, so HR decisions may always be challenged with the base, criteria, or the frontiers on which the decision of recruitment, selection, promotion, and bonus are taken.

As John Hawksworth [18], PwC's chief economist, made it specific that "legal and regulatory hurdles, in regard to organizational apathy and legal systems might cause a delay in moving toward AI and Robotics" [18]. According to Minon [4] it might be there that HR leaders may feel the need of the more digital tools to outpace the existing one with lot of more correction [19].

Indeed, the lust of HR leaders for being on the digital front and to acquire the mastery on the new tools may outperforms their ability of getting the tools [19]. Again, one more hurdle lies in the shortage of the AI-skilled employees and again the shortage of trainers to provide training in this regard.

AI-enhanced HR is also going to challenge the white collar job like lawyers, teachers, traders, sale and marketing, and doctors.

3.11   Conclusion

As AI and machine learning are playing with the technological landscape of the HR, it is becoming very crucial for the HR manager to find a way out to bring equilibrium in between the advancement of the technologies and the human pace. Drenched with mounting data and robust but affordable computing technologies, like AI, it is branching out into more and more diverse industries and areas of life. Luckily, the AI possesses the capability of improvement in almost all sectors and operation all the functions of any business. AI, by acquiring more and more capabilities, can indeed learn quickly; then, humans in long run may diminish human capability and they may change in their conditions, too.

The successful implementation becomes more crucial then the adoption. At end of the day, AI is not the answer of the every question neither it is a *"Jin of Aladdin"*, with *"HUKUM mere AKKA"*. The HR must find out the best way to use this *"magical Lamp"*. It is the tool and nothing more, the tool which works based on the data, and to be effective, the data must be effectively handled. Likewise, there is always two side of the coin, and it depends upon the user to use it wistfully so lies with AI in HR. A thoughtful use of the machines in combining the people can result in a solution for the managerial conflict which going on in totally believing a machine for "devolving" people management tasks as an HR function or to took up a strategic challenge by totally believing upon it.

References

1. McCarthy, J., What is AI, Personal website (formal.stanford.edu/jmc/index.html) last updated Nov.12, 2007.
2. Deloitte Human Capital Trends, AI, Robotics, and Cognitive Computing Are Changing Business Faster Than You Thought, 2017.
3. IBM, *Build AI chatbots employees want to talk to*, 2019.
4. Minon, J.-A., HR Tech Talk, Artificial intelligence, On boarding, HR software, HR Technology "Ten ways HR tech leaders can make the most of artificial intelligence, 2017.
5. Davenport, T. and Ronanki, R., *Artificial intelligence for the real world*, Harvard Business Review, January-February, 2018.
6. Buranyi, S., *"Dehumanising, impenetrable, frustrating": the grim reality of job hunting in the age of AI*, The Guardian [Online], 2018.
7. Reilly, P. and Williams, T., *Strategic HR: Building The capability to deliver*, Routledge, 2006.
8. Sony, T.S., *The next generation organizations*, Beyond Thinking [Online], 2018, Available at: https://medium.com/beyond-thinking/the-next-generation-organizations-60688e8b34e2.
9. Williams, R., *How dying offers us a chance to live the fullest life*, New Statesman [Online], 2018.
10. Wood, J., *The death of HR is just part of its resurrection*, The Globe and Mail [Online], 2017.

11. Ledford, G.E., Benson, G., Lawler, E.E., Aligning research and the current practice of performance management. *Ind. Organ. Psychol.*, 9, 2, 2016.

12. Tata, *Cognitive Diversity: AI and The Future of Work*, Tata Communications, 2018.

13. Mewald, C., *No machine learning in your product? Start here*, The Lever [Online], 2018, Available at: https://medium.com/the-lever/no-machine-learning-in-your-product-start-here2df776d10a5c.

14. O'Shea, L., *Tech has no moral code. It is everyone's job now to fight for one*, The Guardian, 2018.

15. Harkaway, N., *Will computers be able to think? Five books to help us understand AI*, The Guardian [Online], 2018, Available at: https://www.theguardian.com/books/2018/jul/23/willcomputers-be-able-to-think-five-books-to-help-us-understand-ai.

16. McKinsey, *Smartening up with artificial intelligence*, McKinsey & Company [Online], 2017.

17. Kissinger, H., *How the Enlightenment Ends*, The Atlantic [Online], 2017, Available at: https://www.theatlantic.com/magazine/archive/2018/06/henry-kissinger-ai-could-mean-theend-of-human-history/559124.

18. Hawksworth, J., PwC's chief economist. (https://www.employment-studies.co.uk/system/files/resources/files/mp142_The_impact_of_Artificial_Intelligence_on_the_HR_function-Peter_Reilly.pdf)

19. Heric, M., *HR new digital mandate*, Bain & Company [Online], 2018, Available at: https://www.bain.com/insights/hrs-new-digital-mandate/.

4

Effect of Artificial Intelligence on Human Resource Profession: A Paradigm Shift

Jyoti Dashora[1*] and Karunesh Saxena[2, 3†]

[1]School of Management Studies, Sangam University, Bhilwara, Rajasthan, India
[2]Sangam University, Bhilwara, Rajasrhan, India
[3]ICCR, New Delhi, India

Abstract

Human Resources are one of the most important resources in a business organization. Due to the advent of Information Technology, Human Resource Management (HRM) has witnessed a paradigm shift. The unprecedented development in the field of IT has positively influenced organizational practices. Artificial Intelligence (AI) which is IT-based technology has come to be recognized as a great boon for business organizations. AI has evolved to emerge as a game changer in the past few decades. AI has great potential for multifarious applications in the field of HRM. There are many routines and monotonous administrative tasks that can be efficiently handled by chatbots. An attempt has been made in this paper to discuss the symbiotic relationship between AI and the HR profession as well as the limitations of AI with reference to HRM Practices. Authors conclude that AI cannot and should not replace HR professionals as it lacks emotional intelligence.

Keywords: Artificial Intelligence, automation, Human Resource professional, Human Resource Management, symbiotic relationship

Corresponding author: jtdashora1@gmail.com
†*Corresponding author*: karuneshsaxena@gmail.com

S. Balamurugan, Sonal Pathak, Anupriya Jain, Sachin Gupta, Sachin Sharma, Sonia Duggal (eds.) *Impact of Artificial Intelligence on Organizational Transformation*, (57–72) © 2022 Scrivener Publishing LLC

4.1   Introduction

Information Technology (IT) is a broad term that means a system used to store, retrieve, and sending information. A system includes computer and telecommunication technology through which the exchange of information is possible.

The IT industry deals with manufacturing and selling the various software and hardware components, as well as process the data. Artificial Intelligence (AI) is one of the essential parts of IT as well as a branch of computer science that aims to develop intelligent machines that think logically and act like the human brain. AI uses many algorithms and impressions [1]. AI is a technology which is used to increase the speed of control mechanism. It is IT-based automation in the organization. AI is a blend of many disciplines such as Psychology, Mathematics, and Philosophy. Simply, it is a software programming by which anyone can create a machine that has the power of problem-solving, initiating common sense, and reasoning. Machine Learning (ML) is an essential part of AI. In recent times, AI has become an integral part of organizational practices. It becomes a vital part of the innovative technology in industries. In common words, AI is a new way to develop a computer through a software that thinks similar to a human brain.

In this fiercely competitive business era, Human Resource (HR) is an important asset for a business organization. This is the only living and active resource of any organization. HR Department (HRD) is handing the entire workforce from recruitment to retirement though it is very essential to make it more employee-friendly through incorporating innovative technology. AI has greater significance for HR Management (HRM) profession to complement its multifarious functions [2]. Customer satisfaction is the vital key for prospering in market place and organizations must embrace innovative HR practices. It was explained that AI-based HR practices make work of HR professionals much relaxed and productive by competent use of Chatbots [3, 4].

The world has witnessed great changes taking place in the organization, due to the increased use of innovative IT-based tools and technologies [5]. The profession of HR has come a long way from its administrative functions to the behavioral consideration and is now entering the era of automation. AI and Augmented Reality (AR) have completely redefined and reshaped the way organizations do their work.

An attempt has been made in this paper to:

- Trace the evolution of AI.
- Discuss the changing role of HR professionals.
- Assess the impact of AI on the HR profession.
- Elaborate the symbiotic relationship between AI and HR professionals.
- Outline some of the limitations of applications of AI in the field of HR.

4.2   Evolution of Artificial Intelligence

Although AI is everywhere in the world from centuries, it came into fame after the 1950s. The term AI has been devised by John McCarthy and his co-founders in 1955. The AI introduced in 1950 and because of excessive expectation use of AI became immobile from 1970 to 1990s [1]. In the year 2012, a new revolutionary wave of AI-generated. Alan Turing has developed a testing technique to make a difference between the intelligence behavior of machines and humans. The test has been conducted including three components such as *human foil, computer, and human interrogator*. The role of the interrogator is to ask a series of questions repeatedly to the rest of the components (human foil and computer), and by this process, anyone can differentiate the humans from the computer. Monitor and keyboard play a key role during communication. This testing technique gave the strength of the idea of AI. The basic idea used in this technique was that humans are capable to store information and solve various problems whereas computers cannot do this.

Till 1974, machines could not able to store information, they face many difficulties in executing different commands. After 1974, more developed machines were introduced. These machines were ready to store more data as well as information.

In the 1980s, tools with large reserves and algorithmic commands have developed, the John Hop field and David Rumlhald implemented the "Deep Learning" method which made the device more independent in terms of independent-learning through previous understanding.

Figure 4.1 describes the year wise progressive evolution of Artificial intelligence is as follows:

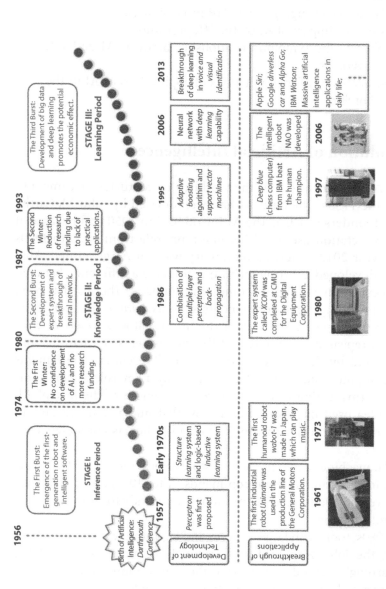

Figure 4.1 Evolution of Artificial Intelligence.

Note: Three stages of Artificial Intelligence are three stages is Inference, Knowledge, and Learning period. It describes the various stages of implementation of Artificial Intelligence in previous years. It also shows the evolution of AI in a periodical and systematic manner from simple to complex technology. Source: https://www.researchgate.net/publication/323591839_State-of-the- Art_Mobile_Intelligence_Enabling_Robots_to_Move_Like_Humans_by_Estimating_Mobility_with_Artificial_Intelligence/ figures?lo=1.

4.2.1   Phases of Artificial Intelligence

Figure 4.2 describes three phases of AI as follows:

- **Artificial Narrow Intelligence (ANI):** It is the initial stage where there is no power of logical reasoning and problem-solving ability. It covers only one functional area.
- **Artificial General Intelligence (AGI):** Currently, this phase is working which works on more than one functional area with advance features and starts working as human brain means thinking logically with problem-solving skill.
- **Artificial Super Intelligence (ASI):** It is a very advance stage where it works equally as human intelligence.

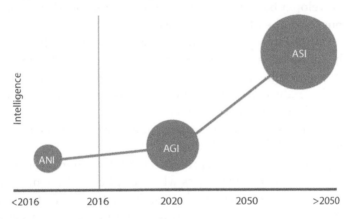

Figure 4.2 Phases of Artificial Intelligence.
Note: It explains that the changeover gap is shorter during the development of ANI to AGI while longer between II and III phases. The ASI has the intelligence of humans and machines in an equal manner. Source: UBS, https://www.ubs.com/microsites/artificial-intelligence/en/new-dawn.html, 2016.

4.3   Changing Role of Human Resource Professionals

HRM has come a long way from the traditional nomenclature of Personnel Management. HR managers are nowadays viewed as catalytic agents who facilitate organizational work. Previously, companies were not so concern about the welfare, fulfillment, and happiness of their professionals but the focus was on maintaining discipline, punctuality, and wage administration. Lately, the companies realize that the employees are not like machines but they are a vital resource of the organization. Consequently, the focus shifted on attracting and retaining the talented HRs to their organization.

Due to these environmental changes, the role of HR professionals in an organization has become very complex. Therefore, it is logical that they make use of advanced IT tools and techniques such as AI for facilitating their work. Before, the implementation of AI-based technology HR professional should

- List out the problems and areas where its requirement is more.
- Form a team of significant stakeholders and communicate them the benefit of AI implementation in business areas to solve crucial problems.
- Assess the requirement of new jobs and skilled professionals to work with AI-based technology.
- Develop a basic understanding of the uses of AI in various phases of the life of an employee.

  Applicability of AI in the entire area of Human Resources has completely transformed the entire work process of HRM. AI is enough capable to make HR professionals work easy and to reduce their manual workload but it will never be able to replace the HR managers [6].

  AI is re-shaping and transforming the profession of HRM and it can be introduced in the HR process [7]. The increasing use of AI in the HR profession results in more time being available for HR managers which can be used for motivating and mentoring employees. Now, the HRD becomes more efficient by implementing AI supporting systems in its work area, and therefore, recent technologies are the key to making a workplace less categorized, more open, and more innovative as well. The HRD must align their policies and practices with technology and employees need similarly that the marketing as per customer needs.

On the other side, the HR professional should implement AI to increase the employees' performance. There are two important functions of HRM where AI can be effectively used:

- Recruitment and selection of employees.
- Increasing the efficiency of employees.

It is an immense need to have deep knowledge and capability to articulate the influence of AI-based technology on HRM and its practices [8]. Similarly, those who are responsible for HRs must clear the doubts and make workers free from the stress who see AI as an enemy.

All the three systems of AI that are Robotic Process Automation (RPA), ML, and Natural Language Processing (NLP) have proved to be highly successful in HR profession. AI has become the latest buzz word in the global business arena which has completely transformed the HRM profession [9].

4.4   Effect of Artificial Intelligence on Human Resource Profession

In the age of recent innovative technology advancement and development, the modern and fresh In-Technology is AI. It is a progressive level of technology, developed with the aim of better economic growth, high productivity at all levels, and to help humans get over their monotonous task. AI is mainly based on big data and a set of algorithms, analyses, and study and executes the task, as a human would normally do. The interaction between humans and robots signifies as a great challenge for AI [10]. Although, all kinds of work physically performed by humans can be performed by AI-based technology in a similar way but AI lacks emotional intelligence. AI is a catchword, and everywhere, there is talk of innovative technology; it also comes with its pros and cones. AI is radically transforming HRM functions. Figure 4.3 describes the role of AI and Data analytics in various functions of Human resource management. In the future, by applying AI will detect a drastic change in the way of applying the HR practices in the organization [11]. The big challenge is of its usage, application, and its impact on HR to persist and sustain in the competitive environment. AI plays an important role in HRM; it chiefly helps us in productivity management and manpower planning [12]. It is very necessary to understand that the purpose of AI implementation is not to eliminate the HR professionals but the work performed by the HR professionals is going to be more fruitful if assisted by AI. Human interference is constantly required all the time in each area of HR. AI is purposefully not developed for replacing the human being but it directly or indirectly supports and praises the skill, efforts, and talent of HR professionals. World Economic Forum report also explains that 75 million present jobs were loosened due to AI, but simultaneously, it creates 133 million new employments such as AI Trainer and Chief Officer of Moral and Humanitarian where skill and perfection are required. AI is a fundamental part of the Industrial Revolution. There are many difficulties faced by HR professionals before the implementation of new technology such as AI in the organization. Are employees ready to adopt the implementation of AI and understand their uses? The relationship between both these questions is a critical consideration for the entire management of HRs and organization as well. The only implementation is not enough. HR

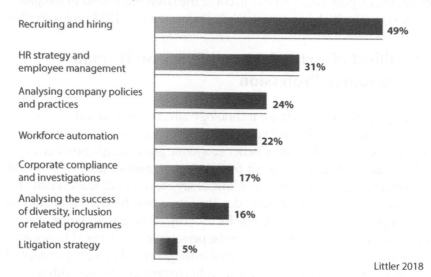

Artificial intelligence and data analytics in HR

Areas where AI and data analytics are being used to improve workforce management decisions

Recruiting and hiring	49%
HR strategy and employee management	31%
Analysing company policies and practices	24%
Workforce automation	22%
Corporate compliance and investigations	17%
Analysing the success of diversity, inclusion or related programmes	16%
Litigation strategy	5%

Littler 2018

Figure 4.3 The role of AI in Human Resource.
Note: It shows that AI is mostly used in recruiting and hiring (49%). Source: Littler (2018), https://www.raconteur.net/hr/Artificial Intelligence-hr-human.

professionals should think about the recruitment of technical experts, who operate the AI-based machines or software.

Human interaction is a dominant aspect for the HR profession. The participation of AI is not isolate HR professionals from their work but support them in transforming the process of recruitment, skilling, and performance assessment in reasonably radical ways. The impact of IT on HRM is in three categories: Operational, Relational, and Transformational impacts, which embrace all the areas of HRM [13]. Some of the aspects positively impacted on HRM include the following:

1. **Enrich the recruitment and orientation process:** Acquiring talent is an area where HR professionals require specific, quick, and measurable results to reduce the time for the hiring process. Discovering talent is a crucial part of AI application in HRM. AI-enriched HRM can process and examine more numbers of resumes to recognize and rate the talent before the process of interview. AI-based technology is applicable to a cross-section in their business [14]. By using AI through automation in the recruitment process, an organization can save

time, as well as rest on an accurate assessment of applicants like experience, skills, values, and performance to generate a perfect match. A very popular example of using technology in the recruitment process is the amalgamation of Linked in tools and Microsoft's Talent 365. First, post the hiring stage and target them. Then, the AI-supported onboarding process helps the organizations to establish a perfect working relationship with new employees. The behavior of employees can also be analyzed and understand better using AI modeling during the process of hiring and onboarding stages of an HR team member. Using AI in the recruitment process, reduce behavioral and observant biases at great extent.

2. **Ongoing employee satisfaction and talent retention:** Recently, more attention is being paid toward the retention of talent. The talent acquisition as an important activity in the organization, AI can easily remove tons of stressful and repetitive work [15]. It can also help to predict retention and beneficial training program for employees. Losing talent in terms of specific skilling and experience due to employees' dissatisfaction adds a significant insufficiency and drain of resources.

   AI empowers HR departments to monitor performance, employee feedback, and work-life balance in real time. Enterprise flexibility along with AI has played a great role in employee engagement and their need to be associated with their colleagues and peers through organizational social networks that develop a sense of belongingness.

3. **Enriched management of performance and skilling:** Rapid signs of progress in technology are placing the obligation on a current organization and its workforce, to persist competitive and relevant. AI enables the improvement of employees' skills through exact and on- schedule training. Training and skilling have also turned from classrooms to innovative smart apps. During performance analysis, AI plays a greater role to focus on the individual employee, by empowering the precise processing of high volumes data and also helps to recognize and reward individual accomplishments that would have been overlooked by traditional models. Performance management requires the use of large and separate data sets. This data sets analyzed by AI and discard unparalleled employee's data, by connecting dots that may have been invisible to evaluators or appraisers.

4. **Decreasing administrative load by introducing automation and innovations such as smart chatbots:** By replacing human involvement in monotonous processes, AI can permit an HR professional to provide free time to more concentrate on value-adding talent management doings. The use of chatbots has been found to drastically boost human relationships and also increase workforce engagement. Shifting from the outdated employee portal to an employee chatbot model ensures improved communication also.

5. **Increased compliance and dependable practices:** Compliant documentation, which helps to safeguard the rights of employees as well as empowering their optimal performance, is the ultimate facet of HR functions. The capability to deliver these consequences can often be challenging in the enormously data-dense world of HRM. AI supports an advanced order of employee-specific compliance that merges best HR practices with talent engagement.

Figure 4.4 describe the effect of AI on various functions of Human Resource Management. The future of HRM with an application of AI will lead to the following developments:

- **Artificial Intelligence for employee engagement:** Using online fast games and quizzes using intranet can engage employees in better ways.

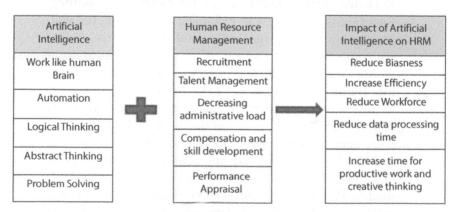

Figure 4.4 Effect of AI on Human Resource management.
Note: AI contributes toward increase in efficiency, reduction of workforce, better time management, and more objectivity in the functioning HR. Source: Researchers 'Creation.

- **Artificial Intelligence for exit management:** It is the area where HR professionals have to take exit interviews of those employees who are leaving the organization. Employees who have previously left their exit interviews can be taken through audio and video recording with the help of AI.
- **Artificial Intelligence for succession planning:** It is the process where a lot of studies have to be done to finding the right candidate for the future unoccupied position. As traditional succession planning process holds out of human error. AI-based succession planning more suitable to find out the perfect fit for the future vacant position.

4.4.1 Symbiotic Relationship Between Artificial Intelligence and Human Resource Profession

The term symbiosis is associated with the discipline of science, where living organisms exhibit interdependence for their survival and flourishing. During this relationship, both the organisms gain equal benefits. Similarly, the researchers are focusing on the relationship between AI and HR professionals. Figure 4.5 describes the prediction by Human Resource Professional for involvement of artificial intelligence. As per the above synthesis, the impact of AI on the HR profession is clear, but for another part (AI), benefits are observed as the popularity of innovative technology, the establishment of new software companies, increased employability in the field of Software Developer, the establishment of IT based technical institute, etc. As it is clear that both the components are getting equal benefits by implementing AI-based technology for the HR professionals, so it is a symbiotic relationship between both the components. ML, AI-based technology, and automation are complements for every HR professional.

The symbiotic relationship of human empathy and decision, collectively with the dominant analytical and advance predictive abilities of AI, is a formula for success in HRM.

AI role in HR domain for companies is important but no one yet mentioned AI application in removing biases in performance appraisal and management of talent because biasness has been harming the organization at extreme level up to the attrition of talent [16, 17].

There is a serious necessity that HR professionals start thinking deliberately about their roles and essentially to be more data-driven to stay applicable to future organizations. For this, there is a need to change the culture of decision-making about employees and their work.

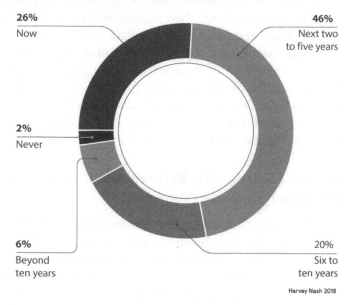

HR predictions about AI
When HR professionals think AI and automation
will be advanced enough to impact workforce planning

26%
Now

46%
Next two
to five years

2%
Never

6%
Beyond
ten years

20%
Six to
ten years

Harvey Nash 2018

Figure 4.5 Forecasting of Human Resource Professional.
Note: Forecasting of Human Resource Professional about the involvement of AI in percentage. It depicts that the next 5 years for the AI boom in HRM, and gradually, the use of AI will decrease. Source: Harvey Nash (2018), https://www.raconteur.net/hr/ai-hr-human.

4.5   Limitations of Artificial Intelligence in HRM

Even though AI is beneficial in all the aspects of HRM, it still has some limitations like other advanced technologies and machines which are enumerated below.

- **Unable to accommodate differences:** Application of AI in the recruitment and selection process is not free from blemishes. The robot fails to identify the finer nuances in applicants resume; hence, the risk remains that some good quality candidates could be rejected at the initial level itself. The interview should be taken by human expert as they are capable of judging even the nonverbal responses of the applicants such as nervousness, confidence, sincerity honesty, and transparency of the personality. AI-based technology may not pick up these cues so efficiently.

- **Lack of understanding:** AI-based systems are usually working on previous data to analyze them and draw some conclusion. AI is capable to provide data that exhibit a specific pattern after crunching big data. AI is not capable of handling the HR functions independently but it can support the decision-making of HR professionals by means of expert systems (also known as Executive Support system).
- **Lack of human-like sense:** It is a well-known fact that AI is smart enough to do work efficiently. But it lacks emotional intelligence which is very important for interpersonal relations. It fails to empathize with "fellow colleague". Further, AI lacks the qualities of creativity and innovation which human beings are endowed with.
- **System dependent:** AI is software-based system which is susceptible to system errors. The failure of AI may lead to the failure of entire HR subsystem, causing rampant dissatisfaction among the employees, leading to the increase rate of attrition.

4.6   Conclusion

In view of the above discussion, it can be concluded that HRs are an integral part of any organization because it is dealing with live resources. The transformation in HR practices through IT-based technology is responsible for automation. AI is one of the innovative IT-based technologies which have been helping HR professionals to make their task easy. AI is capable enough of handling routine monotonous administrative tasks but it lacks emotional intelligence. Emotional intelligence is a core characteristic of human beings which is not yet possible to be replaced by any other smart technology. However, AI is advance in its feature but human also has own peculiar characteristics which cannot be replaced by any technology. A blending of the analytical ability of AI and human expertise of decision-making can do a miracle in the field of HRM. Ultimately, the collaborative relationship between both human and AI is a wonderful concept to get victory over unwanted pressure of work and data handling. Symbiotic relationship of both AI and HR profession can increase efficiency and reduce biases and uncertainty in HR-related decisions. HR professionals will now have more time to focus on creativity and strategic decision-making in the area of HRM. Those organizations which are embracing AI must understand that it is not jobs but the tasks that are being automated. Organizations should also understand that automated job roles make a new way for job transformation rather than exclusion. Some limitations also exist while using AI in the field of HR. It is expected that both AI and HR professionals will co-exist and complement each other rather than competing with each other. In the end, it can be concluded that the application of AI in the field of HR will yield best results only when it is used intelligently by HR professionals.

References

1. Milani, L., Rahmati, D., Nurakbarianti, R., von Klitzing, P., *Exploring the Impact of Artificial Intelligence (AI) on Human Resource Management (HRM): A Cross-Industry Analysis*, The London school of Economics and Political science, Oracle, London, Accessed 15th April, 20, 4.30 pm, from https://www.oracle.com/webfolder/s/delivery_production/docs/FY16h1/doc36/AC-20170121-OracleAI.pdf, 2017.

2. Iqbal, M.F., Can Artificial Intelligence Change the Way in Which Companies Recruit, Train, Develop and Manage Human Resources in Workplace?, Asian Journal of Social Sciences and Management Studies. *Asian Online J. Publishing Group*, 5, 3, 102–110, 2018.

3. Jauhari, A., How AI and Machine learning will impact HR practices, Retrieved 23rd April, 20 from https://www.vccircle.com/how-ai-and-machine-learning-will-impact-hr-practices, 2017.

4. Sheila, L.M., Steven, G., Chad, M., Mayank, G., *The new age: Artificial Intelligence for human resource opportunities and functions*, pp. 1–8, Ernst & Young global limited, U.S. LLP, Accessed 15th April, 20 from https://hrlens.org/wp-ontent/uploads/2019/11/EY-the-new-age-artificial-intelligence-for-human-resource-opportunities-and-functions.pdf, 2018.

5. Saxena, K. and Bhadu, S.P.S., IT has come......to stay. *Paper presented at 29th National Convention of ISTD held at Udaipur*, 2018.

6. Merlin, R. and Jayam, R., Artificial Intelligence in Human Resource Management. *International Journal of Pure and Applied Mathematics*, Vol. 119, No. 17, pp. 1891–1895, Retrieve 15th April, 20 from https://acadpubl.eu/hub/2018-119-17/2/153.pdf, 2018.

7. Bhardwaj, R., *How AI is Revolutionizing the Human Resource Functions*, Entrepreneur Asia Pacific, Retrieve 4th May 2020, 3.00 PM, from https://www.entrepreneur.com/article/325715, 2019.

8. Nunn, J., The Emerging Impact of AI on HR. Accessed from https://www.forbes.com/sites/forbestechcouncil/2019/02/06/the-emerging-impact-of-aion-hr/6d23a2ca5496 accessed on 16th April 20, 5.00 pm.

9. Heric, M., HR's New Digital Mandate-Digital technologies have become essential for HR to engage top talent and add value to the business, Accessed 15th April 2020 from https://www.bain.com/insights/hrs-new-digital-mandate/, 2018.

10. Lemaignan, S., Warnier, M., Sisbot, A., Clodic, A., Alami, R., Artificial cognition for social human–robot interaction: An implementation, in: *Artificial Intelligence*, R. Kanna and S. Alessandro (Eds.), pp. 45–69, Elsevier B.V., 2017.

11. Reilly, P., The impact of artificial intelligence on the HR function, in: *IES Perspectives on HR*, Institute for Employment Studies, Brighton, Available at: www.employmentstudies.co.uk/resource/impact-artificial-intelligence-hr-function., 2018.

12. Srivastava, P., Impact of AI on strategic HR Decision Making, https://www.peoplematters.in/article/technology/impact-of-artificial-intelligence-on-strategic-hr-decision-making-17935, 2018.

13. Saxena, K. and Bhadu, S.P.S., *IT & HRM-The Flourishing of a Symbiotic Relationship*, Nirma Institute of Management, Tata McGraw- Hill publishing company, New Delhi, India, 2000.

14. Van pay, B., How AI is reinventing HR, Accessed 20th April, 20 from https://www.entrepreneur.com/article/320763, 2018.

15. Wislow, E., Top 5 ways to use Artificial Intelligence (AI) in human resources, Retrieved 10th April 2020 from https://bigdata-madesimple.com/5-ways-to-use-artificial-intelligence-ai-in-human-resources/, 2017.

16. Ahmed, O., Artificial Intelligence in HR. *Int. J. Res. Anal. Rev.*, 5, 4, 971–978, 2018.

17. Jain, S., Human Resource Management and Artificial Intelligence. *Int. J. Manage. Soc. Sci. Res.*, 7, 3, 56–59, 2018.

5

Artificial Intelligence in Animal Surveillance and Conservation

Devendra Kumar* and Saha Dev Jakhar

Department of Zoology, Mohanlal Sukhadia University,
Udaipur, Rajasthan, India

Abstract

Artificial Intelligence (AI) is a mainframe or any computer system which has potential to work equal or better than human being in all scenarios. The use of AI has been adopted by several organizations like healthcare, industries, business, education, tourism, animal surveillance, and their conservation. AI has aptitudes to be a precious implement for animal surveillance and conservation. In present time, AI is the basic need rather than additional things in animal surveillance because of the lack of manpower and some work limitation of human being. The use of AI is needful and fruitful for animal conservation due to several reasons like it can work better than human being in typical environment conditions without any disturbance in animal habitat and it saves human life from animal attack and reduces illegal animal trafficking and saves animal from poachers. There are several AI tools established for livestock and wildlife monitoring. The animal surveillance becomes easier with AI tools. Through AI tools, we can easily trace the animal activity and location and collect data about behavior, habitat, and their health conditions.

Keywords: Artificial Intelligence, animal surveillance, tools, monitoring, conservation

**Corresponding author:* devendrak35@gmail.com

S. Balamurugan, Sonal Pathak, Anupriya Jain, Sachin Gupta, Sachin Sharma, Sonia Duggal (eds.)
Impact of Artificial Intelligence on Organizational Transformation, (73–86) © 2022 Scrivener Publishing LLC

5.1   History

The word Artificial Intelligence (AI) was first described in 1956 by John McCarthy in the first academic conference. He was a computer scientist and cognitive scientist. He is known as father or founder of AI. AI is the broad branch of computer science. It is very useful in the today's world. In recent few years, the use of AI is increased simultaneous. In present time, the AI becomes necessity for almost all organizations. Our future will be fully dependent on AI. AI means any computer system or machine which can perform the work equal or better than the human being in any organization or field.

Image 5.1 John McCarthy (4 Sept. 1927-24 Oct. 2011).

5.2   Introduction

The main concept of AI is to create a very helpful creature which is fun-loving, caring, and flexibility for human life, which will be able to think like human being and make decision for himself without any help. The goal of AI is to create the system that work intelligently and independently. In AI, the main objective is to develop the capacity of thinking and learning. The speech recognition in AI by statically based (natural language processing). The AI work by computer vision, symbolic ways, image processing, and pattern recognition by use data. The system collects the data and codes and converts them in algorithm and then makes a decision. AI tries to break the barrier between human being and machine.

AI is very important for India. Solving major problems prevailing in developing country like India can only be possible through it. Recently, the NITI Aayog (National Institution for Transforming India) makes a decision to prepare a machine learning ecosystem at national level and makes a platform of research work in this field. AI can prove very useful in every field of life, from medical to general health care, wildlife to livestock, and from space to army. But still, it is at an early stage in the world. India has full potential to play a leading role in the field of AI. According to some opinion, there are some risk factor of AI such as job loss and fear of inferiority. But in reality, the situation is just opposite; there is no risk of jobs being lost due to excessive use of AI and it will create new job opportunities for our society. The AI is to generate the ability to think, understand, and act like humans within machines. AI is used for betterment of wildlife, livestock, and machines in adverse places like country border, large desert areas, and betterment for human life.

5.3   Need of Artificial Intelligence

In our world, there is enormous number of works that is so typical and impossible for human being. These works are required high man power and technologies. But if we observe deeply, we found that it is so typical to higher huge number of workers for one organization. In another ways, the human being is having their limitations of work and power and the time consumption is so high. Whereas the same work can be completed by machine is in less time and less money. From several years ago, the human being used machine for their work. But these machineries required human being for order or handling (Figure 5.1).

But now, in this era, we need a machine which can make their own decision and do not require human interference. We require the machine

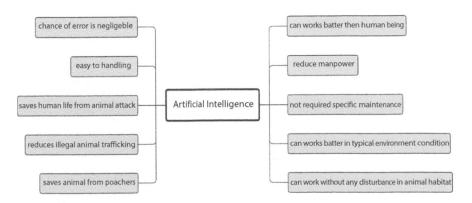

Figure 5.1 Specifications of Artificial Intelligence.

which having power of think, observe, learn the things and understand the situations, and take a decision either good or bad. In present time, the AI is very needful and useful in wildlife conservation, animal surveillance, health care, country border, security, educational organizations, health organizations, and in commercial organizations.

5.4   Applications of AI in Animal Surveillance and Conservation

Animal surveillance is a methodology by which the animal observations will be carried out for any disease and animal behavior and facilitates for its prevention and control. Animal conservation means to protect the animal and its habitat (ecosystem and environment) from human interference (Figure 5.2).

The earth planet is a very big ecosystem which can be subdivided in several other ecosystem like aquatic ecosystem and terrestrial ecosystem. These ecosystems consist several miles areas and thousands of animals. These animals are distributed in scattered and clustered form in their habitat. So, the disease surveillance and for other study of these animals is about impossible for human being [1].

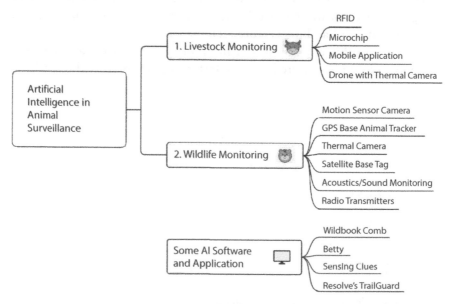

Figure 5.2 Use of Artificial Intelligence in animal surveillance.

In aquatic ecosystem, some animal such as deep see fishes are rarely seen on surface water and the behavioral study is just impossible for human being because the marine ecosystem is very large and very deep where the water pressure is so high and this ecosystem is still so far from human being. So, these fields require some technologies which helpful in these studies and make this easier for human being. The AI is very useful in these fields because

- It works in typical environment conditions;
- It works without any disturbance in animal habitat;
- It works better than human being and in less time consumption;
- It saves human life from animal attack and typical environment condition;
- It reduces illegal animal trafficking; and
- It saves animal from poachers.

5.4.1 In Livestock Monitoring

Livestock animals such as cow, buffalo, sheep, pigs, hen, and goats are the general necessity of human being. Generally, these animal productivities are very less due to their illness and disease, and because of these, the farmers do not get full profit from their cattles. Monitoring means to observe each and every moment of animal to collect information about animal location and trace their activity, their feeding behavior, and animal health status. It is impossible to monitor each animal for human being, so the human requires some help from machine. They need a machine which can work proper and independently. The weighing machine and other identifications machine is already available for animal monitoring but it is not a significant tool for other observations.

The farmer needs a tool which helps them in animal monitoring. Many computer scientists developed different tools such as sensor, chip, mobile app, tracking device, and drone with thermal sensor, which are very helpful and significant for human being. These devices are example of AI. They build up by wires and other some small hardware. They collect the data from sensor and convert them statically in natural language processing. These devices can sense the animal body temperature, their heart beat, and also sometime detect some infections in their body. With the help of these devices, the farmer can easily detect the problem and try to solve them in proper systematic ways. Some devices are already available for some particular animal such as pig; these devices also available at commercial level.

These are some example of AI which used in Livestock Monitoring as follows.

Image 5.2 RFID ear tag.

5.4.1.1   Chip and Sensor (RFID)

RFID means the radio frequency identification. It is a basic example of AI. It is a wireless communication which made up by plastic which contains a chip. It is a high-quality device in which frequency is detected by reader in a particular area range and used for animal tracing. Generally, it is an ear tag of animal and consist unique code which help in reading the data. It is commercially available in wide range. Its available in yellow and pink color. It is very simple technologies and easily handles by farmers. The animal ear-pinna just punch and then fix this RFID ear tag [2]. This ear tag protocol is so simple, it uses the electromagnetic coupling in the radio frequency portion of the electromagnetic spectrum to uniquely identify the animal.

In recent, the RFID technology uses in honey bee tagging. In this tagging, the radio chip is very small and it can easily fit on the upper surface of honey bee [3].

Image 5.3 Honey bee with radio chips.

5.4.1.2   Microchip (GPS Tracker)

It is a very tiny device which is specially designated for pet animal. It is a better example of AI. Its size is about 0.5 mm and look like grain. It is a computer chip which consist a special unique code. The unique code contains all the detailed about the animal. It is very handy and easy to fix on animal. It is just implanted under the skin mostly near the neck region with the help of needle. It is a GPS tracker chip which track the animal with the help of computer or tracker devices. It can be scanned by simple scanner. Many times, these pets are missing and without proper identification the reunites with their owner is just impossible but with the help of this microchip the pet is easily identify and reunite easily. For the pet the AI is as a god gift.

Image 5.4 GPS tracker microchip.

5.4.1.3   Mobile Application

The scientist constructs a chip with a sensor which can detect the RFID, and this chip can connect directly to our mobile application and in our computer. Several different mobile apps are designated for farmer which is so simple and easy to understand and use.

5.4.1.4   Drone With Thermal Camera

It is a simple thermal camera which fitted on drone. It is also an example of AI which broadly use in the livestock monitoring. The thermal camera can detect the surface temperature of any object like animal by detect an infrared signal which reach to the camera. It is a very powerful AI device which broadly use in animal monitoring [4].

Image 5.5 Drone with thermal camera.

5.4.2   In Wildlife Animal Monitoring

Wildlife means animal which borne, grow, and develop in wild area, also known as undomesticated animal. All ecosystem can consist wildlife. The wildlife monitoring is so typical for human being because the area is very wide and the animal number is also high. The ranger in forest area is very few in number as compare to animal number or area. Only one ranger posted in about 1,000 ft^2 area. So, there is impossible to monitoring each animal or every spot area. That is why the poacher activity is high in wildlife areas. To control the illegal animal trafficking and poaching, the AI is required. The AI tools are very helpful in these areas. Recently, from few years, the poaching activity is increase in number for animal body parts.

The AI helps in animal tracking, detects the poaching activity, traces the missing animal, observes the animal activity in particular area, etc. The common and basic tools of AI which are used in the wildlife are as follows.

5.4.2.1   Motion Sensor Camera

In the wildlife, the animal identification plays the key role in animal study and about their occupied habitat. Manually, this identification is about

Image 5.6 Motion sensor camera.

to impossible so there are some need the machine which can detect the organism and able to differentiate between them and then isolate them. The automatic identification is occurred by Motion Sensor Camera in wildlife [5]. The motion sensor camera having a sensor which capable to detect the movement. In this camera, the sensor is very powerful which designated for sense a particular animal movement. That is why this camera easily identifies the animal. The camera setup can be handled very easily. Just fix the camera where the animal movement occurs simultaneously. It detects the motion and convert them automatically in pictures.

5.4.2.2   GPS Base Animal Tracker

The increasing number of poaching cases in wildlife park and conservation areas is very problematic in this time. So, to solve this problem, the GPS tracker is attached on the wild animal. The GPS tracker is normally use for trace the animal location in particular area. It is mostly use in wildlife reserve or sanctuary or any conservation areas. This fitted on neck region of animal. The GPS tracker requires about three satellites to receive exact longitudinal or latitudinal location of the animal. In this GPS tracker, the temperature sensor can also fit for animal health conscious. A message alert also enabled in this tracker to receive location and temperature alert. Whenever the animal body temperature is rise from normal temperature by fever or any wound, then a message automatically sent to registered mobile number and the ranger get alert message and resolve the problem. Sometimes, it also helps in vaccination by trace the animal again.

Image 5.7 Telemetry system [6].

5.4.2.3   Smart Camera (Thermal Camera)

Smart camera or thermal camera means the temperature sensing camera which do not required light. It is mainly made up for night vision, also known as night vision camera. It detects the heat which produces on the body surface of animal. This camera ignores the visual camouflage. It produces picture by heat and known as thermogram which may be different color and shape [7].

Poaching, encroachment, and illegal animal trafficking are also detected by thermal camera. The thermal camera detects the human body by heal producing by body and forming an image, the ranger gets alert by this illegal activity or human movement in restricted areas, and they can trace them and arrest them.

5.4.2.4   Satellite Base Tag (Ringing, Callers)

This type of tag mainly uses for known the migration pattern of animal or bird. It is radio-based transmitter technology which broadly use in migration study. A small radio transmitter fit on animal leg and the signal receive by RDF receiver. When the bird migrates from one place to another place, then the scientist or researcher can locate their geographical location [8, 9].

The callers its primitive technology to tag a wild animal for their geographical location. A small transmitter consists in this caller and it emits signal which can receive by receiver by ranger. But it is not a so much useful technology because the wireless transmitter signal range is very less about miter to some kilometer. The ranger has a wireless receiver to receive theses signal.

Image 5.8 Bird ringing [10].

5.4.2.5   Acoustics/Sound Monitoring

It is the advance example of AI. It is a sound monitoring device which can capable to detect the individual sound and or couple of sound and able to

Image 5.9 Audio moth [11].

differentiate between them. It used in wildlife for ecosystem monitoring and to stop illegal poaching and to know the animal movement in particular area. The different sound recognition system already installed in it, and whenever the sound repeats in area, it captures and records it. Such as it detects and differentiate automatically individual sound like lion roar and gunshot, etc., and it can fit easily on tree or any stable hard places. It is commercially available in market such as Audio Moth.

5.4.2.6   Radio Transmitter (Transponder)

Transponder (Transmitter + Responder) is tiny devices which mainly use for endangered species like honey bee tagging. Honey bee is known as best friend of farmer so their conservation should be our need or necessity. It is a wireless device which transmit signal automatically and receive it. It is use in monitoring and communication devices. It is a good example of telecommunication.

Image 5.10 Transponder [12].

5.5   Some Other Tools of Artificial Intelligence

5.5.1   Computer Software and Application

5.5.1.1   Wildbook Comb (Bot)

It is an intelligent agent which work automatically on database. The Wild book Comb is an advance technology of AI. It is a computer software and can detect the particular animal by its specific coat color or patches or specific body shape. It filters the animal from photos and videos which uploaded in 2 to 3 days on social media or on own computer. Australia uses this Wild book Comb to count the giraffe number and differentiate them between profit and nonprofit giraffe.

5.5.1.2   Betty

It is also an intelligent agent and advanced example of AI which specially designated for cow. It is also known as the mobile cow app. It is very useful for dairy farming. It detects the sick and ill cow. It helps in diagnosis the disease in cow. First, it is launched in New Zealand.

5.5.1.3   Sensing Clues

It is advance example of AI in the wildlife platform. It is developed for prohibit the poaching and illegal animal trafficking. It is a computer software which can detect the human activity in prohibited areas.

5.5.2   Resolve's Trail Guard

The trail guard is the small belt-like device that is the better example of AI. It is a security base system. It used in the wildlife for detect the illegal

Image 5.11 Trail guard.

human activity, poacher activity, and illegal animal trafficking in restricted areas like national park and sanctuaries. They designated as detect the specific individuals as human creature. It can fit on any tree or any hard surface. It is very light weight and easy to handle. Whenever any poacher crosses the specific area, the trail guard device detects them and alerts the ranger. So, it helps to control the illegal activity and arrest the poacher [13].

References

1. Lalooses, F., Susanto, H., Chang, C.H., Chang, C., An Approach for Tracking Wildlife Using Wireless Sensor Networks, 2007.
2. Park, M.-C., Jung, H.-C., Ha, O.-K., Development of Livestock Monitoring Device based on Biosensors for Preventing Livestock Diseases. *J. Korea Soc. Comput. Inform.*, 21, 10, 91–98, 2016.
3. Gawel, R., August 29, 2014. *RFID Tags Track Bee Behavior*, Electronic Design, California, 2014, https://www.electronicdesign.com/technologies/components/article/21800189/rfid-tags-track-bee behavior.
4. Chen, C.S. and W.C., Research and Development of Automatic Monitoring System for Livestock Farms. *Appl. Sci.*, 9, 1132, 2019.
5. Norouzzadeh, M.S., Nguyen, A., Kosmala, M., Swanson, A., Packer, C., Clune, J., Automatically identifying wild animals in camera trap images with deep learning. *PNAS*, 115, 5713–5725, 2017.
6. Emslie's, K., *GPS and VHF Tracking Collars used for Wildlife Monitoring*, Wildlife ACT Blog, South Africa, April 17, 2014, https://wildlifeact.com/blog/gps-and-vhf-tracking-collars-used-for-wildlife-monitoring/.
7. Gonzalez, L., Montes, G., Puig, E., Johnson, S., Mengersen, K., Gaston, K., Unmanned Aerial Vehicles (UAVs) and Artificial Intelligence Revolutionizing Wildlife Monitoring and Conservation. *Sensors*, 16, 97, 2016.
8. Anderson, G. and Green, R., The value of ringing for bird conservation. *Br. Trust Ornith. Ringing Migr.*, 24, 205–212, 2009.
9. Awad, S., Farhoud, M., Saada, R., Busse, P., Long-term bird ringing in Palestine. *Ring*, 39, 83–102, 2017.
10. Picture Source: https://www.hkbws.org.hk/web/eng/bird_ringing_eng.htm.
11. Prince, P., Hill, A., Piña Covarrubias, E., Doncaster, P., Snaddon, J.L., Rogers, A., Deploying Acoustic Detection Algorithms on Low-Cost, Open-Source Acoustic Sensors for Environmental Monitoring. *Sensors*, 19, 3, 553, 2019.
12. Murray, L., Science Photo Library, 2014, https://www.sciencephoto.com/media/619862/view/honeybee-radar-tagging.
13. Dinerstein, E., *Stopping Poachers and Protecting Parks and Communities*, Resolve, Washington, 2019.

6

Impact of Artificial Intelligence on Digital Marketing

Giuseppe Granata[1]* and Vincenzo Palumbo[2]

[1]Business Management and Marketing – University Mercatorum, Dept. of Economics, Rome, Italy
[2]University of Naples, Dept. of Economics, Naples, Italy

Abstract

Artificial Intelligence Marketing is the area of marketing that uses artificial intelligence (AI) to improve the interpretation of the B2B and B2C market. It suggests the actions to be taken in order to achieve the results that have been programmed. This includes a specific area of marketing able to exploit the most modern technologies that work together with the AI and have the same final objective, like Machine Learning and NLP (acronym for Natural Language Processing), integrated with mathematical/statistical techniques and behavioral marketing. This union allows you to apply marketing choices tailored to the individual user and gradually improved. For each interaction, the algorithm acquires new data and learns from the actions that are performed, in order to develop the most specific content for the user. The goal is to transform users into customers in order to obtain a benefit both in economic and behavioral terms, since in addition to the economic result of the company, above all, the consumer will derive satisfaction from the purchase of the product or service.[1]

Keywords: Content marketing, digital marketing, cloud computing, chatbot, big data

Corresponding author: giuseppe.granata@unimercatorum.it

S. Balamurugan, Sonal Pathak, Anupriya Jain, Sachin Gupta, Sachin Sharma, Sonia Duggal (eds.) Impact of Artificial Intelligence on Organizational Transformation, (87–108) © 2022 Scrivener Publishing LLC

6.1   Introduction

At this time, the main steps will be synthesized which will then be recovered and analyzed more specifically later. The steps consist of three phases:

- The first is the collection of data about everyone who could potentially be converted into future customers.
- The second consists of the analysis of the amount of data obtained, and through the use of machine learning and of AI, they will be transformed into light signals for the management. Once you organized the data, you can implement targeted action plans.
- The action is the last step in the process, and through this, you try to involve the right target audience. It will correspond to a targeted communication campaign that will deliver superior results in terms of effectiveness.

In essence, the rule of the AI is both to aggregate and analyze the data after they are collected, and this kind of process results to be in a continuous learning and improvement task used for identifying from time to time things like the actions, the strategies, and the communication and sales techniques that have the highest potential effectiveness/success for individual segments of users. In modern organizations, there are some activities taking advantage of the AI that are developing considerable advantages over its competitors in the relevant fields. Between these are as follows:

- Content Marketing: Automatic creation of content such as articles and news and presenting them to the public at the right time is one of the most promising areas of the Artificial Intelligence Marketing (AIM). This is because through a content marketing plan that encourages conversations between the prospect, the credibility of the company is increased and brand awareness, thereby improving the credibility and reliability to the public [1]. A process is made possible only by creating a flow of information and content aimed at educating buyers B2B through a wide variety of communication tools such as articles, books, case studies, guides, online courses, podcasts, videos, webinars, and presentations able to create added value and increase the leadership of a company in a sensitive directing the purchasing process.[2]

- Voice Search: Voice Search has always established itself more as a new research method and approach to search engines, mainly because of the voice assistants like Cortana, Google, and Siri assistant. In fact, it is easier to use and more intuitive than traditional research methods. Suffice it to say that the voice is three times faster than writing and allows you to multi-task. AI that guides screen readers makes them able to interpret the semantic meaning of the research of users based on previous queries, the user's location, and the interaction with the device.

- Programmatic Advertising: It is a digital process based on the acquisition of data supplied by cookies and monitoring systems that allow to identify the user/customer target by recording every single action that takes place. Then, based on the obtained information, those involved in the marketing area from data acquired can buy banners and other forms of advertising on portals, search engines, or social channels, showing the right ads and then communicating in a more targeted to the user. In this way, companies using machine learning can have more control over the purchase and distribution of their ads, identifying with more accuracy the sites and the types of users who surf in order to verify the reliability or alignment with the positioning, the strategy, and the reputation of the own company.[3]

6.2   The Impact That AI Has on Marketing

AI, as you can guess, is one of the revolutionary elements that revolutionized the world of marketing in recent years. Thanks to increasingly sophisticated and precise algorithms in every single aspect regarding the identification of needs, the Engagement Marketers improve personalization and individual issues, automatically transforming consumer insights into messages based on their tastes [2].

Spending on AI technology worldwide currently stands at $7.409 trillion in 2019, rising by "only" $1.534 trillion of 2016.[4]

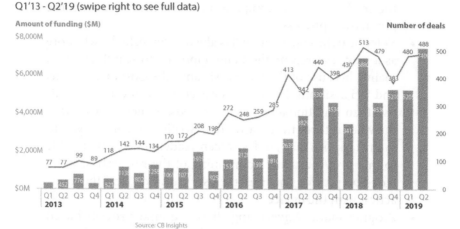

Q2'19 sees record funding to AI startups at $7.4B

Q1'13 - Q2'19 (swipe right to see full data)

Source: CB Insights

Source: https://www.selligent.com/sites/default/files/media/ebook-artificial-intelligence-it.pdf

Only 18.9% of marketers currently has a good understanding of the differences between the terms of AI, machine learning, and predictive models, while 37.4% admit to not knowing clearly both differences and advantages.[5]

6.2.1   The Data of Artificial Intelligence in Marketing

In 2020, the AI in Marketing had been crucial, and in fact, the relationships among the brands and the consumers are for the 85% conducted without the help of human interaction.

In addition, 82% of those who make the decisions of international marketing say that the predictive marketing is crucial to remain competitive in the future.

Moreover, 52% of marketers in the retail world use AI in dialogues with customers in real time, and 54% use it to personalize customer experiences on various channels.

The 70.5% of B2B marketers in North America is expected that the AI will assist in customizing marketing strategies, 63.4% in the identification of trends, and 58.1% in customization.[6]

The American Heritage Dictionary of the English Language defines AI as "The ability of a computer or other machine to perform those activities that normally require intelligence believes". Beneath the surface, computers rely on algorithms and statistical models for analyzing data and studying performance parameters and adjust future behavior (this is the "intelligent" part).

If you look around in the market, most of the "AI" solutions now available are not self-learning systems in its own right. In marketing, the AI solutions must be able to automatically identify attributes and consumer behaviors that grow their main KPIs of the campaign and to correct initiatives accordingly. But only very few are able to do this because it takes time to "train" the AI engine that behaves like a marketer and better constantly learning independently.

As we speak of "learning", it is needed to do some order: there is a fundamental difference between AI and machine learning. Elaborating on the automatic nature of learning, the AI uses a lot of data from different sources to learn and form.

A machine is usually programmed in this case and instead the AI is programmed to automatically learn. The apprehension process is done through the reception of data derived from user behavior and uses a certain set of algorithms to improve.

The marketing has a future in which the customer is the center of a super customized plan; in fact, the consumers, in general, today are used to get personal assistance during all the period, both before and after the sales. In a current study on the retail segment, 44% of shoppers in the US would become repetitive after buyer a personalized experience, while 71% expressed frustration after impersonal experience. Furthermore, 54% of the buyers expect to get a personal and customized coupon code in the next 24 hours after they identify themselves, that is not much because the 32% would like and expect to get it only after one hour.[7]

Thanks to specific AI engines for marketing, marketers now have all the tools to make real the hyper-personalization, and the thing you notice on the turnover: The e-commerce leader Amazon is already using AI advanced features for create more than 35% of its total revenue with personalized tips on shopping. The main advantage of Amazon is that its online ecosystem captures a myriad of data on interests, desires, and actual purchases of its customers, ready to be turned into tips from AI engine owner.

The AI is able to resolve the critical problem that actually is hitting the Marketing: the analysis of the big data, AI is able to understand what to do with a growing amount of quality customer data. Machine learning actually opens the world to a new generation of AI and is being part of an automated marketing system.

Instead of manually defining segments based on the people and conjecture, marketers can leverage to AI to reach a highly targeted segmentation and automatically create their own targeted messages to these customers.

Rather than designing static customer journey, based on assumptions and past experiences, marketers can now make use of AI engines to build customer journey "on the go", constantly updated with the latest data in real time. This immediate personal response level is a daunting task for companies and virtually impossible to satisfy with conventional methods.

By replacing humans' commitment with a smart and automated system, the AI brain is mainly composed for working on three segments:

6.2.1.1   The Audience: Highly Targeted Marketing Segmentation

Previously, creating audiences meant only working on demographics. Today, however, the public is segmented according to many more data and parameters that is being provided and processed by AI. AI engine gives a lot of more possibilities to create more personalized campaigns based on users' tastes, and therefore, these campaigns are obviously converting more. Larger companies would be unable to operate with conventional marketing automation as they have a need to reach a larger audience and therefore a more targeted scale of segmentation. A simple market segment which can, for example, be "female 28–32" obviously cannot have the same performance as the one created by AI which includes many other features and details that allow the customer to be better framed.

6.2.1.2   Journey to: The Customer's Road

Consumers today use different communication channels to take an interest in the things of their interest that they have already purchased or want to buy in the future. In this, the AI is gold for Marketing as it is possible to set up many different campaigns and, at the same time, understand which the right channels are and which the right moments for reaching customers are. These data affect the consumer because each of them could potentially have different preferences. This particular functioning of the AI derives from the fact that it can study the behavior on the devices and compare it with real-time actions made on the platforms in order to have precious information and therefore improve the personalization of future messages.

6.2.1.3   Offer to: Advice-Based Behavioral Marketing

The algorithms store and process large volumes of data capable of generating future personalized messages that derive from past actions. It has been statistically found that the data that have been elaborated by the AI and transformed into real automated Marketing strategies have increased the conversion rates up to 20%. AI to observe all customer behaviors, and through these, it is able to generate recommendations that are automatically inserted in Marketing campaigns, for example, if a user adds items to a wish list that will certainly be a valuable given that the AI stores in a first moment and then processes. The suggestion on the products to recommend is of fundamental importance and is part of a real-time personalization process that significantly increases conversions. Take Amazon as an example, where thanks to AI and Machine Learning, it is almost always able to hit the customer's attention with the customization of the recommended products section; in fact, when we are looking for an article we almost always notice that we are also interested in what the platform is recommending us.

In this way, thanks to the collected and processed data, many universal consumer profiles are created, and thanks to these, AI and Machine Learning always improve and are able to give accurate and updated suggestions in real time.

In addition, marketers maintain full control over which offers are displayed the most and which have the best conversions so that it is possible for them to understand which categories of products or services to focus and which ones they have to insert the most. All the rest is left to the AI engine and is easy to understand that AI and marketing experts' figures will work always more and more in symbiosis.

The data that the consumer leaves on the platforms are therefore the future of marketing in commutation with the AI, the conversion levels that are reached today have always been impossible to obtain previously, and the most surprising thing is that all this is possible thanks to the consumer himself who acts as the gasoline for this new "marketing machine", the Artificial Intelligence.

For years, marketing experts have tried to do this job manually and therefore obtain the same results, but all this on a large scale has always been, obviously, impossible. While today, even a company that has millions and millions of users can have a one-to-one marketing customized service.

But even here, the AI is not a panacea to a consumer fuzzy intelligence. The marketing initiatives generated by the AI are positive only if the data are available on customers. According to a recent edition of the Marketing Over Coffee podcast, regardless of how advanced their AI engines are, marketers still spend an average of 80% of the time cleaning and preparing data so that AI engines can start to analyze them. Proper organization of the data is only part of the attempt to make the best out by the AI. Data integration is an even bigger problem, because most marketers today still rely on technology from manufacturers mixed stack and data integration suffers. Even the best AI engines are unlikely to create product suggestions when crucial data streams—such as the purchasing records—are locked in data silos out of reach. Last but not least, another problematic technological mix-and-match stack data reliability. One study found that only 29% of third-party data providers are accurate more than half of the time. Needless to say, this level of accuracy is not the database that makes AI engines thrive for hyper-personalized marketing.[8]

6.2.2   Number of Efficiency Powered by the AI Global Consumer Statistics

The marketers are discovering the Customer Data Platform (CDP). The CDP is specifically built for the needs of marketers' engagement and to give priority to the free flow of reliable data and properties of all customer touchpoints, beyond the boundaries of the various offices in a company. The CDP also complement and verify the data by third parties and maintain profiles of customers accurate and updated in real time. As a basis for all these features, the platform creates rich universal profiles for each consumer, both for known customers, both anonymous visitors to websites. All data stored in the CDP contain behaviors, preferences, and actions of every person. Collecting big data is the perfect solution, because when the AI will analyze them, it can be able to customize the messages with the features that the consumers actually are looking for. Also if the data of one person are not enough to customize a lot his experience, they are still enough, for example, for showing him some recommended products based on what he previously searched. Starting with these basic customization features, the one-to-one marketing is automatically put in place and optimized once that draws from the rich data of universal customer profiles.[9]

For example, optimization of the send time on favorite devices: The AI engine after it has gathered long-term data on the time and the preferred device for each customer, combined with situational data in real time, sends messages as ideal canal ideal. In other words, the CDP provides the perfect fuel for AI engine.

Meanwhile, the AI that studies the content identifies them and provides them so that people are statistically shown that materials are interesting for their interests.

Also, the AI engines measure the intent to purchase (buying intent) to provide customized promotions, not only based on previous purchases, but on that which probably individual customers will buy later. The self-learning system always turns out more about consumers and how to create a one-to-one personalization that generates measurable results.

Marketers can intervene at any time and retain full control over the type of content and offers that a customer sees. Or they can simply monitor the AI engine and merely track the results at every step.

Getting the real and consistent impact from the capabilities of AI means to build this system integrated in a cloud solution marketing platform, actually this is one of the powerful tools that the marketing expert have because they are able to scale up their engine every time they want. So if the business actually grows with some simple steps, they are able to process more and more data. Also, the cloud solution allows them to manage and plan the automation strategy of the AI itself. The engine offers all AI capabilities for user engagement across all channels. The learning algorithms analyze the data in real time and uses machine learning algorithms to increase conversion of visitors' engagement and loyalty.

From the automatic user segmentation by optimizing the customer journey you select of the best offer for the right person at the right time.

In any case, it is to emphasize that today, 69% of currency marketer performance suppliers are "bad" when it comes to AI. Most solutions AI "live" still isolated in technological marketing stack, and many have integration problems.[10]

Marketing experts predict that the AI will soon become a standard for every company, and that is not all because it will also provide the only way to give personal data relevance in relationship marketing scale. Before long, the use of AI will not only be "just an option" but a must.

The contemporary history of online businesses shows us that those who are currently successful online are those who are investing in AI and machine learning; these are the innovations needed to facilitate the customer's journey in the sales process and encouraging conversions [3].

6.2.3 Cloud Computing: How it Interfaces to Marketing Thanks to Big Data

Another key pillar of the digital revolution is Cloud Computing.

The "Cloud" technology is simply not comparable to an Internet user whose sole purpose is to save data and information on a remote server. The Cloud Computing[11] is instead a new model of organizing IT resources that restores from basics the way a company is usually used to manage IT systems in order to speed up the entire management of IT: from fastest and most simple operations, such as a simple backup of information and data, to its more complex tasks, such as managing a data center.

Through the Cloud Computing technology, all the data that are created in the network converge: in the last 2 years, it has increased so much to take the name of Big Data.[12]

The Big Data is another fundamental element of the "digital disruption" and widely relevant in the growth of companies and markets, as much as the advent of the Internet. The reason is related to the possibility that provide these data can be made more accurate analysis, leading to similar levels of decision-making to the absolute accuracy.

Companies are no longer owners of their clients nor are they able to influence them as before, and the only alternative is the dialogue with them. Listening is key because it determines the future of the company, the consumer has become a "Citizen Marketer" as it has become the one who does marketing for the company; this is the note through the increasing influence that leads in the important decisions such as sending the company feedback; the ability to affect sales through word of mouth; the ability to determine the innovation of products or contribute to the improvement of existing ones; the same ability with which some figures determine the failure or otherwise manage to save businesses in crisis [4].

A learning algorithm is good if it produces hypotheses that are able to accurately predict examples of events never met previously. The quality of these is evaluated by comparing its predictions with correct classifications.

This is accomplished through a set of tests, collecting a phenomenology of cases the fullest possible extent. These results may be transposed graphically going to form what is defined as a learning curve.

The meeting point was when the marketing strategies have begun to follow more and more technological development and then keep up with the times going to seek out the consumer in new media through an increasingly important use of computer techniques.

The application areas of this fascinating field with that of marketing are numerous, as are a number of decision-making that artificial agents can play in supporting business decisions.

Some of the areas that have grown the most are as follows:

1. Market Segmentation and target.
2. Management of relationships with consumers.
3. Management in procurement and supply chain.
4. Custom Sales Management.
5. Communication B2B.
6. Pricing Strategies.
7. Development of new products, creativity, and innovation.

8. Service management.
9. Management of the web and e-commerce.

In order to achieve these objectives, the agents make use of information from behavioral targeting marketing techniques (behavioral marketing).

In the man-machine interaction process, the agent AIM uses machine learning models to find the best sales strategy probabilistically.

After each attempt, the algorithm improves its knowledge, acquiring new data and learn from experience (Machine Learning).

The use of AIs, then, is revolutionizing the way we do marketing making increasingly central customer experience, which in the past was put aside, but now with the digital revolution and the technology available to make it a real point of which to compete.

So, the relationship between companies and consumers is based on modern digital channels of interaction, particularly through Social Media App; therefore, an excellent customer care service provides for the presence of these channels [5].

The greatest contribution that these give the marketing is the ability to keep track of the results obtained, as well as the investment's ROI through the following:

- Brand monitoring.
- Customer care management.
- Collecting feedback from users.
- Instant monitoring competitors.
- Monitoring of real-time metrics.

But to be really performing and being able to keep up with all consumers' demand is not enough to man's supply but required the integration of modern AIs based on the following:

- Interactive Voice Response (IVR).
- Improvement of the identification process.
- Natural Language Understanding (NLU).
- Chatbot.

The main reason is the explosion of data in the network, which are difficult manageable and analyzable.

It is estimated that 2.5 Exabyte every day (2 and a half billion Gigabytes). Growth is exponential when you consider that 90% of the data produced in the world was created over the past 2 years.

6.2.4   AI World is Made Also With BOT. Exactly What Are BOT?

A software bot is a type of software agent in the service of software project management and software engineering. A software bot has an identity and potentially personified aspects in order to serve their stakeholders. Software bots often compose software services and provide an alternative user interface, which is sometimes, but not necessarily conversational.

Software bots are typically used to execute tasks, suggest actions, engage in dialogue, and promote social and cultural aspects of a software project.

The term *bot* is derived from robot. However, robots act in the physical world and software bots act only in digital spaces. Some software bots are designed and behave as chatbots, but not all chatbots are software bots. Erlenhov *et al.* discuss the past and future of software bots and show that software bots have been adopted for many years.[13]

They are normally used for simple and repetitive tasks, to which we dedicated a lot of time, or to which it is not worth assigning a human resource. Skype, instant messaging and VoIP software, bots define as AI programs useful to perform any type of operation such as searching for information, a summary of web pages, games, and more. You can start chatting with a bot as if it were one of your friends: you simply select it and start writing.

Some bots are considered "good", and among these, we can find the Web Crawler Spider or Spider. The first program of this kind was born in 1994 as the WebCrawler; the most famous is called crawlers GoogleBot77, known as BackRub when it was created in 1996. These robots start from the analysis of a few web pages and then follow all the hyperlinks related to them, continuing in this way until the observation of billions of pages and the creation of a "spider's web" of Internet pages; then, following a request from a user, the search engine selects all the pages that include the terms used, providing tens of thousands of results; subsequently, through the use of an algorithm that analyzes a variety of factors, including how many times one of the keywords is repeated within the site and where (URL78, title, text etc.) or how important a page can be considered based on the external links that branch out from it, finally and not less important the search indexed pages.

As said, these bots are extremely important; Crawlers of Google (the new generation of Google's spiders) are used by search engines for visiting automatically website's pages and index them on the Google search engine.

The Uniform Resource Locator: A sequence of characters identifies the location of a Web document, a picture, or a video.

Others are used with less than noble intentions; a "malicious" bot has the characteristic of self-propagate by infecting the host and creating a connection to the central server that acts as a control room for a compromise device networks, called "botnets". Thanks to Botnet that can be launched generalized seizures, remotely to the chosen target. Moreover, in addition to the ability to self-propagating, bots can be able to capture passwords, retrieve and analyze mailboxes, obtain financial information, and launch attacks DoS79. This kind of software is even used for spam, either through the mail or on social platforms such as Twitter or forums. A Twitterbot, for example, is a program that is used to publish post and follow Twitter users automatically; some are set to "answer" or "retweet" automatically based on the words or phrases contained in the post.

In 2007, a bot could infect a network of about 50 million computers, making numerous crimes, including fraud and identity theft.

6.2.5   The Chatbot: Service Robot as Support of Customer Care

The chatbots, also called chatterbot, are computer programs able to conduct a conversation through an exchange of text messages or audio messages. In particular, they have the task to simulate an intelligent conversation with humans and have various applications.[14]

The bots can be divided into two types:

- Smart Bot: through AI and machine learning learn over time and according to research carried out by users.
- Simple Bot: are based on standard rules and have the task of leading the conversation in a linear fashion along a specified route. Although, these types of internet bots have spread recently and have margins of huge growth.

Over the past decade, smartphones have been the catalysts of numerous intelligent chatbot that can interact with the user through voice commands. In particular, between 2010 and 2012, Apple's Siri and Google Now were launched by Google; in 2015 however, Amazon and Windows have introduced respectively Alexa and Cortana. In particular, born in 2010, "Siri is a faster and easier way to do everything. It's always with you, on your iPhone, iPad, Mac, Apple Watch, and Apple TV, to help you out in a thousand different ways and gradually learn to know better yourself and your needs. You ask: Siri does the rest" [Apple].

The peculiarities of modern AI systems and the bot is this: through the machine learning processes, these products are able to assist and improve continuously through the acquisition and analysis of data that we supply; reading the privacy policy just a few lines to understand that "What you say and such will be recorded and sent to Apple to process your request. Your device will send to Apple rather the information, such as your name and your username. All these data, collectively 'User Data', are used to help Siri understand you better if you've enabled location services, will be sent to Apple also the location of your device when making a request to allow Siri to improve accuracy answers".

In this way, the organization manages to acquire a number of personal data very high, so we can offer personalized services. However, not limited to data derived from digital assistant through the use of Apple applications, but also through different applications, in fact, "if you choose to enable integration with Siri to third-party applications, data from these apps, they may be sent to Apple to help Siri understand your request. Part of your request will be shared with the app to provide a response or trigger an action. If you choose to allow the app to use Siri for transcription, the transcribed voice data may be sent to Apple". The Cupertino company provides the ability to disable data acquisition services, but doing so will not be possible to use Siri or Dictation. In the above disclosure is specified that "using Siri or Dictation, accept and authorize the transmission, collection, storage, processing and the use of such information (including: voice input, user data, and other data that may be sent to Apple the apps you have enabled the integration with Siri) by Apple and on partners and licensees in order to improve and provide features such as Siri, dictation and dictation for other Apple products and services".

It was the reference to "other Apple products and services" that is the measure of how all the data collected by all individuals could be used beyond the borders of the chatbot Siri.[15]

On the same model of Siri, Google launched in 2012, Google Now, a support tool that allows you to take advantage of the full power of the search engine but not only through the analysis of information about the user, is able to provide personalized content before they are required. It allows the use of voice commands as well as text and interacts, such as the Apple program, with third party applications.[16]

In 2015, Facebook launched the Messenger test, a digital assistant that by the time working in the San Francisco, and is designed to integrate with the Messenger instant messaging platform. Messenger interacts with users through chat conversations and provides for the supervision of a team of technicians to allow the chatbot to also understand more complex sentences while maintaining the natural conversation and perform work which, alone, would not be able to accomplish. The implementation of this bot has had many positive effects for Facebook, since it has allowed us to create a foundation for developing new generation of bots and provided information about user preferences, which can be used by businesses to produce mirate ads.[17]

The opportunities that are provided by these products are manifold, especially when you consider that the development may have with the progress in AI and machine learning. To seize them, it is necessary to insert these intelligent agents within an overall strategic plan with the definition of channels and platforms, the objectives, and the monitoring and analysis processes [6].

6.3   The Community Regulation "GDPE" and Artificial Intelligence: Here's How Technology is Governed

European legislation establishes a bridge to the future by regulating the protection of personal data human-computer interaction.[18] An overview of the areas of action and the impact they will have on the rules "of the 21st century commodity".

The inevitable spread of AI systems and the impact on the lives are pos-ing significant questions in several respects: ethical, legal, social, and, of course, the protection of personal data. Hence, the need to manage, nor-malize, and regularize the flow of personal data is necessary to feed the AI. At this need, the European legislator has given a positive reply with the EU Regulation 2016/679 (GDPR).

AI, as already discussed, to be smart enough needs of the users' per-sonal data or information that identifies or make them identifiable, directly or indirectly, a natural person and who can provide information about its characteristics even particular, his habits, his lifestyle, his personal rela-tionships, his health, his financial situation, his preferences, its location, etc.

Particularly, important for AI are precisely the data: the direct identifi-cation, such as patient demographics (e.g., name), pictures, and other per-sonal data.

With regard to the indirect identification, these data may be an identifi-cation number (e.g., the tax code, the IP address, the license plate number, and IBAN) and fall into particular categories: namely, those that revealing racial or ethnic origin, religious, philosophical, political opinions, trade union membership, concerning health or sex life, genetic data, biometric data, and those relating to sexual orientation relating to criminal convictions and offenses or related security measures: these are the so-called data "judicial", i.e., those that can reveal the existence of certain judicial orders subject to registration in the criminal records (e.g., the penal provisions of the final sentence, conditional release, ban or residence requirement, and alternatives to detention measures) or the quality of accused or investigated.

With the evolution of new technologies, other data have taken on a significant role, such as those related to electronic communications and those that allow the geolocation, providing information on popular places, their movements and their frequency (a reservation on Airbnb, l' purchase of a flight, a Trip Advisor review, etc.) [7].

As was pointed out earlier today, the impact of new technologies and AI science of living is high. The AI has data needs to be put in place ("exist"): the personal data. It is equally understandable (even measurable) because, with great superficiality, users give personal information in exchange for that you can define the 21st century commodities. Too bad, this trading occurs often without proper assessment of the impact on the lives.

Over time, the European legislator intervened, first with Directive 95/46 and subsequently with the EU Regulation 2016/679, and the same thing, they did national legislators with the regulations transposing and adapting, to try to keep pace technological and scientific. Attempt, to keep up, only partially successful because, above all, the technology has a geometric progression well represented by the Moore's Law [The complexity of a microcircuit, as measured, for example, by the number of transistors per chip doubles every 18 months (and hence quadruples every 3 years)] that determines the capacity and data processing speed and this means comparison of "examples of data" and "personal data" more and more numerous (more accurately), and faster and faster.

Just this addresses the GDPR, mandatory from May 26, 2016 and applicable to all citizens of the European Economic Area (the EU plus Norway and Iceland) and citizens of the Swiss Confederation, which can be considered the norm rather new, advanced, evolved, and adapted what concerns the processing of personal data.

The GDPR pays particular attention to the automatic processing of personal data. Art. 22 GDPR (automated decision-making process related to individuals, including the profiling) reaffirms, as a general principle, that the subject has the right not to be subjected to a decision based solely on automated processing of their data, starting with the profiling, defined in Art. 4 of GDPR (Definitions), which produces legal effects concerning him or affecting the same way on his person significantly.

About the first paragraph of Art. 22, it seems clear that no AI technology conforms to GDPR without human intervention. What it is in fact required of users of IA systems to acquire and process personal information from individuals (affected) is:

- Define the purpose of treatment.
- Inform on use that is done of the IA technology.
- Collect the consent to the automated processing and profiling.
- Determine the legal basis.
- Assess the impact that the use of AI exerts on individuals (DPIA).
- Giving prospectus completed and full operation of the technology, to identify the criteria of reasoning (and possibly some starting bias).
- Intervene when you present possible opportunities for violation of the rights of those concerned.
- Communicate and inform in case of breach date.

It is worth noting that it is necessary to define the purpose of treatment. A system based on AI and machine learning (self-learning) could start treating the data even for purposes other than those first notified on which, or the interested party (owner policy) but, in some cases, not even the holder of the processing of data, news, and would therefore no possibility to exercise the rights or control which affect the lawfulness of the legal basis invoked earlier.

6.4   The Case Study Estée Lauder

The Estée Lauder brand is a world of cosmetics brand, and its beauty products and skin care products are popular all over the world.[19]

To increase your online brand awareness among young women, the company has encouraged potential customers to subscribe to their newsletter and encouraged the audience to leave contact information to receive samples of their products.

The marketing strategy was extended to all devices. In addition, the brand wanted to strongly keep costs of the promotional campaign, requiring the optimization of the cost per click (CPC) and cost per contact (CPL).

The Appier, through its CrossX platform, identified the devices owned by individual users and, through the functionality "Lookalike", reached and identified new potential profiles that correspond to the desired profile by Estée Lauder.

The result was obtained by analyzing data stored in the database CrossX, data collected from over 3,000 directly managed campaigns Appier over the years.

The use of AI has allowed Estée Lauder to reduce not only the cost of the marketing campaign but also the time of conversion of users into customers.

In addition, the brand has been able to discover that the majority of users, who have left their information in exchange for free samples offered, were people who came from ads dedicated to the theme of aesthetics and not so much in skin care.

The analysis of data, practically in real time, has made it possible to correct the campaign settings, enabling significant cost savings.

So, through advertisements devoted to "appearance", the French brand has managed to increase sales of products for skin care with "minimal effort".

The partnership with Appier allowed to Estée Lauder a 300% increase in the attractiveness of its ads promotional cross-screen, reaching in some cases spiked 1,100%.

Compared to its KPI (Key Performance Indicator), Estée Lauder has obtained the following results:

- CPC reduced by 43%.
- CPL reduced by 63%.
- The number of clicks increased by 74%.
- The number of conversions increased by 167%.

The cross-screen conversion devices were considering at least 3:

- 11 times higher than the average for the PC;
- 4 times higher than the average for the tablet;
- 3 times higher than the average for smartphones.

6.5   Conclusion

The chapter allows us to understand what the main advantages of AI are and how you can integrate these technologies into the business. Thanks to the business models and case studies, it will be much easier for an entrepreneur to understand and implement the integration process. The multiple examples will boost the managerial experience; also thanks to the very important issue addressed on GDPR regulation, it will therefore not possible to lie in legislative issues arising from the use of AI.

In particular, the case study that has been treated is reported to be very important because it allows us to understand that technological progress in the field of AI increasingly requires the marketing consultant vision "holistic", a global vision of marketing strategy, and then to his aid AI and is being more readily platforms capable of analyzing data by providing very accurate profiles of consumers.

Platforms that take advantage of neural networks to classify consumers, making predictions of behavior, suggest the best decisions to make. Platforms which may (and already are) to automate all the mechanisms "manual" adapting them according to the change in consumer behavior themselves.

The customer care, sales, can become ever more delegates to AI thanks to the "virtual assistants", including Siri, Cortana, Google Now, and Alexia that are just precursors.

What AI cannot do is replace that which characterizes the human, instinct, creativity, and his being "human".

References

1. Rancati, E. and Gordini, N., Content Marketing Metrics: Theoretical Aspects and Empirical Evidence. *Eur. Sci. J.*, 10, 34, pp. 96–99, 2014.
2. Alavinasab, S.M. and Kamal, S.H., Studying the Influencing Factors on Online Brand Trust. *Int. J. Econ. Manage. Soc. Sci.*, 4, 1, pp. 42–45, January 2015.
3. Mangold, W.G. and Faulds, D.J., Social media: The new hybrid element of the promotion mix. *Bus. Horiz.*, 52, 357–365, 2009.
4. Budikova, J., How digital trends are changing the marketing landscape. *Cent. Eur. Bus. Rev.*, 3, 2, pp. 57–58, 2014.
5. Holliman, G. and Rowley, J., Business to business digital content marketing: marketers' perceptions of best practice. *J. Res. Interact. Mark.*, 8, 4, pp. 269–293, 2014.
6. Granata, G. and Scozzeze, G., The Influence of Virtual Communities in Marketing Decision. *Int. Bus. Res.*, 10, 12, 192–194, 2017.
7. Granata, G. and Scozzeze, G., The actions of e-branding and content marketing to improve consumer relationships. *Eur. Sci. J., ESJ*, 15, 1, No. 2 No. 3, 2019.

Sitography

[1] [In depth: "The Impact of AI in Business", by "Diego Pineda", "https://medium.com/swlh/the-impact-of-ai-in-business-a14d8e98b7b9"].

[2] [In depth: "The 3 Ways That Artificial Intelligence Will Change Content Marketing", by "Lilach Bullock","https://www.forbes.com/sites/lilachbullock/2018/11/12/the-3-ways-that-artificial-intelligence-will-change-content-marketing/#5e5cc0a9618f"].

[3] [In depth: "What is Programmatic Advertising", by "Charlotte Rogers", "https://www.marketingweek.com/programmatic-advertising/"].

[4] [In depth: "What Artificial Intelligence Will Look Like In 2030", by "World Economic Forum", "https://www.weforum.org/agenda/2016/09/what-artificial-intelligence-will-look-like-in-2030/"].

[5] [In depth: "What means Indeed AI In Marketing", by "Selligent.com Marketing Cloud", "https://www.selligent.com/sites/default/files/media/ebook-artificial-intelligence-it.pdf"].

[6] [In depth: "Recognizing And Engaging Customers Demanding Of Today", by "Gian Musolino, Selligent Marketing Cloud", "https://www.cmimagazine.it/18055-riconoscere-e-coinvolgere-i-clienti-esigenti-di-oggi/"].

[7] [In depth: "Digital Marketing Strategies", by "Selligent.com, Marketing Cloud", "https://www.selligent.com/sites/default/files/media/ebook-holiday-marketing-2-it.pdf"].

[8] [In depth: "8 Million Facebook Posts", by "Marketingovercoffee.com", "https://www.marketingovercoffee.com/2018/05/25/8-million-facebook-posts/.
"Predictably inaccurate: The prevalence and perils of bad big data," by "Deloitte.com", "https://www2.deloitte.com/us/en/insights/deloitte-review/issue-21/analytics-bad-data-quality.html"].

[9] [In depth: "What Is A Customer Data Platform", by "Jordie van Rijn", "https://econsultancy.com/what-is-a-customer-data-platform-how-is-it-different-from-a-dmp-or-crm/"].

[10] [In depth: "Welcome Into The Future Iperpersonalizzato Marketing", by "Selligent.com, Marketing Cloud", "https://www.selligent.com/sites/default/files/media/ebook-artificial-intelligence-it.pdf"].

[11] [In depth: "Cloud Computing" By "Jake Frankefield", "https://www.investopedia.com/terms/c/cloud-computing.asp"].

[12] [In depth: "What is Big Data" By "Oracle.com" "https://www.oracle.com/it/big-data/guide/what-is-big-data.html"].

[13] [In depth: "Bot Software", by "Wikipedia", "https://en.wikipedia.org/wiki/Software_bot"].

[14] [In depth: "What Is A Chatbot And How To Use It In Your Business", by "Anadea, Medium.com", "https://medium.com/swlh/what-is-a-chatbot-and-how-to-use-it-for-your-business-976ec2e0a99f"].

[15] [In depth: "Siri Does More Than Ever", by "Apple", "https://www.apple.com/siri/"].

16 [In depth: "Google Now", by "WordStream.com", "https://www.wordstream. com/google-now"].

17 [In depth: "Facebook Messenger Chatbot Marketing: The Definitive Guide", by "Larry Kim, Medium.com", "https://medium.com/marketing-and-entrepreneurship/facebook-messenger-chatbot-marketing-the-definitive-guide-28aaa77e5078"].

18 [In depth: "Artificial Intelligence And The GDPR: How Do They Interact", by "Avocats-Mathias.com", "https://www.avocats-mathias.com/technologies-avancees/artificial-intelligence-gdpr"].

19 [In depth: "Estée Lauder Case Study" By "Mohd Hariz", "https://www.academia. edu/7280960/Estee_Lauder_2011_Case_Study_U.S._"].

7

Role of Artificial Intelligence in Transforming the Face of Banking Organizations

Shweta Solanki[1*], MeeraMathur[1,2] and BhumikaRathore[1]

[1]*Management Department, Faculty of Management Studies- MLSU, Udaipur, Rajasthan, India*
[2]*Faculty of Management Studies, MLSU Udaipur, Rajasthan, India*

Abstract

The phenomenon of technological revolution is taking place in the present scenario and the term is known as Artificial Intelligence (AI), which is the center of the Fourth Industrial Revolution. The dream of technology that makes machines to imitate and develop intelligence like human has now turned into reality. AI is a stream of technology that permits machines to replicate human activities and task. AI is being adopted by almost business operations and sectors; banking sector is also marking medium degree of adoption and acceptance level of this technology. Undoubtedly, AI is going to bring enormous business value to banking operations. The dynamic nature of the banking and needs of the customers at different conditions and the obstacles encountered with the traditional methods of banking have given rise to the transformation of the banking operations. AI system is capable to transform the operations of banking business, reason being that it can take decisions like human and can avoid errors unlike human. So, are we entering an age of fidelity on artificial versus actual intelligence? Or is this just a new but more accurate and efficient way to present the same information and services to customers?

Keywords: Artificial intelligence, banking, technology, business, operations, machine learning, data, transform

*Corresponding author: Shwetasolanki884@gmail.com

S. Balamurugan, Sonal Pathak, Anupriya Jain, Sachin Gupta, Sachin Sharma, Sonia Duggal (eds.)
Impact of Artificial Intelligence on Organizational Transformation, (109–122) © 2022 Scrivener
Publishing LLC

7.1   Objectives

Objectives of the study are as below:

- **A.** To study the existing knowledge and concept of AI in banking business.
- **B.** To review the existing literature about AI associated with banking.
- **C.** To have the insight about the role of AI in banks.
- **D.** To study and understand that what the future holds for Artificial Intelligence with respect to banking business.

7.2   Introduction

Technology has transformed the way businesses are operating in this decade. Sometimes, in all of our lives, we have all imagined for a robot that could follow all our orders and does work just like us. The human brain separates human beings from machines. The most recent phenomena and base of digital era revolution and recent term of Artificial Intelligence (AI) can be understood as follows.

According to [1] "It is the science and engineering of making intelligent machines, especially intelligent computer programs". (1956) Accenture's [2] defines AI as a system that can do four things: 1. Perceive, 2. Comprehend, 3. Act, and 4. Learn.

In the words of [3] "AI is one of the most important things humanity is working on".

The noun of artificial intelligence was given in 1956 by the father of AI—John McCarthy. AI is a system to make a computer, or a computer controlled robot, a software that can think in intelligent manner, in the same way as an intelligent human being thinks. Or it is a system that can understand the surrounding world, interpret the received information, and can have actions which are based on understanding, improve and enhance its self-performance by observing from what happened before and by making the systems and machines able to interact in natural manner with the outside environment, with people and data. It is the development of computer systems which require human intelligence like visual identification, making decisions, recognition of speech, and translation of different languages.

7.2.1   Three Stages of Artificial Intelligence

1. **Machine Learning:** It is known as set of various algorithms that can be used by intelligent systems that can learn from its experience.
2. **Machine Intelligence:** It is a set of algorithms which are advanced, used by machines to learn from experience. Latest AI technology is at this level.
3. **Machine Consciousness:** It is a self-learning from machine experience where there is no the need of outside data.

7.2.2   Different Types of Artificial Intelligence

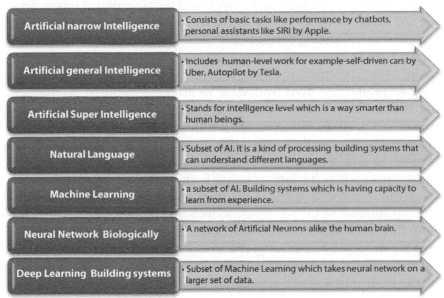

Artificial narrow Intelligence	• Consists of basic tasks like performance by chatbots, personal assistants like SIRI by Apple.
Artificial general Intelligence	• Includes human-level work for example-self-driven cars by Uber, Autopilot by Tesla.
Artificial Super Intelligence	• Stands for intelligence level which is a way smarter than human beings.
Natural Language	• Subset of AI. it is a kind of processing building systems that can understand different languages.
Machine Learning	• a subset of AI. Building systems which is having capacity to learn from experience.
Neural Network Biologically	• A network of Artificial Neurons alike the human brain.
Deep Learning Building systems	• Subset of Machine Learning which takes neural network on a larger set of data.

7.2.3   Trends and Need of Artificial Intelligence in Context of Indian Banking

The scope of AI is so wide and can be utilized by all industries whole over the world with the birth of AI, and banks are having access to improved technology and comparatively decreased costs for processing operations and data storage unlike before. We will study the effects and impact of what AI is having on the banking business and its future scope. The study is exploring the level of adaption of latest technology AI in Indian banking scenario. Both private and public sector banks are showing interest in this recent technology and have begun using it. Banking companies and financial services are also entering into the newly digitized intelligence era. Decisions and automated actions that are taken by AI are helping banks to serve their customers better in a managed way. As there is vast and rapid development in technological field like artificial intelligence, quality outcomes of these technological processes are multilayered in terms of cost, speed, profit, process, competition, and management like never before so it becomes inevitable for banking industries also to adhere these ongoing tech trends. The obvious question that clicks in our minds is: if machines will perform human tasks, then what will the humans do?

The purpose of this study is to understand the benefits that this technology will include without human interference. Albeit AI concept is new and still growing in banking business, but the business value that it is going to fetch is huge and exceptional. It has rippling effect on whole over financial sector. AI has something more than just productivity in banks as it includes a big scope starting from front desk to manage customers. Responsible and ethical AI shall drive the banking organization with profitability and growth in future. By reducing and expelling the repetitive routine work and performing more than expectation in each task, AI enhances the work motivation: skill sets and offers higher roles. AI is having the capacity to transform the whole banking practices from traditional one to newly automated one. Here, data is one of the most crucial key of algorithms which is the foundation of the AI-driven technology. As banks are having enormous data sets and information available to them, accessing these data and working on these by concluding ethical and responsible decisions becomes the major role of AI applications in banks. The technology is overcoming human made mistakes and automating tasks without error simultaneously solving complex and futuristic problems and coming up with innovative and creative ideas. So, it is experiencing positive results on all the fronts of trading, investment and banking, along with providing new doors of opportunities to all employees, employers, as well as to the customers. The paper seeks the role, importance, and impacts of AI application in banking operations and practices.

According to [4], "Indian banking sector is starting to accept AI in the past few years, and AI application's global investment has touched $5.1 billion far more than what was in 2015".

As stated in [5], "83% of Indian bankers thinks that AI will work along with humans in the next two years—a higher than the global average of 79%". "93% bankers in India responded that they increasingly use data to drive automated decision-making. Albeit 77% Indian bankers considers that most firms are not prepared to confront impending waves".

As revealed in [6], "32% of financial service executives assured that they have already started using AI solutions, including predictive analytics, recommendation engine, and voice recognition".

According to [7], "in collaboration with Deloitte, 76% of Chief Experience Officers in the banking industry agree that AI is a top priority because it is critical for differentiation".

7.2.4   Uses and Role of Artificial Intelligence in Banks in the Opinion of [20, 25 26 & 31]

Fraud Detection Task: To improve the accurate results of frauds related to credit cards— identification and activities of anti-money laundering.

Risk Management Facility: Tailored and customized services and products are offered to customers by reviewing past data, performing risk analysis, and removing human errors.

Back Office Work With Digitization and Automation: By capturing the documents using Optical Character Recognition and using machine learning.

Automated Teller Machines: It is based on image recognition and face recognition by using camera images which are real time and advanced AI stages to prevent and detect of fraud and crime.

Customer Friendly and Helpdesk: Humanoid robots and chat bot facility to enhance efficiency and also to have reduction in cost for customers interactions. For example, HDFC's EVA and SBI's SIA.

Security Issues: Doubtful practices and unwanted emails can be identified to predict and prevent security breaks.

Wealth Management Task: Personalized portfolios managements by Bot Advisor to help and assist clients by knowing their lifestyle, courage for taking risk, and expected return on investment.

Smart Wallets: AI-driven future digital cashless payment techniques with major IT companies' connections.

Underwriting: Banking along with financial sector is also upgrading on AI handled machine learning techniques for underwriting and loan application purposes, resulting in more empowered decisions.

Digitization: Gone are the times of traditional banking and physical branch services, machine learning of AI techniques and digitization has made it possible to get banking in your hands 24*7 anytime with a wide open platform.

As [8] explained, "Banking artificial intelligence is technology that makes inferences and decisions that used to require direct human involvement."

As [9] suggested in their studies, technology uses in banks can make better control over bank's administration like risk management, enhance bank's transparency, and reduce cost. So, technology can prove as a key to organizational survival, competition, and differentiation.

According to [10], use of technology in banks can increase the performance and competitive advantages.

As analyzed in [11], banks using AI can increase credit analysis methods, and AI-driven neural networks can processes underwritings and rate loan applications in the credit system of banks. Banks can also have tailored approaches on the basis of their strategies.

As suggested in [12], AI is considered in banks as new technological machine frontier because they seek for greater customer management. Banks like Standard Charted and Citi groups are in process to develop AI applications. Bank employees find potential in AI-based applications and program.

7.2.5 Importance of Artificial Intelligence in Banking Practices and Operation

AI is proving as a boon to banking organization because it increases the efficiency and effectiveness in terms of cost, reduction in risk, enhancing customer and business value, unprecedented profits, saving of time and money, while amalgamating these with new technology. AI applications empower the tasks with automated decisions which are beyond the human capacity. For example, millions of transactions take place on daily basis in fact every minute around the globe but it is just impossible for a single person to learn and remember these data and amount of transactions, it is beyond human capacity to analyze and retrieve the data but AI crosses these obstacles in fractions of seconds leaving no error, thanks to memory technology of AI. The most expensive asset and treasure that banks are having is the innumerable amount of information and data that is lying underutilized, with the help of machine learning this information can be attached with algorithms, behavioral and external information that can prove out something valuable like trust and customers relation with banks. Some of the below technological aspects of AI matters to banking organizations are as follows.

7.2.5.1 Chat Bots

Chat bot technology is the widely used application of AI in banks nowadays. As Padhi [27] says, it works on Natural Language Processing algorithms responding and interacting by text or voice with the customer in human understandable manner. They are being accessed by bank's authority considered as virtual agents. It is generally used to response customer's query.

7.2.5.2 Analytics

This technology relies on large data sets/algorithms and data is the most substantial element of machine learning. Analytics algorithms are based on machine learning technology; for example, underwriting credit application to receive a loan with all terms and conditions. In such case, a well-planned and constructed machine learning program can analyze and assume on the basis of embedded data, thereby taking underwriting decision driven by AI.

7.2.5.3 Robotics Process Automation

Robotics Process Automation (RPA) works on machine learning by imitating the routine human task and works at faster speed. For example, receiving input physically on some query by junior banking staff, processing the required methods, and forwarding the same to next level in manual activities but in AI technology, at this level of interpretation, RPA enters. AI enables RPA to make decisions independently that needs human interference.

7.2.5.4 Generating Reports

It works on NLG (Natural Language Generation) for turning the data into sequential form. Large amount of data and information is narrated and key issues are being highlighted by this AI-driven technology.

7.2.6   Impact of AI in Banking Operations

AI is having potential to transform the whole banking scenario from the very first end to the back end. Some of the banking operation areas that are being affected by the applications of AI are as follows in the views of [29 & 30]:

1. Front office operation
2. Middle office operations
3. Back office Operation

7.2.6.1   Front Office Operations/Customer Centric

The first interaction of bank's customer and bank's employees happen here; it can be approached directly by AI application like virtual chat bots that can solve customer's queries by voice or text interaction. The banks can receive enormous customer satisfaction level as well as value addition. If this application does not work in responsible and ethical manner, then banking organization would get bad experience and feedback from customers.

7.2.6.2   Middle Office/Operation Centric

Middle office includes functions like coordination of work with employees and with customers too, taking time and human interaction; here, AI processes work at faster speed and at lower cost with lesser human interaction and with better results, making banking business dependent on machine decisions.

7.2.6.3   Back Office/Decision Centric

Back office operations are done to check obstacles and reconciliation issues, and AI can detect errors and can make necessary adjustments along with detecting the risk and also mitigation of the risk. But the question of extra dependency over AI comes into picture in back office operations and decisions.

7.2.7   Future of Artificial Intelligence in Banks

AI technology has peaked to the level where it becomes inevitable for financial and banking institutions to abide by it so as to have growth, profitability, and better customer management. Banks are in continuous process to explore more ways in which AI can be empowered in their organizations. As stated earlier, that AI covers a range of technology like analytics, RPA, and NLG. As [23] states, machine learning contains the potential foundation of innovation and development in product and banking services. All these depend upon the greater collaboration between machines and humans. AI decisions shall be significant only when there is balanced supervision over machines decisions. The resultant outcomes of AI applications have to be morally and ethically right for customers to accept. The impacts have already been much on positive sides, so a bright opportunistic future of AI is waiting in banking scenario where lesser human intervention with ethical banking and investment results would be exceptional in terms growth as well as profitability.

7.3 Existing Technology

In this computerized and technological-driven scenario, banking sector is also experiencing a working change in its approach from brick mortar building branches to digital banking. Banks are dramatically spending on AI and Machine Language for personalized customer experiences to fulfill the interests of the technological updated class. According to [24], traditionally, these services included face-to-face contacts and written application proofs but AI is now available to differentiate payments, provide advices to customers based on payment history, offer suggestions, and a facility of chat bots for answering frequently asked customer queries. Banks are using AI like never before to evolve and offer customer's highly personalized, tailored, and customized products and services. Digital channels need to be constantly sync with new technologies to attract and retain customers.

According to [13], "The extended technology acceptance model gives an overview of what factors influence the mindset of individual persons when it comes to new technologies. Since organizations are always made up of people".

In addition, [14] have written articles on the use of RPA in the banking sector. While this is not as sophisticated as AI (e.g., cannot handle unstructured data), it could be considered as an intermediary step to real AI applications, which makes it worth discussing in our opinion. We thus believe that some of the insights with respect to RPA in banking will also hold for AI and that is why we will investigate it nonetheless.

7.4 Methodology

To investigate the transformation in banking business after the introduction of AI and understanding the role of AI in banks, we conducted a systematic extensive review of literature to identify previous conceptual studies on AI and banking. The potential contribution of this study is to identify the level of adoption of AI in banks and how is it changing the business that banks perform and create a framework for future research. The study would be a relevant contribution for researchers and academician who want to explore and study the AI and banking field, for data management and machine learning experts who can develop investment friendly application for future purposes. This study is review based which includes secondary data (newspapers, journals, articles, books, and Google Scholar) and follows systematic review of literature on AI and banking, impacts, benefits, and future of AI in Indian banking organizations.

7.4.1   Search Process

This study is review based (secondary data sources) in which studies from SSRN, ResearchGate, and Google Scholar have been used. Currently published articles related to AI and banking have also been studied. A list of relevant keywords is included: banking business and operations, finance and technology, artificial intelligence, and artificial intelligence and banking.

7.4.2   Selection Criteria and Review Process

Introduction of AI in banks is at the very initial level so only a few number of literature are present in this area, but to understand the concept and changes taking place in banking industry, latest published articles, papers, reports, and the reviews from the experts of IT and banking sectors were used. The review process includes four stages: searching, screening, selecting, and studying. At first stage, the related topics were searched by keywords, and total 50 articles and papers were searched; at second stage of screening, titles and abstract were studied and 20 papers were rejected; at third stage of review process, selection of 30 papers and articles were used and these were studied in detail to reach out the suggestions and findings.

7.5   Findings

Findings of this study point out that AI is entering into almost procedures of banking businesses that require a very low level of intelligence and have high volume in terms of task and profits. Reviewing process revealed that AI techniques are normally used by private sector banks that also in metropolitan areas, public sectors banks and urban areas are lagging behind using AI in comparison. In the views of [28] this innovation is helping banks not only in performing at lower costs but with more accuracy and quicker speed than earlier when they were handled by humans. Using algorithms, AI is being encountered with great success in customer services, risk assessment, and fraud detection. Adaptation of AI in banking sector has certain pros associated with it; some of them are enlisted by [15–19] which observed that it can enable and accelerate automation of all the processes in banking, less room for human errors, it can significantly reduce the cost of banking services, and it can aid in systematically analyzing behavior pattern of customers and offer them more personalized services to cater their needs. With the use of machine learning, AI systems can identify abnormalities in patterns to recognize security threats and responds to them in time.

7.6   Conclusion

Futuristic scenario of AI in banks will be deploying virtual assistants to suggest and guide customer, chat bots, credit appraisal, etc., by making humans free to do more complex task. So, the need of the time emphasizes that employees as well as customers should be well acquainted with AI technologies and operations. There is a wide scope available for expanding awareness about AI because resources are still scarce in this area. The core issues of AI should be strengthen—people, data and process, making trio of these element firm, shall undoubtedly drive any banking organization at par excellence. As AI is an evolving field, this paper cannot answer all questions and inspect all the areas. It is clear that by having an organization-wide approach by implementing AI applications, banks can take huge advantage in terms of cost cutting as well as customer satisfaction. Banking s that are using advance AI are surely going to encompass multilayered effects on cost, competition, profitability, and growth. So, the time has come when banking should embrace and welcome the power of AI in its practices as well as operations.

7.7   Suggestions

Our suggestion for this study would be that the future appraisals systems and evaluation of banking companies should be in terms of degree of adoption of AI systems and technique implementation, in a manner that the outcomes and consequences can be used in better way. [21] says that a knowledge framework of AI should be used widely for both employees and customers. Banks should focus more and more on data acquisition. Human intelligence should control the AI techniques and systems and not the reverse. According to [22] no matter where the technology and machine decisions reach, the sense of attachment and belonging that a human being can maintain with another can never be replaced by machines and AI, though to reach at the pinnacle of success and to beat competitors in cut-throat competition and profit-making scenario, AI is going to spread its wings dramatically and drastically.

References

1. Artificial intelligence, Amazon.com, Rockville, Maryland, USA, Retrieved February 2020, from www.sciencedaily.com: https://www.sciencedaily.com/terms/artificial_intelligence.html.

2. Shook, E.J., *Future Workplace Survey-Realizing the Full Value Of AI*, Accenture., USA, 2017, Retrieved January 2020, from www.accenture.com: https://www.accenture.com/_acnmedia/pdf-79/accenture-insurance-report-ai-future-workforce-survey.pdf.

3. https://theprint.in/tech/sundar-pichai-thinks-ai-will-be-a-more-profound-change-than-fire/353300/. Retrieved February 2020, from www.theprint. in: https://theprint.in/tech/sundar-pichai-thinks-ai-will-be-a-more-profound-change-than-fire/353300/, 2020.

4. Fintech India Report. Asset Publication. https://www.pwc.in/assets/pdfs/publications/2017/fintech-india-report-2017.pdf, 2017.

5. Accenture Techvision Report, Acnmedia, USA, 2018, https://www.accenture.com/se-en/insight-technology-trends-2018.

6. Artificial Intelligence (AI), Adoption Grew Over 60% in the Last Year, 2018. Retrieved 2020, from www.narrativescience.com: https://narrative-science.com/resource/press-release/artificial-intelligence-ai-adoption-grew-over-60-in-the-last-year/.

7. How artificial intelligence is transforming the financial ecosystem, 2018. Retrieved 2020, from www2.deloitte.com: https://www2.deloitte.com/content/dam/Deloitte/uk/Documents/financial-services/deloitte-uk-world-economic-forum-artificial-intelligence-summary-report.pdf.

8. Latimore, D., 2018, September. Retrieved February 2020, from Artificial Intelligence in Banking-Where to Start.: https://cdn2.hubspot.net/hubfs/Marketing Assets/ArtificialIntelligenceinBanking-WheretoStart.pdf.

9. Healy, P., Information Asymmetry, Corporate Disclosure & Capital Markets: A review Of Empirical Disclosure Literature. *J. Account. Econ.*, 31, 405–410, 2001.

10. Koteswara Rao, G., Kumar, R., IIM, I., Framework to Integrate business intelligence and Knowledge management in banking industry. *Rev. Bus. Technol. Res.*, 4, 1–14, 2011.

11. Eletter, S.F., Yaseen, S.G., Elrefae, G.A., Neuro-Based Artificial Intelligence Model for Loan Decisions. *Am. J. Econ. Bus. Admin.*, 2, 1, 27–34, 2010, https://doi.org/10.3844/ajebasp.2010.27.34.

12. Matthew Sainsbury, F.M., *Artificial Intelligence Leading The Way For Finacial Services Technology,* Innovation, Retrieved March 2020, from www.Fst.asia.com: USA, 2013, http://fst.asia/NewsArticle_details.aspx? Articlenewsid=56.

13. Davis, V.V., A Theoretical Extension of the Technology Acceptance Model: Four Longitudinal Field Studies. *Manage. Sci.*, 46, 186–204, 2000, 10.1287/mnsc.46.2.186.11926. Retrieved March 2020 from www. researchgate.com.

14. Bohlke, A., Robotics Process Automation In Finance, 2018. Retrieved February 2020, from www.rolandberger.com: https://www.rolandberger. com/fr/Publications/pub_robotics_process_automation_finance.html.

15. Mannino, A., Althaus, D., Erhardt, J., Gloor, L., Hutter, A., Metzinger, T., *Artificial Intelligence: Opportunities and Risks. Policy Paper*, pp. 1–16, Effective Altruism Foundation, London, 2015, www.foundation-al-research.org. Retrieved March 2020, from Artificial Intelligence: Opportunities And RiskPolicy Paper: www.foundational-research.org.

16. Verma, S., *UAE Banking On AI*, 2017, Khaleej Times, UAE, Retrieved January 2020, from www.khaleejtimes.com: https://www.khaleejtimes. com/editorials-columns/uae-banking-on-ai-and-the-results-are-showing.

17. Ghurair, A., 2018. www.khaleejtimes.com. Retrieved December 2019, from Embracing Artificial Intelligence: Do UAE banks Have a Choice: https://www.khaleejtimes.com/business/banking-finance/embracing-artificial-intelligence-do-uae-banks-have-a-choice.

18. Manning, 2018. internationalbanker.com. Retrieved January 2019, from How AI is Disrupting Banking Industry: https://internationalbanker. com/banking/how-ai-is-disrupting-the-banking-industry/.

19. Punamaraju, R., How Artificial Intelligence Is Changing The Banking Sector - CXOtoday.com, CXOtoday: http://www.cxotoday.com/story/ impact-ofartificial-intelligence-on-the-banking-sector, 2018.

20. Alzaidi, A.A., Impact of Artificial Intelligence on Performance of Banking Industry in Middle East. *Int. J. Comput. Sci. Netw. Secur.*, 18, 140–148, 2018.

21. Bhushan, K., 2018. Retrieved January 2020, from www.livemint.com: https://www.livemint.com/AI/Artificial-Intelligence-in-Indian-banking-Challenges-and-op.html.

22. Bilton, N., Artificial Intelligence As A Threat. *N. Y. Times*, Section E, 4.101, Page 2, 2014, November.

23. Clifford, C., 2018, Feb. Retrieved December 2019, from www.analyticsinsight.net: https://www.analyticsinsight.net/five-ways-ai-and-ml-technology-can-revolutionise-the-banking-experience-for-better.

24. Comes, A., How is Artificial Intelligence Changing the Banking Industry?, 2019. Retrieved 2020, from www.bobsguide.com: https://www.bobsguide.com/guide/news/2019/Jun/27/how-is-artificial-intelligence-changing-the-banking-industry/.

25. Jewandah, S., How Artificial Intelligence Is Changing The Banking Sector–A Case Study of top four Commercial Indian Banks. *Int. J. Manage. Technol. Eng.*, 8, 7, 525–530, 2018.

26. Deshpande, B.N., Digitalization In Banking Sector. *Int. J. Trend Sci. Res. Dev.*, 4.101, 80–85, 2018.

27. Padhi, U., *Future Of Artificial Intelligence In The Banking Sector*, 2019, Youth Ki Awaaz, Self Published, India, Retrieved February 2020, from www.youthkiawaaz.com: https://www.youthkiawaaz.com/2019/07/future-of-artificial-intelligence-in-banks.

28. Sabharwal, M., The use of Artificial Intelligence (AI) based technological applications by Indian Banks. *Int. J. Artif. Intell. Agent Technol.*, 2, 1–5, 2014.

29. Saman Goudarzi, A.S., *AI In Banking & Finance*, The Centre for Internet and Society, India, 2018.

30. Uyttendale, J., *Artificial Intelligence In Corporate Banking-A Closer Look At The Potential Impact On E- Business Process*, Gent University, Belgium, 2018, Retrieved January 2020, from lib.ugent.b: https://lib.ugent.be/.

31. Vijai, D.C., Artificial Intelligence in Indian Banking Sector: Challenges and Opportunities. *Int. J. Adv. Res.*, Belgium, Gent University, Belgium, 7, 5, 1581–1587, 2019.

8

Artificial Intelligence and Energy Sector

Oum Kumari R

Department of Economics, Manipal University Jaipur, Jaipur, India

Abstract

Energy sector occupies a central role in the path of development of any nation as economic growth and energy supply are very closely correlated with one another. All the economies are striving hard to grow and attain the status of development, and this could be achieved only through uninterrupted supply of power in the economies.

Energy sector forms a critical component of infrastructure that influences the growth and development of economy. India ranks fifth in terms of energy consumption and it also comprises of 3.4% of total global consumption. The growth in the consumption of energy is an effective indicator of growth but this increase in the per capita consumption of power/energy has given rise to many problems. The present chapter is divided into three sections: Section 8.1 gives an overview of energy scenario in India, and challenges of energy sector are discussed in Section 8.2. Section 8.3 provides some strategic measurement to overcome energy crisis without harming the environment and compromising the development of nation.

Keywords: Energy sector, infrastructure, economic growth, environment, energy crisis, economic development

8.1 Introduction

Tremendous efforts have been taken by Indian power sector since independence to provide adequate energy/power supply to take the economy to greater heights and keep ourselves at par with the other developed and developing nations. The growth in the installed capacity in last seven

---

Email: Oum.kumari@jaipur.manipal.edu

S. Balamurugan, Sonal Pathak, Anupriya Jain, Sachin Gupta, Sachin Sharma, Sonia Duggal (eds.)
Impact of Artificial Intelligence on Organizational Transformation, (123–130) © 2022 Scrivener Publishing LLC

decades and increase in the per capita consumption of power clearly indicates the fact that India is no more an underdeveloped nation but a developing nation. But the price paid for the development witnessed in last few decades if very high in terms of environment, resources, health, productivity, etc. The various threats from Indian power sector is discussed in detail in this section.

8.1.1 Increase in the Emission of Greenhouse Gases

More than 70% of energy needs is met from fossil fuel especially coal which is a significant emitter of harmful gases like carbon monoxide, sulfur dioxide, carbon dioxide, and nitrogen oxide. India is ranked as the third biggest emitter of greenhouse gases in the world. There is an urgent need to fight the battle against adverse environmental issues either by curbing the excess demand for power through artificial intelligence or by switching over to renewables through AI.

8.1.2 Increase in the Financial Burden

The cost of generating thermal power is very high as compared to other fuel sources as coal of good quality is imported from other countries to meet our energy demand. Inefficient thermal power plants also fail to utilize our full capacity resulting addition to our existing financial stress.

8.1.3 Huge Power Deficit

Demand for power has always been exceeding supply as witnessed in last few decades in many of the states and because of this majority of villages are not provided with adequate power which, in turn, hampers the development process of rural areas. AI can help us to forecast the demand for power which will help us to allocate the load more effectively and efficiently.

8.1.4 Water Scarcity

This is one of the issues caused by thermal power plants. Thermal power plants are known as great pollutants but they are also consuming excessive water causing excessive water stress which affects households and industries, ultimately slowing the pace of development. India has 269 thermal power plants, and these plants consume 88% of total water consumed in industrial sector [1]. If sufficient efforts such as use of renewable energy like solar and wind energy would supplement our energy needs without water stress, therefore water that is utilized in thermal power plants could be used for meeting the basic water needs of the people.

Researches all over the world in the past two decades have been emphasizing on the use of renewables as the only solution to fight the battle against climate change. Switching over to renewables will help us not only to reduce our dependence on fossil fuel but also to achieve self-sufficiency of power as renewable energy sources like solar and wind have huge potential in country like India. But in spite of inventions, innovations, and policy making in the areas of renewables, country like India has failed to tap the potential of renewable energy sources.

8.2   Challenges of Indian Power Sector

In order to achieve steady growth, an economy is therefore forced to increase its installed capacity so as to meet the ever increasing demand for power. The ambition to make India a $5 trillion economy by 2024 would not be possible without increase in the supply of energy to meet out the growing demand. But this increase in the supply of power has led to various other serious issues listed below.

8.2.1   Global Warming

More than 70% of energy needs is still met out from coal and other conventional energy sources. Electricity demand has increased by 36% since 2012 but the generation from coal fired plants have increased by 74%, thereby contributing toward environmental degradation [2]. As shown in Figure 8.2, majority of our energy needs are met from conventional sources like coal and oil, resulting in the emission of harmful gases like sulfur dioxide, carbon monoxide, nitrogen oxide, carbon dioxide, ozone, lead, and non-methane hydro carbons. Thermal power plants are considered to be one of the major contributors of pollutants released in the atmosphere, resulting in global warming.

8.2.2   Depletion of Coal

India ranks second in the world after China in the production of coal but the reserves available would not be sufficient to produce the needed electricity in future. Heavy dependence on coal for energy needs has definitely decreased the reserves of coal in India to a larger extent. It is estimated that one ton of coal can generate 2,460 KWh of electricity and the current installed capacity of power from coal is 198,495 MW as on 31st January 2020 [3] which means requirement of 80,000 tons of coal. But it is also found that the total reserves of coal in India would not be sufficient to generate power for more than 35 years.

8.2.3   Huge Financial Stress

Economies are continuously increasing the investment on generation of power either by borrowing from external source or by allocating a significant portion of the annual budget which is not only adding on to existing debt but also imposes severe financial stress on the government. This could be seen from the fact that the Rajasthan State Electricity board is under a debt of more than one Lakh crore and also is failing to revive for more than one decade. Electricity theft, free electricity for farmers, transmission, and distribution losses also add on to the problems and aggravate the financial stress of government further.

8.2.4   Power Crisis

Per capita consumption of power has been increasing rapidly since independence. In 2001, the per capita consumption of power was just 559 KWh, and now, it has increased manifold to 1,100 KWh, i.e., around 100% rise in 20 years. Ministry of power has been trying very hard to increase the supply of power in order to meet the growing demand for power.

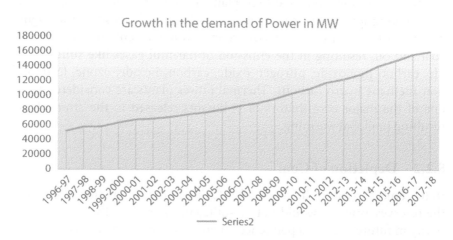

Figure 8.1 Increase in the demand for power since 1996 to 2018. Source: Annual Reports, Ministry of Power.

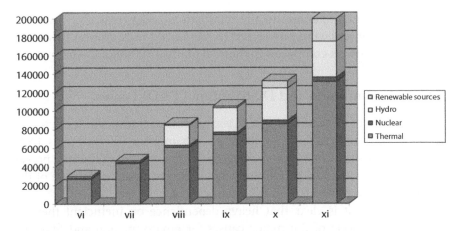

Figure 8.2 Growth in installed capacity during planning period. Source: Central Electricity Authority.

Figures 8.1 and 8.2 clearly bring out the increase in the power consumption in India since 1996 and increase in installed capacity. The table shows that electricity as an important energy source has occupied a very important role leading to increase in the per capita consumption of power manifold in last six decades. This continuous increase in power consumption has resulted in increase in the installed capacity so as to keep pace with the growing demand.

8.2.5 Health Issues

Coal is widely used all over the world as it has the highest energy generation potential. The pollutants released from coal fired plants are said to be the cause for serious health issues in an economy. The harmful gases released from burning of coal have led to skin, cardiovascular, brain, blood, and lung diseases [4]. Sulfur in coal pollutes air, water, and land extensively which accelerates the rate of diseases and also decreases the life expectancy of people around the power plants diseases [5].

8.2.6 Plant Load Factor

Plant load factor (PLF) is a measure widely used to assess the capacity of power plants. It is the percentage of energy generated and supplied corresponding to the installed capacity in that period. The PLF factor of thermal power plants is reported between 65% and 70% [6] which is considered to be very high in comparison to the international standards. PLF factor in the case of solar and wind power T&D losses is said to be around 18%–20% which is very low as compared to thermal plants [7] (Shika Lakhanpal).

8.2.7   Transmission and Distribution (T&D) Losses

Some amount of electricity is lost in the process of transporting electricity from the point of generation to point of consumption referred to as T&D losses. This loss is estimated to be 22% in the case of Indian thermal power plants [8]. This 20% loss is definitely adding to the financial burden of the Ministry of Power but also on the environment.

From above, it is clear that heavy dependence on inefficient thermal power plants is one of the major causes for environmental and financial issues in India. If timely measures are taken to supplement our energy needs through renewable, then we would not only take the economy to toward the path of development but also protect our environment from global warming and climate change. But there are various issues related to the use of renewable energy sources which could be easily overcome by integrating Artificial Intelligence and renewable energy sector. Section 8.3 provides the solutions that could be offered in the field of renewable energy system.

8.3   Artificial Intelligence for Energy Solutions

Renewable energy sources account for one-fifth of total installed capacity but it has contributed only to one-tenth to the electricity generated (CEA) and the target to achieve 40% of the total installed capacity by 2030 in renewables seems to be difficult. Solar and wind energy together have a huge potential of 300 GW and 750 GW in total 1,050 GW but generating only 68 GW in total [9]. In order to keep pace with the growing demand for power on one hand and to protect our environment on the other, efforts have to be made to understand the bottlenecks in exploring the renewables and find some strategic ways to overcome the difficulties addressed in the renewable energy sector. In the present chapter, efforts have been made to identify the use of artificial intelligence to solve the problems in renewable energy sources.

No doubt, renewable energy is a solution which would make our world a safe place to live but also energy proficient. Artificial intelligence in renewable energy sector can help us not only to meet our energy demand but also protect our environment from global warming and climatic change by reducing our dependence on conventional fuels such as coal and oil.

AI would help us to develop smart entities which would provide accurate predictions for all energy related issues. AI algorithms are much successful in solving various problems such as predicting, forecasting, modelling, and control of renewable energy systems. AI will help us to develop technologies to improve the following:

a) Net load forecasting
b) Line loss prediction
c) Decision process
d) Energy efficiency
e) Renewable energy operations
f) Equipment failure prediction, etc.

All the current issues of energy sector like heavy dependence on conventional fuel, ever increasing demand for power, financial stress toward increase in the installed capacity, and adverse environmental issues could be very well tackled by artificial intelligence. Policymakers therefore should encourage and motivate the researchers to come up with feasible solutions to tackle all energy related issues through AI.

References

1.   Annual Report- TERI.
2.   Kumari, O. *et al.*, Environmetal kuznet's Curve for Sustainable Development. *Int. J. Innov. Technol. Exploring Eng.*, 12(s), 8, 813, 2019.
3.   Central Electricity Authority, Annual Reports, 2019.
4.   Badman, and Jaffe, Blood and Air pollution; State of knowledge and research needs. *Otolaryngol.-Head Neck Surg.*, 114, 205, 1996.
5.   Kelsall, *et al.*, Air Pollution and Mortality in Philadelphia, 1974-1988. *Am. J. Epidemiol.*, 146, 9, 750, 1997.
6.   Central Electricity Authority (CEA), Annual Report, 2020.
7.   Seetharaman, G., Why India may not achieve its 2022 clean energy targets, The Economic Times, Nov 3, 2019.
8.   Central Electricity Authority (CEA), Annual Report, 2019.
9.   Business Today, New Delhi, December 27, 2019.

Impact of Artificial Intelligence on Development and Growth of Entrepreneurship

Pooja Meena[1]*, Ankita Chaturvedi[2] and Sachin Gupta[1†]

[1]Department of Business Administration, Mohanlal Sukhadia University, Udaipur, Rajasthan, India
[2]Department of Accounting & Taxation, IIS deemed to be University, Jaipur, Rajasthan, India

Abstract

"In changing global scenery, where digital technology is the centerpiece of every economy, the focus now should be on entrepreneurship."

The continuous uses of Artificial Intelligence (AI) in every field of life are the second wave of digital transformation. Companies around the world are taking advantage of the new capabilities that technologies such as machine learning can provide to optimize their current operations or create new business models. As a result of the proliferation of large amounts of data, there has been a tendency to leverage AI to process them cheaply, conduct open research, and raise funds on a large scale, a virtuous cycle that has only accelerated in recent years used to be. AI has already firmly penetrated in so many fields of our businesses, our professional, personal, and even our daily life. It has an amazing ability to modernize business activities, develop new ideas, products and services, and solve production problems to achieve large-scale entrepreneurial activities.

Entrepreneurial activities were inspired in AI where knowledge is the main source of production to understand the whole scenario for better production and it is necessary to assess the entrepreneurial process from a new field. The aim and main objective of the paper is to discover the character of the knowledge and activity-based entrepreneurial process and its components. The outline and

---

*Corresponding author: Pooja.meena9@yahoo.com
†Corresponding author: sachinguptabusadm@gmail.com

S. Balamurugan, Sonal Pathak, Anupriya Jain, Sachin Gupta, Sachin Sharma, Sonia Duggal (eds.) *Impact of Artificial Intelligence on Organizational Transformation*, (131–146) © 2022 Scrivener Publishing LLC

structure process includes the opportunity identification, opportunity development, growth, and opportunity exploitation.

AI in the field of entrepreneurship is considered as one of the most essential force that determines the health of the economy of a country even for a tribal place too. This article aims to review the current scenario of entrepreneurship and AI system in tribal areas to propose an effective environment for integrating and promoting AI education awareness and knowledge as essential to mainstream business education for a developing country like India and for tribal areas, too.

Keywords: Artificial intelligence, entrepreneurship, business, innovation, information, technology, ability

9.1   Introduction

In present era of changing scientific technology advances, business and entrepreneurship is not only a source of creating new products and services but also they are reshaping and creating industries, small and big business, blurring geographical boundaries and challenging the existing regulatory frameworks.

At the time of the 20th century, the world saw the structured development of many new creation and inventions like microcomputers, telecommunications and mobile phones, information technology, globalization restructures after 1991, and the Internet and Intranet. Since the business is not far from these developments, it has been greatly influenced. It has essentially moved the phases of trade and business to include electronic and online commerce rather than the typical older stages.

As the speed of the business environment are moving rapidly, and as a result, costumers are needed, there has been a huge amount of specific and relevant data that can be analyzed toward intelligent decision-making, information gathering, and knowledge creation. This means too much time and effort. This has open up doors broadly for data pulling out processes to arrange out irrelevant business data. Also, the development in other software systems has added a new edge, founding of business intelligence toward upgrading the performance of business organization.

The present industries and businesses being powered by high advanced technologies like Artificial Intelligence (AI), robotics, and Internet are developing so quickly that it can be difficult for industry analysts and experts to keep pace.

AI cannot always perform the best on its own; but humans make them able to do the best. AI technologies are vast and huge at replacing heavy or even lower-level cyclical or boring tasks, but when a humans being and machines work together, businesses often get the best performance changes improvements.

9.2   Entrepreneurship

Entrepreneurial business is the ability to develop, organize, and run an enterprise as well as to make profit with its uncertainties. In simple terms, entrepreneurship means starting new businesses to earn profit. In the economical way, labor, natural resources, land, and entrepreneurship involving capital can generate a profit. The entrepreneurial image is defined by discovery and researches risk taking ability; it is also very important for a country's ability to succeed in a fast-changing and more competitive global market. Entrepreneurs by placing profitable business proposition attract investment to ensure private participation in the industrialization process [1].

Role of entrepreneurship in economic development of a country:

- To the economic development of a nation
- For job creation
- To improve standard of living
- To growth in capita income
- For improvements in infrastructural facilities
- To export products
- To raise national income
- To fetch new technologies.

9.3   Artificial Intelligence

In modern age, AI is an integral part of robotics and science that focuses on the creation and invention of self-working intelligent machines and tools that reacts and works like a human. Computers and robots are designed for many activities like problem solving, forecasting etc., for this many technical and specialized research work is done by AI. There are so many reasons why AI is a mandatory for new era business such as follows:

- Speech recognition
- Learning
- Planning

- Knowledge
- Reasoning
- Problem solving
- Perception
- Ability to manipulate and move objects etc.

There are some reasons why AI is necessary for new startups and for new entrepreneurs:

- Accuracy: With AI, the chances of errors are negligible. Its accuracy is very high.
- Less work load: The use of AI reduces the work load of human, and the risk of human life also decreases.
- Efficiency: AI has very high power and efficiency to calculate. But they are very weak in daily life experiences.
- Following orders: AI does not have any feelings like humans. They do many things for us every day, but they do not know what they are doing. They just follow their orders.
- Problem solving: AI has a very large set of solutions. Man faces many problems including technical and economic problems in his work, and AI is very useful for that purpose.

9.4   Artificial Intelligence and Entrepreneurship

According to Timmons, Entrepreneurship as a practice embedded with three main components, namely, taking risk, innovation, and commercialization of the products and services for getting profit (Timmons, 78AD). To that knowledge, ideas, innovation, and technological change are important factors in entrepreneurship and economic development of a nation. Success and entrepreneurship are interrelated behind the success of any entrepreneur. Apart from this, innovations and creations are unique tools of entrepreneurs through which they transform as a separate opportunity business. It is capable of being presented as a discipline, capable of learning, and capable of practice. Entrepreneurs always need to hunt for innovation, change, and their traits that signal for opportunities, i.e., successful innovation [2]. AI education and awareness in the field of entrepreneurship have gained importance in today's environment. AI awareness, education, and knowledge in the field of business and entrepreneurship can help people to increase their knowledge and skills for doing their business; it could help those new entrepreneurs for starting, managing, and organizing their own enterprises and new startups. No one can turn into job creator overnight. To be a tech entrepreneur, one only needs to be a sensible entrepreneur or business man. They not only need to understand the technologies, and they are creating and developing but the wider and broader technology system too. Where they will provide opportunities and where these technologies will develop, they also need to be able to see these.

For established industries, AI could always continue to update business models. So many new startups, MSMEs, and small business make their importance scheme on these latest and updated technologies with AI. This digitalization asks for skilled, well-trained, and zealous entrepreneurs to create innovative solutions which can improve their business and personal lives too.

9.5   Process of Entrepreneurship

According to Moore's model, the entrepreneurial process as a level follow each other for the growth of the business and even shed light on the important factors that drive growth business at each stage. For contribution and understanding of identity and behavior that can lead an entrepreneur to success, it has been agreed that certain personal characteristics, like the necessity for achievement, the tendency to bear risks, and control entrepreneurs, are seen in successful entrepreneurs. Mostly, the literature suggests that entrepreneurs are much more adapted to achieving goals, most likely to develop creativity and inability to get opportunities in different business scenarios. The contributed to dedication, money, planning, aim for values, and vision.

9.5.1   Entrepreneurial Recognition

First in the process of recognition, it means that an opportunity is a combination of external conditions and subjective thoughts and ideas of the entrepreneur. They are a bunch of possibilities and potential to create new products, ideas, services, processes, business models, inventions, and strategies that give entrepreneurs the ability to make a profit from the gap between the selling price and the cost of the product.

Opportunities arises from the different sources as a need of new product, updated technology, uncertain problems, a procedure of business model updating and improvements, market policy or business structure changes, environment changes awareness, and creation, invention, and blend of knowledge. The expansion of modern AI and digitalization is an expandable innovative creation in business activities, which is a brilliant source of entrepreneurial and business opportunities that have optimistic growth and innovative AI and robotics–based goods and services. The most essential is that business model is a central production in the recognition of entrepreneurship.

9.5.2   Human Capital

Another key is that knowledge-based people are embedded in experience and highly competitive technology by doing research and development activities.

9.5.3   Technology Requirements and Idea Generation

In AI and robotics-based entrepreneurship, technology plays a very important role in knowledge entrepreneurship to the extent of achieving competitive advantage that is important in the era of technology.

9.5.4   Opportunity Recognition Phase

It allows entrepreneurs to thrive their ideas. AI is the method of externalizing the opportunity and idea to the whole world. A business model describes how the entrepreneur plans to build generating economic or social value and revenue and profit by using a new or improved product or service. The discovery process of the opportunity includes knowledge incorporation and decision-making about optimal resource allocation for maximizing the possibility of product commercialization with profit.

9.5.5   Opportunity Development

Having a clear picture of the business model, opportunity development creates market demand for products and services. This will increase resource requirements and research and development requirements.

9.5.6   Resource Requirements

Firms achieve competitive advantage through resource-based theory. The resource that entrepreneurs need in the process of starting an enterprise is called entrepreneurial resource and the success of an entrepreneur depends highly on resources and their use.

9.5.7 Entrepreneurship

Entrepreneurship in the age of AI and Robotics is a process of outcomes which means the critical process of developing and disseminating commercially finished products, services and innovation. All innovative processes start with the idea of generation.

9.5.8 Financial Resources

Any entrepreneurial aspiration requires money in many ways; at the stage of financial need discovery depending on the size, technology and human resources, and length of the project, the development phase may be minimal and the development period and various sources are required to develop the entrepreneurial effort.

9.5.9 Opportunity Exploitation

Stage of opportunity exploitation is an entrepreneurial step with social functions. This includes starting an enterprise based on a business model by developing product validation and being close to the market services. It is a phase of generating revenue and growth of the organization.

9.5.10 Knowledge Networks

Entrepreneurship is a social endeavor that relies on interaction with other members of society. This development of wealth begins at entrepreneurial endeavor by the pursuit of opportunity; marketing entrepreneurs need products and receive various ways of support from their knowledge network; it is called commercialization through participation, i.e., the use of social networks and the last technique to introduce to the market to increase sales, marketing, and excellent support to the customer.

9.5.11 Validation of the Product

Any product that is made through a research and development process must be validated. In particular, AI-based product validation is done through prototyping, creating a viable product with minimal functionality and testing. The market and reaction will take place to ensure that the market is ready and results in legitimacy.

9.6   The Need of Artificial Intelligence for Business Development

In present era, digitalization and AI have full the whole world with a thunder storm. In recent time, our business and most of human activities are continuously rotating around AI, where humans' every single need has completely dependent on AI [3]. The force of AI is achieving fast improvements in the area of entrepreneurial development also, due to which big financial houses and many marketing sources are mesmerizing. In a latest study, it was revealed that within 1 or 2 years, most of the consumer–shop keeper interaction will end almost all human intervention; all thanks to AI and digitalization. The finest technique to recognize the complex and difficult element of any technological factor is to establish the easiest use of AI that is growing in the business.

9.6.1   Consumer Satisfaction

The process and progress of a business are depending on its consumer and what a customer feels about the product and brand. A customer will come back to the shop only when he feels connected with the product and be loyal about the brand. Nowadays, lots of many companies are exploring this through the help of voice messenger chat bots, IVRs (voice recorders), etc. This helps consumers in providing the best possible solutions by making calls to customer cares, browsing the websites, and from the CRMs customer support desk. These activities provide better experience to customers and increase screen time too. The more they interact, the more they connect. Different phase of AI is the arrangement of information according to each single customer; lots of many business firms provide customer interaction through data analysis or customer representative managers of their priority option and choice. This works on ever-increasing customer fulfillments and satisfaction. These kinds of business allow the business enterprises to conclude researches on a regular point to extend its business.

9.6.2   Cybercrime Protection

More transactions can help to grow a business. In that scenario, every customer wants a secure and safe online experience, and this is the main reason that most of the companies spend a huge portion on fraud exposure. In this digital era, AI-based applications make it easy to detect fraud information to create any blueprint expertise and alertness for the same. So, many enterprises are using updated technologies that function on a systematic system to detect cyber security crimes.

9.6.3   CRMs

Customer relationship management system is a very complex, but important part of every business development, as new prospects with older customers, is the generation gap trending pressure which faces by every business. Lots of new applications are now being created and developed with the help of digitalization and AI which enables information to be gathered in just one click. All this interaction increases the possibility of creating major and most important probability data.

9.6.4   AI-Based Analytics

In the current scenario, consumer databases and information necessitate to be analyzed for business expansion. If a business person cannot use it for achieve his business goals, then there is no use of collecting such information. The translation of a bulky data file is next to impossible by human; it always requires a new and updated technology. This can be dealt easily with the help of machine learning or knowledge of AI. It is very important to find out the value of your data in the business world and use it to speed up your business growth.

9.6.5   Demand and Supply Management

The use of mechanism and computerization with the help of AI in present time can help retailers and whole sellers to improve maintain their demand and supply chains in such a way that it will diminish product losses at the customary level. This can automatically optimize the demand and supply chain by automatic refilling orders. For an improved performance, an entrepreneur can move to such applications which are completely based on AI, for inventory management, and demand and supply chain issues. AI has been effectively used in projection and forecasting [4].

So, many businesses and new entrepreneurs are using computerization and machine learning for the application of logistics and supply chain movement predictions.

9.6.6   Improved Maintenance and Better Equipment Safety

In manufacturing, construction, and transportation business, AI can definitely help by managing and organizing by healthier safety and protection options. Checking of the maintenance schedule before action can save you from major losses of money and even source of production.

A more customer-modified lineup reduces the possibility of delays and prevents almost business stoppages. As far as the construction and manufacturing industry uses, AI has been used for protection, manufacture, and protection units since ages [5].

9.6.7   Searching Capable Employees

Searching for the right and eligible person for business expansion component is always time-consuming. The use of AI can help here. We have lots of applications which allow for face and eyes reorganization that can help to evaluate an interviewee's emotions and performance. Lots of business enterprises already use AI for screening eligible and qualified candidates at the first stage itself. Some of them companies announced its AI-aided hiring which was a huge success here candidates give their interviews on their mobile phones using those applications. The app takes necessary data itself (video and audio) which is related to the interview and analyzes the data for better results.

9.6.8   Virtual Assistance for Sales

Without investing in an actual labor force AI has the ability to increase sales productivity with the help of fundamental business support that can improve sales and expand business. To generate information regarding market and customers these programs and applications can be used, that contact these leads through various means like calls, messages, email, chats etc. The best part of AI sustain applications is that it can cooperate with geographic borders and demographic data in any intervening language.

This essentially works on analytical examination of consumer data which enabled well-organized work of the entire process.

9.6.9   Improvements With Self-Driven Technologies

An entrepreneur that is completely based on the transportation system and can carefully use AI's self-powered expertise to enhance the logistics producer manages time by low investment at high cost of skilled labor. So many changes has come in the business development and sales industry from last few years, with the use of AI in their systems and a variety of uses of computerization, machine learning applications increasing the productivity of the sales team in any industry by up to trice. AI can handle various aspects of the business development industry, from information creation, analysis, sorting and processing of information.

9.7   Some Important Facts About AI

- AI technology can increase business productivity by up to **40% (Source: Accenture, 2019)**.
- The number of AI startups since 2000 has **magnified to 14 times. (Source: Forbes, 2018)**.
- AI will **automate 16%** of American jobs **(Source: Forrester, 2018)**.
- 15% of enterprises are using AI, and 31% of them say that it is their agenda for the next 12 months **(Source: Adobe, 2018)**.

It is true, to a large extent, that AI is not only limited to experimental labs only but it is being praised for its wonderful ability to convert entrepreneurs to a successful business person. Yes, a business always has to meet some difficult tasks before finding out the right prospective of this technology.

9.8   Opportunities for Artificial Intelligence in Business

AI is a hot topic in business technology. Industrial companies, small business startups, and MSMEs notice this. There are so many risks and challenges that are associated with AI implementation in business and startups. But, like two different faces of a coin, AI also has many opportunities for businesses. Due to the opportunities associated with AI, many businesses employ dedicated Indian developers to have their own AI-based apps. Let us look at them one by one.

9.8.1   AI in the Field of Marketing

Maximizing your marketing budget and focusing on high achieving marketing strategies is the dream of every small business. In addition, all business desires to know which activities of marketing provide the maximum result on savings and investment, although monitoring and analysis the information from different media sources can take a lot of space and time. At this point comes the part of AI Marketing resolution. AI in the field of marketing can enable the surface from different channels like internet and television; different websites can easily help manage marketing operations [6]. Computers and machines are used for analyses and comparisons of live campaign primary data with the assistance of emotion and reaction analysis algorithms and help to suggest the delivery of marketing actions ensuing in the best results.

It monitors and manages the whole marketing expenses so that the entrepreneurs and new business persons can reduce the time it takes to track marketing campaigns and focus on other key fields.

9.8.2   For Track Competitors

It is very important to maintain track of our competitors on what they are doing. But most of the entrepreneurs and business persons are unable to analyze the opposition activity due to their busy schedules. At this place, the role of AI comes. There are so many analysis tools that are available for tracking completion. For track competitors, they take help of various sources such as internet, different websites, applications, and social media. In addition, they monitor business persons and well-settled entrepreneurs for any changes in competitors' marketing plans, such as cost changes, PR activities, and micro-message modifications.

9.8.3   Make Less Work of Huge Data

It is not surprising that, like big businesses, small entrepreneurs are also ready to get benefit of huge amounts of offline and online information and data-driven decisions that will grow up their enterprises and business. AI is a powerful tool for business that can be fitted into every data production workflow and provides close insights that are fairly appropriate and applicable as well as actionable.

9.8.4   AI as Customer Support System

Customer care services and automated call and chat systems allow small entrepreneurs to free up the resources needed for their customer service efforts and more complicated customer interactions. AI customer support system such as Digital IVR (voice recorders), genius people advice, or computerize responses to received customer queries helps employees to categorize queries and send inquiries, messages, or information directly to the correct department.

The average handling time of the customer support when using AI is reduced. In addition, this increases the whole accountability of customer support service team.

9.8.5   Artificial Intelligence in CRMs

If a business person wants to take his CRM to the next stage and wants to expand valuable insights, then AI can help to manage relations with existing and potential customers. Integrating AI into CRM can also computerize customer data, info, reports, emails, and more. It is fixed with AI functionality that can execute immediate data examination to offer forecasts and similarly recommendations based on entrepreneurs' business processes and customer information. An AI-powered CRM will be able to gain knowledge from previous results and historical patterns to achieve the best leads for success. After some time, AI will also be able to forecast future customer behaviors.

AI Is shaping the future for all types businesses. Figure 9.1 shows how an entrepreneur or a businessman takes advantages with the opportunities of AI. You can use AI to increase customer retention, sales close rate, and pre-qualified leads. It is difficult to know where AI will be in a decade or two. But, it is already playing a big role in the daily operations of many businesses. This can play a big, beneficial role in your business as well as in the future.

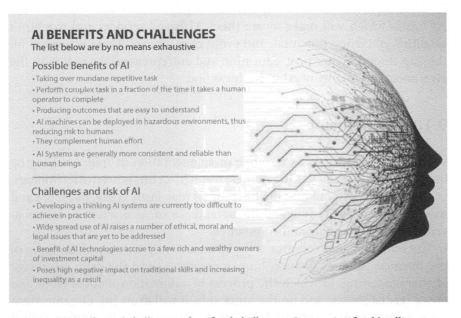

AI BENEFITS AND CHALLENGES
The list below are by no means exhaustive

Possible Benefits of AI
• Taking over mundane repetitive task
• Perform complex task in a fraction of the time it takes a human operator to complete
• Producing outcomes that are easy to understand
• AI machines can be deployed in hazardous environments, thus reducing risk to humans
• They complement human effort
• AI Systems are generally more consistent and reliable than human beings

Challenges and risk of AI
• Developing a thinking AI systems are currently too difficult to achieve in practice
• Wide spread use of AI raises a number of ethical, moral and legal issues that are yet to be addressed
• Benefit of AI technologies accrue to a few rich and wealthy owners of investment capital
• Poses high negative impact on traditional skills and increasing inequality as a result

Figure 9.1 Benefits and challenges of artificial challenges. Source: Artificial Intelligence Opportunities & Challenges in Businesses (Robert Adixon 2019).

9.9   Further Research Possibilities

AI and mechanism have the capacity to refurbish technology and dramatically modify the organizational structure. The adoption of AI in the field of entrepreneurship and business technologies will likely change the skill and bundle of tasks that many businesses comprise. From that aspect alone, these technology institutions will reorganize organizations and military firms to further consolidate these changes.

This study will lead to future research possibilities, AI and robotics have to maintain big data such way, and it will be exploited by the entrepreneurs and businessmen. New digitalized industries should concentrate on designing an artificial network for the building of knowledge economy. AI-related skills are future skills. Strategies are required to be identified and implemented for future preparation. Some initiatives we suggest which can be occupied to create a huge pond of skilled and trained professionals of AI. At the essential primary level, researchers can be uncovered to compulsory information-intensive programs: mechanism, computer learning, and AI courses. Proper settled digital classrooms can be set up in educational institutions. So, many countries already started AI education at their schools, colleges, and universities [7]. For making a strong and healthy digital environment and influence, most powerful and capable government leaders, departments, and experts and equipment heads must provide AI basics which will make aware them AI-based services and machine's qualities, efficiency, potential, and profit of machines. There is need to fill the gap among higher post-education and entrepreneurial needs with the awareness and quality of AI in business line.

9.10   Conclusion

We should consider AI as a source of augmentation in spite of changing human capabilities for getting the best result from this powerful technology.

Therefore, we found that the time for AI may lastly come, but more and more evolution is needed, and the acceptance of AI is irregular in transversely different sectors and companies.

Currently, AI and robotics techniques are fully automated in many of the business, such as finance, human resources, and the main advantage of manufacturing, in which the process of automation reduces labor and other related shores, and on the other side, it will grow [8]. Organizations have a huge opportunity to keep huge amounts of data and to collect lots of knowledge using collected data, and data mining will be useful in advertising machine learning algorithms. In a short time, we can see that AI is going to change humans of almost all organizations. AI's knowledge is an opportunity for entrepreneurs, they have to come for unique mission and vision and strategic planning of product process. AI and robotics are changing to the next level, where products and service are moving fast. There is no doubt that the high speed of AI and robotics facilitates more innovations and entrepreneurship.

All schools and universities must include AI as a mandatory subject in all their programs to get ready for the next generation. AI is not propaganda, but it has the potential to transform the worldwide financial system through technological creation and innovations, digital knowledge, and entrepreneurial business activities. The progressive expansion of mechanization, computerization, and AI over the past decade has been recognized, and some most important factors are hardware accelerators and the escalating accessibility of large data.

Both these two elements are building AI as the main technology responsible for intense mechanization and connectivity. This will surely impact on businesses, entrepreneurs, governments, and individuals. AI has a high efficiency in the field of sports, recognition, new innovation; making and classification of new products tasks make available new opportunities etc. It also provides an open-up chance for the expansion of technologies and ideas for disabled and aged people too. This study explains how automation and AI industries can create more opportunities in the upcoming future, in the field of cyber intelligence, healthcare, security, center AI, entrepreneurial skills, and intelligence. The rising curve in investment in automation and AI from the last few years visibly means that it has the right possibility to transform the world and financial system.

References

1. Sarabu, V.K., Rural Development in India through Entrepreneurship: An Overview of the Problems and Challenges. *Technology, Innovation Management and Entrepreneurship Development*, p. 23, 2016.
2. Nawaz, N., Entrepreneurship In The Age Of Artificial Intelligence And Robotics. *Int. J. Hum. Resour. Manage. Res. (IJHRMR)*, 9, 28–33, 2019.
3. Anurag., "Why Business Development needs Artificial Intelligence, *Newgenapps*", Accessed 25th March, 20, from https://www.newgenapps.com/blog/why-business-development-needs-artificial-intelligence, 2020.
5. He, B., Artificial Intelligent for Intelligent Manufacturing and Robotics. *Robot. Autom. Eng. J.*, 1, 5, 123–125, 2018.

4. Rupa, D.M., Application of Artificial Intelligence in Automation of Supply Chain Management. *J. Strategic Innov. Sustainability*, 14, 3, 43–53, 2019.

6. Hargude, N.V. and N.R., Modern Trends in marketing management- A Review. *Int. J. Sci. Technol. Manage.*, 05, 3, 225–229, 2016.

7. Tattwamasi, P., Education in India: Need for policy interventions Entrepreneurship. *Advances and Trends in Entrepreneurship Research*, p. 8, 2005.

8. Raj, M. and Seamans, R., Primer on artificial intelligence and robotics. *J. Organ. Des.*, 8, 11, 1–14, 2019.

10

An Exploratory Study on Role of Artificial Intelligence in Overcoming Biases to Promote Diversity and Inclusion Practices

Bhumika Rathore*, Meeera Mathur and Shweta Solanki

Faculty of Management Studies, Mohanlal Sukhadia University, Udaipur, India

Abstract

The main aim of this study is to find out challenges of workforce diversity and to investigate biases created by human interventions and by machine algorithms. Another important purpose of this paper is to study role of Artificial Intelligence (AI) in overcoming biases to promote Diversity and Inclusion (D&I) practices. The objectives of this study were achieved by doing a systematic review of literature. Relevant studies were rigorously identified with screening and eligibility criteria process. Studies which were published between year 2000 and 2019 with special context to AI and D&I were referred for systematic literature review process. In this process 25 relevant studies were found to be eligible to be included in current study. It was concluded that leaders, managers, and engineers must work toward where systems need to be taught to ignore data about race, gender, sexual orientation, and other characteristics. There should be an increase in D&I in AI development. This paper fulfills an identified need to study how AI can help in overcoming biases to promote D&I practices at workplace and in balanced decision-making for more inclusive workforce.

Keywords: Human resources, diversity and inclusion, workforce diversity, biases, systematic literature review, artificial intelligence, virtual communication, decision-making

Corresponding author: bhumi04.bhumi@gmail.com

S. Balamurugan, Sonal Pathak, Anupriya Jain, Sachin Gupta, Sachin Sharma, Sonia Duggal (eds.)
Impact of Artificial Intelligence on Organizational Transformation, (147–164) © 2022 Scrivener Publishing LLC

10.1   Introduction

Workforce diversity (WFD) managerial and inclusive practices are creating a buzz all around. A diverse workforce has been recognized as one of the most important antecedent for improving the performance of organization as it has both tangible and intangible values. If broadly categorized, diversity has two dimensions: visible (ethnicity, gender, age, physical disabilities, etc.) and non-visible (sexual orientation or gender identity or expression, attitudes, prejudice, perception, mental ability, psychological factors, values, beliefs, behaviors, experiences, expectations, etc.). It is so important to look for all types of dimensions of diversity when we are talking for inclusive practices. Many Indian organizations like Infosys, ONGC, HCL technologies, Wipro, TATA, and Genpact are inclined toward working for employees with physical disability, gender, and cultural diversity.

WFD has been extensively studied and researched by scholars, academicians, and industrialist in different geographical areas with different perspectives and context. It has been studied widely for investigating diversity dimensions, classification of WFD, with special context to gender and racial diversity, significance of diversity at workplace, approaches for effective management of diversity, efforts of Indian organizations in implementing diversity managerial practices, WFD and organizational effectiveness, diversity as civil rights, affirmative action, socio-cultural and demographic dimensions of diversity, increasing awareness, significance of DM, ongoing global demographic changes, shift in DM concept from equal opportunities to valuing diversity issues, etc.

With the increased use of technology at workplace where many of the HR practices are being conducted with the help of automated process. There are pros and cons of diminishing human interventions in recruitment, promotion, or any other HR policies.

Hence, in this era of technology, it is necessary to study role of Artificial Intelligence (AI) and virtual communication in Diversity and Inclusion (D&I) practices. Our study mainly focuses on role of AI in overcoming biases to promote D&I practices.

Research design of this study is exploratory in nature. We conducted a systematic review of literature of previous qualitative and quantitative studies. Relevant studies were rigorously identified with screening and eligibility criteria process. Studies which were published from year 2000 to 2019 with special context to AI and D&I were referred for systematic literature review process. We included total 25 studies out of 75 for qualitative synthesis and review of literature.

10.1.1   Objectives of the Study

This study aims to identify role of AI in overcoming biases to promote D&I practices at workplace. The following objectives were framed to fulfill research question:

> ➢ To study existing literature of WFD dimensions.
> ➢ To find out biases created by human interventions and machine algorithm.
> ➢ To study existing literature of AI in management studies.
> ➢ To investigate role of AI in promoting D&I practices.

10.1.2   Background of the Study

Along with this issue of WFD, AI is probably the most complex and latest creation of humanity yet. In this study, we are trying to create a picture about relationship between WFD and AI. Since diversity starts with a society and we cannot ignore the fact that AI has greatest impact on the society. According to [1], there are four types of AI: reactive (memory less, it only reacts to different stimuli), limited memory (uses memory to learn and improve its responses), theory of mind (understands the need of other intelligent entities), and self-aware (has humans like intelligence). But somehow, human biases are creating errors in D&I practices and AI can help in mitigating the biases. So, in this paper, we are including a conceptual framework having WFD, benefits, challenges and barriers of diversity, biases as obstacles in D&I practice, types of biases, AI as a tool to prevent biases, research methodology, synthesis, and conclusion.

10.1.3   Relevance and Scope of the Study

We are living in the era where technology is infused in our everyday life. We are unknowingly became a part of AI, e.g., smart phones, smart cars, social media feed, online ads network, music and media streaming services, navigation, banking, and finance. Because of the technology and virtual communication, physical boundaries are no longer important. Organizations are becoming rich in diversity. There are different types of people working for same organization and for a common objective. Hence, to study WFD with the context of AI becomes significant.

This study can provide hypotheses to test as it is in exploratory in nature. This study may give a direction to the scholars to find out the relationship between AI and D&I practices.

10.2   Research Gaps Identified

On the basis of systematic review of literature, it was found that WFD has been studied with different context, e.g., employee performance, organizational effectiveness, models to improve, as civil rights and affirmative action, dimensions, and perceptions, and the following are the research gaps that need to be filled:

> ➢ Workforce D&I practices are still untapped in the area of AI.
> ➢ The available studies have been originated from few geographical areas, and there is no study regarding role of AI in D&I practices in India.

10.3   Experiential Work

This part of study includes a research methodology, systematic representation of literature review, understanding WFD, benefits, challenges, biases as barriers, types of biases, AI as a tool to prevent and overcome biases, discussion, and conclusion.

Following is the framework of this article:

(a) Type of Research: Exploratory Research: Exploratory research is also known as formulative research that is different from descriptive type of research. According to [2], the aim of this research is to generate a problem for more accurate investigation and study. This type of research focuses on discovery of new ideas and insights.

(b) Research Question: To find out role of AI in overcoming biases to promote D&I practices.

(c) Research Design: An exploratory research may comprise of three methods—survey of concerning literature, the experience survey, or the analysis of insight-stimulating examples. In this paper, we have used survey of existing literature.

(d)   Sources of Data and Information: Secondary sources.
(e)   Tools and Techniques: Literature Review.
(f)   Type of Literature Review: Systematic Literature Review.

Systematic literature review is different from narrative literature review. Systematic literature review follows a predefined protocol-based search process. There is also a predefined selection, eligibility, screening, and inclusion criteria of the articles.

(g)   Type of Systematic Literature Review: Meta-Synthesis.

There are two types of systematic literature review—meta-analysis and meta-synthesis. Meta-analysis is a statistical technique of literature review in which specific patterns and relationships of variables are detected, and conclusions and discussions are interpreted. It is a deductive approach. Meta-synthesis is a non-statistical technique of literature review which combines, assesses, and explains findings of various qualitative research studies. This is an inductive approach.

(h)   Analysis and Evaluation: Qualitative.

10.3.1   Hypothetical Research Model

The predefined protocol of search process and synthesis of literature review were framed after developing the following hypothetical research model (Figure 10.1).

In this model, we consider that due to WFD, there are biases created by human or machine algorithms at workplace. AI can be helpful to prevent these biases and obstacles and can promote D&I practices. For that, algorithms must be taught to be free from traditional ideologies (e.g., gender discrimination, racism, and sexism). After accomplishing these steps, managers and leaders can have a balanced decision-making process for organization development.

10.3.2   Methodology

To examine the role of AI in overcoming biases to promote D&I practices, we conducted a systematic review of literature to identify previous qualitative studies in AI research focusing on D&I practices. The potential contribution of this study is to map the field of AI with special reference to D&I practices, synthesize the state of knowledge, and create an agenda for

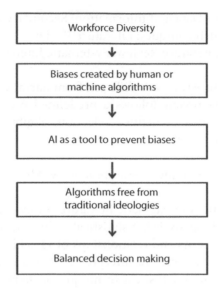

Figure 10.1 Hypothetical research model for the study.

further research by using Cooper's Taxonomy. (Cooper's Taxonomy generally comprises of focus, goal, perspective, coverage of relevant studies, paper organization, and intended audience or readers.)

10.3.3 Search Process

This study is exploratory in nature and review based (secondary data sources) in which studies from EBSCO (academic libraries and research database), ProQuest, SSRN (Social Science Research Network), Shodhganga (a reservoir of Indian thesis), and Google Scholar have been used and relevant studies are cited. Relevant keywords were used to identify research articles: Human Resources, Diversity and Inclusion, Workforce Diversity, Biases, Systematic Literature Review, Artificial Intelligence, Virtual Communication, Decision-Making. Search was also made with the help of reference work of these articles. Studies published between year 2000 and 2019 were used to identify previous research studies.

10.3.4 Selection Criteria and Review Process

The first stage was to identify articles from keywords and from reference work. Second stage was to screen those articles which were duplicates, published before year 2000 and not in D&I context. Now, full text articles which were not in HR context excluded deciding their eligibility. Finally, remaining articles were included for literature review and qualitative synthesis. We reviewed total 25 studies in this research paper.

An extensive review of literature has been done and the studies were divided into four parts:

a) General studies on WFD and its dimensions.
b) Studies on benefits and challenges of WFD.
c) Studies on biases as obstacles in D&I practices.
d) Studies on AI to promote D&I practices.

10.3.5   Systematic Representation of Literature Review

The process of selecting 25 articles out of 75 went through a rigorous process. Figure 10.2 depicts a systematic representation of literature review that is compiled by researcher. First, 52 articles were identified from selected keywords and 23 articles were identified from reference work. Total of 75

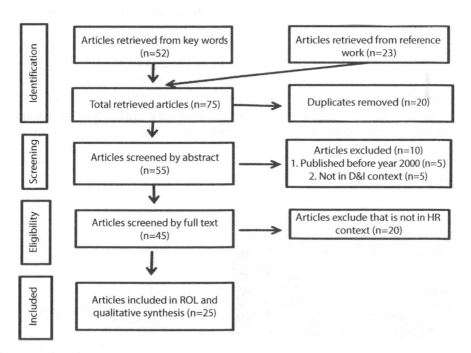

Figure 10.2 Flow diagram of literature selection process. Source: compiled by researcher.

studies were identified for this particular study. Second, 20 duplicate studies were removed in identification stage. When we went through 55 studies from its abstract, 10 studies were excluded at screening stage. Out of those 10 studies, 5 were published before year 2000 and 5 were not in D&I context. Third, 45 studies were found eligible by full text after screening stage and 20 studies were excluded as it was not in HR context. Finally, total 25 articles were included for review of literature and qualitative synthesis.

Out of 25 articles, maximum of 15 articles from year 2015 to 2019 met our inclusion criteria. We found only one relevant study from year 2005 to 2009.

10.3.6   Understanding Workforce Diversity

A heterogeneous workforce is now working in different organizations having various dimensions, for example, age, educational, gender diversity, physical disabilities, regional, language, and social background diversity. Hence, when diversity is present in the organizations, it creates a healthy and professional image. But if diversity is not appreciated in any organization, then it has a huge impact on the productivity and efficiency. The world is becoming a global village due to globalization. Geographical barriers are not anymore a challenge because of increased transportation and telecommunication techniques.

Now, to understand diversity, we should determine various dimensions of diversity, and for that, [3] indicated that diversity has more than two dimensions. It was described from the analogy of an iceberg. The most visible dimensions or the primary dimensions (race, ethnicity, gender, age, disability). Just below the surface lie the secondary dimensions (religion, culture, sexual orientation, thinking style, geographic orientation, family

Figure 10.3 Diversity iceberg.

status, lifestyle, economic condition, political belief, work experience, education, etc.) which are revealed with time, and the tertiary dimensions (beliefs, assumption, perceptions, attitudes, feelings, values, group norms) lie much below the surface. The following diagram shows all three dimensions in diversity iceberg (Figure 10.3).

There is also a kaleidoscope model of diversity which elaborates this diversity iceberg model. Just as a kaleidoscope contains certain amounts of particles of varied shapes and colors, personality of an individual may be a composition of varied diverse attributes. According to [4], humans are different on the basis of their different personality and psychological dimension.

The current scenario suggests that every national or global organization is taking effort to include people from various geographical background, creed, and people with disabilities or gender. According to [5], diversity is now in the form of inclusion practices not exclusion.

India is the most diversified country in the world due to various environmental conditions, various geographical patterns, system of castes which is followed by reservation policies, and many more. As [6] suggested that the concept of diversity has always been very vulnerable in India since it is rich in diverse cultures, race, caste, and religion. So, there is no doubt that even a local organization of India consists of varied workforce. A diverse workforce is good for overall productivity of organization as it provides an opportunity to have brainstorming with different minds from different background. In the opinion of [7], diversity at workplace is not only good for ethical and social approach but it also useful in developing novel business insights. Diversity always starts from society and it can be understood by Social Identity theory. Diversity is not just about visible dimensions; a deeper perspective for invisible dimension with special context to psychological dimensions must be there.

10.3.7   Benefits and Challenges of Workforce Diversity

A diverse workforce has both pros and cons. If diversity is very well managed, then it can improve organizational effectiveness and its productivity. But if diversity is poorly handled, then the results can be chaotic. After an in depth research, it was found that outcomes of diversity range from negative to positive. As some studies showed, there are only benefits that we count for diversity but similarly many studies stated negative impacts of it. For example, diversity creates innovation and creativity but it results into reverse discrimination against the members of majority group.

There is a much greater impact on an economy of the country. As [8] stated, a diverse workforce is an integral to a strong economy. For building strong and lasting economy diversity can play a key role. A diverse workforce drives economic growth.

- Diversity at workplace increases a greater share of the consumer market.
- More qualified diverse workforce.
- D&I practices help in reducing employee turnover cost.
- More creativity, innovation, and brainstorming at workplace.

A diverse workforce not just impact the economy but it plays an important role in overall productivity of the organizations be it national or multinational company. In the view of [9], a diverse workplace can contribute to an organization's efficiency and create a competitive advantage. The following diagram shows benefits of having a diverse workforce at workplace (Figure 10.4).

According to the above diagram, having a diverse workforce leads to higher morale of employees, and it gives varying perspectives and opportunity of having brainstorming. Diversity also has a global impact and it can also increase community relations.

Due to globalization and technology revolution, there are no physical boundaries for communication and for business. This increases WFD, and the challenge is to manage them in fair and equitable manner. Every coin has two sides: having a diverse workforce also contains pros and cons. There is a need to understand both sides and managers must implement transparency and flexibility in diversity managerial practices. Similarly, [10] argued that employees are feeling increased frustration, disappointments, and anger because of different implemented policies in the name of diversity management. According to [11], the goal of managing WFD is to create a positive work environment for all employees. If WFD is handled poorly, then it can easily turn into a losing situation for all involved, leading to devaluation of employees who are perceived as culturally different, reverse discrimination against members of the majority group, demoralization and reinforcement, and increased exposure to legal risks.

Figure 10.4 Benefits of diversity.

Managers and leaders must rethink, redefine, and reconceptualize dimensions of diversity for better strategy development in Human Resources Management. In the opinion of [12], awareness and recognition for diversity management have increased in IT industries of India. The real challenge they found is to develop a healthy attitude toward minority including women and employee from different culture, religion, geographical area, and LGBT.

If there is cultural sensitivity among employees at workplace, then they can better work with harmony. Acceptance is the key that people are different in every aspect to the other. According to [13], the biggest challenges for accepting WFD are prejudice, ethnocentrism, stereotypes, blaming the victim, discrimination, harassment, backlash, etc.

India is the most diversified country in the world so managing WFD in this type of competitive environment becomes very important. The most important dimensions that need to be focused by managers are concept of gender identity or sexual orientation, people with disabilities (physical or mental), and gender equality. We are still behind in promoting gender equality at workplace and now this is not just limited to male or female. One has a choice to express their gender identity in any form of LGBT (Lesbian, Gay, Bisexual, and Transgender), and in the opinion of [14], Indian organizations are working toward inclusion practices but many still do not include LGBT candidates in their corporate diversity agenda. Many organizations of India are now including women advancement in diversity management practices but PWDs are still an untapped area.

The range of impact of WFD can be deeper, but here, we are studying only positive and negative impacts. Sometimes, impact of diversity can be seen as neutral since employees are not much affected by D&I practices. [15] stated that employees in Singapore have neutral perception for WFD managerial practices.

After an in depth review of relevant articles, benefits and challenges of a diverse workforce are quite apparent. A diverse workforce gives an opportunity to create healthy brainstorming and exchange of ideas within the employees. It has a huge impact on business and economy. While to manage a diverse pool of employees in a fair and equitable manner is still a challenge.

10.3.8   Biases as Obstacles in Diversity and Inclusion Practices

Apart from above stated challenges, implicit and unconscious biases play a very important role in inhibiting D&I practices. Unconscious biases are the inaccurate assessment based on faulty perception. Unconscious biases are typically outside of our awareness and can affect the whole recruitment process of an applicant. Affinity bias (feeling of connection or similarity), halo effect, horns effect, attribution bias, confirmation bias are the commonly unconscious biases that directly or indirectly inhibit D&I practices. Organizations cannot completely free from implicit or unconscious bias until it is not well identified and corrected. According to [16], by identifying and acknowledging unconscious bias, managers, executives, leaders, and HR practitioners can eliminate it from creating a hurdle in D&I practices. In the view of [17], implicit bias in the workplace can be pervasive. It can hinder D&I initiatives and HR practices and unintentionally create a biased organization culture. Implicit bias affects recruitment, orientation, transfer, and promotion of employees. Most probably, implicit bias is related to race and gender.

Biases can affect a whole lifecycle of an employee during the tenure. It includes common HR practices, for example, interview, talent acquisition, recruitment, training and induction, salary and compensation, merit rating, transfer, retirement policies, and termination. In the opinion of [18], conscious or unconscious bias, inhibit every type of D&I practices, e.g., discrimination against a job applicant for diversity in race, caste, religion, region of origin, age, and gender identity or sexual orientation.

Implicit bias may be so infused within organizational culture that awareness about it requires a major fundamental change. Getting and accepting diversity at conscious level may require a tedious work on everyone. But one good thing is that millennial worldwide is the most cultural and racial diverse generation who have better sensitivity toward diversity.

Above stated biases are created by human intervention but the challenge that is in front of many organization is the biases created by AI. These unconscious biases are created by AI where the technology is the reflection of its designer. Whatever is coded into the machine for HR practices, if it is developed in a biased manner, the organizations will go along with it even without knowing. Similar study done by [19] interpreting that in the absence of balanced inclusion datasets, there is a full scope that machine algorithms are going to create biases among diverse pool of employees. [20] stated that women, LGBT community, other minorities from different geographical background, race, or religion face bias as of part of their workplace experience.

Unconscious gender biases can also be seen where sequencing or order in filling a form (nowadays, online and digital platforms) always follow a traditional ideology writing male as first and female as second. Some applications need to correct those gender biases, for example, writing chairman in place of chairperson and always writing he or him without specifically mentioning gender identity and many more.

There are examples of Facebook advertisement which are coded based on gender identity and follow the old stereotypes. Making automated voice assistants in female voice and naming like Alexa or Siri (female names) show that AI system is still following human unconscious biases for gender inequality. Some navigation apps are also addressing gender biases. These apps are not just gender biased; many dating and gaming apps available digitally are showing biases toward different races. Apart from gender or racial biases, these applications are marginalizing people with disabilities whether it is physical or mental.

Hence, unconscious bias, if created by human interventions, is quite visible, but automated bias generated by AI is not easily detectable. Say, a talent attraction AI system created by an Asian engineer, it will indirectly create a biased system for job applicants of different geographical background.

10.3.9   AI as a Tool to Prevent Bias and Promote D&I Practices

The post-modern society cannot imagine their life without the support of machines. Organizations are living with this reality and working with AI. In this whole situation where the possibility of biases and discriminations becomes higher and higher, leaders must think about using AI as a tool to prevent bias and promote D&I practices. Also, experts and engineers who develop an algorithm must include all inclusion criteria and must generate a system free from personal bias [21] argued that our systems must be trained and generated in such a manner that cannot create bias based on diversity of employees, e.g., color, religion, race, caste, education, marital status, family background, political belief, gender identity, sexual orientation, and other characteristics that are not completely relevant in tenure of the employee at workplace. Not just at workplace, AI can be helpful in other fields also for more inclusion. There are some worst examples of a faux-pas of applications created by machine algorithms, for example, facial recognition app which promotes racial, color, or gender biases. These researchers also brought the issue of a program that suggests longer duration of imprisonment for blacks rather than whites, and this program was based on some influenced and flawed coding and bots. For example, sentencing software suggests high risk for blacks when there is a prior offense of resisting arrest without violence and there is no subsequent offense. The same software suggests lower risk for whites even after some serious prior and subsequent offense.

AI is able to do this if it is recreated and refined by human experts and engineers. The system must be bias free and more inclusive about diversity of employees. Not just at workplace, when these systems and applications are developed for general public it must be inclusive for women and people with physical disability. In the view of [22], there should be an increase in D&I in AI development, policy, and research. The homogeneous culture in AI, limited awareness of the field, lack of exposure to technical concepts early, and few relatable role models are the obstacles in D&I practices.

The following diagram in Figure 10.5 shows how an engineer can develop a responsible AI system.

In case of ensuring a responsible AI system, organizations must test it before implementation and a regular monitoring is a must. Now, there is need to adopt a fair concept of ethical standards, so that heterogeneity can find a fair place in this technology era.

Gender diversity (including gender identity and LGBT community) is suffering the most due to traditional ideologies at workplace. Though organizations are doing quite well by running programs for women and other minorities in order to hire and retain them, still there is a huge lacuna where algorithms and database were taught in unbiased manner. Experts can work where database can ignore previous ideologies. As suggested by [23], AI learns from observing data. The design of these technologies sometimes represents over representation of men leading gender inequality and can destroy the efforts done by organizations. In the opinion of [24], AI can play a key role in creating unbiased mechanisms. It can overcome the personal errors done by human interventions. In the view of [25], human bias is intentional or unintentional, implicit, or unconscious. These biases can destructively affect hiring process of job applicants. AI can ensure that hiring process must be done on the basis of applicant's skills, experience, and talent.

AI has an ability to influence perception and thinking style of each and every individual, and this issue becomes much to ponder as AI was once influenced by human unconscious and conscious biases.

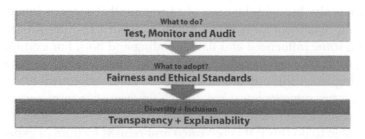

Figure 10.5 Ensuring responsible AI.

Hence, to prevent human bias at workplace AI can be helpful, simultaneously previous database and machine algorithms must taught to ignore traditional ideologies regarding diversity issue. It is helpful in creating a gender balanced applicant tool by replacing text with the help of language intelligent agents. It can recommend a proper salary range free from gender, ethnicity, race, religion, or caste. AI can help in balanced decision-making for more inclusive workforce.

10.4   Synthesis of the Study

This study is trying to depict a picture about role of AI in promoting D&I practices. Total 75 articles were identified for the study, out of these 25 studies were reviewed for this research. Articles published before year 2000, duplicates, not in HR and D&I context were excluded. In introduction section, WFD and AI were studied thoroughly. An experiential work was conducted in which there is research methodology, general studies of WFD, benefits and challenges of diversity, biases as obstacles in D&I practices, and role of AI in promoting these practices. A hypothetical research model was developed for existing literature survey. A predefined protocol was established for a specific search process with the help of relevant keywords and reference work from authentic research database.

10.5   Managerial Implications and Conclusion

The significance of a diverse workforce is that organizations can have a healthy brainstorming; different notions with a variety of solutions are the major outcomes. It can also foster innovation and employees can gain exposure to wide varieties of perspectives and values. So, many studies have been done on different issues of WFD at global, national, and regional level as it is an interdisciplinary approach. These literatures reveal that WFD is unavoidable and an important concept of Human Resources Management. Despite the fact that extensive studies have been done in the area of WFD management, still there are some untapped areas which demand a new perspective for research. For example, role of AI in mitigating diversity biases, Indian perspective of unity and inclusion in diversity, in sustaining a diverse workforce, and in overcoming reverse discrimination against member of majority group focuses on dimensions like sexual orientation, physical disability, and age diversity because cultural and gender diversity has been studied many times linking with differing issues.

Also, there is a need to understand that there is a fine line between diversity and inclusion. It is not just enough to have a diverse workforce but to make them feel included in the organizational environment is also very important. Apart from above stated challenges and biases, sometimes, it is seen that employees are being cyber bullied because of their different personality, race, color, and religion or gender identity. There is need to accept and understand perspectives of diversity dimensions. These types of cyber bullying are now a part of organizational culture whether it is corporate or educational institutes. It has been seen that cyber bullying happens within the organizations by colleagues (as nowadays, there is no specific boundaries between personal and professional life due to increased use of social media) or by customers (as there is no specific identity; it triggers customers to misbehave). Not just corporate sectors, educational institutes also come under various cases of cyber bullying where teachers face cyber aggression, defaming email circulations, and bullying on their race or color.

India is the most diversified country in the world, and more and more MNCs are attracted toward setting up their business in India. But diversity has been always a sensitive issue here and often discussed under labels such as racism, castes, civil rights, and reservation policies. There is no study of AI with context in D&I practices in India.

A diverse workforce can drive economic growth, for competitive economy, greater share of consumer market, boost healthy brainstorming, and creative outcomes. But there can be frustration and disappointments within employees because of diversity intervention programs. Apart from challenges, there are unconscious and implicit biases that create inhibition in D&I practices. Due to these biases, no organization is successful to achieve its D&I goals. These biases can skew its HR practices and complete life cycle tenure of an employee. There are some biases which are created by AI itself, which is actually a reflection of its designer. For example, if the design is created by a man, then it will reflect gender inequality in its programs.

For this purpose, systems need to be taught to ignore data about race, gender, sexual orientation, and other characteristics. There should be an increase in D&I in AI development. Also, there is a need to include more diverse team in development of AI programs. Diversity training programs in collaboration with AI system is the need of the hour.

Hence, an unbiased mechanism can be developed by running certain key words in machine algorithm. AI can help enormously by implementing consistent and fair assessment and screening criteria.

References

1. Joshi, N., *7 Types Of Artificial Intelligence*, 2019, June 19, Retrieved March 1, 2020, from https://www.forbes.com/sites/cognitive-world/2019/06/19/7-types-of-artificial-intelligence/#7afff4e8233e.

2. Kothari, C. and Garg, G., *Research Methedology: Methedology and Techniques*, New Age International (P) Limited Publishers, New Delhi, 2019.

3. Rijamampianina, R. and Carmichael, T., A Pragmatic and Holistic Approach to Managing Diversity. *Probl. Perspect. Manage.*, 3, 1, 109–117, 2005, January.

4. Saxena, A., Workforce Diversity: A Key to Improve Productivity. *Proc. Econ. Financ.*, 11, 76–85, 2014.

5. Deshwal, P. and Choudhary, S., Workforce Diversity Management: Biggest Challenge for 21st Centuary Managers. *Int. J. Multidiscip. Res.*, 2, 4, 74–87, 2012.

6. Nagar, M., Managing Diversity at the Workplace in a Global Economy: Challenges & Opportunities. *Prabandhan: Indian J. Manage.*, 5, 2, 47–54, 2012.

7. Kundu, S.C., Bansal, J., Pruthi, M., Perceived Workforce Diversity and Firm Performance: A Study of An Indian Public Sector Organization. *J. Strateg. Hum. Resour. Manage.*, 8, 1, 47–60, 2019.

8. Kerby, S. and Burns, C., *Center for American Progress*, 2012, July 12, Retrieved April 15, 2019, from Center for American Progress Website: https://www.americanprogress.org/issues/economy/news/2012/07/12/11900/the-top-10-economic-facts-of-diversity-in-the-workplace/.

9. Smith, H., *Global LT*, 2017, March 21, Retrieved April 15, 2019, from Global LT Website: https://global-lt.com/diversity-workplace/.

10. Lorbiecki, A. and Jack, G., Criticle Turns in the Evolutin of Diversity Management. *Br. J. Manage.*, 11, Special Issue, 17–31, 2000.

11. Bergen, C.V., Soper, B., Foster, T., Unintended Negative Effects of Diversity Management. *Public Pers. Manage.*, 31, 2, 239–251, 2002.

12. Buddhapriya, S., Diversity Management Practices in Select Firms in India: A Critical Analysis. *Indian J. Ind. Relat.*, 48, 4, 597–610, 2013.

13. Bedi, P., Lakra, P., Gupta, E., Workforce Diversity Management: Biggest Challenge Or Opportunity For 21st Century Organizations. *IOSR J. Bus. Manage.*, 16, 4, 102–107, 2014.

14. Dixit, P. and Bajpai, B.L., Managing Workforce Diversity in Competitive Environment. *Int. J. Bus. Manage. Invent.*, 4, 1, 01–011, 2015.

15. Joseph R., D. and Selvaraj, P.C., The Effects of Work Force Diversity on Employee Performance in Singapore Organisations. *Int. J. Bus. Adm.*, 6, 2, 17–29, 2015.

16. Harnandez, P.A., *American Management Association*, 2018, February 22, Retrieved March 6, 2020, from https://playbook.amanet.org/training-articles-unconscious-bias-diversity-inclusion/.

17. TIAA Institute, *Managing Implicit Bias with Diversity and Inclusion: An Imperative for Future Success*, Council on Foundations, New York, 2018.

18. Zhang, H., Feinzig, S., Raisbeck, L., McCombe, I., *The role of AI in mitigating bias to enhance diversity and inclusion*, Armonk: IBM Talent Management Solutions, Unites States, 2019.

19. Madaka, C., *Diversity & Ethics In AI: A Reflection Of Its Designer*, University of Texas, 2019, July 4, Retrieved December 13, 2019, from https://blog.strands.com/ethics-diversity-in-ai.

20. Krentz, M., *Harvard Business Review*, Massachusetts, 2019, February 5, Retrieved March 5, 2020, from https://hbr.org/2019/02/survey-what-diversity-and-inclusion-policies-do-employees-actually-want.

21. Daugherty, P. R., Wilson, H. J., & Chowdhury, R. (2018, November 18). *MIT Sloan Management Review*. Retrieved Decemeber 21, 2019, from MIT Sloan Management Review: https://sloanreview.mit.edu/article/using-artificial-intelligence-to-promote-diversity/

22. Posner, T., *AI will Change the World. Who will Change AI? Ethics and Diversity in AI*, Gallup Northeastern University: Microsoft Research, 2018.

23. Leavy, S., *Gender Bias in Artificial lIntelligence:The Need for Diversity and Gender Theory in Machine Learning*, GE'18, Gothenburg, Sweden, 2018.

24. Rizzi, R., *Digitalist*, 2018, November 20, Retrieved February 27, 2020, from https://www.digitalistmag.com/future-of-work/2018/11/20/ai-helping-organizations-overcome-bias-embrace-inclusive-culture-06194307.

25. Sambandan, S., *HR Technologist*, 2019, November 12, Retrieved 2020 March 1, 2019, from https://www.hrtechnologist.com/articles/digital-transformation/combining-human-and-artificial-intelligence-for-a-more-inclusive-work-environment/.

11

Artificial Intelligence: Revolutionizing India Byte by Byte

Priyanka Jingar[1]*, Anju Singh[2] and Sachin Gupta[1]

¹Department of Business Administration, Mohanlal Sukhadia University, Udaipur, Rajasthan, India
²Department of Financial Studies, IIS Deemed to be University, Jaipur, Rajasthan, India

Abstract

India has open-heartedly adopted Artificial Intelligence (AI) which leads our nation to become smarter and pioneering. AI is piercing in every sector at an incredible pace to meet up the global trend of technology and innovation. India, being the swiftly flourishing nation with the second largest population on the globe, has a major contribution to the AI revolution. Whether it is the healthcare sector, agriculture, education, and transportation, the gamut of AI has reached to every nook and corner in India. AI presents the prospect to harmonize and complement human intelligence and augment the manner people live and work. The focus of this chapter is to know the chief role of AI to strengthen the Indian economy. While, this chapter contains the objectives, role of AI to India's transformation, numerous initiatives taken by the Indian government to introduce AI, the economic impact of AI to lead India on the road of growth and development, the impact of AI on various sectors, and its SWOT analysis.

Keywords: Artificial intelligence, revolution, India, innovation, technology

11.1 Introduction

Artificial Intelligence (AI) transformed the approach to persons' live and work. The fourth industrial revolution is the result of adoption of AI which

---

Corresponding author: priyajingar@gmail.com

S. Balamurugan, Sonal Pathak, Anupriya Jain, Sachin Gupta, Sachin Sharma, Sonia Duggal (eds.)
Impact of Artificial Intelligence on Organizational Transformation, (165–182) © 2022 Scrivener Publishing LLC

leads to a rise in the socio-economic expansion of India. AI is all about imitating the temperament of human intelligence. AI is a vibrant tool that is driving our nation toward productivity and economic enlargement. AI amplifies the efficiency and effectiveness of humans and greatly perked up the decision-making by evaluating a large amount of unstructured data. AI helps to boost customer demand and generate sales and create demand for new products and services.

India has witnessed a sharp and continuous development in technological advancement and innovation. India has been an emerging hub for new businesses and ranks among the prominent investment purpose for technology transactions across the globe. Technology and innovation is the prime ingredient for attaining wealth maximization for an economy. India has recognized the need for AI and its power to transform economies. In this context, NITI Aayog launched the National Program on Artificial Intelligence in 2018–2019 for channelizing research and development in the novel and budding technology.

AI has the strength to give huge incremental worth to an extensive variety of sectors. NITI Aayog has focused on five major sectors that are highly impacted by AI. These are as follows:

❖ Healthcare sector: Improved access and quality of healthcare services in terms of affordability.
❖ Agriculture sector: Improved income of farmers, greater than before the yield of farm and lessening of waste.
❖ Education sector: Enhanced scope and excellence.
❖ Infrastructure sector and smart cities: well-organized and connectivity for the swiftly mounting metropolitan populace.
❖ Transportation sector and smart mobility: Elegant and secure means of transportation and improved traffic and overcrowding nuisance.

11.2   Objectives of the Chapter

1. To study the status of adoption of AI in India.
2. To study the impact of AI on various sectors in India.
3. To study the contribution of AI in the economic development of our nation.
4. To study the SWOT analysis of AI (Figure 11.1).

Emerging AI technologies

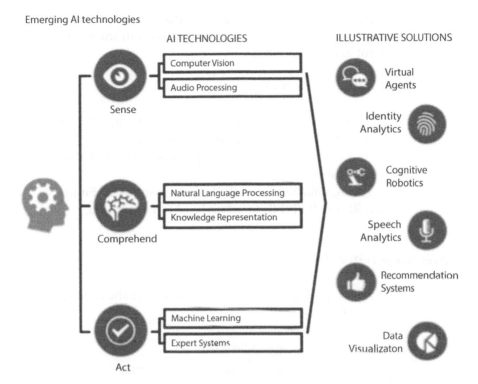

Figure 11.1 What is Artificial Intelligence. Source: NITI Aayog Discussion Paper, 2018. https://niti.gov.in/writereaddata/files/document_publication/NationalStrategy-for-AI-Discussion-Paper.pdf

11.3   AI for India's Transformation

Artificial Intelligence is behind the curtain to make user experience graceful. The notion of AI relies on the idea of building machines, competent of thinking, performing, and learning like human being. A universal strategy is introduced by NITI Aayog for AI in India with a primary focus on financial enlargement and social inclusion. The Government of India has taken a numerous initiatives toward AI.

They are as follows:

Government Initiatives in 2017

- Commerce and Industry Department, Government of India formed AI Task Force that primarily focuses on the economic transformation of India.

- "Kaizala" is an initiative introduced by one of the state government for the residents of the state to assist in work management and communications.

Government Initiatives in 2018

- NITI Aayog has signed a statement of intent to integrate the most modern enlargement in robotics and AI.
- Memorandum of understanding signed by Invest India and the UAE Minister for AI.
- NITI Aayog collaborates with the Tata Institute of Fundamental Research (TIFR) to set up ICTAI in Karnataka.

Government Initiatives in 2019

- NITI Aayog announced a national program for the development of AI.

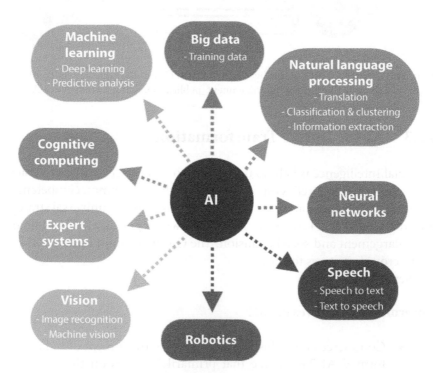

Figure 11.2 The branches of Artificial Intelligence. Source: Syam and Nguyen, 2019 [1].

- AI 4 All Global Hackathon launched by NITI Aayog to endorse knowledge and build up solutions to deal with the infrastructure confronts, with no compromising on the data privacy (Figure 11.2).

11.4   Economic Impact of Artificial Intelligence

AI is rising as the latest factor of production, enlarging the conventional factors of production such as manual labor, capital, innovation, and technological modification detained in entire factor productivity. Restrictions of labor, capital, etc., can be overcome with the strength of AI and unlock fresh avenues for growth and development. From an economic point of view, AI possesses the possibility to impel development all the way through allowing.

(a) Intelligent mechanization: the aptitude to mechanize complex physical tasks that necessitate flexibility and quickness across industries.
(b) Labor and capital augmentation: facilitate human beings to give spotlight on parts of their role that adjoin the most value, harmonizing individual ability and recovering capital efficiency.
(c) Innovation diffusion: AI innovations on an individual sector will have optimistic consequences on an additional sector.

According to Accenture report to analyze the financial impact of AI for G20 nations, and projected that by 2035, AI will perk up the yearly growth rate of India by 1.3% points [2]. AI has put a feather in the golden cap of India. The epoch of AI has appeared. According to the report "Rewire For Growth" launched by Accenture, India has the capacity to add US$987 billion or 15% of India's current gross value in 2035. AI has the revolutionary strength to makeover the industries by advancing productivity and expansion, for example, manufacturing sector witnessed a vibrant 39% increase in profit share because of an AI-enabled system whose aptitude to learn, adjust, and develop with the passage of time can remove inactive machines and defective equipment. India has again witnessed an energetic boost up in the number of AI startups as India stands on the third rank out of all G20 countries, which have shown progress since 2011 at a composite

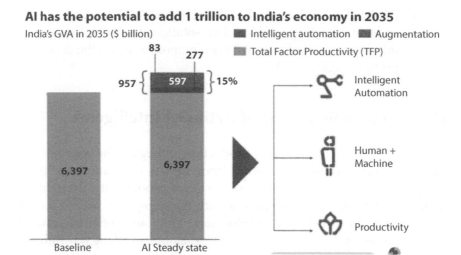

Figure 11.3 India's GVA in 2035. Source: The Financial Express, 2018 [4].

annual growth rate of 86% which is way upper than the universal standard [3] (Figure 11.3).

11.5   Artificial Intelligence and its Impact on Various Sectors

As intellectual gear continues to move forward in capacity and range, AI possesses the power to give magnificent benefits for both business and the general masses. In the trade and customer space, AI proposes superior mechanization, immediate support, predictive study, and accurate data mining abilities. 24*7 availability, minimized inaccuracy, improved speed and precision, and data application and the aptitude to carry out monotonous and dangerous jobs are few key benefits of AI. As per the report of Microsoft, 90% of international businesses look forward to AI to encompass a constructive impact on development. In addition, 86% look ahead to AI to improve efficiency [5].

AI has significantly impacted many sectors to boost their growth and development. AI is revolutionizing a range of industries in various sphere, for example, banking, telecommunication, healthcare, educational, retail, consumer and package goods, and transportation. Few are as follows.

11.5.1   AI in Healthcare

Healthcare is the segment that is greatly impacted with by implementation of AI. However, AI assists to analyze large amount of unstructured data and can aid doctors to make better decisions. AI can give wings to the doctors and healthcare professionals turn into heroes by equipping them with the latest technology to go ahead of traditional practices of patient care. AI-enabled applications can work as a digital assistant to assist patients as well as medical professionals. AI leads to improve in patient result and helps to minimize the medication cost. With the help of AI chatbots, patient can get a precise, safe, and suitable reply in seconds that can help to save money too. AI made the healthcare facilities much handier and reasonably priced.

According to few reports, the doctor-patient ratio in India is very less, i.e., 1,000:6, which means there are only six doctors on every 1,000 patients. AI-based system for rural areas can just be the solution to curtail this issue. Enabling doctors and other hospital staff with technology and gadgets would save time and speed up the process of healthcare.

Right from the word go, everything can be connected centrally to hospital software; doctors can perform their routines such as attending the patients, writing prescriptions and recommendations, or transferring the patient to other departments if needed. All the tasks that a healthcare center needs will get a lot easier by the means of AI, transmission of large size files (MRI, CT scans, and other reports) through various departments, and their access to the respective departmental doctors would be an added advantage, thus resulting in improved productivity and overall healthcare development.

AI is bringing revolution in the healthcare industry. Below mentioned are few areas where AI is performing a decisive role (Figure 11.4):

- Heart echostudy
- Drug management
- Modeling cure plans
- Robot-assisted surgery
- Automated image diagnosis
- Dosage error reduction
- Drug testing simulations
- Virtual nursing assistants
- Clinical trial participation
- Fraud detection
- Intelligent administrative workflows
- Give precise medication by viewing medical records

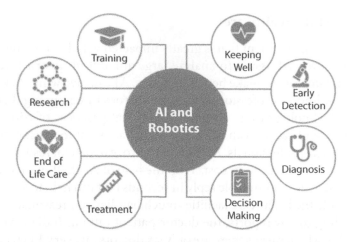

Figure 11.4 Relevance of AI in the healthcare industry. Source: NITI Aayog Report, 2018 [2].

- Forecasting evolution of HIV's effects on affected individuals
- Rendering virtual consultation
- Performing medical education with the help of Avatars rather than patients
- Virtual analysis of medical images
- Craft and encode friendly robots to take care of old age persons
- Assist in administrative managing processes
- Developing advanced medicines for severe as well as curable diseases.

11.5.2   AI in Banking and Finance

The banking and finance industry has witnessed growth by introducing AI in every segment. From enhancing customer experience to boosting banking sector productivity, AI has reached every nook and corner. Robotic process automation makes the business processes more efficient and eliminates the boring physical interventions. Concurrently, AI-enabled virtual personal assistants such as chatbots assist to lift the client or user experience with extremely modified communications and customized offerings. AI facilitates the workforce to concentrate on higher-value activities instead of focusing on a dull or ordinary task such as day-to-day customer call.

AI and automation, machine learning, and data analytics have drawn a supreme impact on the banking and financial sector. Whether it is personal finance, underwriting, portfolio management, capital market, trading, and financing, AI has become a principal component of Fintech. For example, AI systems are competent of doing millions of dealings without any individual intervention, in a flawless mode within a span of a single day. Fintech installed the AI-focused trading system in which robot advisors are assisting in the function like portfolio management.

AI perks up the competency of the financial and banking sector. By investigating the past data, AI-enabled software is perfect in advising if the investment is worthy or not. AI also assist the investors about the market based on the past market trends. The adoption of AI in the banking sector has led to maximization in their wealth. AI can also recognize legal and deceptive dealings precisely than any human being on the globe. AI not only minimizes the losses but also amplifies the goodwill of banking organizations.

11.5.3   Artificial Intelligence in Education

An efficient education sector possesses the power to renovate a nation through the expansion of human wealth and augmented efficiency. In developing countries, the altitude of education and literacy rate plays a significant role in the overall growth and progress of an economy (Figure 11.5).

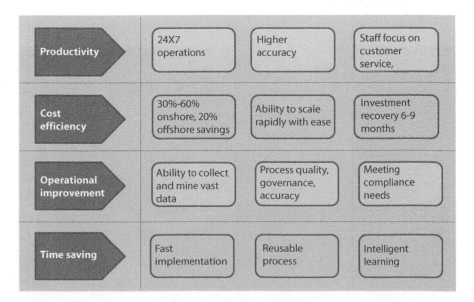

Figure 11.5 Benefits from robotic process automation. Source: Asian Banker Research.

Nowadays, the educational sector is highly influenced by digitalization and innovations. Thus, entrusting and modernizing educational systems with AI has resulted in enhanced impartment of information.

According to the US Educational Sector Report, by the end of 2021, AI will grow up to 47.5% [6]. The digital market of India was recorded at USD2 billion in 2016 and is planned to rise at a CAGR of 30%, in 2020 [15]. According to a survey held in the US, 75% teachers want to replace their traditional printed book by digital learning tools. Adopting machine learning and AI is fostering students to expand their knowledge and to become a good human being. Not every student understands same teaching technique and every student has some unique features so AI facilitates to recognize the plus and minus of every student to formulate customized teaching methods (Figure 11.6).

AI can bring revolution in the education sector in followings ways:

- Universal access to educational content for all students
- Automate admin task
- Personalized learning
- Support teachers and students
- Automate grading
- Identify the strength and weakness of student and offer content accordingly
- Smart content

Figure 11.6 AI in education. Source: Johnson, 2019 [7].

11.5.4   Artificial Intelligence in Agriculture Sector

Gone are those days where agriculture is only related to traditional farming techniques, technology is transforming the agriculture sector in India. Technological upgradations have renovated farming techniques with the passage of time and amplify the agriculture sector in countless aspects.

Agriculture is the core employment in countless nations universally and with mounting people, according to UN projection, the population will rise from 7.5 billion to 9.7 billion in 2050. It means to meet this aggressive demand of further 2 billion population, farmers have to raise their output by 60%. The AI-equipped solutions will not merely facilitate farmers to perk up their productivity but also helps to advance in quantity, superiority, etc.

Nowadays, availability of laborers is a major issue in agro-industry. AI-enabled machines can take off the weight of farmers and manage the deficiency of workers in the field. AI can boost farming experience in the following ways (Figure 11.7):

- AI technology can also monitor the health of a crop and keep proper track of crop health. AI can identify the weed and pests that are harming the crops at an early stage so that various recommendations can be given to curtail the effect.
- AI can advise farmers to place the right crop at the right time and also give proper knowledge regarding climate conditions.
- AI can take the revenue of the agriculture industry to the next level by suggesting the right harvesting period.

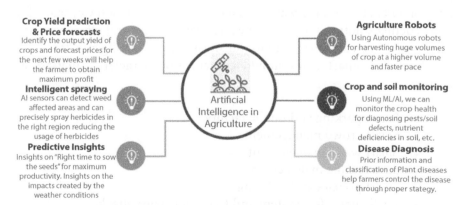

Figure 11.7 AI benefits in agriculture sector. Source: Revanth, 2019 [8].

Worldwide, AI and digitalization is resolving the issues of agro-industry. Farmers of India are moving toward digitalization. More than 30 million farmers in India possess smartphones which is likely to reach three times by 2020 and the reach of internet in rural India is vast. A survey was conducted by Accenture and found that 70 million Indian farmers will be impacted by digital farming and connected farm services and can add 9 billion US dollars to farmer's revenue [2].

11.5.5   Artificial Intelligence in Smart Cities and Infrastructure

India is enrooting to urbanization. In 2011, only 31% Indian population lives in urban areas, while recent study shows that, in 2018, nearly 45% population moves toward urban areas, and it is expected that around 60% population will reside in urban areas by 2050 [2]. Unplanned urbaniza-tion will cause overpopulation, jamming, increase in crime rate, deprived living standard, infrastructural burden, etc. To combat these challenges, few initiatives are taken up by the Indian government. Initiatives include set up of Smart Cities across India, designed to augment the economic development and quality of life. Initially, 99 cities across India have been selected under the Smart City Mission with the investment of 2.04 lakh crore rupees. Few components are included as Smart City Mission such as improvement of the city, redevelopment of the city, and green-field extension.

Some Smart Cities have already introduced AI features to boost their growth. For example, Pune city introduced The Pune Street Light Project to install power saver street lights which are controlled by remote via supervisory control system. The Smart City of India, Surat, has constructed a network of more than 600 cameras for observation located to all major cites of Surat city. Surat city also collaborated with Microsoft Company for constructing solution for effective water management and efficient urban planning. AI can aid smart city to transform into an intelligent city.

AI-enabled smart cities should contain few characters. They are as follows:

- Smart parking and public facility
- Smart crowd management
- Smart waste management
- Smart traffic management
- Smart policies and building
- Intelligent safety system and free from cyber-attack.

11.5.6   AI in Smart Mobility and Transportation

The transportation industry usually faces various issues because of deprived infrastructure, rapidly increasing population, growing traffic in cities due to urbanization, pollution, etc. AI helps to get rid of these challenges

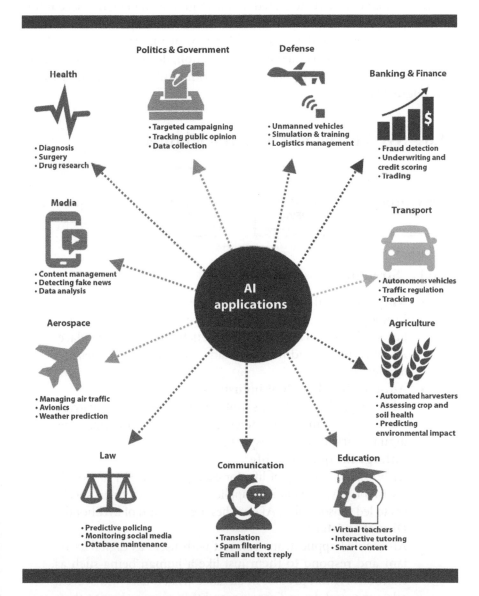

Figure 11.8 Applications of AI to various sectors. Source: Syam and Nguyen, Everything you need to know about artificial intelligence, 2019 [10].

easily by integrating transportation facilities with technology and innovation. Nowadays, AI bought a revolutionary transformation in this sector where vehicles can plot a route and move without any support of human being. Introduction of AI benefited the transportation sector in many ways such as reduce traffic jamming and accidents, augmented passenger safety, reduction in carbon emissions by vehicles, reduce the requirement of high-priced infrastructure, and diminish the total financial cost of traveling [9].

Below mentioned is the image which is showing application of AI in numerous sectors such as media, law, education, defense, politics and government, health, aerospace, agriculture, communication, law, and transport (Figure 11.8).

11.6   SWOT Analysis of Artificial Intelligence

STRENGTH OF AI	WEAKNESS OF AI	OPPORTUNITY OF AI	THREAT OF AI

11.6.1   Strength

- **Amplify the efficiency at workplace**
  Employees spend plenty of their precious time on manual tasks; AI helps to magnify the productivity at the workplace. AI let employees administer a large number of activities in a flawless manner.
- **Adopted by a bunch of industries**
  AI has significantly left its footprint to a range of industries, starting from media to defense, healthcare to agriculture, digital marketing to transportation, etc.
- **Enlarge the quality of life**
  AI boosts the quality of life, for example, from Siri to Google Assistant, payment banking applications to Alexa, smart speakers to led sensor bulbs; AI enriches the standard of livelihood.
- **Digital assistant**
  AI-enabled applications connect with users as digital assistant and respond to them just like a human being such as chatbots. AI can predict in advance what a user will search, ask, type, and do and recommend things according to their past behavior.

- **Prompt decision**
  AI has an incredible accuracy, appropriateness, and swiftness. Human being reacts in both manners emotionally and practically but AI-powered machines only react on the programmed algorithm which leads in faster decision making.
- **24*7 Availability**
  AI machines do not get bored just like humans and can work day and night without getting tired.
- **Enhanced risk taking capacity**
  With the support of AI-powered machines or robots, numerous risk taking limitations of human being can be removed. Whether it is reaching to mars or to explore the deep gigantic ocean, rescue a blast, etc. AI can effectively manage all risks [11].

11.6.2   Weakness

- **Making human lethargic**
  In every big organization, majority of the work is performed with the help of AI techniques which results in laziness on the part of humans. Human beings possess supreme ability to judge, think, listen, analyze, etc. If AI will perform the entire task, then human capabilities will go in vein.
- **Involves huge cost**
  AI-enabled machine need to be updated on a regular basis to cope with the flaunting external environment which requires huge cost.
- **In human**
  AI can communicate effectively but not includes personal and emotional touch in the communication. Machines cannot work in group and unable to create personal bond with humans.
- **Restrictive approach**
  AI-enabled machine can only perform those activities for which they are coded. Anything out of the box can diminish their relevance.

11.6.3   Opportunity

- **AI can be used to track competitor**
  In a globe filled with full of competition, it is important for an organization to know its existing as well as budding

competitor. Here, the role of AI comes into scene, for example, Crayon is an AI-enabled tool which facilitates an organization to track its competitor regularly via social networking websites and many more [12].

- **Take customer relationship management to the next level**
  AI brings CRM to the level of par excellence. AI-powered CRM platforms perform real-time data analysis and assist customers with precise or fruitful recommendations and suggestions.
- **Motivation of digital marketing**
  AI helps organization to track its target audience or customers according to their past behavior such as interest, past data searched, and hobbies. AI leads to boost the brand awareness among customers and also enhance the customer experience by providing appropriate product according to their taste and preference.

11.6.4   Threat

- **Unemployment**
  AI is hampering the level of employment because majority of the activities are done by AI-enabled machines or robots which are decreasing the importance of humans in an organization. Every industry is in the race to replace less qualified employees with AI machines or robots which can perform similar task more precision.
- **AI could get wrong**
  AI can become a serious threat for all human kind. AI is widely adopted in the healthcare sector to analyze and diagnose disease. But in case the diagnosis by technology gets it wrong and is corrupted by virus, then the entire diagnosis process goes bad and may cause serious injury to the patient.
- **Misuse of technology**
  In some situations, technology can go against human being. AI could cause mass losses if goes in the hands of an immoral person. This risk will continue grows up as the level of technology will reach sky.
- **Risk of cyber attacks**
  Most of the AI applications relied on the huge number of information of their clients or user base. Hackers can easily hack personal and sensitive data which leads to a major disruption among all users and can cause major loss.

- **Risk to our planet**
  Expansion of tools and gadgets are swiftly may cause critical challenges to our planet. Currently, the wastage of electronic and computer parts are creating a major problem in the growth of our environment and planet.

11.7   Conclusion

India is on its way to becoming a key global leader in terms of technology, innovation, and AI. AI is a significant vehicle for India through which our country may move toward socio-economic growth and development. AI is acting as a motivation for innumerable business and industries. There is no domain left which is untouched by AI. Hence, AI is revolutionizing India byte by byte.

According to McKinsey Global Institute Report, AI has the power to boost the global economic output by 16%, and by the end of 2030, AI can add 1.2% of an annual standard contribution to growth productivity [13]. According to the recent report launched by PwC, AI advancement will amplify the global GDP to 14% by 2030 and will contribute additional $15.7 trillion to the world's economy [14].

In nutshell, AI will double down the growth of all nations around the globe. In India, AI has colossal possibility to enlarge human intelligence and to drastically amend the approach to access commodities and services, to interrelate, assemble data, etc. AI is continuously setting up the milestones toward excellence.

References

1. Syam, N. and Nguyen, L., *Everything you need to know about artificial intelligence*, CGTN, 2019, June 13.
2. Roy, A., *National Strategy for Artificial Intelligence*, NITI Aayog, 2018.
3. Menon, R.M., Vazirani, M., Roy, P., *Rewire For Growth*, Accenture, 2017.
4. *Artificial Intelligence has the potential to add 1 trillion to India's economy in 2035*, The Financial Express, Noida, Delhi. 2018, June 9. (https://www.financialexpress.com/opinion/artificial-intelligence-has-the-potential-to-add-1-trillion-to-indias-economy-in-2035/1199249/)
5. Narayanan, A., *Top 5 industries impacted by artificial intelligence and data*, DataQuest, New Delhi, India, 2019, October 25, Retrieved February 10, 2020, from DataQuest: https://www.dqindia.com/top-5-industries-impacted-artificial-intelligence-data/.

6.   Lynch, M., *Roles For Artificial Intelligence In Education*, The Tech Edvocate, 2018, May 5, Retrieved February 10, 2020, from The Tech Edvocate: https://www.thetechedvocate.org/7-roles-for-artificial-intelligence-in-education/.

7.   Johnson, A., *5 Ways AI Is Changing The Education Industry*, E Learning Industry, 2019, February 6, Retrieved February 10, 2020, from E Learning Industry: https://elearningindustry.com/ai-is-changing-the-education-industry-5-ways.

8.   Revanth, *Towards Future Farming: How Artificial Intelligence is Transforming the Agriculture Industry*, Wipro, 2019, November, Retrieved February 10, 2020, from Wipro: https://www.wipro.com/holmes/towards-future-farming-how-artificial-intelligence-is-transforming-the-agriculture-industry/.

9.   Joshi, N., *How AI Can Transform The Transportation Industry*, Forbes, 2019, July 26, Retrieved February 10, 2020, from Forbes: https://www.forbes.com/sites/cognitiveworld/2019/07/26/how-ai-can-transform-the-transportation-industry/#a5b53bc49640.

10.   Syam, N. and Nguyen, L., *Everything you need to know about artificial intelligence*, CGTA, 2019, June 13, Retrieved February 2, 2020, from CGTA: https://news.cgtn.com/news/2019-06-12/Everything-you-need-to-know-about-artificial-intelligence-HswDK6aQdW/index.html.

11.   Kumar, S., *Advantages and Disadvantages of Artificial Intelligence*, Towards Data Science, 2019, November 25.

12.   Adixon, R., *Artificial Intelligence Opportunities & Challenges in Businesses*, Towards Data Science, Canada, 2019, July 24.

13.   Berger, I.W., *The Impact of Artificial Intelligence on the World Economy*, The Wall Street Journal, New York City, 2018, November 16. https://www.wsj.com/articles/the-impact-of-artificial-intelligence-on-the-world-economy-1542398991

14.   Byrd, B., *The Economic Value of Artificial Intelligence*, Pricewaterhouse Coopers, New York City, 2018. https://www.theexperience.work/wp-content/uploads/2018/06/WSJ-economic-value-of-AI.pdf

15.   Sarwal, R., Prasad, U., Madangopal, K., Kalal, S., Kaur, D., Kumar, A., Regy, P., Sharma, J., *Investment Opportunities in India's Healthcare Sector.* NITI Aayog, 2017.

12

AI: A New Strategic Method for Marketing and Sales Platforms

**Ravindar Meena[1]*, Ashmi Chhabra[2], Sachin Gupta[3]
and Manoj Gupta[4]**

[1]*Doctoral Studies, Department of Business Administration, Mohanlal Sukhadia
University, Udaipur, Rajasthan, India*
[2]*IIS Deemed to be University, Jaipur, Rajasthan, India*
[3]*Department of Business Administration, Mohanlal Sukhadia University, Udaipur,
Rajasthan, India*
[4]*Department of Electronics & Communication, JECRC University, Jaipur,
Rajasthan, India*

Abstract

Marketing changed dramatically in the past 10 years as technology evolved, but
as we enter a new decade, B2B marketing professionals appear to be relying on
many of the tools and strategies they have employed in the past couple of years.
Technology is gradually creating the tools for your opponents that are used to
build new digital products and services that target and release hidden demand
and serve important needs. That interruption may happen quickly that is likely to
have started already. With the impact of AI estimation for the economic growth
of developed countries between 2017 and 2035, it potentially adds $7.4 trillion to
the U.S. economy alone.

Businesses that use AI will be able to forecast demographic compatibility, track
consumer movement, foresee purchases, and offer excellent customer service.
Sales will rely on data and insights more than ever before, and to overcome these
challenges, AI provides analytic systems that explore existing customer graphs
to find new customers. To overcome these challenges of marketing, AI provides
rank or cluster existing customers according to interests. It acquires reports about
activity impact, identifies profitable product areas, and captures new and trending
product concepts.

**Corresponding author*: meena.ravi2606@gmail.com

S. Balamurugan, Sonal Pathak, Anupriya Jain, Sachin Gupta, Sachin Sharma, Sonia Duggal (eds.)
Impact of Artificial Intelligence on Organizational Transformation, (183–200) © 2022 Scrivener
Publishing LLC

In this chapter, we are trying to explain the impact of Artificial Intelligence in marketing field where it is going toward the better lead, predictive analysis that improves pitches, better upsell opportunities, and the challenges that arise while performing the AI tools in marketing area.

Keywords: Artificial intelligence, technologies, opportunities, marketing, sales, economy

12.1   Introduction

AI has reached, but it is mostly been applied on consumer goods and services companies to mark the marketing messages, increase the knowledge of customers, manage inventory and increase customer loyalty. AI has equally powerful impacts on B2B sales and marketing, but it is in its early stages. AI is the new strategic method of all sales, but it is still lacking behind to reach the B2B space. Many businesses gradually improving the accessing power of collecting the data across multiple sources. The fast-growing digital analytics firm helps companies toward forecasting the new revenue, accelerating the new product and enhancing the product popularity, maintaining the consistency in retaining the customers, and also helps in taking the correct investment decisions. B2B companies are making important decisions in solutions that safeguard the company's vision of accessing the data across all platforms. These investments contain technologies and platforms that safeguard the predictions which are followed in a B2B world.

The adoption of AI for B2B marketing may be promising, it leads to be believing in the substantial progress in the coming years because of the investments being made in data and technology. In addition, 54% of B2B marketer respondents said they have not tried AI. While other B2B service companies and product companies are the top user of AI tools such as content personalization which is 62.2%, some other features of AI such as face recognition, visual search, augmented, and virtual reality are used which are controlled more than any other business types like B2C companies when it comes to using AI for most marketing activities [1].

12.2   Objectives of the Chapter

1. To analysis the impact of Artificial Intelligence (AI) in marketing and sales field.
2. Recognizing the significant value of AI in marketing and sales field.

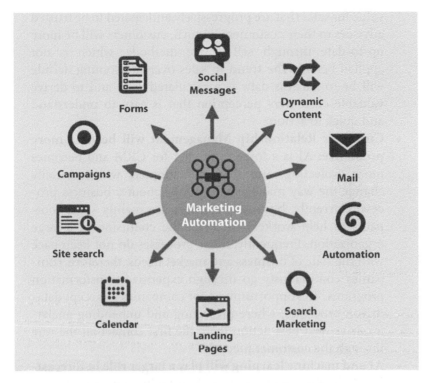

Figure 12.1 Marketing automation. Source: https://senitih.com [9].

3. To know the future prospect of predictive analytics on marketing and sales field.
4. To know the potential value of AI.
5. To study the contribution of AI on B2B growth and to study the traditional methods of marketing and sales (Figure 12.1).

12.3   Importance of Artificial Intelligence

AI helps many companies to forecast the demographic compatibility, tracks consumer movement, foresees purchases, and offers excellent customer service. An AI consulting services company, using AI, businesses will not only communicate with individuals directly but also convert the information collected from them into a framework to help serve them efficiently in the future. Three ways the technological advancements in AI will reshape sales:

- **Sales will rely on data and insights more than ever before:** The level of perceptions that AI delivers has far-fetched value for sales that are progressively anticipated to be trusted advisors to their customers. In turn, customers will be more up-to-date through self-service methods, which is not applied before. The trend in sales over the coming decade will be to harness data as a calculated asset and to derive valuable customers perception that is easy to understand and quick to action.

- **Customer Relationship Management will become more predictive:** AI is a force multiplier for CRM and becomes more projecting, and the early adopters will essentially change the way management thinks about a business process. Currently, business processes are mainly static footpaths to help workers to direct the confusion of a large organization. Frequently, those processes do not keep pace with the state of business and market needs; therefore, companies continuously go through expensive transformation programs. The opportunity is for companies to accept data-driven processes, where projecting and unbending analytics drive next best action from the first contact all the way through the customer lifecycle.

- **AI and machine learning will play a larger role in forecasting:** One of the first places of AI is taking the root for forecasting. Statistics methods are used by companies for decades to assist their forecasting efforts, which tend to become very expensive and time-consuming, and efforts were led by small back-office teams. The assistances of such efforts could not be operationalized at a scale that has all transformed in the previous years and will remain to progress.

What is most important about the maturity of AI-enabled forecast tools over the years is that it is helpful in explaining our predictions and makes them actionable to a broad array of workers, from sales representatives to channel managers to sales operations. Forecasting has developed as one of the most popular AI use cases and expected that to continue for the coming years [2].

12.4   Research Methodology

Qualitative research methodology and case studies are used here to recognize the effect of AI on the uprising and growth of marketing and sales

Figure 12.2 AI inbuilt Robot. Source: Alex Knight | Unsplash.

filed. AI is a new innovation concept, which gets the complete performance and let the researchers to cooperate with the interviewees which turn out to be easy in qualitative research. Qualitative research surveying the existing knowledge and theoretical foundations become easy which cannot put on AI. Several case studies are showed in many marketing and sales field in various organizations (Figure 12.2) [3].

12.5   AI: The Ultimate B2B Growth Accelerator

AI is an instrument which is vastly increases their contribution in many industries and some part of our lives. In most cases, we have not yet reached the widely discussed point where AI is replacing humans, but it is helping a lot of companies across a broad cross-section of industries to accomplish tasks more efficiently and effectively. How AI can help with sales? AI is a tool which speeds up the sales processes and helps sales teams stay ahead of the game.

The finest method to expand sales is by meeting data to examine and make data-driven decisions, and that is what AI is all about [4]. AI can help in raising the business by increasing sales in some different ways as follows.

12.5.1   AI Can Help Get Better Leads

Possible leads are found using platforms such as Google or LinkedIn; when AI is involved, it can cross-reference the data you collect against many other sources so you get the most accurate data for your business.

12.5.2   Predictive Analysis Improves Pitches

An AI system allows you to build customer profiles that are separated by behavior and their habits. This additional information helps your sales system to more accurately predict what customers need or may wish to buy.

12.5.3   Better Upsell Opportunities

Businesses must be able to balance getting new sales while still retaining their current customers so they can keep growing. AI can help salespeople figure out when customers should be buying again and how they can use a product. For example, Amazon uses AI to figure out customer buying patterns and anticipate the needs of their clients before they even arise. Uber is doing similar things by using heat maps and AI to get their drivers in the right areas at the right times.

12.5.4   AI is an Excessive Digital Assistant

To be more creative, AI can become your digital assistant. You can use AI as voice-controlled digital sales assistants so that your salesperson can record key information on any of their devices, day and night. These assistants can also ask key questions and help your salesperson to get through the process in the right way. While your sales person is busy in any conversation or any other key activities, at that time, AI assistants can do crucial data entry by itself. Many businesses have fully embraced the developments that AI has given the sales industry, while others are concerned and anxious about the changes it is bringing. The good thing about AI is that it can help businesses boost their presence and improve sales.

12.5.5   AI and Improved Customer Conversations

AI reveals people's motivations, communication styles, and other behavioral traits. The biggest benefits of AI for sales and marketing experts are refining the conversations and messages they present to prospective customers. In this hyper-connected economy of a global market where every salesperson, marketing experts and their managers are chasing after the same thing successful conversations. Technology like email, messaging, and other social media activities have created as many encounters for sales and marketing professionals as it has provided benefits, including a massive confusion of messaging [5].

12.6   The Existing Methods of Marketing and Sales

Many new campaign and product launches fail because sellers do not understand the new solution or did not even know about the launch in the first place. An email outlining the new product, services, and messages is easy to overlook, leaving many sellers unable to fully understand the uniqueness and positioning of the new offering. In order to resonate with customers, your announcement must be seen, messaging captivated and content leveraged with the sales team. However, more often than not, the announcement and content get lost in the shuffle, or sellers create their own off-base content. For an effective product launch, you will want the correct content and up-to-date information at the fingertips of your salesperson. By optimizing messaging, collateral, and communication through effective sales enablement, sellers can better communicate the differentiating value of your new solution, showcase marketplace positioning, and properly advise prospects.

Many small unit businesses are continuously, making the same blunders in their performance of sales and marketing activities some of them are:

12.6.1   Being Lazy About Self-Promotion

Many small and medium-sized companies attained the mistake of self-promotion. Many CEO senior staff hate self-promoting. It wonders that, so many small- and medium-sized companies make this curious marketing error. Your existence should be shouted and louder your name in every newspaper, advertisement, blogs, and street corner. Every customer should be aware about the seller, shop, and product offered. Social media platform like Quora, Reddit, Chatbot, and Yahoo answers the questions of your daily customers and opportunities that strengthen to your business.

12.6.2   Avoiding Networking

Many small-sized businesses attempt the error of avoiding network with other units related to their businesses. It is very essential for the marketers to find measures that narrate to their productions. For example, fashion businesses, you must reach out to all fashion and clothing event. Influencers are continuously watching for the good content to help them endorse their own business but they are curious to forget to ask for interviews. Connecting yourself to the social media networking platform and other event managers related to your businesses helps in generating the more prospects to speak about your business and the products you are offering.

12.6.3   Bridging the New Product Launch Gap

Businesses provide their sellers about the product with excess information, throwing lots of new content at the sales team and hoping that all of the news is top of mind. To help alleviate this overload, companies can leverage a sales enablement platform.

- **Customized workspace:** You can present a customized workspace to your sellers, sharing news and content that is filtered for each seller's specific needs and providing a special section for new and relevant announcements. Sellers can personalize the workspace to refine their experiences. For announcements, organizations can link to all the right content and tools to help educate the seller, helping them understand, position, and articulate the value of the new solution to prospects.
- **Sales playbooks and collections:** Sales enablement platforms can also help package all launch materials into an interactive sales playbook to guide sellers to all the right content situationally. For example, a playbook could be based on industries, roles and stages of the prospect. By having all the approved materials in one location, sellers are prepared with the content they need to effectively understand a new product launch, showcasing the benefits and potential outcomes of implementing the new solution for their customers.
- **Business value selling tools:** Your sales enablement solution can promote and integrate interactive value selling tools, helping empower sellers to effectively quantify things like total cost of ownership (TCO) savings, business value outcomes, and return on investment (ROI) for prospective buyers [6].

Marketing is not difficult if we perform it according to the plan. If we halt making these vast unusual mistakes, then we will be on path to lift our business.

12.7   AI Will Shape Marketing Strategies of Startup in the Future

AI is a tool that easily transforms the marketing plans of startups and the actions of customers. AI helps in expanding the customer service opportunities, new business models, and sales methods. In the future, AI is the future course of action that permit online trading and marketers to estimate the requirements of customers with exact accuracy. AI helps supplier to identify the customers taste and preferences. With such kind of tools of AI, sellers can refer the exact products even without proper instructions, which provide option in front of customer to accept the delivery or return. Many marketing firms are often to adopt AI to lift the efficiency of their promotions. While the technology is still lacking behind to achieve the marketing objectives in its early stages, the upcoming of AI in marketing field is optimistic.

The marketing field will derive the profit through analytical scoring, buying through digital advertisement, and many discounting offers to customers. Some small business units like travel agencies, retailer, and packaged goods to customers are expected to getting more profit. These segments produce a large amount of customer dealing and a quality data.

AI to inspect the massive amount of data helps small business units to get more benefit of it (Figure 12.3).

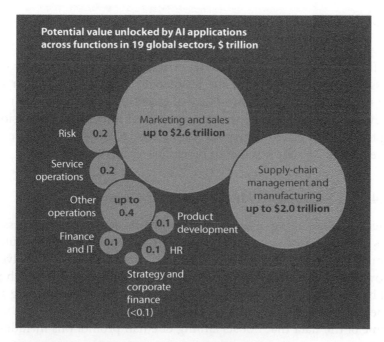

Figure 12.3 Scoring in different sector. Source: McKinsey.

12.7.1   Winning the Loots of Artificial Intelligence

The new startup businesses that adopted AI over digital marketing planning are more likely to be benefited. The advancement of AI allows the small business units to get a significant benefit in compare to other challengers. Many new startups will enjoy the high level of supremacy that would be unreachable without AI. The startups that adopted the AI in their earlier stages will accept business models that demands to investors and startups can get up a significant profit from listed data than AI.

12.7.2   The Control of Artificial Intelligence and Recorded Data

Exclusive data and AI boost the processes of small business units. The highly precise product endorsements yield benefit from large amount of customer data. For example, Google benefited from exclusive data in the form of search providing the most appropriate results. With the help of large amount of user's data allows the firm to train its systems. AI is a game changer tool for upcoming, as they can challenging a huge business-like Netflix, Amazon prime, and Google.

12.7.3   Artificial Intelligence the Game Changer for Small Businesses

AI is the advancement of technology which should be learned by every professional person who runs the business to train others in their firm. There must be a complete knowledge of essential technology required by the new startup to bring the wroth proposal. AI must be a compulsion to bring the value of price of the product and service. New businesses can be a game changer if their product or service necessitates AI to work.

12.7.4   AI Selling and Marketing for E-Commerce

AI affects the upcoming of digital marketing policies for new business that stands with AI-based company, resulting in marketing robotics solutions. E-commerce traders depend on automatic email marketing resolves to improve their promotions. The AI-based service result in the worth proposal by allowing traders to sell additional products. The projecting scrutiny permits marketers to mark the exact audience.

Some of the data that boosts aiming of email promotions includes the following:

- Description of price
- Subject outline
- Alteration charges
- Copy of email
- Promotions
- Marketplace

The data helps AI to modify their software, in such a manner that it improves the quality of promotions launched by new startup businesses in the e-commerce segment. The AI-based features also bring access to actual subject outlines that surge the open rates.

12.7.5   Marketing Computerization to Modified Knowledge

AI offers a technique for small business units to move from marketing computerization to modified knowledge. For several years, the digital marketing unable to bring any new revolutionary concepts to retain customers. Acceptance of AI pushes the new startups into new stage as they chase to gain a modest benefit. AI will boost significant variations in marketing area [8].

12.8   Artificial Intelligence is Shaking up the Job Market

By tracking the speed of technological modification as it stretches escalation to new work role, professions, and trades, the account measures the shifting outlines of work in the Fourth Industrial Revolution. The new machineries in the labor market convey further clearness to discussion about how AI brings changes in both produce and economic breakthrough. Social media platform like LinkedIn delivers an exclusive idea into world labor market growths, allowing investigations that will outline the upcoming efforts.

Technical jobs like computer software and data forecasters, technical knowledge such as cloud computing, mobile application on a software like Android & iOS, software inspection, and AI are on the path of trending in many industries across all areas. The automatic jobs decline professions, i.e., the jobs that are facing the huge reduction in the share of appointing over the last 5 years. These professions comprise of managerial supporters, customer care, accounts department, and technicians like electrical and mechanical, and many of them are depended on repetitive responsibilities [12].

The estimation effect of AI on the labor market turns out to be a separated description that trending globally. It is projected that by 2025, the most of the work done by machines which is 50% from 29% at present. This rapid change will be convoyed by new labor demands that may result in jobs opportunities.

Although AI is doubtful to exchange human jobs, ambiguity ruins about what types of job opportunities will be designed, how long-lasting they will be, and what kind of training program may require. Making the labor force for these variations will rest on a data-based method to considerate the requirements that are essential for future labor market and a pledge to participating in permanent knowledge prospects that can benefit labors to quick economical change (Figure 12.4).

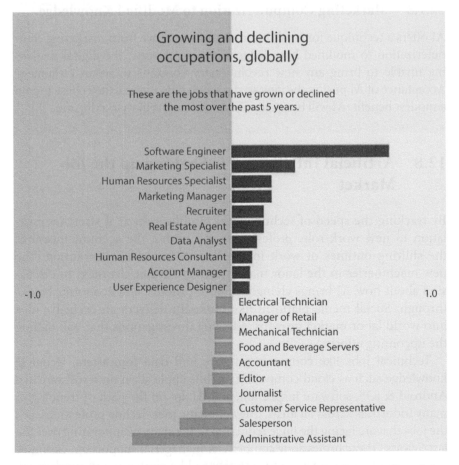

Figure 12.4 Growing and declining sectors. Source: https://www.weforum.org/agenda/2018/09/artificial-intelligence-shaking-up-job-market/.

In the given diagram below where AI skills are global, these the nations with maximum usage of AI skills are United States, China, India, Israel, and Germany.

The world endures toward participating in AI machineries, and we will remain in the direction of judging their consequence in industries and the effect on labor work force. As the new technology arise, the governments should conduct various skill program compulsory for educational institutions, employers of the different firms should consider the most successfully development skill that they will be desired to retain up with the current economy [7].

12.9   The Role of Artificial Intelligence and Machine Learning on Marketing

Artificial Intelligence: Learning of creation of our machines extra knowledgeable and capable of resolving glitches in the same manner a human does (Figure 12.5).

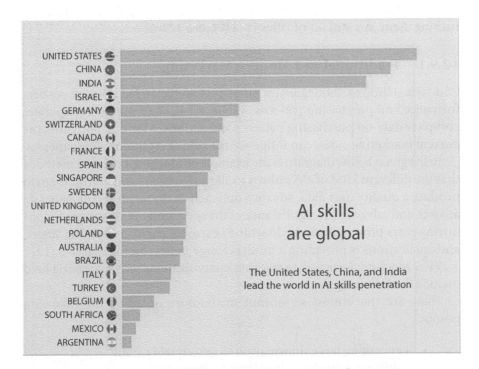

Figure 12.5 Ranking of AI usage globally. Source: https://www.weforum.org/agenda/2018/09/artificial-intelligence-shaking-up-job-market/.

ARTIFICIAL INTELLIGENCE   MACHINE LEARNING

Figure 12.6 Artificial Intelligence & Machine Learning. Source:https://www.grazitti.com/blog/the-impact-of-ai-ml-on-marketing/.

Machine Learning: Innovative mode of producing resolutions; at this point, we impart computers to acquire from remaining data without disturbing them in a stiff set of rules [11] (Figure 12.6).

12.9.1   Traditional and Modern Marketing

Old-style selling method takes incomplete vision addicted to employer performance and purchasing patterns. While, AI-derived marketing operates complete data on purchasing patterns and actions. Machine Learning, the current marketing sides, can influence the rule of AI into their businesses.

In the given below diagram is the example of Machine Learning methods that use different kind of algorithms to allow marketers and permit them to produce a quality user data, advance outreach in the target sector, generate answer, and advance the significance of the spectators. Wide range of monitoring gears power-driven by Machine Learning, cloud-computing stages, and applications is providing a model change in developing markets [13].

View Machine Learning marketing methods in current marketing field include the following.

These are the utmost significant methods recorded in the following points:

- Leveraging large information to get a quality result
- Additional modest advantages to discover
- Better buyer relations

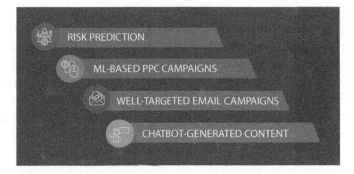

Figure 12.7 AI marketing strategies. Source: https://www.grazitti.com/blog/the-impact-of-ai-ml-on-marketing/ [10].

- Exact market predictions and sales estimates
- Data-based, enhanced marketing promotions
- Marketing qualified leads
- Sales qualified leads
- Visions to advance placing
- Augmented significance at measures
- Decrease in buyer mix amount
- Reduce demand variability
- Keener point-of-sale structures
- 360-degree opinion of client requests
- Generating new business opportunities
- Consumer satisfaction with better-quality practice
- Decrease in marketing prices for improved ROI

Marketing and publicity administrators around the world consume one goal: Attain significance at scale (Figure 12.7).

12.10   Conclusion

As we have provided functional benefits, we also have to occupy the emotional space in the minds of the consumers. The way we interconnect with consumers has reformed marketing field. It is adjusting every single day and somewhere it is the huge change that taken place. Big change trending in the marketing field is AI and Machine Learning. Thus, marketers must familiarize AI structures in their promotion policies toward current digital marketing. It helps marketers and consumer to saves together the time and money and resides the attentions of consumers without human interference.

AI technologies allow you to advance an all-inclusive, actual opinion of your clients and their related networks during your sales expedition. AI improves your prime development procedure and permits you to emphasize on planning the sales method and to determine the exact results. Digital conversion through AI is generating sales opportunities to moving forward. AI is unquestionably transforming in marketing and sales field. In revolutionary determination to classify the influence of AI on the ground, the results of this research drive to advise instructors about the institutional changes affected by AI.

References

1. Bronski, P., Business-to-machine (B2M). *business-to-machine (B2M) the next marketing frontier*, Mike Murrell, 2020, February Thursday.
2. Chapungu, G., *AI will Shape Marketing Strategies of Startups in the Future*, Medium, 2020.
3. Yin Yang, K.S., A Qualitative Research on Marketing and Sales in the Artificial Intelligence Age. *Proceedings of the Thirteenth Midwest Association for Information Systems Conference*, Midwest (MWAIS), Missouri, Saint Louis, p. 7, 2018.
4. John F. Gantz, G.M., *A Trillion-Dollar Boost: The Economic Impact of AI on Customer Relationship Management*, p. 20, IDC Analyze the Future, 2017.
5. Dinesh, *alavi.ai*, 2020, February Friday, Retrieved from www.alavi.ai: https://alavi.ai/blog/3-bizarre-marketing-mistakes-that-stop-small-and-medium-sized-companies-from-growing-and-how-to-prevent-them/?utm_source=marketing&utm_medium=twitter&utm_campaign=post.
6. Kaput, M., 4 Marketing AI Predictions for 2020. *4 Marketing AI Predictions for 2020, According to Experts*, 2020, February Tuesday.
7. Maechler, N., Finding the right digital balance in B2B. *Finding the right digital balance in B2B customer experience*, Lori Gardner, 2017, April, Retrieved from mckinsey.com.
8. Mayekar, S., Global market value of artificial intelligence. *Global market value of artificial intelligence to hit US$1.2 Trillion IN 2018*, 2018, May Wednesday.
9. McKendrick, J., 7 business areas ripe for an artificial intelligence boost, 12.1, 2020, February Saturday.
10. Michael Chui, J.M., McKinsey & Company, 2018, April, Retrieved from https://www.mckinsey.com: https://www.mckinsey.com/featured-insights/artificial-intelligence/notes-from-the-ai-frontier-applications-and-value-of-deep-learning?cid=other-soc-twi-mgi-mgi-oth-1807.

11.   Newman, S., Artificial Intelligence in Retail Market. *Artificial Intelligence in Retail Market to Show Great Impact in Future by Key Players Anaqua, Inc.,* Cardinal IP, Patrix AB, WebTMS, 2019, August tuesday, Retrieved from https://www.theinnovativereport.com/2019/08/27/artificial-intelligence-in-retail-market-to-show-great-impact-in-future-by-key-players-anaqua-inc-cardinal-ip-patrix-ab-webtms/.

12.   Nolan, P., *AI's role in sales and marketing,* SMMonline, 2020, Retrieved from salesandmarketing.com.

13.   Perisic, I., artificial intelligence is shaking up the job market. *How artificial intelligence is shaking up the job market,* p. 7, 2018, September Monday.

Website

1.   https://www.mckinscy.com/business-functions/marketing-and-sales/our-insights/finding-the-right-digital-balance-in-b2b-customer-experience

2.   https://medium.com/inflection-point-perspectives/is-business-to-machine-b2m-the-next-marketing-frontier-84f9078fd50e

3.   https://www.softwebsolutions.com/resources/5-strategies-to empower-your-sales-team.html?platform=hootsuite&utm_source=MarComKPC

4.   https://www.theinnovativereport.com/2019/08/27/artificial-intelligence-in-retail-market-to-show-great-impact-in-future-by-key-players-anaqua-inc-cardinal-ip-patrix-ab-webtms/

5.   https://www.mckinsey.com/featured-insights/artificial-intelligence/notes-from-the-ai-frontier-applications-and-value-of-deep-learning?cid=other-soc-twi-mgi-mgi-oth-1807

6.   https://medium.com/@gcneophil9/how-ai-will-shape-marketing-strategies-of-startups-in-the-future-21aa2f0280ae

7.   https://www.weforum.org/agenda/2018/09/artificial-intelligence-shaking-up-job-market/

8.   https://alavi.ai/blog/3-bizarre-marketing-mistakes-that-stop-small-and-medium-sized-companies-from-growing-and-how-to-prevent-them/

9.   Michael Chui, J.M., McKinsey & Company, 2018, April, Retrieved from https://www.mckinsey.com:https://www.mckinsey.com/featured-insights/artificial-intelligence/notes-from-the-ai-frontier-applications-and-value-of-deep-learning?cid=other-soc-twi-mgi-mgi-oth-1807.

13

Brain and Behavior: Blending of Human and Artificial Minds Toward Stress Recognition and Intervention in Organizational Well-Being

Manisha D. Solanky* and Sachin Gupta

Department of Business Administration, Mohanlal Sukhadia University, Udaipur (Rajasthan), India

Abstract

Stress attracts significant attention in the era of Artificial Intelligence (AI). Stress has become a part of every human and its consequences are severe if left untouched. The chapter pens down the impressions of AI as an enabler of human-technology interaction through various facilitators like sensor technology and wearable devices with physiological and psychological signals. Stress at workplace is a phenomenon that can neither be avoided nor be ignored but can be condensed to a great extent. In this chapter, attempt is made to explore all possible AI-powered stress recognition techniques and effective stress management interventions toward organizational well-being. The chapter is purely descriptive in nature following a qualitative approach. The intention of the study is to carry systematic literature review on AI-powered stress recognition and stress management interventions and its role in mental and physical well-being of employees. AI-powered devices and app are developed to manage stress, depression, and anxiety, even to prevent suicidal risk. After extensive literature review, it has been concluded that AI plays a positive and an impactful role in real time, and accurate stress recognition and interventions through chatbot, virtual therapist, biofeedback systems, wearable devices with sensor technology, and smart phone apps are effective in reducing the stress at workplace.

Corresponding author: solankymanisha21@gmail.com

S. Balamurugan, Sonal Pathak, Anupriya Jain, Sachin Gupta, Sachin Sharma, Sonia Duggal (eds.) Impact of Artificial Intelligence on Organizational Transformation, (201–228) © 2022 Scrivener Publishing LLC

Keywords: Stress, stress management intervention, artificial intelligence, sensor devices, wearable smart devices, stress recognition, machine learning

13.1 Introduction

> *"A confused mind is the main cause of all Stress"*
>
> verses from Bhagavad Gita

In the epoch of cut throat competition, stress has become a part of life. The mind can go in either direction under stress, either positive or negative; if negative, it will lead to obliteration, and if positive, it will lead to creation. According to Wrike's U.S. stress figures from 2019, 94% of employees feel stressed at workplace. Around 23% of employees feel highly stressed, according to the reports the American Institute of Stress [11]. Around 1 out of 75 persons experiences panic disorder due to stress at workplace, which depicts the report of National Institute of Mental Health, knowing the crucial fact that it has become important to take initiatives to reduce the stress before it causes physical and mental harm. Physiological and psychological stress is common and has an unpleasant health outcome such as heart related disease, diabetes, depression, and burnout anxiety, and the severe outcome is suicidal risk. Despite the evidence that stress negatively affects health, there are few effective and practical stress management solutions that can be seamlessly integrated into an individual's daily life. In order to develop truly personalized, targeted stress management solutions, we need to be able to accurately and reliably identify occasions of stress in real-world settings [14]. Detection of stress in real world setting is possible only when technology interacts with humans.

The universe is crossing verifiable extension spreading over human and Artificial Intelligence (AI) and the result is meeting of two brains: one human and one artificial. Human and technology associations have end up being an aid to mankind. The interaction between human and computer has been tremendously utilized in industries, health care, and homes. Emotions have "significant" influence on cognitive processes of the human brain such as knowledge, remembrance, observation and problem solving, and psychological and physiological connections that benefit different applications [40]. Depending on the application, many devices monitor heart rate (HR), galvanic skin response (GSR), blood vessel pulse, etc., which has to recognize the stress level of an individual, and these are known as physiological signals. Smart devices like smart watches, smart phones, and sensor-based wrist bands have in built facility to track stress related symptoms. With connecting the physiological and psychological signals with these smart devices, it has been easy to track stress at initial stage. When two minds interact, one natural and other being artificial, then the result will no doubt help the man kind immensely. In same way, stress has been detected through the coordination of psychological signals and with machine algorithms. In this chapter, an attempt is made to explore all possible AI-facilitated technology that helps in real-time stress recognition and accordingly provides interventions.

13.2   Research Methodology

Objective: This chapter aims at evaluating the stress faced by employees at workplace and its impact on the overall organization well-being.

To explore the role of AI-powered stress assessment techniques and stress management interventions and its impact on employees and organizations well-being.

Research Design: This study is descriptive in nature. Descriptive research is an attempt to spotlight on the current issues and problem by collecting data either through primary or secondary data that describes the complete situation or phenomenon. The purpose of descriptive research is to describe, elucidate, and validate research findings.

Type of Data: Secondary data has been used to complete the study.

Sources of Data: Secondary data has been collected from various journal, articles, websites, and E-libraries. Data has been accessed from IEEE Xplore, Procedia, Jstor, Springer link, Google Scholar, etc., to gain quality journals and articles. Examples of e-libraries are Wiley Online Library, ACM digital Library, and NDL.

13.3   Fundamentals of Stress

Stress is the most common phenomenon that has been faced nowadays at every stage of life by a person. Stress is a "Contagion, a block plague spreading like wildfire and sprewing large numbers of organizational members across the world" [1]. Stress is the growing concern for the organization as employees are the backbone of successful organization. Nowadays, organizations are paying keen interest toward the well-being of their human capital. According to a recent survey, in India, approximately, two million people suffer from heart attack every year and one person dies every 33 seconds. People common suffering is due to stress and depression through negative emotions, which dramatically weakens health and performance [17]. The study of man's reactions to deep psycho-social stresses has become a key concern of psychological investigation in current scenario. The accessible literature and researches present the occurrence and severity of stress and its ill consequences on employees and organization. Stress is a physiological reaction to human beings' psychological, emotional, or other physiological challenges, including their workplace [26]. Stress is concerned with two elements constraints and demand; these both leads to potential stress. Mixture of uncertainty and importance of outcome results in *Actual Stress*. Prolonged unexpected and unmanageable stress causes major damage to an individual's mental and physical health. One of the most important capitals of an organization is their employees and efficient manpower is a main index of excellence of an organization. Hence, organizations try their best to provide a healthy work environment to employees, but still lack in many perspectives [18]. Organizations are facing problem of stress at workplace and large number of employees experience unacceptable level of stress. Excessive stress can ruin an individual's life and can adversely affect his personal and professional life. In the competitive era, stress has become an inevitable outcome that affects everyone at some point of times. Urbanized world undergoes radical transformation,

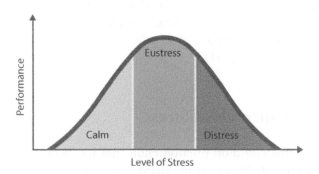

Figure 13.1 Relationship of performance and stress. Source: www.psychology. stackexchange.com.

and as organizations scale down, de-layers, the stresses and strains on employees increase gradually [7]. Stress cannot be completely eliminated out of life but initiatives can be taken by organization to reduce the occupational stress to the extent where one's life becomes worth living.

Stress has always held a negative side whose outcomes are negative feelings and negative emotions. Negative stress or unpleasant stress is termed as *distress*. Distress can be caused due to unhappy married life, divorce, punishment, accident, financial crisis, work conflict, etc. *Eustress* is the other side of coin also known as optimistic stress that accompanies attainment, high spirits, and job satisfaction. Stress has direct relationship with performance, if an individual is likely to face eustress, then the performance of individual is likely to increase. If an individual comes across distress, then his/her performances will gradually decline according to the amount of stress that is perceived (Figure 13.1).

13.3.1   Stress at Workplace

According to the American Psychological Association (APA), stress is divided into three, namely, acute stress, episodic acute stress, and chronic stress. There are severe consequences of stress which, if left untreated, may even uplift the risk of suicides. Some major outcome of stress are migraine, panic attacks, lack of concentration, hypertension, sleep problems, strokes, sleep issues, memory and concentration issues, burn out, anxiety, and depression. Workplace stress is mostly caused due to the various circumstances encountered at work as any other stress workplace stress also adversely affects a healthy mind and healthy body. Workplace stress needs to be addressed from a larger perspective since the workforce in organization is tremendously increasing and causing susceptibility to different chronic illness in certain cases death too. The sources of workplace stress to employees are highly individualistic. To some, a happening of event may be a stress, but to some, it may be chance of opportunity. Mostly, workplace stress arises due to disparity between demand of job and competency of an individual against the job. Anything that causes stress or some different working conditions that follow distress are stressors. Three stressors have been identified by researcher (Cooper); these are psychosocial stressors (e.g., unsatisfactory job design, inappropriate working environment, deprived social interaction, and societal circumstances at work), physical stressors in the workplace (e.g., need of security and stressful ambient factor), and psychological health problems related to workplace (e.g., mental strain, lack of concentration, and short temper).

13.3.2 Symptoms and Outcome of Stress

In the epoch of technology, life seems to be more challenging and exigent, and therefore, to be competent enough, the demands of current workplace prerequisite are always high. Consequently, it becomes really difficult to manage the psychological stress and physical stress. Here, the role of organization becomes critical in identifying the symptoms of stress that prevails at the workplace among the employees. Symptoms of stress can be distinctive, as it may differ from person to person [28].

Stress symptoms can be categorized into three broad headings as follows:

- Emotional symptoms
- Physical symptoms
- Behavioral symptoms

The symptoms of stress are the methods to understand the level of stress an employee or a workforce is undergoing. Symptoms are the ways to identify the mode in which the situation has been perceived by an employee. Stress symptoms may vary from employee to employee. It is really important for an organization as well as an employee to be aware of the stress through the symptoms to avoid worst consequences of stress on mental and physical health.

Emotional symptoms: When we converse about well-being, the employees need to be emotionally sound. Numerous studies conclude that emotional well-being at workplace is directly linked to higher productivity, creativity, good relationships, and good health. The root cause of emotional stress can be due to long-lasting unresolved and unmanageable circumstances. It is therefore important for organization to identify the stress and manage before the situation worsens.

Physical symptoms: One of the major outcome of stress is physical illness like migraine, frequent headaches, muscle tension, changes in libido, fatigueness, sweaty palms, dry mouth, shaky hands, dizzy spell and the list is never ending [28]. Research also proves that stress can be silent killer. Prolonged physical stress may lead to severe physical disorders.

Behavioral symptoms: Stress in workplace can also lead to behavioral changes. Its always better that the problem is diagnosed earlier in order. Behavioral changes in an employee at workplace can be result of stress. All behavioral changes may not be due to stress but, all of sudden and unexpected changes, should be examined to know whether it is due to stress. Managers of organization need to be vigilant enough in identifying frequent behavioral changes in employees and accordingly can draw conclusions whether the employees are under any type chronic stress or not.

Table 13.1 Types of symptoms and outcomes.

S. no.	Emotional symptoms	Physical symptoms	Behavioral symptoms
1	Mood swings	Insomnia	Sleeping difficulties
2	Irritation	Hemorrhoids	Lack of punctuality
3	Lack of memory and concentration	High or low blood pressure	Absenteeism and withdrawal
4	Depression	Panic attacks	Risk taking behaviors
5	Short temper	Ulcers	Unhealthy eating habits
6	Anxiety	Migraine	Accident
7	Excessive sadness	Low energy	Addictive/excessive behavior
8	Isolation	Nervousness	Exhaustion

Source: Researcher Self.

Through these above-mentioned (Table 13.1) stress symptoms, it is very important to tackle these crucial problems at the initial stages as ignoring would pull down the well-being of employees at workplace. Stress has an adverse effect physically and mentally. The outcome of stress can cause serious ailment to physical body as well as psychologically like heart attacks, suppress of immune system, shrink brain areas, fatigueness, depression, and anxiety. Organization success depends completely on human capital employed, and if human capital is not well, then it will have adverse effect on organization. Organization needs to provide healthier workplace ambience so that employees can be healthy. Stress needs to be identified at an initial stage before it corrupts the individual and organization.

13.4 Embracing AI Opportunity in Stress Management Interventions

AI is the limb of computer science. It is the study of association between computation and cognition. Imperative tool of AI is programming language which stipulates the objects and procedure to solve definite classes of problem. AI is the current and the future of every dilemma. AI is defined as the "mental faculties through the use of computational models" [4]. AI deals with "intelligent behavior in artifacts" [39], and intelligent behavior revolves around insight, interpretation, learning ability, perception, and communicating and acting in complex environment. AI revolves around engineering and scientific goals. The use of AI for the self-driven physiological and psychological well-being has developed exponentially in recent years as per the findings of [23]. Sensor technology is gaining popularity among the crowd for detection and measurement of stress. AI plays a tremendous role in all meadow; AI has reduced the role of human to great extent. Nowadays, robots can teach students, robots can perform surgeries, and heartbeats and blood pressure can be checked through wearing sensor-enabled technology.

AI is a tool that can renovate the future workplace, by sinking recurring task and supporting employees with its smart tools [38]. Some of the universal forms of technology that AI adopts are as follows:

- Machine learning
- Automation
- Natural language process

To build up a stress recognition structure, there is the need to comprehend the stress procedure. When human undertake a fervent event, the body is prone to extensive physiological and psychological stressor, provoking a reaction of the responsive nervous system to meet the augmented metabolic demand. The sensitive nervous structure fundamentally speeds up certain processes within the body ("fight-or-flight" response); it raises the HR, sweating rate, hypertension, etc., which can be detected using wearable smart sensors according to the findings of [12]. Therefore, AI and its important technology forms are combined with other smart devices and technology to help us detect real-time stress at workplace. Through this technology, blending stress can be recognized at early stage before it causes severe harm to employees as well as to organization.

13.5   Existing Technology for Stress Recognition

With growing technology, the stress detection devices have also grown immensely. Stress recognitions are based on self-tracking system where individual can detect stress at their own level and only few stress detection system are developed based on organization purpose where they can take initiative to explore the level of stress faced by employees.

13.5.1   Smart Detection Devices

Internet of Everything (IoE) is combination of sensing, computation, data mining, and communication functionalities together in a device according to the author [22]. The role of smart devices, sensor supported devices, portable devices, and wireless devices has been increased in the era of AI, and these devices play an elementary role in IoE. Smart devices are equipped with multicommunication interface like Wi-Fi, Bluetooth, and cellular communication and most important part massive number of in built sensors, With expansion of semi-conductor technologies, electronic devices take the smaller shape but act more powerfully [41]. Smart devices like smart watches, smart phones, and smart wristbands play an immense role in detecting the behavioral changes, emotional changes, and physiological changes in an individual. These devices adopt the technology of sensors to identify the sudden and unexpected changes happening in the internal state of body. Sensor technologies are simple yet complex devices that convert physical variable into electrical signals. Sensors have a property of self-validation, self-identification, self-diagnostic, self-healing, and self calibrating, and due to these rich properties, it has become easy to detect the patterns of changes that occur due to stress.

13.5.2   Stress Detection Through Physiological Signals

Automatic stress detection through physiological signals can be a useful tool to solve the problem of human stress. Stress may perhaps be detected by monitoring many physiological changes, such as blood volume pressure (BVP) and HR that could be obtained through electrocardiogram (ECG) and photoplethysmograph (PPG), pupil diameter (PD), respiration (RESP), skin temperature (ST), and GSR as a consequence of sweat-gland activity, muscle activities measured by electromyogram (EMG), and brain activities recorded through electroencephalogram (EEG) as described by author [2, 30].

Through physiological signals, recognizing stress would be more accurate, and through these signals, it becomes possible for human to interact with technology comfortably. Physiological signals are the best source to analyze human behavior, cognitive science, social psychology, and group perception. Many products are available in market which support interaction of computers with physiological signals. Smart devices and wearable sensor-based devices take aid of physiological signals, GSR, respiratory rate, electromyography, and BVP to detect the emotional state of human body [41].

13.5.3   Sensor-Based Detection

Sensor technology is gaining space in recognizing, detecting, and measuring stress through biological signals such one technology is biofeedback method for monitoring stress level. Sensor-based technologies are proving to be best and most accurate technique in detecting stress by interacting with physiological signals like HR variability, blood vessel pulse, respiration rate and GSR. Autosense is one such example of an unobtrusive, flexible band worn around chest which helps to detect stress through the physiological signals. This device provides respiration data by expansion and contraction of chest [27]. Sensor technologies have potential capacity to augment e-therapies experience through objective, automatic monitoring, and feedback. Biofeedback is a real-time self-tracking sensor-based technology that captures biological signal of a person and detects the stress through the data monitored [19, 23].

13.5.4   Deep Learning Approaches for Stress Detection

Deep learning is one of the most powerful tools of AI. Deep learning approach is widely used in image processing and natural language processing to detect or recognize stress, yet no study has yet applied this approach to analyzing multiple signals.

Deep learning approaches are basically based on ECG and RESP data to recognize mental stress at workplace. Sensor-based deep ECG net is also used by many organizations to recognize the stress at workplace. Deep ER net structure identifies stress by identifying unique pattern of ECG and RESP measurement in employees according to researcher [31]. Using the multiple dataset, Deep ER net performance is better than predictable machine learning models that require the extraction of handcrafted features. By visualizing the network's activation, its neurons activate by unique and specific patterns. Deep learning–based technology is a great technology that can help employees in reducing the stress, anxiety, and distress at workplace as per the findings of [31].

13.5.5   Stress Detection Through Biofeedback Systems

Biofeedback is an interdisciplinary procedure through which patrons train themselves to mount up a group of skills, the training of which is elaborated through the information gained by biofeedback equipment. Biofeedback system is one of the most frequently used stress management intervention and also the most promising intervention [8] techniques and documented to facilitate treatment for a good sort of disorders related to mental and physical such as asthma, panic attacks, hypertension, depression, anxiety, concentration problem, loneliness, and migraine and the intervention provided through this method along with sensor devices, and the results obtained are notably positive according to the study of [19, 37].

As per [12] the author mentioned that "substantial amount of studies were conducted to implement stress detection employing a grouping of psychological and physiological signal processing and machine-learning. Most of them used data from a respiration sensor, ECG sensor, HR sensor, acceleration sensor, GSR sensor, BVP sensor, and EMG sensor. Some are more constrained, either physically (e.g., brain activity analysis) or with reference to privacy (e.g., analyzing the user's audio or video)". Smart watches are often worn to detect stress on a continuous basis, e.g., Empatica wrist watches has in-built app for continuous stress assessment, and this device provides acceleration to blood vessel Pulse, GSR, and HR data, and ST.

Types of biofeedback techniques consistent with researcher [17] are as follows:

- Breathing: Airborne biofeedback means monitoring breathing rates and patterns with sensor belts round the chest and abdomen.

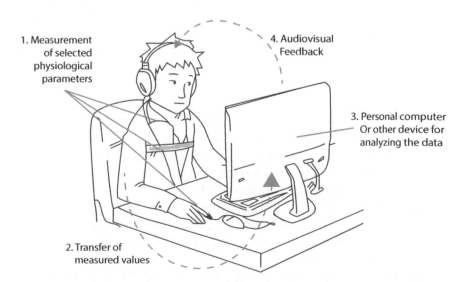

1. Measurement of selected physiological parameters

4. Audiovisual Feedback

3. Personal computer Or other device for analyzing the data

2. Transfer of measured values

Figure 13.2 Biofeedback detection system. Source: www.frontiersin.org/journals/ict.

- HR: Patients with this sort of biofeedback wear a sensor-connected device, which is either within the ears or in their fingers or in their sensors placed in the wrists, chest, or torso.
- GSR: Biofeedback of this sort involves measuring the quantity of sweat on the skin's surface. GSR may be useful marker for detecting levels of emotional excitement, also referred to as skin conductance.
- Brain waves: The scalp-sensor system uses an electroencephalograph (EEG) to watch your brain waves.
- Muscle tension: This suggest placing sensors with an electromyography (EMG) over your skeletal muscles for monitoring the electrical activity causing muscular contraction (Figure 13.2).

13.5.6   Stress Detection Through Virtual Reality

Stress can be detected through computer game or virtual reality (VR). Spirit of mind is often effectively identified by using VR. VR has made commendable contribution in stress management and training [33]. Stress is induced by different state of body like physical strain, mental tension and the different state of body causes changes within body's response. VR environment can additionally activate unusual stimuli for subjects, and numerous phenomena like the nervousness, lack of concentration, and easiness as considered symptoms of stress in a broad sense [5].

VR environment are rich in sensory thus providing opportunities to capture the minds and behaviour of humans according to [6]. VR facilitates by shifting the sensory input that the brain collects, changing brain understanding of existing reality. The approach to VR aims at achieving relaxation, stress reduction, and emotion regulation. Subsequent are the approaches to VR:

- Relaxing VR: The user is presented with imitative of conventional relaxation techniques like progressive muscle relaxation, autogenic therapy, yoga, and meditation. The user is shown with these environments to support them to feel safe, and as a result, it makes them feel relaxed.
- Engaging Virtual Reality: Engaging VR interact with the virtual contents to coach emotional regulation during this approach. The environment is flexible and adaptable depending on the users' interactions.
- Personalized Virtual Reality: Personalized VR is a recent approach to VR, which is a user-centered approach, is built

on unique quality picked up by users' recollections related to life events.

Helium XR acclaims as the first podium that differentiate itself from the remainder by using real-time EEG feedback to extend feelings of positivity. This virtual-based platform tries to evaluate the brain activity. This is often achieved by placing the viewer in environments that are healed and transformed by their changing biometrics. To try this, the platform uses devices such as the **Muse headband**, or smart watches [11].

Relax VR is app with advanced design to assist the one that wants to relax and/or elope the negative emotions. By merging peaceful 360° videos consisting of instinctive scenes, music, and sounds with meditation techniques (like Yoga Nidra), through this effective app, the user can relax their physical and mental state round the clock. Users of the app are trained with numerous relaxation techniques within a selection of serene scenes which they are going to then apply in stressful situations in lifestyle. As a result, users can improve their emotional well-being and quality of life!

13.5.7   Stress Detection Through Keyboard Strokes

As the amount of employees using computers continues to grow spectacularly, the level of stress can be identified by keystrokes too. The hardwares of the PC are additionally being researched as how to assess the consequences of stress. Specially designed keyboards are developed to extract further features that standard keyboards do not comply with. There is a pressure-sensitive keyboards that give, for every keystroke, a value of pressure between 0 (no pressure) and 255 (maximum pressure). The more the pressure on the keyboard, the more significant is the stress. Combination of keyboard strokes and linguistic features of unprompted generated text measures the substantial and cognitive stress of an individual [3]. Detecting cognitive and physical stress through keyboard interactions with the ultimate goal of detecting acute or gradual behavioral changes can be the effective way to recognize and identify stress and anxiety level [36].

13.5.7.1   *Chatbots for Depression, Stress, and Anxiety*

"A chatbots could be a bug that uses AI that simulates human conversation through voice commands or text chats or both". There are a spread of chatbot synonyms, together with "talkbot", "bot", "IM bot", "interactive agent", or "artificial conversation entity", "conversational agents", "machine conversation systems", "dialogue systems", "digital assistants", and "virtual agents [35].

As the space amid the supply of psychological health professional and the cost of each therapy session keep growing and this insists for digitized healthcare solutions. Even in their low times, more and more people are adopting app experience over the important therapy session.

13.5.7.2   WYSA Chatbot

The startup from India and UK is a health-supported startup introduced by Wysa, an AI-facilitated chatbot or "emotionally intelligent" bot that the corporate says can "facilitate in managing emotions and thoughts." Similar to Woebot, Wysa's design supports the ideology of Cognitive Behavioral Techniques to help users confront and alter their behaviors. Wysa chatbot incorporates dialectical behavioral therapy (DBT), and it gets input from chat of user and accordingly provides mediation training and also boosts users' morale through motivational chat. Wysa frequently utilizes input from user while they chat and interpret according to the dialects and provide dialectal behavioral therapy. Wysa chat bots are gaining popularity in few organization, as this platform provides dialect between artificial agent and natural human, therefore employees can freely express their worries to the with the chatbot without fearing of any higher officials.

13.5.8   Stress Intervention Based on Human-Technology Interaction

A group of activities adopted by organization to enhance employees mental and physical well-being by addressing the strain at right time and by reducing its impact on the employees to an immense extent is defined as stress management intervention. Concentrating on employees' well-being and reducing their stress to a great extent can have enormous benefits for an organization in terms of employees performance at workplace, productivity, relationships, absenteeism, employees turnover rate, and lot of more. Stress management interventions are bifurcated into three categories; they are as primary intervention, secondary intervention, and tertiary interventions. The primary stress interventions aspire to put off stress from stirring by reducing the root cause of stress and promoting a healthy workplace. Secondary stress interventions aspire to condense the relentlessness or period of stress once it has occurred and to put a stop the altitude of stress becoming challenging. Tertiary interventions seek to recover and take advantage of implementation of intervention on employees previously suffering from psychological ill-health [16].

Table 13.2 App-based interventions.

App	Intervention technique
Calm app	Mindfulness therapy
Pacifica	Cognitive behavioral therapy
Happify	Cognitive behavioral therapy
Headspace	Mindfulness therapy
Aura	Mindfulness therapy
10% Happier	Mindfulness therapy
What's up	Cognitive behavior therapy

Source: Researcher Designed.

13.5.8.1   Individual Level of Intervention

Intervention opted by a particular person to prevent stress. Individual interventions are a type of self-help programs that help in managing stress and promoting mental and physical well-being at workplace. Techniques that are popularly helps individual at reducing stress are meditation, cognitive behavioral therapy, mindfulness training, exercise programs, yoga, emotion regulation technique, and many more techniques that keep evolving. Trending interventions nowadays are Web/Internet-based interventions and app-based Interventions and also proven effective in reducing the stress levels among highly stressed individuals [15, 21]. As smart phones are part of everyone life, they can be utilized to recognize stress and they facilitate stress relieving techniques anywhere and anytime. Web or Internet-based intervention involves intervention program through online wellness programs like *Healthy Minds* [24], *Healthy paths, Studicare stress*, and *Get.On Stress* that provide online E-coach that will listen to the problems and provide feasible solutions and also include different session along with booster session that will help in reducing stress. Smart phone application like the Loom, Relax and Race [9], Happify and many other as mentioned in above Table 13.2 are effective stress management interventions which can be used easily by any individual.

13.5.8.2   Organization Level Intervention

At organization level, endless attempts are made by management to make stress-free environment. Organization tries their best to eliminate the causes of stress and ensure well-being of employees. Many studies prove that interventions at organization mainly concentrate on job redesign as the mean of employees well-being. Other methods adopted at organization level are peer support group where employees can freely, without any hesitation, interact with peers and discuss any issue which is causing stress to them. Social Support Groups are also made to encourage social interaction among employees through recreation activities. Intervention at organization level is difficult and complex and also an expensive affair. AI-based interventions at organization level are very few and organizations still follow traditional method of stress intervention focusing on job redesign, managing conflict through peer support groups. AI-powered stress interventions at organizational level are not feasible due to complexity involved at various levels. Tech-oriented organizations can easily implement stress recognition support system through ambient intelligence. Ambient intelligence is technologically empowered environment. In this environment, employees are in continuous contact with various devices like computer, microphones, and cameras, and through these devices, movement patterns, facial expressions, posture patterns of sitting, and interactions with others can be used as input to detect and assess stress art workplace [3]. Organization according to the level of stress can provide stress management intervention through web-based or app-based intervention. Virtual therapist, online stress intervention program, and virtual-based interventions can be effective intervention to reduce stress at workplace.

13.5.8.3   Devices Supporting Stress Interventions

Empatica wrist device is a smart sensible device that actively, with its machine learning algorithms, detects stress by assessing user activities (Figure 13.3). The stress is detected through physiological signals like respiration sensor, ECG sensor, HR sensor, acceleration sensor, GSR sensor, BVP, sensor, and EMG sensor [10, 12]. Many sensor-enabled wrist devices are available like seismotracker which senses heart rate, respiration rate and micro-vibrations [13] for recognition of stress, depression, and other symptoms of stress in real-time setting to know the actual state of stress. Where the stress is measured high at workplace, employees can be asked to wear such sensible and smart devices to track their stress level and act sensibly before stress cause major damage to health.

An additional commercially available product is **Stress Eraser**, a relaxation-based training product. This product is used to measure pulse rate by placing it on fingertip and it uses the real-time state to detect the stress and provides relaxation training depending on the level of stress faced by user. A pilot study was conducted on Stress Eraser's effectiveness

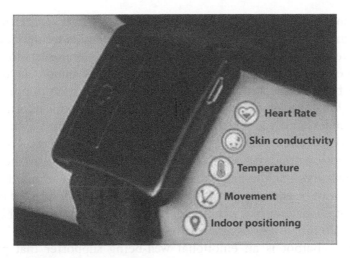

Heart Rate

Skin conductivity

Temperature

Movement

Indoor positioning

Figure 13.3 Empatica sensor-based wrist device. Source: https://tatourian.blog/2014/04/03/your-future-smart-wristband/.

and it was found it gradually reduces the long-term anxiety, stress, and depression, and therefore, the device was more positively received by participants than other techniques according to the study of [20]. Mobile apps that take advantage of sensors present in smart phones for detecting stress in individual can be of great help to employees in reducing their stress. Smart phone apps are developed with an insight to use the in-built sensor system of smart phones to help in recognizing the stress using physiological and psychological signals of users. **Azumio's Stress Check** is one of the effective apps that, with the help of the camera and light characteristics of the smart devices, allows the user to determine real-time pulse rate. **StressViewer** is an app that follows identical approach of Azumio's stress check. **StressSense** is one among the applications, supported by a classifier that can vigorously recognize stress across various individuals in different acoustic environment [3].

Stress Hacker is a wearable biosensor device that helps in detecting stress in real-time setting as well as provides personalized interventions to reduce stress. Stress Hacker detects stress through identifying the sources of stress by recognizing patterns and this was evaluated by researcher [14].

WOEBOT, mentioned as an automatic conversational agent, is also one of the known and widely used chatbots. It is intended to provide expedient care to folks battling with anxiety and depression by mimicking human conversation; it is a chatbot that can be used by employees at personal level as this is based on self-help program. WoeBot works on IOS-supported operating system and allows chatting through Facebook Messenger. This chatbot follows cognitive-behavioral therapy (CBT), as intervention techniques to help user in reducing their stress level. Cognitive behavioral interventions are also one of the most effective stress management interventions as compared to other types of interventions [34]. Source of information to process data is through natural language processing (NLP) and uses this information to urge to understand you better. The composed information allows the program to detect stress accurately and meet emotional needs at a given time, offering personalized resources, self-help guidance according to the need of user. Employees may hesitate in showing their real state of mind but this hesitation can be eliminated if AI-powered chatbot at workplace is installed as colleague. Chatbots play a counselor role in many organization of UK, and they are into Employees Assistance Program.

Youper chatbot is an emotional well-being supporter that provides tailored response and insight supported with input depending on the whole-day text-based conversations with users. For instant, the user may be feeling depressed or nervous or anxious; here, the chatbot will present interventions to reduce anxiousness, depression, or nervousness. **Ginger.io** is a smartphone-supported application and works on machine algorithms and provides clinical networks that identify the exact state of stress. This platform allows user to interact with clinicians and provide online CBT, mindfulness, and resilience training [29]. Ginger.io app provides team of coaches like emotional support coaches to help them anytime anywhere round the clock. The users are also allowed to interact to licensed therapists or board-certified psychiatrists, through video conferencing. Interactions with coaches and therapists can range from unlimited live chats to video sessions, depending on the needs of the individual [29].

13.6   Discussion and Findings

Critically reviewing the prevailing literature, it has been found that AI interference in the managing stress is commendable to a great extent. Only few organizations adopt AI-supported technology for managing stress at workplace. If organizations are to realize the consequences of stress at workplace and the impact of stress on organizational effectiveness and goals, then it is indispensable that organizations should implement positive and anticipatory approach toward AI-based stress management techniques.

Many organizations has made technological transformation supporting digital methods of working; with the technological advancement, these organizations can monitor stress of employees through computers, laptops, microphones camera, etc., and smart environment supporting smart devices can be of great help in detecting stress at workplace like keyboard and mouse dynamics that can be monitored to detect stress through rhythm of typing. Mouse dynamics like moving of pointer on screen and clicking can be monitored to detect stress in employees. Other dynamics includes facial expression through cameras, and speech dynamics like monitoring the pitch of the speaker which helps immensely in detecting the level of stress. Very few studies have been carried out on these dynamics but these dynamics, if applied in organization, can help in monitoring stress at early stage.

Studies reveal that many organizations has taken an initiative toward wellness programs like yoga, meditation, and exercises, but there are few organizations heading toward AI-based systems for stress management. The biofeedback device, like emWavePS, which easily calculates every minor and major changes in heart beat (i.e., HRV) to determine the coherence of physiological signals, which can be used by organizations to detect stress and manage it timely before it causes huge damage to an individual as well as organization. AI-facilitated approaches that support smart portable devices, incorporated with physiological sensors, are generally more accurate and allow the user to maneuver freely round the environment [3]. Employees are always assisted with their personal assistant and popularly known as the smart phones. Smart phones can be used to detect stress and these smart phone app can provide stress intervention if employee are facing high level stress.

It has also been found that very few organizations adopt AI-based stress management interventions. As applying these approaches is an upscale for organizations. Still, organizations follow traditional method of stress management interventions. It was found in the existing literature that it is not possible for organization to implement AI-enhanced approach for stress management as it may require one camera per employees to monitor their movement patterns, facial expression, interaction with others, etc. There can also be issue of privacy that may be threatening to employees and AI-enhanced technology may need to acquire their images for detecting stress which may not appreciated by those employees who are not comfortable with this type of approaches.

Overall review of literature suggests that AI-facilitated stress detection smart devices, sensor-based detection devices, biofeedback techniques, chat bots, VR based techniques are helpful in assessing and detecting real-time stress at workplace. Therefore, to transform organization to a healthy workplace, these above-mentioned approaches can be adopted to detect stress at initial stage and provide interventions accordingly for the overall well-being of organization.

13.7   An AI—Eye to the Future

With advanced machine learning and deep learning algorithms, smart technologies, and wireless networks, the future AI could be much more efficient, powerful, and smarter than the present ones. AI systems could monitor an employee's enunciation of words and tone of voice for stress, detecting linguistic cues that might predict depression and analyzing spikes in HR, an increased typing speed, or a slowdown in productive output, which could all be warning signs for an employer [42]. Smart watches or biometric data, including facial expression, for example, could also come into play, to aid real-time detection of mental health issues. With this information, tasks could be delivered that are appropriate to an individual's stress levels. Above all, the rise of AI has the potential to enable workers to feel more engaged in their role and happier in their workplace. There will be obstacles, including privacy concerns, as well as ensuring workers are comfortable and willing to accept various levels of monitoring. It will be essential that there are protocols in place to ensure that AI development is safe and relevant, with contextual understanding, built with the individual and their well-being in mind. However, if managed responsibly, then the overall benefits could significantly help toward reducing the growing mental health crisis within the workplace.

Forthcoming 5G systems are developing to shore up explosion mobile traffic volumes, concurrent mining of fine-grained analytics, and agile administration of network resources, so as to take full advantage of user experience. The role of smart devices, mobile networking, and deep learning algorithms will increase with increasing complexity of stress in the future, incorporating general intelligence, bodily intelligence, emotional intelligence, spiritual intelligence, political intelligence, social intelligence in AI system that are part of the future deep learning research.

Application of Ambient Intelligence and Ambient Assisted Living role will also increase in the near future. Ambient Intelligence system allows organization in monitoring the real-time stress as employees perform their routine work, without any disruption. Organization needs to work on Ambient Intelligence as this can easily assess the behavior of employees in the real environment.

13.7.1   Implications to Managers

Stress management interventions are an investment in employees' well-being and have positive and healthy impact on organization [32]. Emotions and moods of employees are priceless, the most long-lasting impact would likely emerge from helping employees to cultivate the skills to respond effectively to stress [32]. Therefore, managers are advice to implement sensor-based wearable technology for effective stress control among the employees.

Managers can take initiative to develop IoT for employees' stress management. A centralized system or application can be developed which can monitor stress of employees if any employee is facing high stress level and then it can be reported to center, and accordingly, interventions can be given to reduce their stress. After all, "prevention is better than cure".

Many studies reveal that approaches of stress recognition based on sensor and supported by smart devices and incorporate physiological signals are generally more accurate. Therefore, managers can provide such wearable devices to employees or can make it mandatory for employees to wear feasible devices which allow them to self-monitor their stress.

Ambient Intelligence system can also be implemented in the organization where environment of organization is technologically supported and can monitor every employee's behavior through the Ambient Intelligence system along with sensor technologies without disrupting the employee's daily activities.

Initiative can be taken by managers for assessment of stress though biofeedback methods under controlled and uncontrolled environments as biofeedback methods are most reliable method to assess stress among employees. Stress management program's effectiveness can also be checked through biofeedback wearable sensor devices. After all, employees' well-being reflected organizations' well-being. Neuro biofeedback methods can also be applied at workplace to reduce physical symptoms like migraine which is mainly caused by overstressing situations.

Managers are also advised to develop a customized web-based or app-based interventions that fulfill the requirement of their employees, as organisation-focused intervention lack individually tailored interventions [34]. Web-based and app-based intervention are also effective way of managing the stress of employees. If it is not feasible to develop personalized web-based or app-based intervention, then they can opt any of the existing intervention available on smart phone or on internet. Mobile technologies has become part of everyones life and this technology can be vitally used by managers to transform the stress related issues faced by the employees, like wireless medical sensors, mobile biosensors with real time biometric data and integrated mobile apps [25].

13.7.2 Implication to the Entrepreneurs

After extensive literature survey, customized stress intervention technique at organizational level was not available. Therefore, it can be an opportunity for entrepreneurs to come up with such stress intervention technique supported with AI, according to the requirement of organization to help them in reducing the stress effectively and making workplace environment a better place to work. For example, virtual environment with soothing audios, mediation videos, or chanting can provide mindfulness therapy at workplace. Ambient Intelligence and Ambient Assisted Living is a technology-supported environment along with other smart devices that can be used to monitor stress in real-time setting without disrupting the routine work of an employee. Such devices or such support system need to be developed that can be used to monitor stress without interrupting the routine work. Customized development of app- and web-based interventions can also be develop to support stress-free life. Coupling AI with human brain and developing brain mapping will help a lot more to understand the exact working of neurons. Interaction of human mind and behaviour along with artificial Intelligence can be used as an opportunity to work on developing models on brain mapping. This is mapping of brain circuitry so as to understand how dysfunction, disorder, and disquiet happen and how this can be resolved. There are many opportunities waiting in the meadow and all you need is to keep your hands open to grab these opportunities.

13.8   Conclusion

After extensive and rigorous survey of existing literature, the researchers conclude that AI is evolving as a superpower and its implication of this technology is different from the past technology. This technology has the potential to create a bridge between human and technology. If AI leveraged effectively with humans' physiological and psychological signals, then it will help in creating a complete stress-free workplace and it will also boost employees' morale and productivity. With development of many smart sensor-based technologies, it has become easy to assess stress and contributes to next-generation E-therapies. AI-based intervention is like a magic wand in the hands of managers to control and manage stress. Organizations need to make attempts to detect stress in real-time settings. Therefore, it is very important for organization to adopt any of the mentioned approaches to detect stress and interventions to reduce stress for the well-being of employees as well as the organization. AI is empowered with machine learning, natural language processing, and deep learning algorithms, and through these weapons, AI along with human mind can fight effectively against stress at workplace. Using artificial mind keeps an eye on worker stress, depression, anxiety, and respond to distress and treat workers with compassion. Responding to the anguish of employees in a timely manner enhances employee's well-being, resilience, engagement, commitment, and loyalty. The role of leaders in supporting employees well-being will also expand therefore organizations need to be vigilant in transforming to unhealthy workplace into a healthy workplace.

13.9 Limitations of AI in Human Resource Management

AI plays a significant role in reshaping workplace and enhances productivity employee's engagement. AI handles recruitment, talent acquisition, training and development, performance analysis, and retention strategies effectively. Though AI is the trending phenomenon, it cannot replace human. AI-structured decision can be biased as it completely rely on big data and many a time can be misrepresenting. AI-based technology also lacks human touch because many a times employees may need to talk to real person or need face to face interaction instead of interacting with chatbots and personalized messages. Lack of human direct interaction may bring trustworthy issues among employees and this lack of trust among employees may also prevail due to excess dependence on AI-based technologies. Human interaction is also important while hiring employees as AI can make mistake in selecting the right candidate due to the similar nature of data. Thus, AI completely works on fixed interface but humans are capable enough to redirect themselves toward right decision. Stress recognition of employees through AI is no doubt effective and efficient but a human touch is required to console the human feeling and the real social support is also important to relieve stress comparatively talking to chatbots where there is no feeling and emotions considered while listening to the employees. There is need to make attempts to adopt augmented intelligence where human and technology can integrate together rather than replacing each other.

13.10 Conclusion

AI has emerged as a super power technology that can make decisions as effectively and efficiently as human and its role in recognizing humans' physiological and psychological signals is also commendable. After rigorous review, this paper makes a positive attempt to identify AI-based smart devices and technologies that help in identifying stress of individual and also provide smart intervention that helps in combating the stress effectively. This paper provides an overview of available stress recognition devices and technologies that are based on AI and therefore provides an insight to readers about different technologies that can be effectively used to recognize and identify stress levels. Stress is the most common concern that has been faced in every stage of life by different age of people and there is no doubt employees too face considerable amount of stress due to work life style, and this paper emphasizes on the AI-supported technologies to recognize and combat stress effectively. This paper only lacks empirical testing of devices and has not statistically proven the efficiency and effectiveness of these devices in recognizing stress and stress intervention due to time and resource constraints.

References

1. Aswathappa, K., *Human resource management: text and cases*, McGraw Hill Education, New Delhi, 2013.
2. Betti, S. *et al.*, Evaluation of an Integrated System of Wearable Physiological Sensors for Stress Monitoring in Working Environments by Using Biological Markers. *IEEE Trans. Biomed. Eng.*, 65, 8, 1748–1758, Aug. 2018.
3. Carneiro, D., Novais, P., Augusto, J.C., Payne, N., New Methods for Stress Assessment and Monitoring at the Workplace. *IEEE Trans. Affect. Comput.*, 10, 2, 237–254, Apr. 2019.
4. Charniak, E., *Introduction to Artificial Intelligence*, Pearson Education, Delhi India, 1985.
5. Cho, D. *et al.*, Detection of Stress Levels from Biosignals Measured in Virtual Reality Environments Using a Kernel-Based Extreme Learning Machine. *Sensors*, 17, 10, 2435, Oct. 2017.
6. Difede, J. *et al.*, Virtual reality exposure therapy for the treatment of post-traumatic stress disorder following September 11, 2001. *J. Clin. Psychiatry*, 68, 11, 1639–1647, 2007.
7. Kompier, M. and Cooper, C.L., *Preventing Stress, Improving Productivity: European Case Studies in the Workplace*, Psychology Press, New York, 1999.
8. De Witte, N.A.J., Buyck, I., Van Daele, T., Combining Biofeedback with Stress Management Interventions: A Systematic Review of Physiological and Psychological Effects. *Appl. Psychophysiol. Biofeedback*, 44, 2, 71–82, Jun. 2019.
9. Dillon, A., Kelly, M., Robertson, I.H., Robertson, D.A., Smartphone Applications Utilizing Biofeedback Can Aid Stress Reduction. *Front. Psychol.*, 7, 2016.

10.   Ekiz, D., *Stress recognition in everyday life*, Master of Science. Inst. for Graduate Studies in Science and Engineering, Bogazici University, 2019.

11.   Fourtane, S., Interesting Engineering, 2019, www.interesting engineering. com: https://interestingengineering.com/vr-ar-in-health-applications-powered-by-users-biometrics-eases-stress-and-anxiety.

12.   Gjoreski, M., Gjoreski, H., Luštrek, M., Gams, M., Continuous stress detection using a wrist device: in laboratory and real life, in: *Proceedings of the 2016 ACM International Joint Conference on Pervasive and Ubiquitous Computing: Adjunct*, Heidelberg, Germany, Sep. 2016, pp. 1185–1193.

13.   Haescher, M., Matthies, D.J.C., Trimpop, J., Urban, B., SeismoTracker: Upgrade any Smart Wearable to enable a Sensing of Heart Rate, Respiration Rate, and Microvibrations, in: *Proceedings of the 2016 CHI Conference Extended Abstracts on Human Factors in Computing Systems*, San Jose, California, USA, May 2016, pp. 2209–2216.

14.   Hao, T., Walter, K.N., Ball, M.J., Chang, H.-Y., Sun, S., Zhu, X., StressHacker: Towards Practical Stress Monitoring in the Wild with Smartwatches. *AMIA Annu. Symp. Proc.*, 2017, 830–838, Apr. 2018.

15.   Heber, E., Lehr, D., Ebert, D.D., Berking, M., Riper, H., Web-Based and Mobile Stress Management Intervention for Employees: A Randomized Controlled Trial. *J. Med. Internet Res.*, 18, 1, e21, 2016.

16.   Holman, D., Johnson, S., O'Connor, E., Stress management interventions: Improving subjective psychological well-being in the workplace, in: *Handbook of well-being*, DEF Publishers, Salt Lake City, UT, 2018.

17.   Ingale, K.S. and Gawali, B.W., Stress Management System by using Biofeedback Device–A Review. *Int. J. Inf. Comput. Sci.*, vol. 6, 154–159, 2019.

18.   Khodabakhshi, M., Predicting Occupational Stress for Women Working in the Bank with Assessment of Their Organizational Commitment and Personality Type. *Proc. – Soc. Behav. Sci.*, 84, 1859–1863, Jul. 2013.

19.   Lemaire, J.B., Wallace, J.E., Lewin, A.M., de Grood, J., Schaefer, J.P., The effect of a biofeedback-based stress management tool on physician stress: a randomized controlled clinical trial. *Open Med.*, 5, 4, e154–e165, Oct. 2011.

20.   MacLean, D., Roseway, A., Czerwinski, M., MoodWings: a wearable bio-feedback device for real-time stress intervention, in: *Proceedings of the 6th International Conference on PErvasive Technologies Related to Assistive Environments*, Rhodes, Greece, May 2013, pp. 1–8.

21.   Martín, D.B., Torre, I.D.L., Garcia-Zapirain, B., Lopez-Coronado, M., Rodrigues, J., Managing and Controlling Stress Using mHealth: Systematic Search in App Stores. *JMIR mHealth uHealth*, 6, 5, e111, 2018.

22.   Masoud, M., Jaradat, Y., Manasrah, A., Jannoud, I., Sensors of Smart Devices in the Internet of Everything (IoE) Era: Big Opportunities and Massive Doubts. *J. Sens.*, 2019, May 15, 2019, https://www.hindawi.com/journals/js/2019/6514520/ (accessed Jun. 09, 2020).

23. Millings, A. *et al.*, Can the effectiveness of an online stress management program be augmented by wearable sensor technology?. *Internet Interventions*, 2, 3, 330–339, Sep. 2015.

24. Morrison, L.G. *et al.*, The Effect of Timing and Frequency of Push Notifications on Usage of a Smartphone-Based Stress Management Intervention: An Exploratory Trial. *PLoS One*, 12, 1, e0169162, Jan. 2017.

25. Munos, B. *et al.*, Mobile health: the power of wearables, sensors, and apps to transform clinical trials. *Ann. N. Y. Acad. Sci.*, 1375, 1, 3–18, 2016.

26. Ragav, A., Krishna, N.H., Narayanan, N., Thelly, K., Vijayaraghavan, V., Scalable Deep Learning for Stress and Affect Detection on Resource-Constrained Devices, in: *2019 18th IEEE International Conference On Machine Learning And Applications (ICMLA)*, Dec. 2019, pp. 1585–1592.

27. Rahman, Md. M. *et al.*, Are we there yet? feasibility of continuous stress assessment via wireless physiological sensors, in: *Proceedings of the 5th ACM Conference on Bioinformatics, Computational Biology, and Health Informatics*, Newport Beach, California, Sep. 2014, pp. 479–488.

28. Rout, U.R., Rout, J.K., Occupational stress, *Stress Management for Primary Health Care Professionals*, Springer, pp. 25–39, 2002. https://www.springer.com/gp/book/9780306472404

29. Rucker, M., Very Well Health, 28 Jan. 2020, 15 May 2020 https://www.verywellhealth.com/using-artificial-intelligence-for-mental-health-4144239 (2020).

30. Saidi, M. *et al.*, Mental Arousal Level Recognition Competition on the Shared Database, in: *2019 27th Iranian Conference on Electrical Engineering (ICEE)*, Apr. 2019, pp. 1730–1736.

31. Seo, W., Kim, N., Kim, S., Lee, C., Park, S.-M., Deep ECG-Respiration Network (DeepER Net) for Recognizing Mental Stress. *Sensors*, 19, 13, 3021, Jan. 2019.

32. Smith, E.N., Santoro, E., Moraveji, N., Susi, M., Crum, A.J., Integrating wearables in stress management interventions: Promising evidence from a randomized trial. *Int. J. Stress Manage.*, 27, 2, 172–182, 2020.

33. Tichon, J.G. and Mavin, T., Using the Experience of Evoked Emotion in Virtual Reality to Manage Workplace Stress: Affective Control Theory (ACT), in: *Human Performance Technology: Concepts, Methodologies, Tools, and Applications*, 2019, www.igi-global.com/chapter/using-the-experience-of-evoked-emotion-in-virtual-reality-to-manage-workplace-stress/226563 (accessed Jun. 09, 2020).

34. van der Klink, J.J., Blonk, R.W., Schene, A.H., van Dijk, F.J., The benefits of interventions for work-related stress. *Am. J. Public Health*, 91, 2, 270–276, Feb. 2001.

35. Vijayarani, M. and Balamurugan, G., Chatbot in mental health care. *Indian J. Psychiatr. Nurs.*, 16, 2, 126, Jan. 2019.

36. Vizer, L.M., Zhou, L., Sears, A., Automated stress detection using keystroke and linguistic features: An exploratory study. *Int. J. Hum.-Comput. Stud.*, 67, 10, 870–886, Oct. 2009.

37. Wu, W., Zhang, H., Pirbhulal, S., Mukhopadhyay, S.C., Zhang, Y.-T., Assessment of Biofeedback Training for Emotion Management Through Wearable Textile Physiological Monitoring System. *IEEE Sens. J.*, 15, 12, 7087–7095, Dec. 2015.

38. Yin, D., RingCentral, Retrieved march 15, 2020, from www.ringcentral. com. https://www.ringcentral.co.uk/gb/en/blog/future-of-work/

39. Genesereth, M.R. and Nilsson, N.J., *Logical Foundations of Artificial Intelligence*, Morgan Kaufmann, Palo Alto CA USA, 2012.

40. Egger, M., Ley, M., Hanke, S., Emotion recognition from physiological signal analysis: a review. *Electron. Notes Theor. Comput. Sci.*, 343, 35–55, 2019.

41. Jin, C.Y., A review of AI Technologies for Wearable Devices. *IOP Conf. Ser.: Mater. Sci. Eng.*, 688, 4, IOP Publishing, 2019.

42. Bulpin, J., Citrix, https://www.citrix.com/blogs/2020/02/06/how-ai-could-benefit-mental-health-and-well-being-in-the-workplace/2020.

14

Alternative Financing

Suhasini Verma

*Department of Business Administration, Faculty of Management & Commerce,
Manipal University Jaipur, Jaipur, Rajasthan, India*

Abstract

Alternative financing is a phenomenon which is gaining momentum since last decade. It is a way of dealing in financial requirement on an online platform with or without the intervention of third party. Internet facility, advancement in the information technology, change in the psychology of the individual along with several other factors, and the limitations of the traditional financial organizations gave rise to this segment. Now, alternative financing is fulfilling the need of not only individual lenders and borrowers but also the SMEs to a great extent and being used as a tool of financial inclusion. In this context, it is critical to understand what alternative financing is, how it works, and how it is helping people and SMEs and can be used as a tool of financial inclusion. One important dimension of alternative financing is to see how this segment is being regulated.

Keywords: Alternative finance, traditional finance, business model, financial inclusion, P2P lending, crowdfunding

14.1   Introduction

Alternative financing is a phenomenon which is gaining popularity since past decade. It is an umbrella term of way of dealing with any type of financial requirement on an online platform. Widespread Internet facility, advancement in the (IT) information technology, change in the psychology of the individual along with several other factors, and the limitations of the traditional financial organizations gave rise to this segment

Email: f18suhasiniv@iima.ac.in; verma.suhasini@gmail.com

S. Balamurugan, Sonal Pathak, Anupriya Jain, Sachin Gupta, Sachin Sharma, Sonia Duggal (eds.)
Impact of Artificial Intelligence on Organizational Transformation, (229–244) © 2022 Scrivener Publishing LLC

[9]. Now, alternative financing is fulfilling the need of not only individual lenders and borrowers but also the SMEs to a great extent and being used as a tool of financial inclusion [3]. In this context, it is critical to understand what alternative financing is, how it works, and how it is helping people and SMEs and can be used as a tool of financial inclusion [1]. One important dimension of alternative financing is to see how this segment is being regulated.

Alternative finance is referred to a range of financial products, which are dealt on online marketplace and are developed out of traditional banking system. It is a way of dealing in financial requirement on an online platform with or without the intervention of third party [11]. If an individual or an organization require fund, then they put theirs demand online, whereas there are people or organizations, who wish to lend, process the demand online and if deemed fit provide the fund to the needy. This process may or may not require the intervention of the third party and obviously not the intervention of any bank [6].

The advent of the information technology, availability of internet to masses with good speed, and socio-economic changes help this segment to grow. It is the recession of 2007–2008, which gave rise to this phenomenon, when traditional banking sector was facing dearth of liquidity and was apprehensive to sanction loans [5].

14.1.1   Sources of Funds for Individuals

The traditional sources of finance are very limited for the individuals and the organizations. The sources of finance for individuals are limited to friends and relatives, commercial banks, and non-banking financial institutions [6] (Table 14.1). To get funds from the financial institutions, they need to fulfill their credit requirement—a very good credit score, steady income, and collateral [7, 10]. If the applicant is not able to fulfill all these, then there is less chance that they get fund from them. If they fulfill all the requirements, then, again, they need to wait for the formality to done and the time span for this can span into days.

Table 14.1 Traditional sources of finance.

Traditional sources of finance	
1. Individuals	**2. Organization**
• Friends, relatives	**Debt** - financial Institutions/Financial Market
• Commercial Banks	**Equity** - Venture Capital
• NBFC'	-Private Placement
• Money lenders	-Initial Public Offering

14.1.2   Sources of Funds for Organizations

Organizations may contact either the financial institutions, financial markets, or nowadays venture capital depending upon their need and strategies. They can approach financial market or financial institutions for debt capital or target capital market, qualified institutional investors, or venture capitals for equity fund (Table 14.1).

Whether debt fund expose them to permanent liability, equity may be proving even more costly to them in case of risky businesses. But, again, getting fund from these sources is not guaranteed [10]. Financial institutions have their own criteria to grant or not to grant loan to any organizations. If organizations want to get fund from the IPO route, then there is the need to Financial institutions have their own criteria to grant or not to grant loans to any organizations. To source the fund from the capital market, firms need to fulfill SEBI's requirements, which may not be possible for all the organizations. Again, it is impossible for a new venture to get fund from this route.

Financial institutions have their own limitations to provide loan to any entity—individual of organization—especially so, because they play with the money of others and they are answerable to the safety and growth of the fund. They become extra cautious and want to secure the safety of borrowed fund by credit score, collateral, or stringent appraisal of loan proposal.

14.2   Alternative Financing

Alternative financing relies on the different dynamics powered by the advancement of information technology and their processing and storage capabilities. Now, a slew of data are collected not only from the salary slip of the borrower but also from social media, their payment history, and their purchasing pattern to assess the creditworthiness of the borrower. Also, artificial intelligence is used to proactively assess whether the loan can turn non-performing asset. The borrowers and the lenders meet directly online, or sometimes, a platform helps them to assess the proposal and fixing the rate of interest for a fee. Here, the lender themselves take the decision to lend or not to a particular proposal, and the processing time reduces significantly (Table 14.2).

14.2.1   Features of Alternative Financing

- Speed
  Here, the borrowers and lenders both are available online.
  Either the lender themselves assess the proposal or the

Table 14.2 Conventional lending vs. alternative financing.

Conventional lending examples		Limitations of access to underserved markets	How FinTech lending overcomes the limitations
FORMAL	Banks	Requirement for **physical verification and high costs**.	Utilises **digital footprint as a substitution for physical documents** for verification and/or **usage of third-party** data (e.g. e-commerce) in order to define eligibility, **which lowers operational costs** compared to conventional lending.
	NBFCs		
	Multi-finance companies	The underwriting process requires a **credit history or proof of a steady income or an asset-based collateral**.	Processes the **underwriting assessment** through **digital processing platform with various data points**, to identify **typical attributes for interest rates** to be charged, without prior collateral.
	Cooperatives	Cooperatives are relatively **small in size** and **lack of competitiveness** to attract money suppliers in the market.	Developed a **simple and convenient platform** for attracting investment, as most of the **processes are completed through digital platforms**, which attracts large number of potential lenders.
INFORMAL	Loan sharks	**Risk of irrational credit and limited funding opportunities**	Customised **credit assessment models**, which employ **behavioural data to identify typical attributes for charging interest rates**, supported by large amounts of funding from retail and institutional lenders.

Source: https://www.pwc.in/assets/pdfs/consulting/financial-services/fintech/publications/ a-wider-circle-digital-lending-and-the-changing-landscape-of-financial-inclusion.pdf.

platform, from which they are associated, or provide them the insight, which help the lender to take the decision to check the viability of the proposal. If they deem the proposal fit, then lender intimate their acceptance to the bower within a short span of time. This process makes the execution speedy.

- Simplicity
  With the help of the mobile phones, both the parties can avail the services from the comfort of their home 24/7. EMI calculators, FAQs etc are available on these platforms, which makes the decision making simpler, easier, and faster.
- Affordability
  Mostly, the agreement is done between the lender and borrower, and the intervention of third party curtailed results in the absence of their charges. Also, in crowdfunding type of financing, many lenders provide the fund for the cause may without any reward, so borrower can afford to take up their venture to next level.
- Collection of Data
  Unlike banks, data are collected from various unconventional sources. Online platforms collect the data from social media, e-commerce app, and payment app to check the

spending pattern as well as whether they make payment on time or not.

- Processing of Data

  Advancement of information technology helped this segment to grow at an unprecedented rate. Storage facility of data has increased manifold and their processing capabilities has also increased at an unbelievable rate. Again, there are other technologies, like artificial intelligence, which helps to predict the behavior and chances in advance. It helps the platform to decide loan disbursement.

The alternative finance segment is growing rapidly over the years (Figure 14.1). If we talk about India, here also, it is picking up at very fast rate. In the year 2031, it was only $ 5.09m which has grown to $ 268.58m in the year 2017. If we talk about the popularity of variant of alternative financing, it is Balance Sheet Business Lending which is closely followed by consumer lending. The least popular is property lending.

The data shows that in India, 25% of the platforms significantly changed their business model, whereas 45% slightly changed their business model. In addition, 30% of the platforms showed no change. So largely, in India, 70% of the platforms made changes in their business model (Figure 14.2).

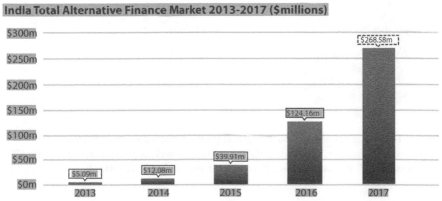

Figure 14.1 Alternative finance over the years. Source: https://www.jbs.cam.ac.uk/ fileadmin/user_upload/research/centres/alternative-finance/downloads/2018-3rd-asia-pacific-alternative-finance-industry-report.pdf.

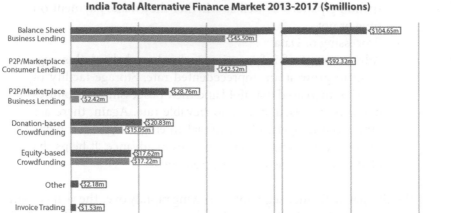

Figure 14.2 Alternative finance's market in India. Source: https://www.jbs.cam.ac.uk/ fileadmin/user_upload/research/centres/alternative-finance/downloads/2018-3rd-asia-pacific-alternative-finance-industry-report.pdf.

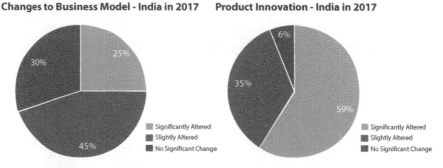

Figure 14.3 Changes in business model and product innovation in India. Source: https://www.jbs.cam.ac.uk/fileadmin/user_upload/research/centres/alternative-finance/ downloads/2018-3rd-asia-pacific-alternative-finance-industry-report.pdf.

Likewise, we see a major change in product innovation. A whopping 59% significant change is seen in the product innovation and 35% slight change was there in product innovation, whereas only 6% products has shown no change.

This change in business model and product innovation has resulted in many fold increase in the market size, which is reflected in Figure 14.3.

14.3   Models of Alternative Financing

The alternative financing segment experiencing an unprecedent growth across the globe and different business models are flourishing to cater the demand of funds.

Peer-to-Peer (P2P) lending and crowdfunding are very popular mechanism, having several variants to cater to diverse type of need of the seekers of the fund.

14.3.1   Peer-to-Peer Lending

This is very popular type of alternative finance. Here, the individual or the organization puts their demand online and either the individual lender or the institute, if they find it profitable, provides loan. Many a time, interest rate is decided mutually. Sometimes, platforms put the funds on bid and the bidder with highest interest payment gives the fund.

14.3.1.1   Peer-to-Peer Lending Types

14.3.1.1.1   Peer-to-Peer Individual Lending
This is the one of the most popular types of P2P lending worldwide. Individuals post their fund requirement with the interest rate they offer. Individual lender or institutional lender assesses their proposal—there are several tools available in this regard and the platforms also help the lender to take decision by their expertise and analytics in this matter. Mostly, the interest rate is decided mutually. Borrower taps this route if their proposal is denied by banks (for petty reasons like bad credit score, it may be because of not paying few rupees; in Rs 100005, the borrower paid Rs 100,000 and Rs 5 is still unpaid making their credit score poor) or absence of credit score. Many a time, individual require fund for the duration until they get next salary [12].

14.3.1.1.2   Peer-to-Peer Business Lending
Here, businesses approach for the loans. Mostly, the lenders are approached by the SMEs for the funds. The demand of the fund is fulfilled

by either the institutional investors or individual investors make a pool of funds for the same.

14.3.1.1.3   Peer-to-Peer Property Lending
It is a type of mortgage loan. The lender funds the individual or businesses against the property. The borrower generates the online application and, in turn, receives a series of loan amount and interest rate. Borrower chooses the most appropriate proposal, get, the property appraised, and, on that basis, signs the deal.

14.3.1.1.4   Balance Sheet Business Lending
The borrower applies for the loan, and on basis of the size of balance sheet of the business, the funder provides the loan to the business.

14.3.2   Crowdfunding

As the name suggests, a crowd or number of unrelated individuals finance a project or a cause. As the popularity of crowdfunding is increasing, so are its types. Depending upon the proposal, funds are being provided with or without benefits [2]. The popular models of crowdfunding are- equity-based crowdfunding, reward-based crowdfunding, and donation-based crowdfunding [14].

14.3.2.1   Equity-Based Crowdfunding

In equity-based crowdfunding, the promoter puts the proposal online and provides the shares of the company to the investors. Normally, startups, who are not able to get the loan form the banks, try this route for funding. Many a time, it happens that new and risky ideas are floated here to check the viability of the same. If many a people put their faith and fund the project, then promoter gets assurance about the idea [8].

It also works as marketing tool for them, as more and more people get to know about the business and put their money in this, they might be a prospective customer of the company.

14.3.2.2   Profit Sharing Crowdfunding

As the name suggest, the promoter agrees to share the profit with the investors. Here, the company promises to share the profit but not to provide them with equity, so there is no dilution of ownership.

14.3.2.3   Reward-Based Crowdfunding

Here, the funder is not given either the share or promises to share the profit among the investor or provider of the fund. Instead, they reward the funder in different manner. For example, they may promise to provide tickets of music concert, if a budding singer wants to organize a music concert, and for that, fund is needed. They may be given signed jersey of a club or replica of the product. Many a time, funder helps someone to achieve their objectives. It also happens that the company or the individual uses this medium to check their popularity or increase the awareness of their brand.

14.3.2.4   Donation-Based Crowdfunding

It is mainly related to charity. The funder does not want anything in lieu of this type of funding. This type of funding is required to, maybe, fund the operation of poor person or where the large amount is required which is beyond the capacity of the person. Or a needy intelligent student wants fund for their study. A sportsperson wants to participate in a sports event and fund is required for training, etc.

Apart from these most popular types of alternative finance, there are other forms which is picking up. The following Table 14.3 has listed various types of alternative finance as well as the volume in Asia Pacific and the leader China.

14.4   Scope of Alternative Financing in India

The alternative financing market is growing as an unprecedent rate in India. But, given the size of the market, its socio-economic features, and regulatory conditions, alternative finance segment still has a wider scope to expand its size. There is still huge mismatch between demand and supply of funds [9]. There is huge untapped market beyond metros in semi-urban and rural areas. Unique business model of alternative financing as well as advancement of information technology have given an edge to alternative financing organization to take under its helm of those small earners or MSMEs who do not have credit access [7].

The alternative finance organizations can address this opportunity by providing tailor made products catering to special needs of this segment. They may enter into collaboration of commercial banks, NBFSc, and technology companies to widen their reach and ensure the

Table 14.3 Models of alternative finance.

Model	Definition	2017 Total volume APAC	2017 Total volume China
Market place/ peer-to-peer consumer/ individual lending	A consumer/ individual borrower is provided the loan by the funders (individual or institutional funder).	$824,552,497.00	$224,431,765,158.86
Market place/ peer-to-peer business lending	A business borrower is provided the loan by the funders (individual or institutional funder).	$623,349,853.00	$97,430,537,311.80
Market place/ peer-to-peer property lending	Loan against the property is provided by the funders (individual or institutional funder).	$667,250,710.00	$5,940,105,541.83
Balance-sheet business lending	Business borrowers are given loan based on their balance sheet by the funders.	$680,313,030.00	$6,868,910,660.65

(*Continued*)

Table 14.3 Models of alternative finance. (*Continued*)

Model	Definition	2017 Total volume APAC	2017 Total volume China
Revenue sharing/ profit sharing crowdfunding	Shares or bonds are purchased by the funders and they share the profits of the business or charge interest to the business.	$176,037.00	$977,885,322.32
Real estate crowdfunding	Fund are provided for real estate by the funders.	$367,914,327.00	
Equity-based crowdfunding	Individuals or institutional funders take part in the business by purchasing the equity issued by the company.	$100,896,122.00	$224,968,323.45
Invoice trading	Businesses are funded based on their invoice. Invoices are purchased by funders at a discount in this type of funding.	$174,795,096.00	$5,605,170,415.75

(*Continued*)

Table 14.3 Models of alternative finance. (*Continued*)

Model	Definition	2017 Total volume APAC	2017 Total volume China
Reward-based crowdfunding	Here, non-monetary rewards or products are provided to the funders.	$71,440,507.00	$5,037,740.24
Donation-based crowdfunding	Funds are provided by the donors purely on philanthropic basis without any expectation of any type of return.	$53,169,352.00	
Debt-based securities	Funders provide the loan to the organization by purchasing the bond or debentures issued by them.	$25,578,193.00	
Balance sheet consumer lending	Individuals are given loan based on their balance-sheet by the funders.	$9,666,370.00	$15,762,790,359.65

Source: https://www.jbs.cam.ac.uk/fileadmin/user_upload/research/centres/alternative-finance/downloads/2018-3rd-asia-pacific-alternative-finance-industry-report.pdf

profitability by process the loan proposal, using the technologies like artificial intelligence and machine learning. They should bring more transparency in their operations, so that a sustainable business can be assured.

14.5   Alternative Finance as a Tool of Financial Inclusion

Alternative finance is seen as a tool of financial inclusion [4]. The traditional financial organizations like banks have their own limitation to fund the requirements of all those who have applied for the fund. They have limited funds, and from that limited fund, they cannot fulfill the need of all. For this reason and for the sake of safety of the fund of deposit holder, they must follow stringent rules while granting the loan.

This makes the speed of pursuit of fund of every needy slow. Alternative finance can be a great help in this regard, as there are various models of financing, and if the investor/funder buys the idea, they can fund without anticipating any return [5]. Apart from that, there is no requirement of physical facility here. Availability of internet and a mobile phone can solve the purpose.

But, in the pursuit of this, financial literacy is pre-requisite and the government must put a strong regulatory system in place to protect the interest of the stakeholder.

14.6   Regulation of Alternative Finance

Alternative financing is largely an unregulated domain. It is a new segment and regulators are learning from each others experiences for better regulation. Malaysia was the first country, who made the regulation in equity crowdfunding, which helped SMEs in the country to access the fund [13].

The main objective of any regulators is to make the domain level playing. Like any other financial sector regulation, emphasis here also is to make the market safe and to protect the interest of the stakeholders. For that, they have made clear the Asset Liability Management and KYC norms. The regulator is keeping an eye on promotion of platforms whether they are making misleading promotions and putting the investors' money at risk.

Lack of data, limited technical expertise, need to coordinate with many supervisory bodies, etc., are few of the limitations of the regulators to provide a framework to the segment.

However, the regulators, all over the world, try to overcome this by innovation, learning from each other's experiences, and use of sandbox. The concept of sandbox is to allow the operation of certain product/service in a controlled manner to see the impact of the operation.

In India, there is no separate law to rule the segment of alternative financing. They are largely regulated by the present related laws of the country. The government has allowed the use of the sandbox.

References

1.　Nemoto, N., Huang, B., Storey, D., *For small and medium-sized enterprises*, vol. 912, Asian Development Bank Institute, Japan, 2019.
2.　Cuesta, C., de Lis, S.F., Roibas, I., Rubio, A., Ruesta, M., Tuesta, D., Urbiola, P., *Crowdfunding in 360°: alternative financing for the digital era*, p. 30, BBVA Research Department, Mexico, 2015.
3.　Casey, E. and Toole, C.M.O., *NU*, J. Corp. Financ., 2014.
4.　Ozili, P.K., Impact of digital finance on financial inclusion and stability. *Borsa Istanbul Rev.*, 18, 4, 329–40, 2018 Dec 1.
5.　Harvey, M., Impact of financial education mandates on younger consumers' use of alternative financial services. *J. Consum. Aff.*, 53, 3, 731–69, 2019 Sep.
6.　Bilan, Y., Rubanov, P., Vasylieva, T.A., Lyeonov, S., The influence of industry 4.0 on financial services: Determinants of alternative finance development. *Pol. J. Manage. Stud.*, 9, 1, 70–92, 2019.
7.　Rubanov, P.M. and Marcantonio, A., Alternative finance business-models: Online platforms. *Financial Mark. Inst. Risks*, 1, 3, 92–98, 2017.
8.　Dziawgo, L. and Dziawgo, D., Crowdfunding in the wider perspective investment crowdfunding: Competition between regulations, institutions, and economic freedom. *e-Finanse*, 15, 2, 1–7, 2019 Jun 1.
9.　Thompson, J., Boschmans, K., Pissareva, L., Alternative Financing Instruments for SMEs and Entrepreneurs: The case of capital market finance, OECD SME and Entrepreneurship Papers, No. 10, OECD Publishing, Paris, 2018. https://doi.org/10.1787/dbdda9b6-en.
10.　Rupeika-Apoga, R. and Danovi, A., Availability of alternative financial resources for SMEs as a critical part of the entrepreneurial eco-system: Latvia and Italy. *Proc. Econom. Finance*, 33, 200–10, 2015 Jan 1.
11.　Gupta, M., Verma, S., Pachare, S., An analysis of Conventional and Alternative financing—Customers' perspective. *Int. J. Financ. Econ.*, 2021 Feb 4.

12. Ramasubramanian, S., A wider circle Message from FICCI, November, 2019. Pwc Report. Retrieved from: https://www.pwc.in/assets/pdfs/consulting/financial-services/fintech/publications/a-wider-circle-digital-lending-and-the-changing-landscape-of-financial-inclusion.pdf

13. World Bank; Cambridge Centre for Alternative Finance, *Regulating Alternative Finance: Results from a Global Regulator Survey. World Bank*, © World Bank, Washington, DC, 2019, https://openknowledge.world-bank.org/handle/10986/32592 License: CC BY 3.0 IGO.

14. World Bank, *Crowdfunding's Potential for the Developing World*, © World Bank, Washington, DC, 2013, https://openknowledge.worldbank.org/handle/10986/17626 License: CC BY 3.0 IGO.

Further Web Links

1. https://www.jbs.cam.ac.uk/faculty-research/centres/alternative-finance/publications/5th-uk-alternative-finance-industry-report/#.XoD5oYgzbIU

2. https://www.jbs.cam.ac.uk/faculty-research/centres/alternative-finance/publications/regulating-alternative-finance/

3. https://openknowledge.worldbank.org/handle/10986/17626

4. https://assets.kpmg/content/dam/kpmg/au/pdf/2018/asia-pacific-alternative-finance-report-2018.pdf

5. https://home.kpmg/au/en/home/insights/2018/12/diversifying-growth-asia-pacific-alternative-finance-report.html

6. https://www.jbs.cam.ac.uk/faculty-research/centres/alternative-finance/publications/2018-global-fintech-hub-report/#.XoCcGIgzbIV

7. https://www.jbs.cam.ac.uk/faculty-research/centres/alternative-finance/publications/regulating-alternative-finance/

8. https://ncfacanada.org/cambridge-global-regulator-survey-results-regulation-of-alternative-finance-is-key-to-make-sector-safe-to-scale-for-the-masses/

9. https://www.refinitiv.com/perspectives/ai-digitalization/accelerating-financial-inclusion-in-india/

Dissertation

1. Weihs, D.C., *Online Peer-to-Peer Lending as an Alternative to Traditional Lending for Small Business Financing* (Doctoral dissertation), Capella University.

2. Li, X., *Essays on the Peer-to-peer Lending Business* (Doctoral dissertation).

15

Application of Machine Learning in Open Government Database

Shantanu P. Chakraborty[1]*, Parul Dashora[2] and Sachin Gupta[3]†

[1]*The Techno India University, Salt Lake & Adjunct Professor Data Analytics IISWBM, Kolkata, India*
[2]*Department of Accountancy and Statistics, Mohanlal Sukhadia University, Udaipur (Rajasthan), India*
[3]*Department of Business Administration, Mohanlal Sukhadia University, Udaipur (Rajasthan), India*

Abstract

Data has become a source of economic and social value. There will be enormous growth of data in coming future as data multiplies exponentially. The staggering amount of data will only continue to grow in future. The abundance of available as well as growing data and the so-called "big data" phenomenon have generated massive interest globally. In this paper, we focus on the value that can be realized from open government data (OGD) around the world and especially on the value-creating mechanisms of data through Artificial Intelligence (AI) and a major subset of AI—Machine Learning (ML). First, we discussed what is OGD, in general, then OGD perspective in Indian context followed by the concept of ML, and finally how ML can be applied in order to evaluate OGD. ML algorithm is useful in understanding and interpreting open government databases.

Keywords: Open government data, machine learning, artificial intelligence, SAS, Python, big data

Corresponding author: shanjdbi.chakraborty@gmail.com
†*Corresponding author*: sachinguptabusadm@gmail.com

S. Balamurugan, Sonal Pathak, Anupriya Jain, Sachin Gupta, Sachin Sharma, Sonia Duggal (eds.)
Impact of Artificial Intelligence on Organizational Transformation, (245–258) © 2022 Scrivener Publishing LLC

15.1 Introduction

Open government databases are available everywhere and to everyone. Public sector undertaking produces huge amount of data for the use of their citizen. The dataset is available by these public institution for encouraging the reuse and distribution of these government datasets that are accountable to the citizen. It is feasible by government to provide value-added services to their citizens. E-governance is largely allowed and facilitated such that every individual gets benefits derived from it. Services include maintaining the land record and maintaining driving licence, vehicle registration, duties and taxes, etc. The dataset used by government is spreading globally and the data is available in machine readable forms for citizens to use and share. This dataset provides scope for civil administration and the community to participate and create value for their public life participation using open government datasets (OGD).

As open government datasets are available that provide a basic resource to various analytical firm to analyze these datasets such that a better insight can be recommended, it provides AI and a subset of Machine Learning (ML) datasets. ML can work on OGD and provides solution and predict outcomes on wide range of datasets.

15.2 Literature Review

Open government databases can be used in a coordinated multilateral. The primary social purpose is to provide transparency, accountability, and civic collaboration to act as a catalyst for innovation and economic growth [1, 2]. Open government databases will be improving the initiative associated with improvement of government services [3] and this will promote scientific development, increasing transparency and accountability in economic growth [6]. As datasets become open, it will allow every stake holder to use the datasets for various purposes [7–9]. Open government databases will benefit society organization and individual and it will enable economy and government making correct and appropriate decision that will add value to the economy as a whole. But still there is a lack of sufficient evidences that will prove how these data will add value to the existing economies and generate values [13, 14]. Open data are inherently an important resource that no one can exclude them from using them [17].

Open government datasets provide ease of replication at marginal cost and instant distribution of datasets. Companies need to work on these open government datasets and to analyze them from various perspectives such that it adds value for their economic sustainability [4, 14]. They will be a source for a sustainable economic value to all its stake holder including government and its citizens.

In recent years, open government databases have attracted the interest in diverse fields. There is an example of open government databases in scientific research [18, 19], business, digital marketing, and understanding its impact on social media marketing and business. From a broader perspective, open government databases [22, 23], its use is remarkable in innovation and implementing issues and policies, this provides a significant impact on accountability for various barriers and problems in different sectors. This includes business sector [11, 23] that can collaborates to bring solution to any real-time problem, this can help in understanding challenges in different domain [20, 31, 32], and it can also help in equality of access such that the data can be fostered to create real-time solutions to any challenges. Open government databases hold out the promise of many potential benefits such as more innovation, stimulating citizen participation, stimulating economic growth, and enhancing transparency [22]. However, some authors, on the other hand [5], take a more cautious view arguing that merely putting open government databases in the public arena will not necessarily foster accountability [24]. This requires both a free press and mechanisms by which citizens can hold rulers accountable [16]. So, while open government databases hold out much promise, several challenges, and problems surround it. Common topics of debate, and sometimes controversy, include implementation challenges, barriers to its release, "dark sides", licensing, and formats [25, 26].

All of the questions that arise with open government databases also bring with them a number of additional problems of their own. One feature of the literature is the variety of definitions of open government databases in circulation; something which is not uncommon in new fields. The common thread in these definitions is that such data should be freely available for use and reuse by the public [27, 29]. Beyond this point of agreement, most definitions are broad, though some [28] try to be more specific as to what types of data open databases encompass.

15.3   Overview of Open Government Data

Public service organizations collect and produce huge volume of public data that makes that data very critical, and these data should be provided to form public transparency and help understand job performed by government and how well government is able to implement its plan and policies

Machine Learning in Government Database

1. **Complete**: All public data are made available. Public data are data that is not subject to valid privacy, security or privilage limitations.

2. **Primary:** Data are as collected at the source, with the highest possible level of granularity, not in aggregate or modified forms.

3. **Timely:** Data are made available as quickly as necessary to preserve the value of the data.

4. **Accessible:** Data are available to the wildest range of users for the widest range of purposes.

5. **Machine processable:** Data are reasonably stuctured to allow automated processing.

6. **Non-discriminatory:** Data are available to anyone, with no requirement of registration.

7. **Non-proprietary:** Data are available in a format over which no entity has exclusive control.

8. **License-free**: Data are not subject to any copyright, patent, trademark or trade secret regulation. Reasonable privacy, security and privilege restrictions may be allowed.

Source: http://resource.org/8_principles.html, adopted in December 2007.

Figure 15.1   Open government data principles. Source: http://resource.org/8_principles. html, adopted in December 2007.

accordingly. OGD can be used to help public understand the functioning of government and brings transparency to the entire process. We can predict public awareness about the government programs and activities that can be supported progressively. This will help to generate an insight into the data and improve government performances (Figure 15.1). This will, in return, help public to collaborate and help government to formulate and create value-added services. This, in turn, helps in decision-making capability of all the stake holders involved in e-governance. OGD will provide framework for economic growth, entrepreneurship, and social innovation.

The fundamental eight principles that were put forwarded for government in December 2007, during an Open Government Working Group Meeting held in Sebastopol, California, United States.

The open data construct has seven key measurable characteristics or dimensions (Figure 15.2), each reflecting a separate affordance of liquid open data [30]. Building on these characteristics, we define openness of data as the degree to which data are available, affordable, and sharable, published in a usable and interoperable format, and made both discoverable and accessible [15].

15.4   Open Government Data in India

Government plays a key role in e-governance as it provides proper environment and OGD acts as a catalyst in the digital development by creating the right environment. In the digital governance, government plays

Characteristic	Description
Available	Data are widely available to stakeholders outside organizational boundaries.
Affordable	Data are affordable and economic barriers are reduced or eliminated.
Shareable	Data are published with open licenses and other legal barriers are reduced.
Interoperable	Data that originate from diverse sources are published with standard identifiers using open data models that explain syntax and semantics.
Usable	Data are accurately, timely, and consistently published in machine-readable formats using open standards with metadata for improved usability.
Discoverable	Data or metadata are published in a central repository and are easily discoverable via a web search or through linkages to other data (linked data).
Accessible	Data are published with multiple, secure access posibilities, including bulk download, web services, and opan APIs.

Figure 15.2 Seven characteristics for measuring the openness of data [Source: Jetzek, T. (2016). Managing complexity across multiple dimensions of open government data: The case of the basic data program. Government Information Quarterly, 33(1), 89104]. Once government Data become public, it can be used in various ways. Data can be turned into fact, information, interface, more data, and service. Jetzek, T. (2016). Managing complexity across multiple dimensions of open government data: The case of the basic data program. Government Information Quarterly, 33(1), 89104].

an important role as it determines the norms, principle, and values that shape human interaction. This determines the cost of transaction and also determines the factors that are essential in determining the cost of transactions to ensure effective and properly utilize OGD. The portal www.data. gov.in is a platform that supports open data initiative by Government of India (Figure 15.3). This portal provides all departments and organizations to publish their datasets for free public use. OGD provides website works in connecting link for government citizens and community. It addresses the issues faced by all its stake holder. To implement OGD, a robust data infrastructure is needed that will combine all datasets and will reward the benefits accordingly to government citizens and community as a whole. Still, OGD is at a very preliminary level in India and has many challenges to face. Still, now in many government sectors, the data is stored in form of paper which restricts its utility. Paper records cannot be accessed by everyone, and it cannot be downloaded and hence analyzed. Data stored and utilized in rural sector cannot be viewed in machine readable form. The data is available at state level or at national level.

The initiative "Digital India" is undertaken to convert paper-based data into digital form [34]. A parallel initiative is taken to convert every process of data collection into digital form. As an integral part of this initiative,

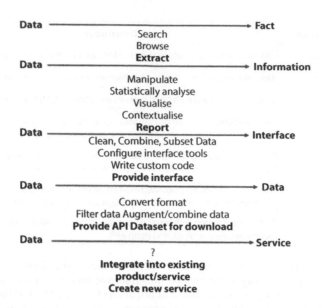

Data ──────────────────────────► Fact
                    Search
                    Browse
                    Extract
Data ──────────────────────────► Information
                Manipulate
             Statistically analyse
                 Visualise
                Contextualise
                  Report
Data ──────────────────────────► Interface
           Clean, Combine, Subset Data
            Configure interface tools
               Write custom code
              Provide interface
Data ──────────────────────────► Data
               Convert format
      Filter data Augment/combine data
      Provide API Dataset for download
Data ──────────────────────────► Service
                    ?
            **Integrate into existing
              product/service
            Create new service**

Figure 15.3 Data transformation in Open Government Databases page. Source: http://resource.org/8_principles.html, adopted in December 2007.

every village, block, district, and state electronic data entry provision is made compulsary. A proper infrastructure and ecosystem will make it feasible when all layers of information, and data is digitized [34]. Real-time storage of data is very important from various contexts as it adds value and yields substantial benefits to all its stake holders. For example, one may consider storing agriculture data where it can predict whether the monsoon was below normal of average based on which yield per hectare can be analyzed; this real-time data can act as a catalyst in improving agricultural productivity and income. Real-time data collection and analysis is much a reality in few sectors [34].

A repository of real-time data at official level, government level, and at village level has a huge potential to transform e-governance. Government official at district level, state level, and block level requires potential analytical skill to make effective use of data in decision-making and exploit data at real time, performing various analysis and coming out with their inferences and interpretation. Ministry of Electronics and Information Technology acts as a nodal department that is trying to translate real-time data into meaningful information using data analytics at national level and at state level [34] (Figure 15.4).

There are various government portals available that provide and effective tools to provide information and data to public. But as a layman, the citizen do not possess analytical skill to interpret data and generate

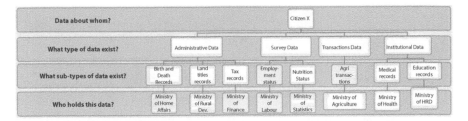

Figure 15.4 Illustration: Dispersion of dataset of hypothetical citizen X across multiple locations. [Source: Jetzek, T. (2016). Managing complexity across multiple dimensions of open government data: The case of the basic data program. Government Information Quarterly, 33(1), 89104]. Once government Data become public, it can be used in various ways. Data can be turned into fact, information, interface, more data, and service.

inferences based on it. Therefore, several data visualization and exploration tools are used to augment this very purpose. Government organization initiating several schemes and projects to collect data on a real-time basis and present data at a granular level based on various government projects and schemes. For example, Swachh Bharat Mission is one of such initiative taken by government where exemplary dash boards provided for public display of data to track the physical and financial performance of welfare schemes [21, 34].

15.5 How to Create Value from Data

High volume of data is not the requirement of the hour, but to make best possible decision, correct data is needed. There is no dearth of data on a real-time basis, but having lot of data will not help in making better and faster decision [10, 12, 35]. With cloud computer massive amount of real-time data that is distributed across various departments, teams, and locations in different formats, so data has to be filtered cleaned before it is used for analysis.

ML and Artificial Intelligence (AI), with their advanced algorithm, are the best mechanisms as on date to govern the OGD and gain key insights from that in a most efficient manner [35] (Figure 15.5).

15.6 Artificial Intelligence

AI is a technique for building system that can simulate human intelligence that includes thinking, behavior, and perception in computer. It is a science of training system to emulate human task through learning and

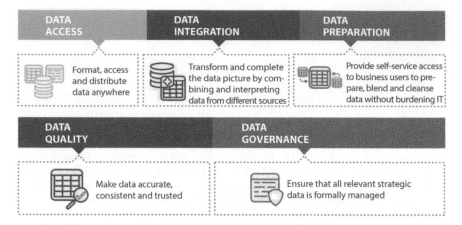

Figure 15.5   Data processing (Source: www.sas.com).

automation. Machine can learn and accomplish task without manual intervention. AI spans a variety of algorithm and methods and it does not. It enables automation and machine learning to all its stake holders. As per report of PWC, by year 2025, AI market will be surpassing $100 billion.

15.7   Why AI is Important?

AI automates machine to program themselves. Robotic automates manual task, but AI automates high volume computing task such as classification and clustering. It adds intelligence to existing products from consumer marketing to security intelligence on investment analysis. For example, an algorithm can train itself to play chess. The technique of back propagation AI models adapts to new data that are given and they start learning from their experiences; for example, building a fraud detection system using AI to algorithm for self-learning. We are excessively using ML by using AI for almost all business process. Every industry is seeing the effect that spans from agriculture, transportation, healthcare, and agricultural sector. It is empowering every sector to be more productive using tools for AI. As per Gartner report, it says that only 4%of all the organization across the world is using AI.

15.8   Machine Learning

ML is a subset of AI. Algorithms learn themselves how to deliver more accurate and better result and accurate predictions. It gives computer the capability to learn explicitly ML algorithms broadly classified in form of supervised learning and unsupervised learning. In supervised learning algorithm, the desired goal or output is known, and there are rules that maps inputs to outputs. The dataset is divided into training dataset and test dataset. The training process continues till the model achieves the desired level of accuracy. Some example is classification algorithm in which previous data is used to predict the outcome. In case of regression, independent and dependent variables can be used to predict the desired outcome from the model. Historical data can be used to predict the price demand and supply of product in near future. Unsupervised learning can be used where the outcome is not known. It discovers hidden pattern in the dataset, and clustering is an example of unsupervised form of learning algorithm. Generative high dimension visualization and be applied to view data on a real life scenario. Once the model captures the probability distribution of input data, it will enable to generate more data. The difference between supervised and unsupervised learning is that the data in supervised form of learning is labeled, whereas in unsupervised form of learning, it is not labeled. The other ML techniques are semi-supervised which is a mix and match between supervised and unsupervised learning. Reinforcement learning interacts with dynamic environment with certain goals. Depending on the ML algorithm, there are three models.

Classification, regression, and clustering; in classification, inputs are divided into two or more classes that produce unseen outputs. For example, filtering an email as a spam mail or a genuine mail and then redirecting it to inbox. Regression is a supervised form of learning where the outputs are continuous rather than discrete. Various kinds of regression model such as linear regression, multiple regression, polynomial regression, and logistic regression. In clustering, input dataset is divided in to groups, these groups are not known beforehand. Some common ML algorithms are decision tree, support vector machines, Naïve Bayes, K-Means, and Random Forest.

This represent ML concept (Figure 15.6).

Hence, a ML system does not just provide insight based on the data that is fed. But they actually change the underlying algorithm based on the data that they see. More the amount of data provided, more tightly they define the algorithm, classify, and predict outcomes. The data provided to the ML, if not managed properly, would result in wrong statements. That results in garbage in and garbage out [33]. ML provides the best return when it is supported by a well governed data management program [35]. Basic principle of ML algorithms is to ingest large amount of data and then determine analyzing the data from different perspective, determining pattern in

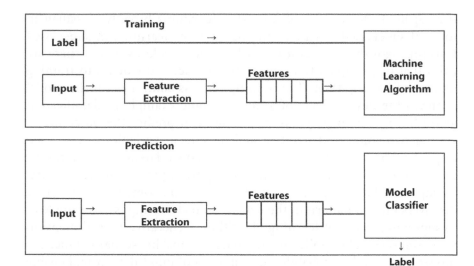

Figure 15.6 Machine learning concept. Source: https://towardsdatascience.com/machine-learning-an-introduction-23b84d51e6d0.

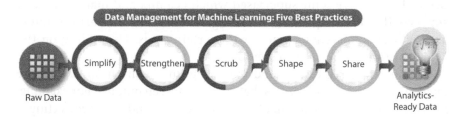

Figure 15.7 Data management (Source: www.sas.com).

data and then learning from those patterns. Finally, producing meaningful output and generating inferences (Figure 15.7).

15.9   Concerns About Machine Learning on Government Database

OGD must be carefully evaluated since the data related to public. A wrong evaluation will result in misinterpretation of any ML model that is used. That will defeat the very purpose if making government data open. The way, we perceive the data before feeding it to the ML model that will definitely make significant impact on the model as a whole. The ML model that we used with OGD needs to be fair and non-discriminatory because the decision they support can expose organization to substantial risk if the classification criteria implemented are unethical, illegal, or publicly unacceptable. Such classification is based on inappropriate criteria.

15.10   Conclusion

Open government database has huge potential in e-governance. It works as an important tool, and by virtue of which, lot of changes will be brought into public service delivery system. A proper infrastructure and comprehensive ecosystem should be built such that the data is available in the form that can be easily accessed and can be used by ML algorithms. But still, there exist lot of challenges to venture open government databases and ML in to different aspect of e-governance a more comprehensive research is needed to venture in to those areas and to get 360 degree view of every possible scenario.

References

1. Davies, T.G. and Bawa, Z.A., The promises and perils of open government data (OGD). *J. Community Inform.*, 8, 2, 1–6, 2012.
2. Janssen, K., Open government data: right to information 2.0 or its rollback version?, *ICRI Research Paper,* (8), 2012.
3. Meijer, A. and Thaens, M., Public information strategies: Making government information available to citizens. *Inf. Polity*, 14, 1–2, 31–45, 2009, https://doi.org/10.3233/IP-2009-0167.
4. Bean, R., How Big Data and AI Are Driving Business Innovation in 2018. Retrieved January 29, 2019, from MIT Sloan Management Review website: https://sloanreview.mit.edu/article/how-big-data-and-ai-are-driving-business-innovat ion-in-2018/, 2018, May2.
5. Peled, A., When transparency and collaboration collide: The USA open data program. *J. Am. Soc. Inf. Sci. Technol.*, 62, 11, 2085–2094, 2011, https://doi.org/10.1002/asi.21622.
6. Zeleti, F.A., Ojo, A., Curry, E., Exploring the economic value of open government data. *Gov. Inf. Q.*, 17, 1, Art. 5, e190049, 2016. Brazilian Administrative review https://doi.org/10.1016/j.giq.2016.01.008.
7. Magalhaes, G. and Roseira, C., Open government data and the private sector: An empirical view on business models and value creation. *Gov. Inf. Q.*, 37, 3, 2020, 101248, 2017, Advance online publication. http://dx.doi.org/10.1016/j. giq.2017.08.004.Government Information Quarterly.

8. Smith, G. and Sandberg, J., Barriers to innovating with open government data: Exploring experiences across service phases and user types. *Inf. Polity*, 23, 3, 249265, 2018.

9. Zeleti, F.A., Ojo, A., Curry, E., Exploring the economic value of open government data. *Gov. Inf. Q.*, 33, 3, 535–551, 2016.

10. European Commission, Open data maturity in Europe 2017. Retrieved from https://www.europeandataportal.eu/sites/default/files/edp_land-scaping_insight_report_n3_2017.pdf, 2017.

11. European Commission, Open data: An engine for innovation, growth and transparent governance. Retrieved from https://eurlex.europa.eu/LexUriServ/LexUriServ.do?uri=COM: 2011:0882: FIN: EN: PDF, 2011.

12. Kundra, V., Digital fuel of the 21st century: Innovation through open data and the network effect. Retrieved from https://shorensteincenter.org/wp-content/uploads/2012/03/d70_ kundra.pdf, 2012.

13. Economist Intelligence Unit, The data directive: How data is driving corporate strategy—and what still lies ahead. Retrieved from: http://www.wipro.com/documents/the-datadirective.pdf, 2013.

14. Lindman, J. and Kuk, G., From open access to open data markets: Increasing the subtractability of open data. *Proceedings of the 48th Hawaii International Conference System Sciences*, 2015.

15. Martin, E.G., Shah, N.R., Birkhead, G.S., Unlocking the power of open health data: A checklist to improve value and promote use. *J. Public Health Manage. Pract.*, 24, 1, 81–84, 2018.

16. McKinsey & Company, Open data: Unlocking innovation and performance with liquid information. Retrieved from https://www.mckinsey.com/business-functions/digitalmckinsey/our-insights/open-data-unlockinginnovation-and-performance-with-liquidinformation, 2013.

17. Hess, C. and Ostrom, E., *Understanding knowledge as a commons: From theory to practice*, MIT Press, Cambridge, MA, 2006.

18. Molloy, J.C., The open knowledge foundation: Open data means better science. *PLoS Biol.*, 9, 12, 1–4, 2011.

19. Murray-Rust, P., Open data in science. *Ser. Rev.*, 34, 1, 52–64, 2008.

20. Bonina, C.M., New business models and the value of open data: Definitions, challenges and opportunities. NEMODE-3K Small Grants Call, 2013.

21. Streeter, L.A., Kraut, R.E., Lucas, H.C., Jr., Caby, L., How open data networks influence business performance and market structure. *Commun. ACM*, 39, 7, 62–73, 1996.

22. Zuiderwijk, A., Helbig, N., Gil-García, J.R., Janssen, M., Special issue on innovation through open data: Guest editors' introduction. *J. Theor. Appl. Electron. Commer. Res.*, 9, 2, i–xiii, 2014.

23. Bertot, J.C., Gorham, U., Jaeger, P.T., Sarin, L.C., Choi, H., Big data, open government and e-government: Issues, policies and recommendations. *Inf. Polity*, 19, 1, 2, 5–16, 2014.

24. Peixoto, T., The Uncertain Relationship between Open Data and Accountability: A Response to Yu and Robinson's 'The New Ambiguity of Open Government', 2013.

25. Khayyat, M. and Bannister, F., Open data licensing: More than meets the eye. *Inf. Polity*, 20, 4, 231–52, 2015.

26. Zuiderwijk, A. and Janssen, M. (Eds.), The negative effects of open government data-investigating the dark side of open data. *Proceedings of the 15th Annual International Conference on Digital Government Research*, ACM, Aguascalientes, Mexico, 2014.

27. Barry, E., Open Government Data: Trinity College Dublin, Ireland, 2012.

28. OKFN, What is Open?, 2015. [Available from: http://okfn.org/opendata/.

29. Klessmann, J., Denker, P., Schieferdecker, I., Schulz, S.E., *Open Government Data Germany: Short Version of the Study on Open Government in Germany*, Federal Ministry of the Interior in Germany, Germany, 2012.

30. Jetzek, T., Managing complexity across multiple dimensions of open government data: The case of the basic data program. *Gov. Inf. Q.*, 33, 1, 89104, 2016.

31. Ind, N., Iglesias, O., Schultz, M., Building brands together. *Calif. Manage. Rev.*, 55, 3, 5–26, 2013.

32. North, D.C., *Institutions, institutional change, and economic performance*, Cambridge University Press, New York, NY, 1990.

33. Granovetter, M., Economic action and social structure: The problem of embeddedness. *Am. J. Sociol.*, 91, 3, 481–510, 1985.

34. Welfare, S., Chapter 4, in: Data *"Of the People, By the People, For the People"*.

35. www.sas.com, 2018.

16

Artificial Intelligence: An Asset for the Financial Sector

Swati Bandi* and Anil Kothari

Faculty of Management Studies, MLSU, Udaipur, India

Abstract

Nothing is permanent except change, and technology change is continuously evolving over the years; we have moved from radio to television and now to the web slowly and gradually where we are adopting AI. AI is nothing but performing its cognitive functions to extract and solve the problem more efficiently and effectively than humans. AI has successfully managed to erect what is thought of as impossible. AI has strengthened its roots within the finance sector which claim to possess benefitted the foremost. "Personal assistant, cognitive computing, machine learning, and chatbots" all are the various fragments of AI which are voluminously worn in the financial sector. This chapter focuses on a paradigm shift of the finance sector using AI within the fields of Insurance, stock exchange and Mutual funds.

At the end of this chapter, one will have deep knowledge about the applications, types, and technologies of AI, and this chapter also will make one understand the various technologies utilized in insurance, open-end fund, and stock exchange which has bought the revolution in finance sector with high accuracy and speed.

Keywords: Artificial intelligence, machine learning, algo trading, mutual funds, insurance, cognitive computing, chatbots, neural network

16.1 Introduction

Artificial Intelligence (AI) is nothing but a computing system which elucidates, exemplifies, and executes exact copy of human intelligence

---

*Corresponding author: swati.dugger86@gmail.com

S. Balamurugan, Sonal Pathak, Anupriya Jain, Sachin Gupta, Sachin Sharma, Sonia Duggal (eds.)
Impact of Artificial Intelligence on Organizational Transformation, (259–288) © 2022 Scrivener
Publishing LLC

which is programmed to stimulate actions. AI is advancing dramatically with the inclusion of applications like speech recognition, machine vision, and expert system, which is transfiguring the world socially and economically.

In 1956, an American Scientist and Professor John McCarthy has invented the concept of AI in his conference which was conducted at The Dartmouth. AI has proved that it can perform better than humans when it involves identifying patterns and neural networks, analyzing the huge data for mapping poverty, globally detecting climatic changes, automated agricultural practices like framing and irrigation, individualizing healthcare and education, predicting consumption motif, and streamlining energy usage and waste management [1]. Today, AI encircles everything from robotic automation to actual performing robotics.

Let us have a look at the evolution of AI from its genesis to the upcoming future.

16.1.1   Phase I 1950–1983 Origin of AI and the First Hype Cycle

The genesis of AI was introduced by professor John McCarthy who organized a conference in 1956 to collect 20 pioneering researchers, and "John McCarthy explores ways to form a machine that would reason sort of a human, was capable of reasoning, problem-solving, and self-improvement". It had been in his 1955 proposal for this conference where the term, "Artificial Intelligence", was coined and it had been at this conference where AI gained its vision, mission, and hype [2].

Many fields and sub-fields of AI were born in between 1956 and 1982, and the keenness of researchers led to seminal work, which gave birth to many subfields of AI (like machine learning, video and image processing, tongue, and speech recognition) which are explained below. Figure 16.1 represents the journey of artificial intelligence from 1950 Genesis to current scenario and also lays down the path for future.

Figure 16.1 History of Artificial Intelligence. Source: Compiled by author.

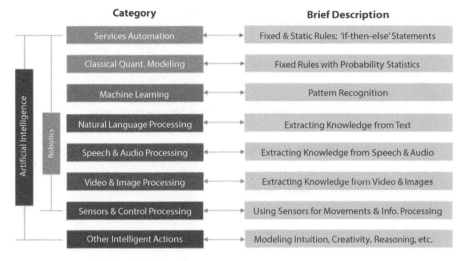

Category	Brief Description
Services Automation	Fixed & Static Rules; 'if-then-else' Statements
Classical Quant. Modeling	Fixed Rules with Probability Statistics
Machine Learning	Pattern Recognition
Natural Language Processing	Extracting Knowledge from Text
Speech & Audio Processing	Extracting Knowledge from Speech & Audio
Video & Image Processing	Extracting Knowledge from Video & Images
Sensors & Control Processing	Using Sensors for Movements & Info. Processing
Other Intelligent Actions	Modeling Intuition, Creativity, Reasoning, etc.

Figure 16.2 Subfields of AI. Source: Compiled by author.

Figure 16.2 gives an idea about various categories of Robotics an Artificial Intelligence and brief description of their sub-fields. Many of those applications (rule-based system, machine learning, single- and multi-layer perceptron networks, tongue processing, speaker recognition and speech to text processing, image processing, and computer vision, chatbots, and robotics, which are explained later) were developed and utilized in different areas which reduced the human effort and led to figure automatically with cent percent accuracy and are not suffering from any human behavior or emotion. Year-wise development of the genesis phase is explained diagrammatically below [15].

16.1.2   II Phase 1983–2010 Reawakening of Artificial Intelligence

In this era of reawakening of AI, tons of researches being instigated and initiated, during this phase, many pioneering researchers done and resolve plenty of AI problems by using many mathematical and economical models. During this phase, development of neural networks was also done by using mathematical descriptions and genetic algorithms also gained its importance during this phase.

In this era of "machine learning", various techniques developed considerably. These techniques were "supervised learning, unsupervised learning, and reinforcement learning, also as shallow and deep neural networks", which left the mark of successfulness during this phase.

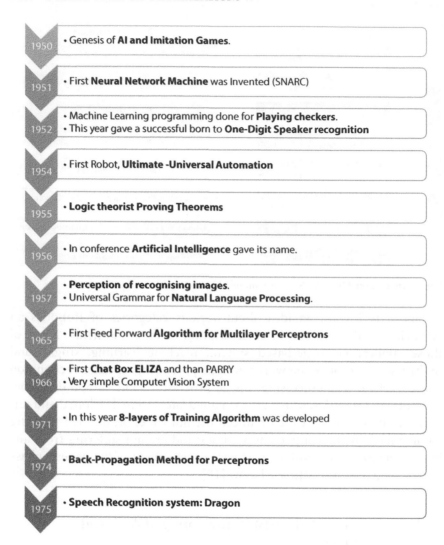

Figure 16.3 Impact of AI on Organisation. Source: Compiled by author.

Figure 16.3 explains the series of events and new invention which gave a push to the second phase of Artificial Intelligence.

16.1.3   III Phase 2011–2017 AI Domains Competing Humans

In this III phase where systems are rivaling humans, which has started from 2011, AI research and development has beholding a continuous hyper-growth, and all researchers have generated many AI solutions and

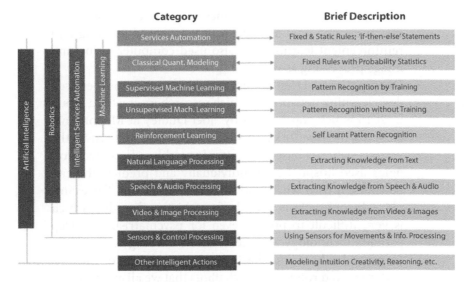

Category	Brief Description
Services Automation	Fixed & Static Rules; 'if-then-else' Statements
Classical Quant. Modeling	Fixed Rules with Probability Statistics
Supervised Machine Learning	Pattern Recognition by Training
Unsupervised Mach. Learning	Pattern Recognition without Training
Reinforcement Learning	Self Learnt Pattern Recognition
Natural Language Processing	Extracting Knowledge from Text
Speech & Audio Processing	Extracting Knowledge from Speech & Audio
Video & Image Processing	Extracting Knowledge from Video & Images
Sensors & Control Processing	Using Sensors for Movements & Info. Processing
Other Intelligent Actions	Modeling Intuition Creativity, Reasoning, etc.

Figure 16.4 Development of techniques of AI. Source: Compiled by author.

techniques which have given equivalent or better results than human brains in the areas of voice recognition, gaming, healthcare industry, computer vision systems, identifying objects, etc. Figure 16.4 depicts the various stages and shows how machine learning has upgraded itself to AI. Some examples of these domains are as follows:

- **IBM Watson beats humans in Jeopardy:** In example of IBM Watson which worked on "feature engineering", it has accommodated around 200 million pages which included the content of many encyclopedias, dictionaries, thesaurus, newswire articles, Bible, Bhagavad Gita, database, and other literature books to beat humans; for an individual, it is very difficult to retain all these pages [12].
- **AlphaGo beats humans in GO:** Researchers introduced AlphaGo Zero which has used the technology of reinforcement learning that was used to build many games. When this gaming was tested against humans, the AlphaGO played around 5 million games against it and other champions and won all the games.
- **AI technique "An Autonomous Car Driving":** Autonomous car driving used two technologies: one was supervised learning and other was reinforcement learning; using these techniques, cars used to follow the traffic rules and operate accordingly. In 2009, researchers at Google have evolved the

concept of self-driven cars. These self-driven autonomous cars were not only assisted with supervised learning and reinforcement learning but also used computer vision and image processing as well.

- **Deep patients:** Deep patient is triple-layered unsupervised deep learning network, in which researchers created a group in 2015 which was headed by "Joel Dudley at Mount Sinai Hospital in New York". This technology was to discover the various patterns based on several variables. These technologies used hospital data individually and predict who can be suffered with what kind of disease in future, For example, schizophrenia is a kind of psychiatric disorders which is very difficult to predict even for psychiatrists but deep patients' technology was successful in tracking it.
- **Improved robots and chatbots:** Now, in the era of chatbots and improved robots, these chatbots that we all are using are in the forms of Siri for Apple iPhones users (in 2010) and Amazon's Alexa, Microsoft's Cortana, Google's Now, Xbox, Skype's Translator, etc., during the phase of 2011–2017.
- **AI-based robotic process automation:** Instead of doing coding through machine language in the phase, RPA software is composed in such a way that it copies all the actions performed by the individual and the robot executes exact same steps while performing a selected task. Through RPA, they made a virtual worker who replaced humans by performing as same as an experienced worker.

These were the six **AI systems which are rivaling humans**.

16.1.4   The Present and the Future Phase (2018–2035)

Over the past decade, AI has seen many ups and downs, but now, the sector of AI has seen striking developments. AI is performing better than or like humans in almost all domains. The huge bust of AI happened between 1956 and 1973 which may be a boom phase of AI hype cycle. Investors are investing billions for enhancing the AI-based researches and startups. Future with AI is at infinity but there is a threat for humans within the job market, because the predications say that AI will again automated by 2033 [10].

Over the past several years, there has been a growing belief that AI may be a limitless, mystical force that is ready to supersede humans and solve any problem. AI is will be a superpower in upcoming next 5 years and that we are summoning the demon.

16.2   Types, Technology, and Application of AI

16.2.1   Types of Artificial Intelligence

Artificial Intelligence (AI) is categorized in two different manner [3]. First one is termed as weak or narrow AI, which is structured to perform a specific task step by step, and the opposite one is robust AI, which is known as "General Artificial Intelligence"; this GAI is intelligent enough intelligence to seek out an answer and may also perform an unfamiliar task (uses generalized human cognitive abilities). At Michigan State University, Professor Arend Hintze has categorized AI majorly into four types, and they are as follows:

- **Type 1:** "Reactive Machines": this deals with gaming as explained earlier.
- **Type 2:** "Limited Memory": this deals with gaming decision-making function, which uses past data to estimate future and take decisions accordingly.
- **Type 3:** "Theory of mind": This theory deals with their own beliefs, intentions, and choices they make, and this theory more relates to psychology term.
- **Type 4:** "Self-awareness": This deal with performing exactly same as human being weather it may be reactions, thought process, etc. This sort of AI does not yet exist, but soon it is going to have its existence.

16.2.2   Artificial Intelligence Technologies

AI technologies are continuously increasing; some of them are as follows [11]:

- **Natural Language Generation:** This technology is used to create an important text document from the personal computer data such as report generation, summarizing some activities related to business, and reminding of customer services.
- **Speech Recognition:** This technology simply transforms human voice into such a format which is useful for operating

system. Presently, this technology is used in mobile application and interactive voice system.

- **Virtual Agent:** This technology of virtual agent is computer-generated or animated which intelligently makes a conversation with customers to solve problems, we can also say that it is a web customer service representative.
- **Machine Learning:** This technology of machine learning is being used in many enterprises who involve themselves in predicting or classifying the data set.
- **Deep Learning Platforms:** This technology is advanced version of machine learning; it deals with neural networks and also is supported by large data sets which are used for recognizing the patterns (multiple abstraction layers) which are followed in multiple layers.
- **Biometrics:** This technology is used to identify the physical or behavioral trait which is unique for each and every individual human being. This biometrics is generally used in private corporation or companies for providing attendance.
- **Robotic Process Automation:** Instead of doing coding through machine language in the phase, RPA software is composed in such a way that it copies all the actions performed by the individual and the robot executes exact same steps while performing a selected task. Through RPA, they made a virtual worker who replaced humans by performing as same as an experienced worker [4].
- **Text Analytics and NLP:** This technology is used to detect sentiments, meaning, intention, so this NLP is currently being used in fraud detection and providing security.

16.2.3   Applications of Artificial Intelligence

a) **AI in Healthcare:** AI is being used in the healthcare industry for better and faster diagnoses than humans. In healthcare industry, technologies which are used maximum are IBM's Watson and NLP. Usage of AI in healthcare industry assists both doctors and patients in following ways [5]:
   - AI provides laboratory for quick and easy making of diagnosis reports.
   - AI also supports researches and decision making.

- AI also helps in integrating activities through cognitive sciences function.
- AI also helps in providing cross-functional discipline for healthcare.

b) **AI in Business:** In business, "robotic process automation" is used to perform monotonous tasks which are normally performed by humans. Machine learning algorithms are used for CRM (customer relationship management) which provides information on the way to better serve customers. Chatbots have already been incorporated into websites and corporations to supply immediate service to customers. Automation of job positions is additionally becoming a point among the teachers and IT consultancies.

c) **AI in Education:** Education industry is also using AI which has made their regular work easier like
- Automatic grading system.
- Automatic calculating of overall attendance.
- Augmented reality can be used to make students understand easily.
- AI is also used to route the map of buses for pick and drop of the students.
- AI is also used in GPS enabled vehicle for parents to detect that where the ward is travelling.

d) **AI in Autonomous Vehicles:** AI is also being used in automobile industry; in this industry, it uses the technologies like supervised learning and reinforcement learning which helps them in behaving like humans. These autonomous self-driving cars have sensors to judge their surroundings and even brain to gather, process, and choose specific actions needed to be performed. Autonomous vehicles are with advanced tools to collect information, including long-range radar, cameras, and LIDAR. AI gathers all information and recruits useless information and useful information and then it utilizes in different capacities that is why AI is compared to human brains. AI has several more applications some of them are as follows:
- AI helps in detecting nearby fuel station and indicating that fuel is running low.

- AI also helps to plan your trip with direction based on shortest route with less traffic.
- AI has incorporated speech recognition for advanced communication with travelers.
- AI also helps in automatic ear shifting depending upon the speed of the cars.

e) **AI in Financial Services:** AI in financial services industry is moving like a storm, because firms have recognized how technology can improve operations, reduce costs, and increase customer satisfaction. AI and advance analytics have capabilities to reshape firm from internal operations to customer experience to treasury services and payments. AI analyzes and understands the saving and investment habits of account holders, through which they will customize the recommendation they provide to their customers.

16.3   Artificial Intelligence and Financial Services

AI has also exceeded its excellence in financial industry. Cognitive computing, machine learning, chatbots, and personal assistant are all peripherals of AI utilized in the finance industry extensively nowadays, and the industry has availed lot of benefits by using these techniques. So, many financial companies are looking forward for investing significantly in AI, and some have already invested to take a position in AI.

AI has started replacing humans by using many of its key features like personal assistants/advisors, webmaster, machine learning, or digital labor etc. AI performs its actions successfully because of its unique features like large data, hyper processing system, cloud services, and many more. Due to which, AI has gained popularity. But still, AI is facing challenges related to lack of trust, biases, and majorly regulatory concern. Hence, companies today are making a combination of technology with human interference in order to make a reliable option with high accuracy and reduced human effort.

AI is being used extensively in the other branches of finance like the process of auditing the monetary transactions and also involves in analyzing huge number of pages of the tax changes. AI proved to be a great help to Indian Financial system. AI is also identifying how customers are reacting to varied situations and problems, and it expected soon that AI will assist companies counting on AI to form significant firm-related decisions and also assist people and firms to make smarter decisions at a really quick pace. But here, the key is to look for the proper balance between humans and technology.

In this study, we are going to discuss three major segments of the finance industry like insurance, stock exchange, and mutual funds.

16.3.1   Artificial Intelligence and Insurance

The insurance sector in India is governed by Insurance Act, 1938, the Life insurance Corporation Act, 1956, and General Insurance Business (Nationalization) Act, 1972, Insurance Regulatory and Development Authority (IRDA) Act, 1999, and other related acts that govern the entire insurance sector.

Insurance in India was introduced in 1818; oriental Life Insurance Company was the first one to start its operations. Later in 1850, General Insurance has also entered into the market and began its operations in India.

Figure 16.5 explains insurance is generally divided into two types as above given all the insurance related to human life comes under life and all the other types lie in the category of non-life. Insurance is nothing but an assurance given by the insurance company that in case of any mishappening, contingency amount/losses will be paid in monetary term by the insurance company according to the contract signed between the parties, against which these insurance companies charge fees called premium. The premium amount is different with the different types of plans and amount of risk involved into it.

This insurance industry is old so it necessitates human intervention for performing manual and paper-based works which are ideally takes lot of time and slow down the process. A customer of Insurance Industry faces many problems like:

Insurance							
Life Insurance (Risk of life is insured)				General Insurance (Apart from life insurance)			
Term Life	Money Life policy	Unit linked Insurance Plan	Retirement Plan	Motor Insurance	Home Insurance	Health Insurance	Fire Insurance

Figure 16.5 Types of insurance. Source: Compiled by author.

- Time consumption;
- Lot of approval has to be taken and paper based;
- Due to which late reimbursement of claim is being made;
- It may be signing up for a replacement policy, etc.

Customers of insurance sector also find themselves paying more for the policies as they are not customized. As the industry is running from the ages due to this, they are slower to embrace technologically change compared to other industries. Once we mention this era of AI where most of our regular activities are online, digitalized, faster, and convenient, providing customer satisfaction, etc., now, we will combine the effect of AI with insurance sector so that transition in the industry takes place with paperless, less time consumption, faster settlement of claims, and high accuracy with tailor-made offering to the customer. Now, insurance sector will provide cheerful customer experience.

The insurance sector has made a worldwide push to reinforce their technological capabilities. The insurance sector is using AI to conduct its operations cheaper and faster with high accuracy. AI has helped the industry to atomize the processes which are more labor-intensive, resulting in cutting down the prices and saving lot of time. AI is also stepping its foot into understanding the customers better, researches being done to identify the need of customers, track their taste and preferences, predict and understand customer behavior, and then offer them with the product which matches exactly according to their needs. AI in insurance is comprised of "machine learning, natural language processing, deep learning, and neural networks", which are improving and setting the trends to realize the new heights for the insurance sector. These technologies have driven savings

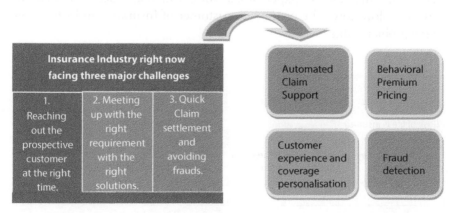

Figure 16.6 The transition of the insurance industry. Source: Compiled by author.

for insurance carriers, policyholders, and brokers, creating an alliance with the insurance industry [13].

We will take a look at three insurance trends using AI, also explained in Figure 16.6, which is bringing a paradigm shift from robust and tedious to faster and quicker processes within the industry [9].

a) **Behavioral Premium Pricing:** Whenever we mention insurance, the primary question that involves our mind is, "What is going to be the premium of the policy?", but now, the insurance sector using AI has enabled customized insurance pricing premiums.

- **Risk less pay less:** This idea deals with wearable and telematic sensor data that permits less premiums for the people that have less risky behavior and better premiums for the more risk-prone behavior, and it also tracks driving less and exercising more.

  For example: A person who is taking a car or auto insurance just must install a telematics sensor in their car. If we mention demonstrating the logic of telematic sensors, then it allows usage-based or pay-per-mile automobile insurance. It allows real-time tracking like, if an individual drives very safely, then he pays less for policies, and if any driver drives rush, then the premium of the policy will increase or they will be charged according to kilometers they run. Policyholders now just needed to pay according to the risk they take. Fundamentally underlying telematics is the technology which is used for these new sorts of insurance products. An individual who is taking this type of insurance just must drive his car safely with average speed and kilometers. For some, it is an excellent bargain, and for a few, it is an excessive amount.

  Another example: Two startups, BioBeats and FitSense, are handling wearable data for insurance with attention on individual health and personalizing these health plans permanently health of the customer.

Changing Insurance Industry from Proxy to Source Data With IoT (Internet of Things) Sensors

- **Bundle Policy and Loss:** Earlier, all financial models were considerably depending upon statistical methods of sampling for measuring past performance, forecasting future, and reaching to outcomes, but now, data analytics and science is enabling predictions which are supported by real-time events because we are now using large set of information instead of making different test and creating assumption against it.

Insurance companies are getting hardware companies because they are providing with many hardware (telematic sensors, BioBeats, FitSense) which we would like to connect the type of insurance which we are taking, and these hardware tools will track us on behalf of the insurance companies and against it, we would like to pay customized premiums. Insurance companies are providing bundle policy because it is a bundle of hardware also because the policy prevents us from upcoming great losses which one can have.

- **Settling and Verifying the Claims:** Internet of Things enables information to access swift and verify risk associated to it, instead of counting on costly assessments and audits with longer and other people engagement.

  Figure 16.7 represents many hardware and software are getting used to detect and manage risk, and all the actions, performance, and movement are being tracked on a real-time basis, and there is no discrepancy in verifying and settlement

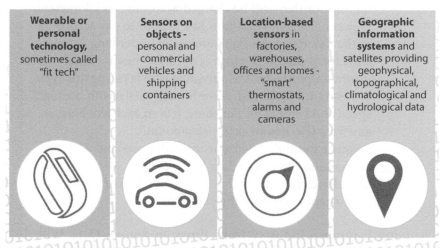

| Wearable or personal technology, sometimes called "fit tech" | Sensors on objects - personal and commercial vehicles and shipping containers | Location-based sensors in factories, warehouses, offices and homes - "smart" thermostats, alarms and cameras | Geographic information systems and satellites providing geophysical, topographical, climatological and hydrological data |

The ability to directly access customer data via the IoT is a new phenomenon for insurers that have traditionally relied on brokers.

Figure 16.7 Insurance hardware devices. Source: https://marutitech.com/ai-in-the-insurance-industry/.

of claims. Hence, this results in a faster settlement of claims which may be a welcome addition to the buyer service within the insurance industry on the opposite side insurance sector also will save themselves from the tedious process of costly assessment and audits.

b) **Customer Experience and Coverage Personalization:** Positive consumer experience is the prime need of a corporation to achieve success, so insurance industry is using three ways in which AI will enhance buying behavior of Insurance products; they are as follows:

- **Chatbots will recognize:** "Buying insurance by just taking one selfie"; the Life Insurance startup Lapetus in 2017 made announcement that you can buy an insurance policy by just taking a selfie. The technology of chatbots provided with advanced image recognition using this technology company could identify the habits like smoking cigarettes, which will predict your period of existence, so using Lapetus gives the score of risk for your life by analyzing your facial attributes by avoiding tedious process.
  One of the examples of image recognition is the startup of Zhong An; in this, both client and customers meet online and they believe machine learning the technique of AI, which leads sell around 7.2 billion insurance products by just being online; it also led to decrease the fraud detection with excellent customized customer experience [8].
- **These platforms used to verify your identity:** Automated identity verification is completed on the varied platforms which may speed up the authentication process which is necessary for quoting and finalizing the premium of the policy.
- **They customize your coverage:** AI technique "machine learning" allows total buying process online or app-based. One can buy any of your policy by just sitting at your home and not going anywhere out.

c) **Faster and Customized Claims Settlement:** AI in insurance helps in settling claims faster with reduction in frauds. Most important factors of insurance are speedy and successful settling of claims which will lead insurance sector to boom, which it would have been never before. Here, there are two key factors through which AI will improve [6]:

- **Swift Settling Claims:** Adopting AI technologies has demonstrated speedy settlement of claims for customer.
- **Decrease the Likelihood of Fraud:** Fraud detection is one among the main reasons for the AI technological adaptation within the insurance industry. There have been around 75% of the businesses reported using automated fraud detection technique, and therefore, the number is increasing. One startup named "Shift Technology" is helping the insurance industry to stop fraud, and they have analyzed around 82 million claims to avoid fraud within the industry.

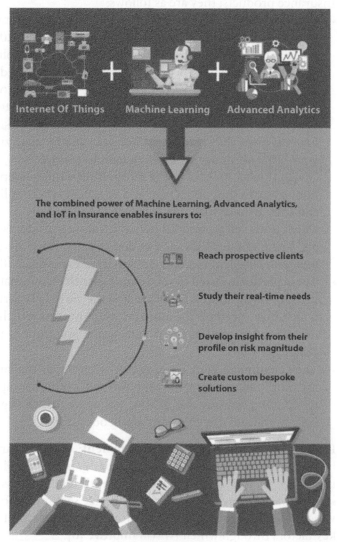

Internet Of Things   Machine Learning   Advanced Analytics

The combined power of Machine Learning, Advanced Analytics, and IoT in Insurance enables insurers to:

Reach prospective clients

Study their real-time needs

Develop insight from their profile on risk magnitude

Create custom bespoke solutions

The future of AI in insurance: AI has potential to modify the industry experience from annoying, procedural, rule bound to faster, flexible, on request, and cheaper. Its tailor-made insurance products approach will attract more customers at fairer premiums. AI technologies are also helping the industry to understand the customer better and serve them according to their needs; through this, insurance will provide more personalized products to its customer. Insurers are going to reduce their cost and will speed up workflows through they will generate more revenue inflows to the companies. AI-driven analysis exposes a replacement business and cross-selling opportunities. AI solutions providing with many of the above positive ingredients might end up making more buys of insurance products with excellent service quality in India.

16.3.2   Artificial Intelligence and Stock Market

"Stock exchange/equity market/share market" is a place where buying, selling, and issuance of the shares take place. These financial activities and transactions are done through regulated exchanges (BSE, NSE, and other regional stock exchanges) and over the counter market place which operates during a predetermined set of rules and regulations. There are often multiple stock trading venues during a country or a neighborhood which allows transaction within the exchange.

"The Securities Contract Regulation Act of 1956 explains a stock market as: An association, organization or body of people, whether incorporated or not, established to help, regulate and control business in buying, selling, and dealing in securities."

Stock exchanges are also defined as "an essential concomitant of the Capitalistic System of the economy. It is indispensable for the right functioning of the company enterprise. It brings together large amounts of capital necessary for the economic progress of a rustic. It is a citadel of capital and a pivot of the cash market. It provides the required mobility to capital and indirect the flow of capital into profitable and successful enterprises. It is the barometer of general economic progress during a country and exerts a strong and significant influence as a depressant or stimulant of commercial activity."

16.3.2.1   From the History of Stock Exchange to the Development of Algo Trading in India

In 1875, India's first biggest and oldest stock market was started in Bombay named "Bombay Stock Exchange", and it was one of the oldest markets in Asia as well. After that, many regional stock exchange opened, like Ahmedabad Stock Exchange in 1894, the Calcutta Stock Exchange in 1908, and the Madras Stock Exchange in 1920. Currently, there are around 23 stock exchanges within the country which includes National stock Exchange (NSE) and Bombay stock Exchange (BSE).

These stock exchanges are supervised by executive chief and governing bodies. All the rules and regulations are controlled by Ministry of Finance. In April 1988, the Indian government formed a regulatory body for stock exchange named "Securities and Exchange Board of India (SEBI)" for smooth functioning, well organization and regulation of the Indian Stock Market (BSE and NSE).

"The Securities and Exchange Board of India (SEBI), on April 3, 2008 introduced algorithmic trading by allowing Direct Market Access facility to institutional clients, to not retail clients". This facility of DMA allows the broker to access the exchange trading system with none intervention from their part.

This power brought down the cost for the institutional investor as they do not have to pay brokerages and also helped in better execution of order. Now, no time is wasted in calling broker giving them order, and then, they will execute the order on exchange.

This modern DMA facility is popularizing and many global players are ready for signing up for registration for using this DMA facility. Many financial institutions and foreign institutional investors like Morgan Stanley, DSP Merrill Lynch, UBS, JP Morgan, Motilal Oswal, Edelweiss Capital, and India Infoline started registering for DMA facility. Following the trend, many other local financial institutions like Global Capital, SMC, and Global Vision also started choosing DMA registration [7].

If you are someone curious about trading within the capital market, the there is a high probability that you may have encountered the term Algo Trading. It may cause you to wonder what this is, which allow us to make you understand about some basics to know it better.

16.3.2.2   What is Algorithmic Trading?

The new invention of AI is "Algorithmic Trading". Algo trading is a computer system–based trading AI strategy which works on specific designated sets of commands referred to as algorithms that automatically submit trades to an exchange with no human intervention. This algorithm uses some pre-described set of rules (technical analysis, indicators, charts, bars, or stock fundamentals) and use historical data for automated trading.

For example, if anyone wants to buy stocks, then they can write the rule of the algorithm and can automate order, so whenever conditions will be satisfied for your order, it will automatically buy/sell your share; you also limit your order by stop loss and put the target within the algorithm which may make your trading easier.

16.3.2.3   Benefits of Algo Trading

a) Algo trades gives you best possible price to execute your order.

b) Execution of the trade is immediate with high accuracy.

c) Hence, the trades are immediate and instant so it avoids price changes.

d) Algo trading provides reduced transaction cost.

e) Algo trading provides continuous and automated check on various conditions of market.

f) Algo trading is also a viable trading strategy because it uses historical and real-time data to predict the future movement and execute on current market conditions.

g) Algo trading omits human intervention does not work on human emotions.

h) Algo trading omits any decisions being made under any psychological influence with minimal human involvement.

i) In Algo trading, simultaneous autonomous market checks are made to execute trades at the best possible prices.

j) The biggest advantage of Algo trading in the introduction of high-frequency trading (HFT).

16.3.2.4   Algorithmic Trading Platforms

- **Omnesys NEST:** This algorithmic trading program provide platform to trade in derivatives, commodities equities, and currency. This algorithmic trading allows in implementing various strategies like ordering slicing, basket trading, and 2L and 3L spreading.
- **Presto ATS:** This algorithm trading platform provides us to trade on all the asset classes available in the market. Presto ATS was developed by Symphony Fintech.

- **ODIN:** This algorithmic trading program provides a platform to trade on a "multi-exchange, multi-segment front-
  office trading, and risk management system" and serves all
  the types of investors.

FlexTrade, AlgoNomics, MetaTrader, and AmiBroker are the other algorithmic trading strategy which has created the automated world for stock
exchange with high accuracy and bulk order placement with condition of
making high profits and stop losses.

16.3.2.5   Algo Trading Strategies

Any strategy for algorithmic trading requires an identified opportunity
that is profitable in terms of improved earnings or cost reduction. The subsequent are common trading strategies utilized in algo-trading:

a) **Trend movement-following strategy:** "Trend-following strategy is most common and one of the simplest strategies to
   implement through algorithmic trading. This strategy
   involves price index movement, follow trends in moving
   averages, channel breakouts, and related technical indicators to establish a well implement trend following strategy.
   As this strategy does not depend upon predictions or price
   forecasts, so it is easy to implement through algorithms".
b) **Arbitrage opportunities:** "The second strategy Arbitrage
   opportunity, we all are aware about the function of arbitrage
   (buying from one market and selling it to another). This
   strategy involves the same function AI helps in buying and
   selling of a dual-listed stock at a lower price from one market and sell it to the another market at a higher price which
   provides us risk-free profits or Arbitrage. Using algorithm to
   identify these price differences and placing orders efficiently
   provides us with profitable deals always".
c) **Index fund restoring balance:** "An Index fund exemplifies
   and equilibrate holdings to bring at par with their respective
   benchmark indices". Algorithmic trading provides profitable
   opportunities for traders and maximizes expected trades the
   key feature of timely execution of the order at best prices
   close the deals with profits.
d) **Model-based strategies:** "This portfolio strategy consisting
   mathematical model of multiple positions with offsetting

positive and negative deltas- a ratio comparing the change within the price of an asset, usually marketable security, to the corresponding change within the price of its derivative— so that the general delta of the assets in question totals zero". It works on mathematical models, as delta-neutral trading strategy which allows trading on a mixture of options and therefore the underlying security.

e) **Trading span (mean reversion):** "Trading Span strategy based on the concept that the high and low prices of an asset are a short lived phenomenon that reverts to their mean (average value) periodically. Identifying and defining a price range and implementing an algorithm supported it allow trades to be placed automatically when the worth of an asset breaks in and out of its defined range".

f) **Volume-weighted and time-weighted average price:** First, we will discuss "volume-weighted average price strategy which breaks up an outsized order and releases dynamically determined smaller chunks of the order to the market using stock-specific historical volume profiles. The aim is to execute the order on the brink of the VWAP".

Secondly, "The strategy of Time-weighted average price breaks up an outsized order and releases dynamically determined smaller chunks of the order to the market using evenly divided time slots between a start and end time. The aim is to execute the order on the brink of the typical price between the beginning and end times thereby minimizing market impact".

g) **Volume percentage:** This strategy is also known as "Steps Strategy" because the order is fulfilled step by step (partial orders are placed) depending on the percentage of the market volume (i.e., demand and supply), it may increase or it may decrease but this strategy will continue its participation till the time the prices of the stock reaches at the level for what of the investor has wished for.

h) **Implementation of inadequacy:** "This strategy aims at minimizing the execution cost of an order by trading off the real-time market, thereby saving on the value of the order and taking advantage of the chance cost of delayed execution. The strategy will increase the targeted participation rate when the stock price moves favorably and reduce it when the stock price moves adversely".

i) **Going beyond the standard trading algorithms:** This is an extraordinary class of Algorithm which spots the happenings on the other side these are known as "sniffing algorithms". These sniffing algorithms are intelligent enough to recognize that is there any prevailing algorithm on the other side. This technique of AI helps to identify order opportunities available which enable us to extract more profits from the market.

16.3.2.6   Impact of Artificial Intelligence on Stock Market

An AI-based tool has already started playing a crucial role in predicting stock exchange trends. AI is additionally used for trade executions, for advisory services, and for discretionary trading. The utilization of AI is not any longer an unrealistic tale. Tools like the Trade Scheduler are already getting used in Asian markets to offer portfolio managers deep insights into when and the way to sell and buy specific stocks. AI not only instigates analyzed data but also studies the pattern of investment done by investors and help to sell or buy the stock; it starts communicating its action in real-time [16].

Well-recognized players on Wall Street like Morgan Stanley and Goldman Sachs have already begun watching narrow AI solutions through data processing, using self-learning algorithms, and Natural Language Processing (NLP) tools, which are capable of far more complex interactions than more well-known applications like "Apple I Phone Siri", "Amazon's Alexa", or "Google Assistant". Many wealth management companies are keeping an in depth eye on the stock exchange because AI offers interesting possibilities just like the rebalancing portfolio. While AI, in its current form, does not completely replace the human workforce, it does augment multiple roles by reducing lower-order work and offering real-time advice.

However, there is a Fintech company called "Aidiya" in Honk Kong which has created a hedge fund capable of creating all stock trades using AI excluding human intervention. While stock markets are using algorithms, automation, and elements of machine learning for several years now, there has always been the necessity for high-skilled human involvement thanks to certain immeasurable factors like emotion and sentiment.

Advanced AI like Machine Learning and deep learning are also getting used to spot, and stop "rogue transactions". "Algorithmic trading is supported by advanced analytics which has continuously detected rogue transactions. AI/ML platforms are maintaining their interest within the capital markets to make sure the operational risk elements and are considered especially when stakeholders would want to validate their current exposure, liquidity, or forex rates among other factors before committing a transaction," said Chiradeep Bhattacharya, Tibco AI and Analytics expert, and Alliance baron.

AI solutions that use artificial neural networks are becoming increasingly "smart" at predicting financial and technical trading trends but still have not reached some extent of accurately predicting sentiment. Humans are still better at locating market signals, understanding emotion, as AI still has not reached some extent of using signals and methods to unravel for causality, a Bloomberg report confirms.

This has not stopped big stock exchange players from attempting to recruit the highest machine learning and AI-based experts from companies like Google, Microsoft, and Apple. Deep learning AI remains being viewed as a breakthrough technology which will create better predictive models to estimate trading, and drive automated investment decisions supported both the info structured and unstructured. Looking forward to Robo-advisors who would integrate behavioral patterns within their financial objectives and make far more targeted trades and investments in our financial sector.

16.3.3   Artificial Intelligence and Mutual Funds

The basic concept of Mutual Fund is to create a "Pool of Money" through NFO (New fund offer); under any scheme, this pool of money is created by the investors' investment who invest in this NFO, that pool of money is given to a professional manager who manages the portfolio in order to gain returns and those returns are again passed back to the investors.

Investment in mutual funds can be made through two strategies SIP (Systematic Investment Plan) and Lumpsum investment; from this pooled money, further investments is being done by professional managers by constructing manual portfolios. With the rapid advancement in technology, our financial sector is transforming around the whole world. AI technologies have been used to automate many paper-based and manual processes to improve its productiveness.

Data science and AI technologies have bought a transition phase regarding the usage of technology. Apart from using technology for reducing human error and defects or improving efficiency of work, AI is extensively used for making smarter, better, and cognitive decisions.

Many other industries like telecom, education, and healthcare are adopting AI technology. Financial Services Industry has also tried their hands on it. We have discussed it for Insurance and Stock market, and now, Mutual Funds

are also using AI technologies at their maximum level to satisfy their investor's needs and desires. In Mutual Fund Industry AMC (Asset Management
company) is using AI technology in replacing Portfolio manager by constructing the portfolio using simple fundamental rules of investing and by
reducing error, sentiment, judgment problem, and emotions, which has led
to provide better investment strategy with optimizing investment goals.

In Mutual Fund portfolio, managers screens huge historical data, checks
out many analytical factors, and uses quantitative techniques, to construct
the portfolio, but still there is always human judgment involved which may
go biased despite of best intentions of portfolio manager, it may involve
errors in judgments while investing. So, to avoid these errors in judgment
which are being made by humans, quantitatively managed funds have
become popular nowadays. They work with AI without any human intervention, emotions, and no error.

Many Asset Management companies like Tata, DSP, Reliance, and ICICI
have launched Quant (Shorten sort of quantitative) Funds which uses a
lively multi-factor quantitative investment model, to provide best decisions with the help of AI modules for current market condition without
any emotions or biasness.

16.3.3.1   Mutual Funds Use AI in the Following Ways

- AI datasets influence and secures large market.
- AI uses many techniques and builds statistical models to
  employ these quantitative strategies of investment.
- AI runs these comprehensive models for testing different
  real-life scenarios of the market.
- AI creates a framework that evaluates and manages these
  quantitative models by predicting high accuracy of time.
- AI uses statistics through which many hidden patterns are
  identified which are running in the market and which is difficult for an individual to track it.
- AI also extracts correlations between two variables which
  play an important role for decision making.

16.3.3.2   Quantitative Fund's Investment Process

The diagram below depicts the investment process of quantitative funds
and quantitative funds, which uses a very high analytical and structured
approach for the management and construction of portfolio. Here, the
picking of stock from the various options is being done on the basis of

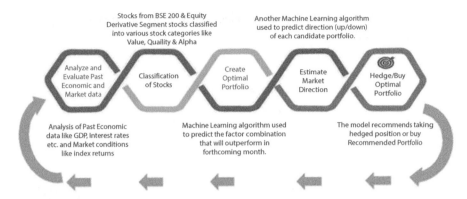

Figure 16.8 Investment process. Source: https://www.advisorkhoj.com/articles/Mutual-Funds/Tata-Quant-Fund:-Artificial-Intelligence-enabled-investing.

generating more returns with reduced risk, through which AI helps in providing stabilized returns with consistent performance throughout. AI involves highly structured, instigative, and well-organized process, as shown in the Figure 16.8 [14].

16.3.3.3   Quantitative Fund—Choosing Stocks Strategy

Many investors tend to target on individual stocks, hoping that they end up to be multi-baggers instead of taking a portfolio view. Portfolio investment, on the opposite hand, may be a diversified approach of investing that seeks to satisfy the investment objectives, regardless of market conditions. Building a portfolio is like selecting a cricket team; different members of the team have played different roles within the team, e.g., we cannot have a winning team by having 11 best batsmen, we must got to have the optimal combination of players (batsmen, bowlers, wicket-keeper, etc.). Similarly, quantitative fund aims to pick optimal portfolio combination of Alpha, Values, and Quality stocks.

Stock selection strategy deals with selecting the combination of top ranked best stocks which creates the optimal (maximizing returns and minimizing risk) portfolio. This selection is done with factor strategy, and this factor strategy evaluates Alpha, Value, and Quality for analysis.

It also checks something out that whether the Macro economic conditions and various other strategy scenarios are in favor of factor strategy investment or not or it may cause a downfall in portfolio performance.

Evaluation-based models make the choice of shopping for or Hedging (Current portfolio). These funds use a quantitative model to create its portfolio which is diagrammatically presented below.

Figure 16.9 represents the stock selection strategy on the basis of predetermined procedure.

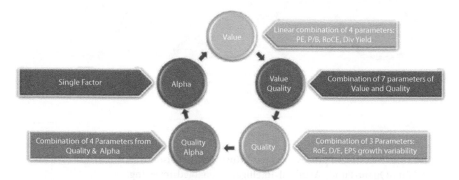

Figure 16.9 Stock Selection Strategy. Source: https://www.advisorkhoj.com/articles/ Mutual-Funds/Tata-Quant-Fund:-Artificial-Intelligence-enabled-investing.

16.3.3.4   *The Other Way Around*

Every coin has two sides so AI is excellent in many areas, yet it has many drawbacks, and they are as follows:

a) High cost and difficulty to understand: The creation of AI requires huge cost and investment and is not easy to understand because of complex machines.
b) Replica of Humans: They will create replicas which will act an equivalent as humans but still human brain is God's gift no machine can replace it.
c) No improvement with experience: A pre-described rule of instructions or algorithms is given to these machines to perform the task and they perform well but they cannot program themselves automatically with a different experience.
d) No original creativity is being done through these complex machines.
e) Leads to unemployment: Humans are being replaced by machines so tons of unemployment is generated in our economy.
f) Lack of personal connections.

16.4   Conclusion

AI is taking the financial services industry by storm. Almost every company within the financial technology sector has already started using

AI to save lots of time, reduce costs, and add value. AI has provided many tools like Robo-advisor, and Wealthfront tracks account activity which uses AI capabilities to research and understand how account holders spend, invest, and make financial decisions, in order that they will customize their products and offer to the investor consistent with their habits.

AI has transformed the finance industry by doing risk management, fraud detection, and management and by providing financial advisory services, algorithmic trading, and private financial management to enable continuous tracking for managing finance.

The future of finance is going to be heavily influenced by emerging Fintech companies and AI technology applications, setting the stage for increasing competitiveness among the industry's leading giants. Within the next decade, AI will deepen its roots by helping finance industry to optimize its resources, reducing risk, and generating more revenue, within the trading, investing, banking, insurance, lending, and other Fintech verticals.

16.5   Glossary

Algorithms: a process or set of rules to be followed in calculations or other problem-solving operations, especially by a computer.

Arbitrage: the simultaneous buying and selling of securities, currency, or commodities in several markets or derivative forms so as to require advantage of differing prices for an equivalent asset.

Chatbots: a computer virus designed to simulate conversation with human users, especially over the web.

Cognitive Computing: describe AI systems that aim to simulate human thought.

Natural Language Processing: may be a subfield of linguistics, computing, information engineering, and AI concerned with the interactions between computers and human.

Premium: is that the amount of cash a private or business pays for a policy.

Quant Funds: is an investment fund that selects securities by utilizing the capabilities of advanced quantitative chemical analysis.

Robo-Advisors: are classes of monetary adviser that provide financial advice or investment management online with moderate to minimal human intervention.

References

1. Point, T., *Artificial Intelligence Overview*, Tutorial Point, 2017, July 23, Retrieved August 22, 2017, from https://www.tutorialspoint.com/artificial_intelligence/artificial_intelligence_overview.htm.
2. McCarty, L.T., A language for legal discourse: I. Basic features, in: *Proceedings of the Second International Conference on Artificial Intelligence and Law, ICAIL*, pp. 180–189, ACM, New York, NY, 1989.
3. Sciglar, P., 2018, April19, https://www.roboticsbusinessreview.com/ai/3-basic-ai-concepts-explain-artificial intelligence/#:~:text=Artificial%20intelligence's%20progress%20is%20staggering.&text=To%20understand%20some%20of%20the%20deeper%20concepts%2C%20such%20as%20data,deep%20learning%2C%20and%20neural%20networks. Retrieved August 22, 2017, from https://beebom.com/examples-of-artificial-intelligence/.
4. Definition from WhatIs.com. Retrieved August 22, 2017, from https://searchcio.techtarget.com/definition/AI.
5. Albright, D., *10 Examples of Artificial Intelligence you are Using in Daily Life*, 2016, September 26. https://www.google.com/search?q=Albright%2C+D.%2C+10+Examples+of+Artificial+Intelligence+you+are+Using+in+Daily+Life%2C+2016%2C+September+26.&oq=Albright%2C+D.%2C+10+Examples+of+Artificial+Intelligence+you+are+Using+in+Daily+Life%2C+2016%2C+September+26.&aqs=chrome..69i57.1155j0j4&sourceid=chrome&ie=UTF-8
6. Bhattacharya, M., Intelligent financial fraud detection: A comprehensive review. *Comput. Secur.*, 2, 47–66, 2016.
7. Li, F. and Z.H., Financial data analysis based on machine learning. *Sci. Wealth*, 6, 624, 2016.
8. https://marutitech.com., Retrieved February 11 2020, from https://marutitech.com: https://marutitech.com/ways-ai-transforming-finance/.
9. Cao, J. and Y.Z., Research Progress on the influence on artificial intelligence on economy. *Economics Information*, pp. 103–115, 2018.
10. Lewis, T., 2014, December 4, https://www.livescience.com. Retrieved February 10, 2020, from https://www.livescience.com: https://www.livescience.com/49007-history-of-artificial-intelligence.html.
11. Makridakis, S., The forthcoming Artificial Intelligence (AI) revolution: Its impact on society and firms. *Futures*, 90, 46–60, 2017.
12. Patterson, M., 2019, September 22. https://hackernoon.com. Retrieved February 21, 2020, from https://hackernoon.com: https://hackernoon.com/how-artificial-intelligence-is-revolutionizing-insurance-9n5e230zp.
13. Shroff, R., 2019, July 1, https://towardsdatascience.com. Retrieved February 20, 2020, from https://towardsdatascience.com: https://towardsdatascience.com/how-are-insurance-companies-implementing-artificial-intelligence-ai-aaf845fce6a7.

14. Team, A.R., 2020, January 13, https://www.advisorkhoj.com/articles. Retrieved February 12, 2020, from https://www.advisorkhoj.com: https://www.advisorkhoj.com/articles/Mutual-Funds/Tata-Quant-Fund:-Artificial-Intelligence-enabled-investing.
15. Lewis, T., 2014, December 4, https://www.livescience.com. Retrieved February 10, 2020, from https://www.livescience.com: https://www.livescience.com/49007-history-of-artificial-intelligence.html.
16. Thomas, M., 2019, March 16, https://builtin.com/artificial-intelligence/ai-trading-stock-market-tech.

Bibliography

1. Jonas, F., *Challenges in Quantitative Equity*, New York, Research Foundation of CFA Institute, 2008.
2. Balci, O., *Introduction to Computer Science Lecture Notes*, p. 129, Department of Computer Science, Virginia Tech, Blacksburg, VA, 1996.
3. Brookshear, J.G., *Computer Science: An Overview*, Fifth Edition, Addison-Wesley, Reading, MA, 1997.
4. Biermann, A.W., *Great Ideas in Computer Science*, p. 376, MIT Press, Cambridge, MA, 1990.
5. Deus, H., *A brief history of tomorrow*, Y.N. Harari (Ed.), p. 445, Hapercollins, New York, 2018.
6. Mariya Yao, M.J., *Applied Artificial Intelligence: A Handbook For Business Leaders*, Topbots, Monrovia, 2018.
7. Prakken, H., A study of accrual of arguments, with applications to evidential reasoning, in: *Proceedings of the Tenth International Conference on Artificial Intelligence and Law*, ACM Press, New York, pp. 85–94, 2005.

Bibliography

17

Artificial Intelligence With Special Reference to Blockchain Technology: A Future of Accounting

Ashish Porwal[1]*, Ankita Chaturvedi[2] and Sachin Gupta[3]†

[1]Finance and Accounting, Institute of Law, Nirma University, Ahmedabad (Gujarat), India
[2]Department of Accounting and Taxation, IIS Deemed to be University, Jaipur (Rajasthan), India
[3]Department of Business Administration, Mohanlal Sukhadia University, Udaipur (Rajasthan), India

Abstract

Blockchain technology is found within value of accounting assets—the information in the database is trustworthy and factual, in spite of the confidence of the opponent. Trading is possible only with the consent of every member. By the support of web accounting, it can be decoded into safe, translucent across groups, and stress-free to use design. Technological advancement requires the need for the protection and validation of the data it brings to the market. It connects markets, suppliers, consumers, and banks by solving the problem of defining multiple ledgers and separately issuing them by providing a reliable distributed ledger. While we associate blockchain with digital currencies, it has various application types in accounting and audit that make up conversion technology.

Keywords: Artificial intelligence, blockchain, accounting, Bitcoin, finance, machine learning, auditing, accountants

*Corresponding author: drashishsporwal@gmail.com
†Corresponding author: sachinguptabusadm@gmail.com

S. Balamurugan, Sonal Pathak, Anupriya Jain, Sachin Gupta, Sachin Sharma, Sonia Duggal (eds.) Impact of Artificial Intelligence on Organizational Transformation, (289–304) © 2022 Scrivener Publishing LLC

17.1   Introduction

17.1.1   Artificial Intelligence and Accounting

Accountants have held the automation waves over the years to improve their efficiency and function. But until now, technology is unable to swap the want for professional acquaintance and policymaking. Certainly, the preceding groups of the "A"-system have universally verified the continuous power of humanoid technology and mechanical limitations. Artificial intelligence (AI) has remained the ambition of computer experts then the 1950 and has grasped great advancement in current era. AI models are now fundamental portion of several of our online actions and will be widely advertised in the whole thing we trace then do [1]. These programs do not duplicate humanoid acumen. Certainly, some scholars would claim against the usage of the word AI to label current schemes of mechanism knowledge. But, depending on performance, systems are increasing to produce far more than the accuracy and consistency of these man-made ones. In the small to middle tenure, AI takes numerous openings aimed at accountants to advance their presentation, deliver more vision, and provide new aid to industries. In the long run, AI presents the latent for drastic transformation, as organizations gradually conquest the roles of people currently making decisions.

It is therefore important to recognize and leverage new know-hows efficiently. Further, zones of technology will interrelate with AI besides having a major impression on industries in the forthcoming, such as "blockchain or quantum computing". Furthermore, the stride of skills transfer can be very hasty, and the nature of data-based learning and data-based programs allows non-stop enhancement. To take full advantage of this influential new technology, we must be clear about their unique physiognomies and how they can assist in solving real glitches. There is typically a long period to go from edifice the know-how to receiving the best worth out of it. Usually, technology can be a clarification that needs a delinquent to solve or merely enable us to imitate our processes using different tools [2].

17.1.2   Blockchain in Finance and Accounting

Blockchain is the folder of archives or communal ledger of all digital activities or events that have been shared and public between participants. Apiece transaction in the open ledger is guaranteed by the accord of the bulk of the program contestants. Blockchain is a publicly distributed fund that is able to store and verify transactions that have occurred on its network. "Public blockchain" means that it does not belong to any organization but somewhat network control is disseminated among its handlers. The process of transaction authentication is performed by so-called sappers who use their computers or devices specifically intended to solve the calculations needed to verify a transaction, and in this way, they are rewarded with a predetermined Bitcoin (or other cryptocurrency) status. The complexity of the calculations increases with the increase in the mining capability to maintain the time needed to write data the specified block of text remains constant. Blockchain is not a solitary technology, but rather a procedure—a method of doing things—for recording transactions. Nothing like the Internet, some place information is shared, and blockchain title can be transmitted from one party to another. Blockchain is a required model for several reasons. For instance, in a market with multiple currency exchange groups, it can eliminate the need to reconcile dividing dividers. Distribution among all users also eliminates the outage and eliminates the costs of paying the chief power to maintain the exactness of the ledger. Any participant in a computer can have access to all of the dealings, allowing for limpidity and block chain to be "self-monitoring" [3].

The idea of using blockchain information and substructure for accounting resolutions comes from the blockchain environment being a ledger for Bitcoin dealings. Since blockchain can handle currency transactions without the trust of a trusted third party agent, be aware that money transfers are one of the most controlled areas of a financial bond, and in the same way, it can grasp dealings of any kind: stocks, bonds, loans, and so on. Now, it is possible, with many companies with blockchain schemes in their operations, and it is conceivable to integrate them into financial reports at any time. Doing accounting as we know it puts a lot of faith in the trust of accountants and auditors who can and sometimes can become corrupt. Nowadays, to authenticate the accounting information GAAP involves auditors to achieve necessary and appropriate indication to support the veracity of the audited dealings without causing a noteworthy expense to the audit. In their quest to lessen the audit costs of their auditing patrons, they have been forced to do less, and to find ways not to actually audit the transaction but to sample more dollars and in a more cost-effective manner as testifies Ellen Masterson, PwC's global head of auditing in a discussion with Frieswick (2003). Though, the rate of communal faith on untrue financial data can be as many times as high a profile con as Enron's testimony. In Enron's instance, the accounting firm remained mortified of hindering justice by altering with important accounting evidence. Opportunely, in blockchain rule, financial information consumers would not need to depend on auditors' judgment for the integrity of their statements [4]. In financial statements, they can know about the accurate financial statements that are timely and perform their own non-cash items, for instance, depreciation and benchmarking. Showing the average loss of companies suffering from accounting errors or intentional alteration of data presents the discoveries of the Bloomberg BNA audits study in 2013, US industries received $ 7 billion of IRS fines due to unfitting reporting with the top two blunders being:

1. To close the books afore the whole thing is needed, correct data is collected.
2. Precise property data since previous years.

These types of errors or occasionally untrue happenings are difficult under the blockchain system; meanwhile, it is not possible to alter the data when it is written and the information is restructured in genuine time [5].

In the lack of an ample accounting info for present blockchain, we need to provide an explanation ourselves. Real-time accounting blockchain structure is a software result that allows financial dealings, based on financials, and additional digital papers between two or more partners, keeps the deal details in legally secured blocks covered by their authenticity verified by the mining process, and lets the creation of financial reports by what time.

17.2 Objectives

The following are the main objectives of this chapter:

1. To explore the usages of AI in accounting.
2. To explore the uses of Blockchain technology in accounting.

17.3 Literature Review

17.3.1 Janling Shi

This paper suggested that with the growth of AI, AI has arrived in the area of accounting intensively, which plays a vital role in refining business performance, sinking employee blunders, preventing and managing business risk, improving business keenness, and improving employee efficacy. AI technology is like a double-sided sword. While endorsing the expansion of accounting, it will also enable accountants to address the problem of joblessness. Founded on the idea of AI and its use to the accounting industry, this paper deliberates the impact of AI in the financial accounting area, and prioritizes the experiments of the digital technology industry. It should lead to the completion of skills development; note the change in the broader role of money management. Start policies such as inventors and directors of synthetic accounting schemes.

17.3.2   Nordgren *et al.*

Their paper established that blockchain technology is widely known for the emergence of Bitcoin in 2009 and has since received a lot of hype as a technology to disrupt the financial services industry. Blockchain was also proposed as a possible solution to the UK border problems after Brexit. While many blockchain developers promise to improve the speed and security of transactions, there are some who question the true functionality of blockchain. Is blockchain the Internet of our time, disruptive technology, or is it just an exaggeration? This paper looks at blockchain technology, its use in the financial and accounting field, and the disruptive power of blockchain in these forums. They provide an overview of the criticisms and issues that need to be addressed with blockchain to realize its potential.

17.3.3   Kiwilinski

This paper discussed that blockchain technology is critical to the value of financial assets—the information is reliable, of course, regardless of the opponent's confidence. Trading is possible only with the consent of all participants. With the help of network accounting, it can be translated into safe, transparent across groups, and easy to use format. Introducing technology into accounting has the following benefits: online transactions are fast and efficient; accounts that can be renewed using smartphone apps. Virtual data recognition systems allow you to change the entire process, starting with the introduction of key documents.

17.3.4   Ahmed Farah

This paper discussed blockchain's new emerging technology in the form of Bitcoin, adding a new way of managing finance. Founded on the achievement of this process from the perspective of Bitcoin, this method has remained trusted upon and has gradually worked on a variety of functions, either public or private, and gained the confidence and satisfaction of customers. This paper highlights the challenges ahead and opportunities in this modern technology that is designed to improve our digital world.

17.3.5   Odoh Longinus Chukwudi

This paper explored that AI is rapidly changing the way financial institutions operate and is expected to greatly expand low-cost jobs due to cost savings and operational efficiency. In recent times, significant improvements have been made in AI especially as it relates to accounting work that has shifted its focus from paper and pencil to computer and software. But the biggest danger of AI is that people conclude early on that they understand it. The purpose of this study is to evaluate the effectiveness of AI in the presentation of accounting functions amid accounting firms in South East Nigeria.

17.3.6   Potekhina and Rumkin

Their study examined the theoretical agenda for blockchain solicitations in accounting, identified the advantages and disadvantages and discussed its audit results and accounting in particular and credit risk management. This example study was preferred as a result as a research plan to add actual impact to our numerical analysis. In an instance where we use the financial record of Nokia organization to determine the results of blockchain accounting in credit score methods, we add value to the research in factual life situations. We then confer the results and try to pull general assumptions and identify the results of the altered groups involved. As it is constantly vital to do once dealing with novel technologies, we confer the potential ethical benefits and glitches arising since technology operation.

This study purposes to analyze the present theoretical framework of blockchain accounting in a lucid way as the present works appear less interesting and many sources are less focused on accounting applications. Observed research aims to classify the quantifiable effect of materiality on a particular complex of credit risk modeling under the wider blockchain paradigm. There are two answers from the study. To reinforce the fact that the possible effect of blockchain accounting credit card trials is locked in the realm of real credit card debt declines and thus technology will have huge consequences for companies with a significant decline in credit measures. The additional discovery is that the effects will not only be optimistic in explaining financial distress and speed of problem solving but can also negatively impact a company by temporarily exacerbating the economic problem, a previously unprecedented issue of blockchain accounting [12].

17.4 Research Methodology

The work is exploratory research approach based on literature analysis. The research method is preferred due to the newness of the topic studied. In leading the research, the concept of AI and blockchain can be defined. It is also probable to intensely scrutinize the phenomenon of the technology in accounting and implications caused by it.

17.5 Usage of Artificial Intelligence in Accounting

Though AI methods like machine erudition are not unique, and the leap of variation is fast, extensive implementation of industry and accounting is in the initial phases. Acceptable to build a better image for the impending, we must grow a deeper accepting in what way AI can solve accounting and industry glitches, practical tasks, and skill writers who need to graft with smart structures [6].

Auditors use their mechanical acquaintance of accounting and finance to assist businesses and interested party make healthier conclusions. To upkeep their conclusion and guidance, accountants require first-class financial and non-financial data and study. This is replicated in the extensive variety of accounting roles through the business and the training of acquiring, processing, monitoring and communicating information, conducting research, and making various decisions. Book keepers have been using technology for numerous ages to help them deliver healthier advice and make better verdicts. Technology can help them do this by solving three wide glitches:

- providing superior and inexpensive information to upkeep decision making;
- creates new information from data analysis; and
- releases tint to emphasize on other important chores such as decision making, problem cracking, mentoring, strategic expansion, association building, and headship.

The characteristic of machine learning skills offers itself to great advances in all zones of accounting and can train artisans with influential new skills and enable them to perform many errands and decisions [7].

Consequently, it is significant to recognize accounting and business glitches wherever machine learning can be fertile especially when snags may not be relevant in these processes. This will ensure that acquisition exertions are obsessed by the need of the business, somewhat than just technical skills. Till day, there has been partial use in actual accounting but initial research and application projects comprise:

- practice machine knowledge to cypher accounting and advance the correctness of procedures followed by guidelines, enabling larger automation of process procedures;
- improve fraud finding by more erudite processes, machine learning replicas of "normal" operations, and improved predictions of fake actions;
- use machine-based forecasting replicas to predict profitability; and

Accounting characters are already varying to respond to new abilities in data analytics. Certainly, accountants are well suited to work well with data analytics, because they cartel high levels of accounting and strong corporate alertness. These processes will speed up with AI [8].

Other roles will last to highlight technical accounting and human decision in dealing with problematic cases and novels. Other roles can be developed to increase teamwork and collaboration with other parts of the group to help them gain accurate insights from data and mockups. There will be new professions. For instance, accountants will need to be intricate in training or testing replicas or in testing procedures. They may berequired to be intricate in projects to help troubleshoot and assimilate results into business procedures [9]. Some accountants may be unswervingly involved in the input or output management, such as exclusion management or configuration record. This output will be reproduced in the services needed for accountants. Other parts, such as training models, may require in-depth information of machine learning strategies.

Within some cases, accounting may require limited machine learning experience to be capable to have informative discussions with experts and additional business units. Precarious thinking and communication abilities are probably the most important. In addition to skills, accountants may need to accept new ways of discerning and doing something to improve machine learning gears. For instance, spending more time on prognostic and energetic tasks—e.g., setting forecasts or the ability to change sequence rapidly—will require diverse ways of discerning.

17.6   Usage of Blockchain in Accounting

Blockchains also sanction for better transparency than outdated conveyors. This is desirable in cases where dishonesty or misuse of possessions is at stake. For instance, value funds can be provided with block-based assets; from there, the previous receiver of the subsidy can be effortlessly recognized.

At present, dealings between companies outcome in a type of "quadruple entry book", in which each company automatically enters a double entry, and in theory, two input sets are equal in value. This model can be meaning fully adapted by blockchain. Through dipping the walls round the interior accounting of apiece company and making admissions directly on the blockchain, bookkeeping permits the transactions to be recorded honestly, genuinely, and authentically by respective party. This may twitch off as something of a deal for Intra Groups, but over time, it can grow across manifold entities, making a kind of "universal book entry" [10].

Essentially, any type of asset ledger will want to be built around the privacy obstacle that a blockchain generates. While the figures in each transaction can be encoded, if the capacity or possession of the goods is at stake, the preceding transaction should be public to settle this. Discovering a way to gauge the competitive significances of allocating other people, secrecy, and security is a present area of research among blockchain professionals. There are numerous areas that still disturb blockchain [11]. When shared with a robust digital identity system, an individuality blockchain can store personal info, abridging the "Know Your Client" and other identity procedures by allowing administrations to occupy in the identification process. Similarly, a record of intellectual property rights can be circulated to facilitate the procedure of identifying IP owners, petitioning and paying for privileges.

17.6.1   Bitcoin

Bitcoin is an accessible online coin, shaped by an unidentified person or people in the alias Satoshi Nakamoto. Succumbing their white paperback in late 2008, and presenting the first code in early 2009, Nakamoto made Bitcoin an electric currency that could be sent to aristocracies deprived of the need for a central bank or other specialist to use and alter a ledger, much less how it used virtual currency. Though it was not the first money online to suggest, the Bitcoin offer solved a number of matters online and turn out to be the most effective version, now accounting for about US $ 69bn in issued Bitcoins, conferring to figures occupied from cryptmarketcap.com in September 2017 [12].

The machine that used the Bitcoin ledger was known as blockchain, which is the word now used to refer to all of the bad ledger technology being dispersed. The unique and big blockchain is the one that lasts to change in Bitcoin transactions now. Some work for a few 100 "altcoins"— some of the same money schemes have different rules—and diverse systems like Ethereum or Ripple. The database has a few structures that have involved investors and disruptors to all financial systems and it is supposed that blockchain, a low-tech, potentially unruly technology and maybe grow into a bed of worldwide record systems.

Bitcoin workings pay miners—which makes a compelling research for sending new transactions—with anew created Bitcoins. If money is desirable, then it feeds itself. The scheme also mechanically adjusts the shipping problems made and the incentive for doing so is to control price rise. Blockchain joins the economic assistances initially made for Bitcoin. Only the addition of the eldest existing chain is satisfied, so that miners are fortified to create new jobs in its place of moving on to diverse smaller groups. But standing still is a trial, as new updates to the Bitcoin client are only active when most members approve to install them.

Bitcoin is attractive to users for many reasons:

- the cost of payers is low;
- Currency accounting has generally been growing steadily since its inception; and
- The system is more restricted than a traditional bank.

Bitcoin does not have "Know Your Client" or identity requirements— anyone with an internet link can join and starts getting and sending Bitcoins. Though this makes the system cheaper and more reachable, it has made and attracted to criminals in much the same way as paper money, the Silk Road "black net" marketplace that made widespread use of Bitcoin before being shut down by the FBI in October 2013 [13].

As a currency founded on the Internet, Bitcoin also does not identify international borders, meaning transmissions between locations are not dissimilar from other payments. There are extra blockchain projects looking to raise funds in this regard containing international payment requests for central banks issued as Ripple.

17.6.2   Interbank Transactions

Blockchains are intended to be useful for systems that necessitate settlement between groups. Most of the top players in the bank upkeep the

R3 Consortium, which is examining the use of blockchain-like block-gerin such as blockgerin for message between finance and other financial schemes. Presently, millions yearly spend refunds among banks; but, if a ledger solution is not able to handle the transaction amount among banks, then this can be expressively abridged [14].

This kind of app will be a private ledger—one in which only invited clutches can view records or cooperate to create new entries. Though, it will permit interbank transactions to create a single, official record that all members can verify. This would decrease the apparent efforts presently spent on restoring books with partners and permit for a more efficient banking system.

An answer of this kind cannot work with the present use of blockchain, either in volume or speed, and in detail, this R3 project has entered some of the dispersed applications of the financial area. Though, considering that these key tests can be overcome, this is an area with the major impact of blockchain application. Others gaze at supply chain incorporation for alike reasons.

17.6.3   Property Registry

Possibly, the most palpable case where blockchain could benefit from the verification and transmission of ownership of assets and terrestrial regis-trations is a very noble case. There have been numerous pilot studies and evidence of idea done, but no one have touched the full maturity level yet. Further indication is that the idea in this arena was the land record in Honduras, which does not presently own a land title and undergoes from scam and unfair removal; some schemes have now been planned or developed in Georgia and Sweden, but none have yet touched the key test. Making a clear and reliable record of ownership and transmission of own-ership will help generate more fluidity in the economy by increasing secu-rity and counter the impression by scattering record keeping to all parties rather than just others.

As a communal register, open blockchain limpidity is not a barrier to land recordings. It is acceptable for members to see who owns, sells, and distributes the land; in accumulation, the verification feature can help to add lucidity when desired.

The worldwide blockchain that registers the land will have to start by designing on the property of the theme in query—that is, generating an exhibition of each piece of land as a legal correspondent of a digital asset, stored in blocks. This will be shadowed by confirming that the existing landlords own the correct tokens allocated to them. This is no minor task as present systems are already complex, and there is a necessity for future elasticity if existing global action is altered or fragmented. In accumulation, if dishonesty in government bureaucrats is a problem, obtaining consent from those bureaucrats for a project that can decrease fraud is a challenge—and that is exactly what has opposed the pilot program in Honduras. There is a better lesson for blockchain in this instance—Bitcoin works because it is a complete online system, with all the members agreeing to the Bitcoin identity and authorizations because of how blockchain works [15]. But many other areas are more complex—ownership still needs to be recorded, but it is also combined with the real world. This poses difficulties for both sides: the register must sincerely reflect the country's physical and intellectual property position, and there must be legal instruments to enforce patents where blockchain records show that this is being held, even against non-blockchain administrations, even if it is not legal.

Supposing that these challenges can be overcome, a world blockchain that registers the land afterward can record the sale of the land (or other similar dealings), creating a reliable and consistent record. In addition, the scattered nature of the ledger will mean that the timeout or server failure will not affect the availability of the facility. While the cost of blockchain interactions can be very high, with a low, high-quality network such as buying and selling land, they are likely to contend.

17.7   Impact of AI on the Field of HRM

Businesses will moreover need admittance to the precise expertise. Obviously, this twitches with technical skill in machine learning. But these technical skills need to be accompanied by deep indulgent of the business background that environs the data and the acumen required. Accounting persons are by this time altering in retort to new abilities in data analytics.

Without a doubt, accountants are fit experienced to effort effectively by data analytics, as they combine high levels of proficiency with robust industry cognizance. These drifts will hasten through AI. Few roles will endure to highlight technical accounting skill and human judgement to deal with tough and unique cases. Additional roles may magnify to upsurge collaboration and partnering with other portions of the establishment to assist them develop the correct meaning from data and replicas. There will also be novel professions. For instance, accountants will need to be intricate in training or testing facsimilia or auditing algorithms. They might need to get convoluted in projects to support frame the difficulties and assimilate results into business processes. Other accountants may be more openly intricate in handling the inputs or outputs, such as exception-handling or formulating data.

This development will be imitated in the expertise mandatory of accountants. Some parts, such as training models, could require profound acquaintance of machine learning systems. In additional areas, accountants might just requisite a more apparent acquaintance of machine learning to be able to have well-versed discussions with experts and other fragments of the trade. Critical thinking and communication skills are likely to become progressively important. In addition to skills, accountants might need to implement novel techniques of thinking and performing in order to mark the utmost of machine learning tools. For instance, spending extra time on predictive and proactive action—for example, putting extrapolations in perspective, or constructing proficiencies to change course quickly—will need diverse means of thinking [16].

17.8   Challenges in Execution

Though blockchain accounting can offer numerous facilities and is able to transform accounting and assessment of new cost efficiency, automation, and more dependable systems, there are some disadvantages to using this know-how.

a) Blockchain technology is extremely reliant on the internet. So, poor arrangement can show misery. Then, an extraordinary level of virtual safety is essential.

b) Accounting and auditing remain highly subject to legislation. Therefore, in order to confirm the complete benefits of blockchain accounting, proper guidelines should also be made. The procedure must be enabled so that any change in rule is immediately accepted.

c) Blockchain capability: In edict to devise a tight link, we want a large sum of pathways. The problematic is that apiece of these traces need to be based on the blockchain [17].

17.9   Conclusion

Based on the conclusions, contemplation is given to the role that AIS researchers should consider in the prospect. The focus emphases on variations in the use of artificial techniques in other arenas than professional programs, information-based systems, etc. In specific, attention should be given to the use of machine learning, which is seen as a new veracity for the forthcoming, and the potential of alternative area of selective intelligence—related to the performance of natural languages. A word of consciousness is provided in this study. While AIS researchers have a character to play in mounting this technology and exploring the restrictions of their use, we claim that researchers have an accountability to step rear and reflect the future potentials of accounting, accounting, and community professionals as a role perfect.

Nowadays, blockchain is a newborn technology, though few stages have been made in its design and global visibility. Originally, technology was supposed to be the basic principle of Bitcoin cryptocurrency in 2008. Though, blockchain is entrenched in the ideas and practices used in the 1980s and 1990s. Thus, blockchain is the result of periods of continuous activity by cryptographers, algorithm researchers, and computer scientists. Technology is extensively used to simplify secure digital payments. Conversely, basic technology has the potential to change almost all main areas of human health.

With respect to the current theoretical framework of blockchain accounting, with literature analysis together with industry reports, book titles, and publications, it is established that blockchain accounting while being extensively combined with technology with many examples of accounting solutions throws significant points. The current conceptual framework includes trustworthiness, flexibility, financial distinction, and cyber-technology security as its most important aspects of use in accounting. However, in spite of looking at the technological challenges of blockchain application, social influence is being met in a more talented way. One of the most vital side effects neglected in the literature is the possible increase in the short-term economic crisis. Documentation and discussion of the problem under the agenda of the account blockchain is our key involvement to the expansion of the present theoretical basis.

References

1. Ahmed Farah, N.A., Blockchain Technology: Classification, Opportunities, and Challenges. *Int. Res. J. Eng. Technol.*, 05, 05, 3423–3426, 2018, May.
2. Andersen, N., *Blockchain Technology: A Game-changer in Accounting?*, Deloitte, Chancellor's Honors Program Projects; Knoxville, USA, 2019.
3. *Artificial Intelligence and the Future of Accountancy*, ICAEW, London, 2018.

4. *Blockchain and the Future of Accountancy*, ICAEW, London, 2018.

5. Coyne, J.G. and McMickle, P.L., Can blockchains serve an accounting purpose? *J. Emerg. Technol. Account.*, *14*, 2, 101–111, 2017.

6. Dai, J. and Vasarhelyi, M.A., Toward blockchain-based accounting and assurance. *J. Inf. Syst.*, *31*, 3, 5–1, 2017.

7. Giles, K., *How Artificial Intelligence and Machine Learning Will Change the Future of Financial Auditing: An Analysis of The University of Tennessee's Accounting Graduate Curriculum*, Chancellor's Honors Program Projects; Knoxville, USA, 2019 Retrieved from https://trace.tennessee.edu/utk_chanhonoproj.

8. Grigg, I., Triple Entry Accounting. [online] Iang.org. Available at: http://iang.org/papers/triple_entry.html, 2005.

9. Haber, S. and Stornetta, W., How to time-stamp a digital document. *J. Cryptol.*, [online] 3, 2, 1991, Available at: https://www.anf.es/pdf/Haber_Stornetta.pdf.

10. Kwilinski, A., Implementation of Blockchain Technology in Accounting Sphere. *Acad. Account. Financial Stud. J.*, *23*, 2, 1–6, 2019.

11. Nordgren, A., Weckstrom, E., Martikainen, M., Lehner, O.M., Blockchain in the Fields of Finance and Accounting: A Disruptive Technology or an Overhyped Phenomenon. *Oxford J. Finance Risk Perspect.*, 7, 47–58, 2018.

12. Potekhina, A. and Riumkin, I., Blockchain – a new accounting paradigm, UMEA University, Sweden, 2017, September.

13. Sarkar, D.S., Blockchain Accounting and Disruption Ahead. *The Management Accountant*, pp. 73–78, 2018, June.

14. Simon, A.D., Kasale, S., Manish, P.M., Blockchain Technology in Accounting & Audit. *IOSR J. Bus. Manage.*, 6, 06–09, 2017.

15. Sutton, S.G., Holt, M., Arnold, V., "The reports of my death are greatly exaggerated"—Artificial intelligence. *Int. J. Account. Inf.*, 20, 60–73, 2016.

16. *The Future of Blockchain: Applications and Implications of Distributed Ledger Technology*, Chartered Accountants, Australia - New Zealand, 2017.

17. Woodside, J.M., Augustine Jr., F.K., Giberson, W., Blockchain technology adoption status and strategies. *J. Int. Technol. Inf. Manage.*, *26*, 2, 65–93, 2017.

18

AI-Implanted E-Learning 4.0: A New Paradigm in Higher Education

Garima Kothari* and B.L. Verma

Department of Business Administration UCCMS, MLSU, Udaipur (Raj), India

Abstract

This chapter investigates the prospects of artificial intelligent (AI) frameworks in the higher education with its mainstay elements: instructing, education, and information; adjacent to the foundation of fast technical reforms and difficulties, universities are dealing in the era of knowledge age to responds to societies. As learning and innovation will steer competitive edge in logically Internet-described system, a new paradigm in higher education is required where telecommunications and PCs supplant infrastructure technology. As the Internet, a worldwide specialized instrument continues influencing each human activity and adventure changing the way in which we shop, bank, cooperate, connect with ourselves, pass on and think, it is in a general sense advancing how, when, and what we appreciate. The chapter has revealed the possibility of a Hyper Class dependent on Hyper-Reality, an enhanced virtual reality. Learners are facilitated by anybody, anyplace, at wherever point learning aided more by "Just in Time Artificially Intelligent Tutors" (JITAITs). AIEd is believed to take a key job in the later phase of educational system restructuring.

Keywords: Higher education paradigm, E-learning, virtual reality, avatars, hyper class, hyper-reality, Just in Time Artificial Intelligent Tutors (JITAITs), Artificial Intelligence in Education (AIEd)

Corresponding author: ariesmini18@gmail.com

S. Balamurugan, Sonal Pathak, Anupriya Jain, Sachin Gupta, Sachin Sharma, Sonia Duggal (eds.)
Impact of Artificial Intelligence on Organizational Transformation, (305–326) © 2022 Scrivener Publishing LLC

18.1 Introduction

Information technology has infused nearly every aspect of human life. To pace with dynamism of modern information technology, E-learning—the learning beyond the physical four-wall setting—is the only feasible elucidation for meeting the diverse learning desires [1]. E-learning is, in the nick of time, training being individualized, complete, and unique learning content, progressively strengthening networks of information and connecting students and teachers with resource persons. The fusion of web in the teaching method of E-learning has made networks of trainings where the network information makes the information society, restructuring the education world. Learning in the information society upshots learners in the conception of new generation in the customary track.

E-learning is the broad utilization of web, electronic devices, and system to multiply the data. The utilization of Internet technologies delivers a broad array of solutions that improve information and execution (Marc Rosenberg, 2001). According to the E-learning action plan (2001) "E-learning is the utilization of new multimedia technologies and the Internet to improve the nature of learning by encouraging access to resources and services together with remote exchanges and collaboration". E-learning or Web-based instruction is the type of electronic education utilizing streaming videos and the highly developed functionalities accessible in educational software and with no physical contact between the concerned parties [2]. The usage of internet advancements conveys an expensive exhibit of arrangements that improve information and execution.

The major outliners of E-learning are reusing, sharing resources, and interoperability. At present, various organizations provide E-learning tools with multiple functionalities, *viz.*, MOODLE (Modular Object Oriented Dynamic Learning Environment) which support the E-learners.

In the regular course of training, corresponding training content is delivered to all learners which do not congregate the learner need certainly. An old saying "Not everyone fits the mould", so learning has to personalized and customized on the learner's desires necessitates. Here, Artificial Intelligence (AI) comes into the picture, trailing the old act of learner, and customized learning package is accessible. Inside an E-learning course, AI can keep tabs on learners' development, which will help recognize the territories where every student needs capability along these lines adjusting the material as needed.

AI being injected to the correct way can ponder the E-learning scene; however, it unquestionably will require some investment to assume control over the whole E-learning industry. It is not only the start, and the future will reveal creative and captivating approaches to make learning significantly more extravagant.

18.2   Research Methodology

18.2.1   Objective

1. To examine current situation of E-learning in the higher educational paradigm.
2. To explore key hi-tech approaches that could help transform the higher educational system in regard to E-learning courses.
3. To propose a potential rational foundation for a new virtual higher educational paradigm.

18.2.2   Research Approach

The research approach is descriptive and conceptual in nature. Let us understand the descriptive and conceptual research in brief. Descriptive research is defined as a method of research that describes the population characteristics or phenomenon that is being studied. This strategy concentrates more on the "what" of the research subject as opposed to the "why" of the research subject. Conceptual research is defined as a research which is used for developing new concepts or in reinterpretation of existing ones by intellectuals. Herein, no practical experiments are conducted.

18.2.3   Types and Sources of Data

Secondary data is collected from various research papers, journals, articles text books, magazines, websites, and E-libraries.

E-sources like ProQuest, JSTOR, ScienceDirect, and IEEE Xplore have been accessed.

18.3   Progression of Web and E-Learning

18.3.1   Some Relevant Definitions Distance Education

Keegan [4] enumerated the characteristic features of Distance Education as follows:

- The distance between learner and instructor

- Influence of an instructive affiliation
- Utilization of electronic-media (TV, radio, etc.) as a medium between an instructor and a student, which facilitates two-way exchange of information
- Instructors happens in the capacity of an individual rather than as a group
- Instructors in an industrialized form

18.3.2   E-Learning

- It depends on a system.
- It centers on the main perspectives of learning.
- Members utilize PCs to acquire data and information.

18.3.3   E-Learning 1.0–4.0

18.3.3.1   *Web 1.0 E-Learning 1.0 (Link to Anything): 1997 to 2003*

Web 1.0 recognized as read-only web with its characteristics like content creation by few, web participation an extravagance, software on the local machine, product pages and confined e-commerce, and personal computers [5]. The thought is to encourage the learning and communication process given the lack of interactivity tools. It was an era of static web pages/reading/owning content. It permits utilizing hypotheses like instructivism, behaviorism, and cognitivist [6]. The fundamental fault here is the production of the content and conferring to other people.

18.3.3.2   *Web 2.0 E-Learning 2.0 (User Involvement): 2004 to 2006*

Web 2.0 is a modification from sites, a fully computerized platform [6]; a Read/Write/Execute Web is where the content is created by the many, and web contribution is a benefit [5, 7]. Dissimilar to Web 1.0, Digital Natives had the option to minister content and it permits the students to take an interest effectively in the learning procedure. Web 2.0 is totally a student-driven reality. It permits utilizing hypotheses like constructivism and social constructionism [6] Table 18.1.

18.3.3.3   *Web 3.0 E-Learning 3.0 (Existing Data Reconnected): 2007 to 2011*

John Markoff coined the phrase "Web 3.0" in the New York Times in year 2006. With no uncertainty, the future has a place with the Web

Table 18.1 Attributes of Web 1.0 to Web 3.0. Source: Dominic, M., Francis.

Web 1.0 CRAWL	Web 2.0 WALK	Web 3.0 RUN
Read	Read/Write	Read/Write/Execute
Client Server	Peer to Peer	
HTML Portals	XML	RSS RDF
Organizations Own	Networks Share	Self
Website Pages	Web Applications	Semantic Applications

3.0, Intelligent Web [8]. Web 1.0 was providing data to clients; web 2.0 was enriching data, creating the contents. Web 3.0 had the capacities of web 1.0 and web 2.0 and enriched 3D atmosphere. Semantic Web and personalization were its significant highlights [9]. It resembles having a personal assistant, concerned for all intents and purposes, every little thing about you, and can get to all the data on the Internet to respond to your inquiry.

18.3.3.4   Web 4.0 (Read/Write/Execute/Concurrency From 2012)

Web 4.0 is a symbiotic web where human brain can help out the machine in symbiosis. The lines among human and gadget will obscure. Association of Web 4.0 will be same as people speak with one another. It will be a "consistently on" associated world. As indicated by PC engineers, Web 4.0 will be similar to the human brain. Regardless of the way advancements in web 4.0, AI would accept an increasingly important job in making the web, which would associate with the people in a highly intellectual manner [10].

18.3.3.4.1   Characteristics of Web 4.0:

- **Intelligent Agents**
  Personal agents manage the expanding volume of electronic data [11]. They serve various functions including emails and sorting of the news, planning a congregation, and data recovery. For ideal use, they must have the option to gain proficiency with a client's inclinations and propensities with the period and to adjust to the varying

needs of the client. So as to produce a precise client profile, data from the same number of various sources must
be utilized [12].
Intelligent agents are user friendly that actively interacts
with users with the aid of computer applications like as in
the case of course management system (CRM) or campus
portal [13]. Intelligent agents are thus a set of software tools
that are independently linked with other database applications within one or multiple computer interface.

- **Mobile Technologies**
  As the name specifies, M-learning means flexible learning, a wing in E-learning context facilitating instant
  access, connection, and learning that is ahead of official
  four-wall setting as in office, house, or other physical
  ambience. M-learning or Mobile E-learning reflects the
  electronic learning which can happen via mobile devices
  like Personal Digital Assistants, Smart Phones, and MP3
  players (e-device meant for playing digital audio files).
  Portable innovation alludes to gadgets that are both trans-
  portable and offer prompt access to data.

The learning happens to be more flexible and convenient with its integration with M-machinery of anywhere and anytime culture. The mix and
match of PC-based learning with new learning instructional methods and
convenient computerized gadgets has constrained significant enthusiasm
from the national training segment in digitalized mobile technologies getting the hang of "M-learning".

E-learning personalization is a significant issue element in the e-learning
arena, and with an aim to arrive at the objective of learning personalization, we must deem learning style, learning curiosity, and more on the gadgets dedicated for learning.

Learning through mobile technologies can react and address the
assorted variety of the learners, adapting requirements and styles.
M-learning ought to be conveyed to give arranged, pertinent, and adaptable learning exercises that improve logical knowledge and correspondence and forward the opportunities between and among students plus
instructors [14].

M-Technology can be demonstrated often by the usage of smart phones
and tablet devices, which are a fundamental part and portion of human life
and the acceptance rate is mounting year to year as referred in Figure 18.1.

(in billions)

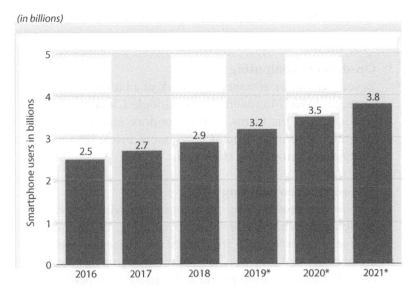

Figure 18.1 Number of smartphone users worldwide from 2016 to 2021 (in billions). Source: Statista 2020, Published by S. O'Dea, Feb 28, 2020, Retrieved on Mar 20, 2020.

- **Cloud Computing**
  Cloud computing has drawn attention of industrialists and academicians during past decades. In the words of National Institute of Standards and Technology (NIST), "Cloud computing as a tool for empowering omnipresent, advantageous, on-request network access to a common pool of configurable assets (e.g., systems, servers, applications, and administrations) quickly provisioned and discharged with insignificant service-provider exertion" [15]. Here, NIST implies cloud computing as a novel delivery model of computing, utilizing the internet communication [16, 17]. Moreover, cloud elucidations are utilized to help collaborative learning by employing PC advances.

Cloud computing encompasses three levels:

1. Infrastructure as a Service
2. Platform as a Service
3. Software as a Service

Contingent upon the prerequisites, the clients can pick one of the services given [18, 19].

Jones [20] enlisted the main features of cloud computing, refer to Figure 18.2:

1. **On-demand computing**
   Resources can be accessed on a click of a button or API call through AWS, Microsoft Azure, Google Cloud, and other public cloud platforms. These vendors envelop gigantic amounts of compute and storage assets, inside data centers everywhere throughout the world.

2. **Self-service provisioning**
   Self-service provisioning goes connected with on-demand computing. With self-service provisioning, in the need of new servers, developers are enabled to choose the assets and apparatuses and they need normally through a cloud supplier's self-administration portal and construct immediately.

3. **Resource pooling**
   To accommodate more clients simultaneously, multi-tenant architectures are relied upon in public cloud providers.

4. **Scalability**
   Asset pooling empowers adaptability for cloud suppliers and clients in light of the fact that computation, storage, and system administration resources can be included or evacuated according to the need.

5. **Pay-per-use pricing**
   Pay-per-use pricing has shifted IT spending from Capex to Opex, as suppliers offer per-second charging.

6. **Resiliency**
   Cloud providers and suppliers provide security by using number of methods.

Figure 18.2 Cloud computing. Source: Researchers.

7. **Security**
   Cloud computing has been said as "the cloud is a security asset". For security purposes, metrics system is being used.

18.4   Artificial Intelligence in Learning

"Know then thyself, presume not God to scan; The proper study of mankind is man." Alexander Pope, An Essay on Man, 1733

18.4.1   What is Artificial Intelligence?

Renowned researchers who had written largely sold books on intelligence, namely, Gardner [21], Gardner [22], and Gardner [23], had defined the word Intelligence as follows.

Intelligence is a blend of the competence to:

1. Learn: To gain proficiency with a wide range of casual and formal learning.
2. Facade problems: To perceive issue circumstances and changing them into all the more visibly characterized issues.
3. Solve problems: To take care of issues and finishing tasks [24].

"Artificial intelligence is the study of making machines does things that would require insight, whenever done by men" [25].

"AI is the computer-based exploration of methods for solving tricky tasks, conventionally being depended on people for its solution. The tasks include multifaceted logical inferences, diagnosis, visual recognitions, comprehension of normal language, game playing, rationalization, and plannings" [26].

The world is witnessing unprecedented technological advancements in the field of data and communication technology transforming us and point of view of the world in an unbelievable manner. The innovative technological advancements while improving nature of our life have likewise carried various confrontations. The world has turned into a (global) town [27]. This perspective has present before some dreadful confrontations due to the under mentioned reality:

- The business patterns, rivalry, and hi-tech advancement are changing at a regularly expanding pace.
- There is exponential escalation of information at a regularly expanding pace.

- The worldwide social worries for opportunity and personal satisfaction.
- Demand for widespread access open doors for pertinent and quality training.
- Demand for widespread access open doors for pertinent and quality training.

For the above-mentioned confrontations, it is essential countrywide to provide means for mass learning/education to at least, its working-age group, outfitted with refreshed desired aptitudes for monetary and logical exercises.

Delivery of the learning content and preparing the majority on vast scope for financial endurance and meeting the dynamism of the general public, the customary arrangement of training dependent on conventional pattern of education would not work. The World Wide Web (WWW) can be a boon for extemporizing correspondence, joint effort, contribution in resources, advancing vigorous learning, and instructions in remote learning. Remote learning, E-learning, and Virtual education might be the ideal arrangements. The point of AI in E-learning is to smoothen the savvy programming to display human conduct, learning, characteristic language, non-monotonic thinking, arranging, and conclusion, thinking under vulnerability and ordered thinking.

A survey by eSchool News reveals that the percent usage of AI while delivering training modules in the industry will enhance by 47.5% through 2021. It is being an elating time in the realm of E-learning. Innovation is continually developing and adjusting to improve everyday productivity, making our lives simpler. New devices enable us to interface from around the world and overpass cracks when they show up.

18.4.2   AI En Routed the Learning

18.4.2.1   Smart Learning Content

The idea of savvy content is a chic subject now as AI can make advanced content with a similar level of linguistic inclination as their human twin. They can be conceptualized from digitized guides of course readings while in transit adaptable to learning digital interfaces and are being presented at all levels from basic to present auxiliary on the professional workplaces.

We can utilize this in an association as AI can consolidate the content of messy guides into increasingly edible examination guides with easy course of action and flash cards. By far, digital curriculum can be designed using smart learning content over an assortment of gadgets, including video, sound, and an online aide.

18.4.2.2   Intelligent Tutoring Systems

Artificial intelligence can supplement more than consolidating a talk into cheat sheets by assuming a job of a tutor for a student for the difficulties he is confronted with. This is known as "Mastery Learning". It supports the adequacy of individualized mentoring and guidance in the homeroom.

Keen coaching frameworks use information from explicit students to give them the criticism and work with them straightforwardly. For example, an Intelligent Tutoring system called "SHERLOCK" is being utilized to encourage air power professionals to analyze electrical framework issues in an airplane. Further propelled form of Intelligent Tutoring System is avatar-based training modules, developed by the University of Southern California for training military personnel being sent on international posts.

These platforms will in a little while be able to adapt to a wide variety of learning styles to help every educator and learner.

18.4.2.3   Virtual Facilitators and Learning Environments

With advent of AI, an actual lecturer may soon be replaced by a robot. Well, not exclusively! But we already have virtual human mentors and facilitators who can think and act like humans. But, how does a virtual facilitator think or act alike a human?

A new technology known as the "touchless technology" or "gesture recognition technology" provides virtual facilitators an ability to respond or act alike humans in a natural way, responding both verbal and nonverbal cues.

Smart learning environments and platforms employ AI, 3-D gaming, and computer animations to create realistic virtual characters and social interactions.

18.4.2.4   Content Analytics

Content analytics refers to AI (specifically machine learning) platforms that optimize learning modules. Through AI, content taught to the learners can be examined for maximum effect and optimized toward learners needs. Content analytics facilitate educators and content providers to just not create and manage their E-learning content but also gain important insights into learner progress and perceptive through a powerful set of analytics.

18.4.2.5   Paving New Learning Pathways in the Coming Decade

Learning is a domain largely governed by human-to-human interaction. The integration of AI has been slower to develop the necessary human-like attributes of receptivity, versatility, and understanding. Nevertheless, there are ample areas where AI's inherent strengths help fill high-need "gaps" in learning and teaching.

AI's ability to analyze large volume of data in real time and automatically provide new content or precise learning parameters helps congregate learners' need for continual, targeted practice and feedback. This enables teachers or trainers to better understand the learner's performance and devise more effective personalized learning plans.

18.5   Impact of Artificial Intelligence in Education (AIEd)

18.5.1   Will AI Take Over From Humans?

Artificial Intelligence's digital and dynamic nature likewise offers open doors for student commitment that cannot be found in regularly obsolete archives or in the fixed condition.

Values, norms, and language have advanced in the course of the most recent eight decades. What has continued as before, notwithstanding, was the dread of the automation. Herbert Simon had spoken in 1956, what various onlookers were convinced of by then "Machines will be proficient, inside twenty years, of accomplishing all work a man can do", and later, those new progressions would make various occupations out of date. Now, we are utilizing PCs in our basic life, at workplace, bank, on travel, and basically requesting meal on drive. Are we considering the occupations which are vanished over to the usage of these PCs and machines? We never again dread the PC that Professor Simon feared, yet something progressively significant: man-made consciousness (AI) or the limit of machines to make forecasts, utilizing a lot of information to take activities in mind boggling, unstructured situations [28].

Intelligent digital assistants, for example, "Google Assistant" who are assigned for arrangements via telephone are nevertheless one potential utilization of AI [29]. Dialogue and picture acknowledgement, natural language handling, and figure interpretation through machine conspicuously are key regions of improvement through AI. Dynamically advanced applications incorporate clinical master frameworks to diagnose and analyze patients' pathologies (medtech), robotized survey of legitimate agreements to design bags (LawTech), and self-driving vehicles or trucks. Without a doubt, even imaginative expressions, a region clearly explicit to individuals is experiencing duplication of uses in AI, from PCs making new bits out of music to work of art in the style of a Rembrandt. In that capacity, AI is substituting mental endeavors rather than substantial ones [30].

Regardless of whether this will remain constant even with quickly creating AI is challenge. A verifiable view gives proof that mechanical change has consistently carried with it a large group of new jobs that we are unable to have recently anticipated or envisioned. We take a hopeful position and accept that AIEd is believed to take a key job in the later phase of educational system restructuring.

Whether or not AI will supplant people will stay a point being talked about. It is the recognizable dread that will school teachers be substituted by AI advancements in the period to come. With the time innovations, we can be sure that AI and humans will be expected to oversee various parts of students' academic and social competencies. It is measured that AI will probably not supplant however will fill in as an emotionally supportive network to the human master. A chronicle gives verification that mechanical change has reliably conveyed with it a huge gathering of new openings that we were unable to foresee or imagine.

18.5.2 AI-Implanted E-Learning

The objective of AIEd is to "make computationally exact and precise types of instructional, psychological, and social knowledge which are regularly left implied" [31]. A large number of AIEd-driven applications are, as of now being, used in the institutes and colleges. AIEd and instructive information mining (EDM) methods are blended to "track" the practices of understudies—for instance, gathering information on class participation and task accommodation so as to distinguish (and offer help) to understudies who are in danger of dumping their investigations.

18.5.2.1 *Avatars*

Avatars are powerful and attractive learning agents capable of transforming a dull subject into a fascinating one. Avatars are competent for showing the six "universal" outward appearances of feeling: happiness, surprise, anger, fear, sadness, and disgust [32], creating a replica of how their human personas interact with others in realities. An added hypothesis to this would be brilliantly designed cyber suits that are shaped as human bodies and talented to fix our physical issues in real life, thus facilitating our guaranteed advancements [33].

Avatars are combination of face-to-face learning aided with computer-based technology, playing the role of mentor, friend, and guide, earning an emotional contact with learners. Immense studies are evident in the zone of robotics, and applications of robotics being functional in assembling, clinical systems, portability gear, and in old age homes are apparent.

Shimohara [34] overviewed the preliminary rapport between human and ALife (Autonomous Intelligent Artificial Life - coupled with Internet) comparable to the rapport of humans to pet.

18.5.2.2   Hyper-Reality

One of the mechanical stages that could help change educating and learning in colleges of things to come is Hyper-Reality. Hyper-Reality is characterized as a state wherein what is genuine and what is fiction are mixed so that there is blur line of difference between ones closure and another's start. Terashima and Tiffin [35] conceptualized Hyper-Reality (HR) as a mechanical stage to mingle augmented reality with physical reality and Artificial Intelligence with human intelligence in a safe mode allowing association.

18.5.2.3   The Hyper Class in Virtual Universities

Hyper class is a Hyper-Reality–supported class that exists in virtual world. Hyper class is supported by Hyper-Reality which exists in real and virtual dimensions, allowing interaction of learners and instructors across the world in education. Student in the real world can either learn in conventional learning methods or through connecting to internet on PC, but with hyper class that is possible. Student and teachers can learn in conventional classes and can connect to internet and interact with other student and teachers across the globe. Hyper class has major advantage that any student who is having interest in some specific domain can interact with other students possessing the same subject interest, and through this, students can learn from different perspective and can enhance their knowledge.

As showed by [36], there are no mechanical cutoff points to the quantity of focuses and nations that can be associated together in a Hyper Class later on. Strauss [37] prophetically observed that while today for all intents and purposes, all web clients are people, and tomorrow clever gadgets working in light of a legitimate concern for people and organizations will order the Web. The world's first Hyper Class was viably coordinated in the year 2000 between Japan, New Zealand and Australia.

18.5.2.4   JITAITs

John Tiffin's book "The Global Virtual University" published in year 2003 conceptualized the possibility of just in time artificial intelligent tutors (JITAITs), and as the name recommends, it can be open at whatever point and wherever an understudy desires them and thus enhances pedagogy. JITAITs rely upon the idea of master frameworks. JITAITs are powerful within the limited areas, paradigmatic, and leaning toward basic reasoning. A JITAIT could henceforth be an expert mentor in regard to an issue that framed the space data on a synergy in Hyper-Reality, like the geometry subject matter in the science zone.

JITAITs enact personal tutors. JITAITs look for information, monitor student's track all through their course, and sort out the leanings for them. They are assigned with scheduling meeting, drafting emails, and coordinating work across the levels in the official frameworks. JITAITs utilize AI strategies to suggest personal human tutoring, conveying learning exercises that best matched to a learner's learning needs with all feedbacks, all this without an individual instructor being available.

For example: BUGGY [38], a system proposed to show fundamental expansion and subtraction, employed a model for the common mistakes by understudy. This "bug library" was used to break down the blunders, and an understudy made with the goal that suitable mentoring could be accessible.

For example: The iTake2Learn framework strengthens math learning for understudies matured 5 to 11 years of age.

18.5.3   Recommendations to Help Unleash Intelligence

AIEd is believed to take a key job in the later phase of educational system restructuring that would not occur by some coincidence. With this, we are moving toward the last segment of this chapter: the viables that ought to be followed now for the insight of AIEd to be unleashed. Refer the AIED dimensions in Figure 18.3.

Figure 18.3 AIEd dimensions. Source: Researchers.

The future capacity of AIEd to handle genuine difficulties in education relies upon how we go about the following measurements that is (a) requiring insightful advancements which epitomize our thinking toward incredible learning in (b) tempting purchaser grade items which (c) can be used sufficiently, taking everything into account, level that combines the best of brain and behavior.

18.5.3.1 Pedagogy

AIEd research has, until this point, for the most part handled the low-balancing product of instruction. For example: learning in exceptionally organized areas, for example, introductory mathematics or physics. These additions are basic; however, they are insufficient. If we have to achieve a deep-seated change in the learning for all understudies, we need to deal with the persevering and odd difficulties of 21st learning, and from this time forward, funders and researchers need to go further and progressively broad.

More or less, AIEd needs in any case the teaching method and be progressively yearning!

18.5.3.1.1 Recommendations

- Begin with the learning.
- Stay focus of the existing AIEd financing on the zones which are presumably going to pass on the deep-seated changes in learning that will make an actual effect.
- Scope out a progression of goal-oriented test prizes that start with bits of information.

18.5.3.2 Technology

AIEd is right now something of a small house industry, and innovations happen in little pockets and at unassuming scale, generally by specialists with restricted subsidizing and without business associations.

To comprehend this, setting up the structures, motivating forces, and subsidizing that will permit an ecosystem of advancement and cooperation to be made in the region of AIEd should be inferred.

18.5.3.2.1 Recommendations

- Build up the infrastructure that empowers advancement, and less activity in AIEd.

- Create smart demand for AIEd technologies. This would open required coordinated efforts between AIEd analysts and professional bodies.
- Find a DARPA (Defence Advanced Research Projects Agency) for training which can quicken the transformation of AIEd tools from the laboratory into reality.

18.5.3.3   System Change

AIEd should be employed in blended learning spaces where digital technologies and homeroom exercises supplement each other.

18.5.3.3.1   Recommendations

- Absorption of learners, instructors, and parents to make sure that potential AIEd frameworks address their issues.
- Take the subsequent stage to emphasize and wisely assess AIEd functionality in true settings.
- Create information benchmarks that organize both the involvement of information and the ethics fundamental for data usage.

18.6   Conclusion

Many facets may give the impression of like "science fiction", flipping the Web to disclose the prospect that is much closer as we presume. It does not indicate to offer responses yet proposes a potential philosophical establishment for a new paradigm in higher education. The essence of higher education is the creation, preparation, and spread and utilization of information where instructors help understudies to apply data to issues. There is a requirement of a novel route in higher education research, independent of interests and devoted to the question of globalization and value.

At last, to cite Lovelock who chains toward improving the University norm:

> "As a researcher, I have been a pioneer searching for new worlds, not a harvester from safe and productive fields, and life at the outskirts has given me that there are no convictions and that dogma is usually wrong [39]."

We ought to continue with our investigation into the fate of instruction that is significant to the growing new understudy desires in the information society.

Concise Summary

Amidst the current world situation subject to the Pandemic, existence is at risk. The only way towards education is technology-based learning opportunities or E-Learning. Touch screens or touching hearts; the soul beings of learning. The chapter envisage the possibility of a Hyper Class dependent on Hyper-Reality, a progressive form of appropriated virtual reality where physical reality and virtual reality and human intelligence and artificial intelligence intermesh and interface and cooperate to give anybody, anyplace, at wherever point learning, in which wisdom should be conceivable by Just in Time Artificially Intelligent Tutors (JITAITs) that will spring up when required. AIEd is believed to take a key job in the later phase of educational system restructuring.

It is apt in the concern: "Technology won't replace educators but educators who use technology will probably replace who do not".

References

1. Liu, Y. and Wang, H., A comparative study on e-learning technologies and products: from the East to the West. *Syst. Res. Behav. Sci.: Official Journal of the International Federation for Systems Research*, 26, 2, 191–209, 2009.
2. Lynch, T.D. and Lynch, C.E., Web-Based Education. *Innovation J.: Public Sector Innovation J.*, www.innovation.cc, 8, 4, 2, 2003.
3. Sheeba, T., Begum, S., Bernard, M., Semantic Web to E-learning Content. *Int. J. Adv. Res. Comput. Sci. Software Eng.*, 2, 10, 58–66, 2012.
4. Keegan, D., On Defining Distance Education. *Distance Educ.*, 1, 1, 13–36, 1980.
5. Larson, L., *Web 4.0: The Era of Online Customer Engagement*, 2012, Published January 5, 2012, http://www.business2community.com/online-marketing/web-4-0-the-era-of-online-customerengagement-0113733.
6. Dominic, M., Francis, S., Pilomenraj, A., E-learning in web 3.0. *Int. J. Mod. Educ. Comput. Sci.*, 6, 2, 8, 2014.
7. Van Looy, A., Definitions, Social Media Types, and Tools, in: *Social Media Management*, pp. 21–47, Springer, Cham, 2016.
8. DeCoufle, B., The impact of cloud computing on schools. *Data Cent. J.*, 50–56, 2009.

9.   Amit, A., *Web 3.0 concepts explained in plain English*, Labnol. org., 2009.
10. Dan, F., From semantic Web (3.0) to the WebOS (4.0). *Int. J. Web Semant. Technol. (IJWesT)*, 3, 1, 2012, http://www.zdnet.com/blog/btl/from-semantic-web-30to-the-webos-40/4499/.
11. Lashkari, Y., Metral, M., Maes, P., Collaborative Interface Agents, in: *Proceedings of the 12th National Conference on Artificial Intelligence*, AAAI Press, Seattle, WA, pp. 444–450, 1994.
12. Crabtree, I.B., Soltysiak, S.J., Thint, M.P., Adaptive personal agents. *Pers. Technol.*, 2, 3, 141–151, 1998.
13. Alsetoohy, O., Ayoun, B., Arous, S., Megahed, F., Nabil, G., Intelligent agent technology: what affects its adoption in hotel food supply chain management? *J. Hosp. Tour. Technol.*, 10, 3, 2019.
14. Nedeva, V. and Dineva, S., New learning innovations with Web 4.0, in: *Proceedings of the 7th International Conference on Virtual Learning (ICVL)*, Bucharest, Romania, pp. 316–321, 2012.
15. Mell, P. and Grance, T., *The NIST definition of cloud computing*, pp. 20899–8930, NIST Special Publication 800-145, National Institute of Standards and Technology, Gaithersburg, MD, 2011.
16. Weiss, A., Computing in the clouds. *networker*, 11, 4, 16–25, 2007.
17. Carlin, S. and Curran, K., Cloud computing technologies. *Int. J. Cloud Comput. Serv. Sci.*, 1, 2, 59, 2012.
18. Creeger, M., CTO roundtable: cloud computing. *Queue*, 7, 5, 1–2, 2009.
19. Pocatilu, P., Alecu, F., Vetrici, M., Using cloud computing for E-learning systems, in: *Proceedings of the 8th WSEAS international conference on Data networks, communications, computers*, 2009, November, vol. 9, No. 1, World Scientific and Engineering Academy and Society (WSEAS).Psom.blogspot.com, pp. 54–59.
20. Jones, T., *Search Cloud Computing*, 2019, July 15, Retrieved March 07, 2020, from https://searchcloudcomputing.techtarget.com/:https://searchcloudcomputing.techtarget.com/feature/7-key-characteristics-of-cloud-computing.
21. Gardner, H., *Multiple intelligences: The theory into practice*, basic books, New York, 1993.
22. Perkins, D., *Outsmarting IQ: The emerging science of learnable intelligence*, The Free PressGardner, NY, 1995, Howard, *Multiple intelligences: The theory in practice*, Basic Books, NY, 1993.
23. Sternberg, R., *The triarchic mind: A new theory of human intelligence*, Penguin Books, NY, 1988, Information about Sternberg and his writings is available at http://www.psy.pdx.edu/PsiCafe/KeyTheorists/Sternberg.htm.
24. Moursund, D.G., *Brief introduction to educational implications of Artificial Intelligence*, David Moursund, University of Oregon, 2006.
25. Minsky, M., Steps toward artificial intelligence. *Proceedings of the IRE, IEEE*, 49 1, 8–30, 1961.

26. Horvitz, E., *Automated reasoning for biology and medicine*, Johns Hopkins University Press, 1993, Napa Valley, California, September 1990, http://research.microsoft.com/~horvitz/AIBIO.HTM.

27. Harasini, L. *et al.*, The Virtual University: A State of the Art. *Adv. Comput.*, 55, 1–47, 2001.

28. Agrawal, A.K., Gans, J.S., Goldfarb, A., *Prediction Machines: The Simple Economics of Artificial Intelligence*, Harvard Business Review Press, Boston, MA, 2018. *Economic Policy for Artificial Intelligence*. NBER Working Paper No. 24690, National Bureau of Economic Research, Cambridge, MA.

29. *Organisation for Economic Co-operation and Development*, Digital Economy Outlook, Paris, 2017.

30. Ernst, E., Merola, R., Samaan, D., Economics of Artificial Intelligence: Implications for the Future of Work. *IZA J. Labor Policy*, 9, 1, 1–35, 2019.

31. Self, J., The Defining Characteristics of Intelligent Tutoring Systems Research: ITSs Care, Precisely. *Int. J. Artif. Intell. Educ. (IJAIEd)*, 10, 350–364, 1999.

32. Ekman, P., Hager, J.C., Friesen, W.V., The symmetry of emotional and deliberate facial actions. *Psychophysiology*, 18, 2, 101–106, 1981.

33. Drexler, E.K., *Engines of Creation*, Fourth Estate, London, UK, 1996.

34. Shimohara, K., Artificial Life in HyperReality, in: *Hyperreality Paradigm For The Third Millenium*, Dalam Tiffin, J. (Ed.), 2001.

35. Terashima, N. and Tiffin, J. (Eds.), *Hyperreality: Paradigm for the third millenium*, Routledge, London, 2001.

36. Tiffin, J. and Terashima, N. (Eds.), *Hyperreality: Paradigm for the third millenium*, Psychology Press, London, 2001.

37. Strauss, H., *The future of the web, intelligent devices and education*, Educause Review, 1999, United States, January/February 2007.

38. Brown, J.S. and Burton, R.R., Diagnostic Models for Procedural Bugs in Basic Mathematical Skills. *Cognit. Sci.*, 2, 155–191, 1978.

39. Lovelock, J., *Homage to Gaia; the life of an independent scientist*, Oxford University Press, Oxford, 2000.

  - Bhuasiri, W., Xaymoungkhoun, O., Zo, H., Rho, J.J., Ciganek, A.P., Critical success factors for E-learning in developing countries: A comparative analysis between ICT experts and faculty. *Comput. Educ.*, 58, 2, 843–855, 2012.

  - Boud, D., Cohen, R., Walker, D., *Using experience for learning*, McGraw-Hill Education (UK), 1993.

  - Dent, L., Boticario, J., McDermott, J. *et al.*, A Personal Learning Apprentice, in: *Proceedings of the 10th National Conference on Artificial Intelligence*, AAAI Press, San Jose, California, pp. 96–103, 1992.

  - Goralski, M.A. and Tan, T.K., Artificial intelligence and sustainable development. *Int. J. Manage. Educ.*, 18, 1, 100330, 2020.

- Harasini, L. *et al.*, The Virtual University: A State of the Art. *Adv. Comput.*, 55, 1–47, 2001.
- https://prezi.com/
- https://www.elearningark.com/mobile-technology-within-higher-education/
- Luckin, R., Holmes, W., Griffiths, M., Forcier, L.B., *Intelligence Unleashed: An argument for AI in Education*, Pearson Education, London, 2016.
- McArthur, D., Lewis, M.W., Bishay, M., *The Roles of Artificial Intelligence in Education: Current Progress and Future Prospects*, RAND, Santa Monica, CA. DRU- 472-NSF.—1993, 2004.
- McArthur, D., Lewis, M., Bishary, M., The roles of artificial intelligence in education: current progress and future prospects. *J. Educ. Technol.*, 1, 4, 42–80, 2005.
- Mircea, M. and Andreescu, A.I., Using cloud computing in higher education: A strategy to improve agility in the current financial crisis. *Commun. IBIMA*, 2011.
- Moursund, D.G., *Brief introduction to educational implications of Artificial Intelligence*, 2006.
- Nedeva, V. and Dineva, S., New learning innovations with Web 4.0, in: *Proceedings of the 7th International Conference on Virtual Learning (ICVL)*, Bucharest, Romania, pp. 316–321, 2012.
- One example of this type of virtual agent can be found in Betty's Brain (http://www.teachableagents.org/research/bettysbrain.php), a computer-based learning environment developed at Vanderbilt University.
- Rajasingham, L., *The Impact of Artificial Intelligence (AI) Systems on Future University Paradigms*, Victoria University of Wellington Wellington, New Zealand, 2009.
- Rana, H. and Lal, M., E-learning: Issues and challenges. *Int. J. Comput. Appl.*, 97, 5, 2014.
- Retrieved from http://www.italk2learn.eu
- Rhodes, B.J. and Starner, T., Remembrance Agent: A continuously running automated information, 1996.
- Rosenberg, M.J., *Beyond E-learning: Approaches and Technologies to Enhance Organizational Knowledge, Learning and Performance*, 2006.
- Rosenberg, M.J. and Foshay, R., E-learning: Strategies for delivering knowledge in the digital age. *Perform. Improv.*, 41, 5, 50–51, 2002.
- Silverman, L.K., Global Learners: Our Forgotten Gifted Children. *7Th World Conference on Gifted and Talented Children*, Salt lake City, UT, 1987.

19

Artificial Intelligence in Banking Industry

GarimaKaneria

Indian Council of Social Science Research (ICSSR), Department of Banking & Business Economics, University College of Commerce & Management Studies, Mohanlal Sukhadia University, Udaipur, Rajasthan, India

Abstract

The most impacted industry by artificial intelligence (AI) is none other than the banking industry. Banks are adopting new technologies for higher boon potentialities and to provide services to the young customers of the society. For each and every operations performed by the bank from sales to accounting to contracts and cyber security, AI is helping in transforming banking day by day. The present chapter defines the role of AI in shaping the banking industry, why these new technologies are highly adaptable by the banking sector, what is its impact on Indian banking, and pros and cons of adopting these techniques by the various bank. AI has made life of the people easier not only of the customer but also of the employees who are working for the banks. The old traditional manual banking has been now transformed into the new technology-based automatic banking with easy access to all the services 24*7 and 365 days. Almost all the banks are using their AI-based chatbots such as Sia [5], Baroda Brainy, Digital Lab, EVA, and emPower.

Keywords: Artificial Intelligence (AI), banking, chatbots

19.1   Introduction

Reality of today's world is "application of artificial intelligence". AI is impacting our lives beyond imagination. There is nothing to deny with if we say that it has become an integral part of our lives. Basically, there are three advanced technologies which are combined together as a part of

Email: Kaneriagarima@gmail.com

S. Balamurugan, Sonal Pathak, Anupriya Jain, Sachin Gupta, Sachin Sharma, Sonia Duggal (eds.)
Impact of Artificial Intelligence on Organizational Transformation, (327–348) © 2022 Scrivener Publishing LLC

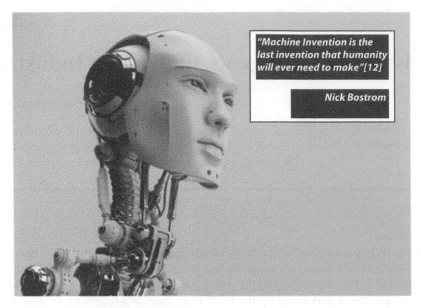

"Machine Invention is the last invention that humanity will ever need to make"[12]

Nick Bostrom

Figure 19.1 Artificial intelligence and machine. Wohl, B. (2017, March 16). How Artificial Intelligence and the robotic revolution will change the workplace of tomorrow. The Conversation. https://theconversation.com/how-artificial-intelligence-and-the-robotic-revolution-will-change-the-workplace-of-tomorrow-72607

artificial intelligence (AI), *viz.*, machine learning (ML), natural language processing, and cognitive computing [4]. What actually AI does is simulation of human intelligence into artificial machines (Figure 19.1). The motive behind this simulation is to speed up the given tasks.

Banks have a very important role to play, in developing the economic lifestyles of the present day society. It acts as a backbone of an economy as it is related with cash dealings, credit agreements, and other monetary affairs. Primary function of bank is to motivate and encourage people to save and earn interest on their savings. This encouragement which bank receives in form of saving is used as a financial assistance for many big industries. Bank plays vital role in the developing various sectors of economic system. Thus, all the financial transactions must be properly documented [6]. The smooth operation of almost all the transactions of banking world can be easily performed with the help of AI. As the name itself indicates, AI refers to the acquiring and making use of natural competencies and knowledge and this capability of copying something is achieved via a system or computer. This capacity to imitate human mind by means of questioning itself is referred to as AI. AI makes a speciality of creating such machines which thinks and acts like a human being. Not only computers, but term can be used for any gadget that reveals human mind trends such as learning and resolving the problems.

Banks are adopting new and improved techniques for better boon potentialities and to provide better services to the customers of new age within the society. For each and every operations performed by the bank from sales to accounting to contracts and cyber security, AI are helping in transforming banking day by day. As in line with the report of IHS Markit on "Artificial Intelligence in Banking", the business cost of AI in banking sector is projected to reach $300 billion by 2030 [1, 8].

19.2   Banking on Artificial Intelligence

Everything in the market revolves around the customer and when we talk about service sector, the key area which plays a vital role is customer service. Rushed working hours, fixed business timings, lack of availability of staffs, and busy schedule have disrupted the customer service. All these things lead to dissatisfaction among the customers and thus affect banker customer relationship [16]. To all these problems, AI has become an only solution [21].

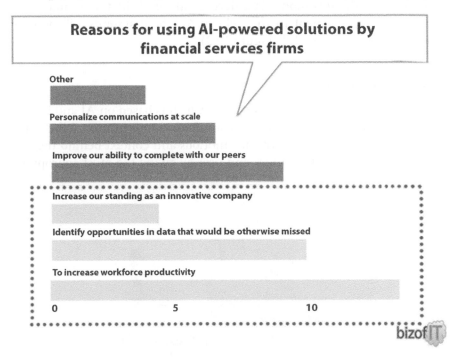

Figure 19.2 Reasons for AI-powered solution used in banking firms [2]. Source: http://www.analyticsvidhya.com/blog/2017/04/5-ai-applications-in-banking-to-look-out-for-in-next-5-years/. Mangnani, D., 5 AI applications in Banking to look out for in next 5 years, Analytics Vidhya, 2017, April 28, https://www.analyticsvidhya.com/blog/2017/04/5-ai-applications-in-banking-to-look-out-for-in-next-5-years/.

In recent years, the industry which is most impacted by AI is none other than the banking industry. It is quite challenging for the organizations working in this sector to cope up with the competition arising out of changing technologies. Figure 19.2 shows the reasons behind adopting AI within the banking industry.

19.3   Role of Artificial Intelligence in Shaping Indian Banking Industry

19.3.1   Detection of Anti-Money Laundering Pattern

Anti-money laundering refers to set of legal rules and guidelines that are designed to forestall the practices of earning creation through unauthorized sources or acts.

Most of the banks were shifted from traditional rule-based banking system to artificial machine–based banking software which is more intelligent in figuring out the anti-money laundering patterns. With the coming year's continuous improvement in the field of AI, these systems will become more exact and accurate [7] (Figure 19.3).

19.3.2   Chatbots

Chatbots are self-regulating chat system which is based on AI and is used in simulation of human chats without any human intervention. What actually they do is identification of the emotions and context behind the text chat and responding the human end user by giving the most appropriate

Figure 19.3 Anti-money laundering and AI. Ostos, G. F. A. A. R. (2020, August 27). Anti-Money Laundering in Financial Services: A Primer. Corporate Compliance Insights. https://www.corporatecomplianceinsights.com/aml-financial-services-lines-of-defense/

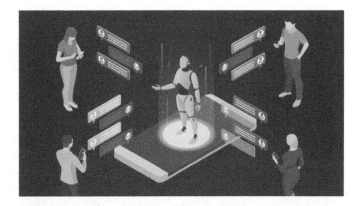

Figure 19.4 Automated chat system. E. (2021, March 10). Best 25 Raspberry Pi 4 Projects in 2020. PCB Assembly, PCB Manufacturing, PCB Design - OURPCB. https://www. ourpcb.com/raspberry-pi.html

explanation or reply. With time, massive data related to the behavior and habit of the used is collected by these chatbots which further helps to understand the wants and state of mind of the end users. They are amply used within the banking industry in order to reform and to deal with customer relationship management at personal level. Google has released "ALLO" as a usual awareness of chatbots [18] (Figure 19.4).

19.3.3   Algorithmic Trading

Across the world, plenty of excessive end structures are utilized by the hedge funds to deploy AI models to learn the versions of changes in financial

Figure 19.5 The rise of algorithm trading. Putnins, M. N. A. T. (2016, November 30). The good, the bad, and the ugly of algorithmic trading. Phys Org. https://phys.org/news/2016-11-good-bad-ugly-algorithmic.html

markets to make investment decisions (Figure 19.5). Trading opportunities and decisions are taken on the basis of inputs received by using different automated AI strategies. Two Sigma, Winton Capital Management, and Ketchum Trading are the most active hedge funds that are being used.

19.3.4   Fraud Detection

Fraud detection is the only field which has received a massive boost in the field of AI because it has provided with the best of its results with cent percent accuracy. This is an important area of the banking sector where AI has outstripped. Falcon Fraud Assessment System is one of the techniques which are used in fraud detection by the banking industry. This field of AI has come a long way and is expected to grow high in near future [19] (Figure 19.6).

19.3.5   Customer Suggestions

Suggestion engines used by the banking industry are the major contribution of AI in this sector. Bank offers or recommends its consumer varied banking products such as debit cards, credit cards, and investment avenues based on the past available data of the user. In recent times, recommendation engines have played a very important role in successful revenue growth by the major banks. These recommendations are based on big data and faster computation machines combined with accurate AI algorithms.

19.3.6   Personalized Banking

Every industry considers customer experience as an integral part of their organization. Today's generation expects a digital experience as the whole

Figure 19.6 Fraud detection and AI.

Figure 19.7 Personalized banking and AI.

world is becoming digital today. The pillar, on which the concept of digitalization is based, is AI, and with the help of AI, banks are providing personalized banking experience to its customers in form of mobile banking, internet banking, and e-mail communication. These services by banks from alerts on transactions to direct bill payments to third party services, etc., has contributed in making the economy a digital economy (Figure 19.7).

19.3.7   Digital Payments

As per Credit Suisse Report, Digital Payment in India will reach $ 1 Trillion by 2023 [3]. Despite of the rise in platforms for online payment

Figure 19.8 Digital banking. Agarwal, M. (2019, December 16). What Are The Most Interesting Fintech Business Models? Inc42 Media. https://inc42.com/features/what-are-the-most-interesting-fintech-business-models/

Figure 19.9 Robo advisors for investments. Can Robo-Advisors change investment behaviour to achieve your financial goals? (2016, June 24). Brighttalk. https://www.brighttalk.com/webcast/1570/204337/can-robo-advisors-change-investment-behaviour-to-achieve-your-financial-goals

(Figure 19.8), AI and ML-based solutions have changed the payment platform more safe and secure [10].

19.3.8   Robo Advisors

A digital platform which provides automated investment services with less or without human supervision is basically what we call robo advisors. Based on some mathematical algorithms, they act as a financial advisor. These algorithms works on the basis of software, and thus, it does not require any or little human intervention. They provides services by considering various aspects such as risk bearing capacity, expectations related to return, objective behind investment, and analysis of product or investment options (Figure 19.9).

19.4   Influence of Artificial Intelligence on Indian Banking Industry

From improved banking operations to introduction of innovative products and services, AI has played an important role. With the improvement and enhancement of system age banks need to compete with upstart Fintech Platform which might be benefiting by the improved technology that from time to time changing human workers with algorithms. To stabilize their role in this competitive world, banking sector requires to embrace AI and to indulge itself toward their business strategy. Some of the AI system includes robotics, computer vision, and ML.

Entering of banking industry within the new age banking through AI has resulted into bulk pressure on numerous states of affairs and targets. For a current technological and digital disruption, follow-ups in AI are nearing in pace of time, and for the control of this effect, it becomes important to make some adjustments and experiences which includes the following:

- Hiring of chief AI officer by growing and hedging banks in the course of investigation process in AI labs and incubators.
- To boom the use of AI-powered banking chatbots so as to increase the accuracy.
- Considering all investment products, best among them should be provided for personal investment purpose.
- To offer help to skilled personnel and robots while dealing with positive choice making aspects, diverse banks, and their collaborations are scaling in the direction of in-house solutions which are generally credited for sophisticated ontologies, probabilistic reasoning algorithms, system learning, pattern recognition, and natural language processing.

Furthermore, various functions related to this field consist of following:

- Automation of procedures through use of choice support and superior algorithms which feel cognitive in nature.
- Improved and enhanced self-studying and understanding competencies to incorporate approach to the problems.
- Developing predictive analysis or sophisticated cognitive hypothesis generation.

Speaking about the today's banking situation, it is facing hardships to reduce the costs, scale to targeted margins and accomplishing the demands of the consumer, and still look forward to more tight experiences and easiness. So, use of AI with such a high costs has become crucial these days. In the survey held by the National Business Research Institute, it was seen that approximately 32% of financial institutions use AI via predictive analysis and voice recognition. Banking sector requires high stake of credit from AI to initiate its business in order to fulfill the improved needs of the developing economy and applications facing society. The AI-based services and products offered by the banks to the society are achieving a strong reach of development. Banks also need to keep a watch on their security and risk management techniques.

19.5   Reasons Behind Elongated Adoption of Artificial Intelligence in Banking Industry

There are varied reasons for extensively adopting AI in the banking industry; some of them are as follows [20]:

19.5.1   Cut-Throat Competition in Banking Sector

There is an immense competition among the all the banks working in an economy. Transformation in technology and operation pattern by one bank encourages another bank to bring something new to the customers in order to meet their growing needs and demands.

19.5.2   Push for Process-Driven Services

All banks declare that they are customer focused and want to provide a customer with best experiences while using the services provided by them. But this is only half way as the number of customers they are dealing with is so large that it is not possible for them to provide personal service to each and every customer. So, they focus on process driven banking.

19.5.3   Introduction of Self-Service at Banks

Self-service banking is a type of banking where the financial transaction such as deposits, withdrawal, transfer, bill payment, and loan is performed by the customer himself by using self-service equipments.

19.5.4   Customer Demand for More Customized Solutions

Bank offers or recommends its consumer various banking products such as debit cards, credit cards, and investment avenues based on the past available data of the user. The past available data can be used to customize the products as per the needs and the preferences of the customer.

19.5.5   Creating Operational Efficiencies

AI has helped banking sector to improve their operational efficiency and to get a clear understanding regarding actually where they are going and what they are doing.

19.5.6   Increasing Employee Productivity

AI has become more popular at workplace as this has helped in increasing the efficiency and productivity of the organization. AI has made the employees free, and thus, they can concentrate on more important tasks which may lead to the growth of the business.

19.5.7   To Help Focus on Profitability and Compliance

AI helps in increasing productivity which in turn helps in improving the profitability of the organization. As the tasks are performed by the software, human mind can focus on other important aspects which in turn improve the profitability and compliance.

19.5.8   Use of Robotics Software

Robo advisors can be defined as a digital platform which deals in automated investment services with least or no human interventions. On the basis of some mathematical algorithms, they operate as Financial consultant. the reason behind least or no human intervention is, use of softwares on whose basis algorithm works. Various aspects are considered while providing the services like risk bearing capacity, return related expectations, investment objectives, product analysis or investment options.

19.5.9   To Reduce Fraud and Risk Associated With Security

This is the key area of the banking sector where AI has outstripped. Falcon Fraud Assessment System is one of the techniques, which is used in fraud detection by the banking industry. This area has come a long way and is anticipated to grow high in the close future.

19.5.10   To Manage Large Information and Derive Value Insight

With the time, huge information associated with the conduct and addiction of the used is accumulated through these chatbots which in addition enables to apprehend the desires and moods of the end users. They are amply utilized by the banking industry for reformation of customer relationship management at personal level.

19.5.11   To Bring in Effective Decision-Making

The physical tasks are done with automation with the assist of AI. It facilitates in faster appearing of tasks as nicely as higher selection making with none human intervention.

19.6   Indian Banks Using Artificial Intelligence

As in step with the joint research conducted by National Business Research Institute and Narrative Science, it was concluded that approximately 32% of the financial services carriers are already using AI technology like predictive analysis and voice recognition. There are many banks operating in an economy in order to be able to satisfy the demands of the distinctive sections of the society. Out of those banks, there are 12 Indian banks that have won media interest over the previous few years for the tasks taken by using them to adopt AI. The list consists of the following [9]:

1. State Bank of India (SBI)
2. Bank of Baroda (BOB)
3. Allahabad Bank
4. Andhra Bank
5. YES Bank
6. Housing Development Finance Corporation (HDFC)
7. Industrial Credit and Investment Corporation of India (ICICI)
8. Axis Bank
9. Canara Bank
10. City Union Bank
11. Punjab National Bank (PNB)
12. IndusInd Bank

19.6.1   State Bank of India

AI-based solution named "Code for Bank", developed through Chapdex who's the triumphing crew from its first countrywide hackathon, is utilized by State Bank of India. Sia Chatbots, an AI powered chat assistant advanced by Payjo, is used by SBI on its front desk. It works simply as a financial institution representative in addressing customer enquiries right away and enables them to carry out their daily transactions with ease [17].

19.6.2   Bank of Baroda

Robot named Baroda Brainy and Digital Lab with unfastened Wi-Fi services is utilized by the Bank of Baroda as a hi-tech virtual branch ready with superior AI gadgets.

19.6.3   Allahabad Bank

An app named "emPower" is utilized by the Allahabad Bank to get important improvements like chatbots and AI-based e-trade payments.

19.6.4   Andhra Bank

AI Chatbot integrated with core banking servers of Andhra Bank had been launched with the aid of Float bot that is a Bengaluru-based AI startup. It turned into released to automate and have interactions with its 5 crore customers digitally. Another chatbot is likewise developed with the aid of float bot to automate the on boarding training for its 20,000 internal employees.

19.6.5   YES Bank

"YES mPower", a banking chatbot for its credit (loan) product, turned into released via YES Bank in partnership with Gupshup. "YES ROBOT" became another AI product which was released to reply the bank associated queries of the customer anytime and anywhere without any waiting or search online. YES Bank changed into the first bank who introduced chatbot primarily based on banking inside the call of "YES TAG" in April 2016. This AI technology permits the customer to carry out the banking transactions on numerous social messengers.

19.6.6   Housing Development Finance Corporation (HDFC)

An AI-based chatbot "EVA" was launched by the HDFC Bank which was built by Bengaluru-based Senseforth AI Research. This chatbot gathers information from various sources and respond to the question in less than 0.4 seconds and also able to deal with the real banking transactions. HDFC Banks has also released a prototype robot IRA (Intelligent Robotic Assistant) which is an in-store robotic application [17].

19.6.7   Industrial Credit and Investment Corporation of India (ICICI)

It has released robotic software in 200+ commercial enterprise approaches across numerous features of the company. It is an AI-based in-house creation primarily based on features like facial and voice recognition, natural language processing, ML, and bots among others. The software program robots at ICICI financial institution facilitates to capture and interpret facts from the system, apprehend sample, and run +commercial enterprise processes across multiple applications to execute activities. iPal is some other AI primarily based chatbot that provides solution to the queries and facilitates in financial transactions.

19.6.8   Axis Bank

An AI primarily based app became released by means of the axis bank which hallows its customers to deal with financial and non-monetary operations, answering the queries and different product associated facts. This app uses natural language processing to permit conversational banking.

19.6.9   Canara Bank

It has released robots named Mitra and Candi. "Mitra" is a humanoid robot which enables customers to navigate the financial institution and this robot was turned to be developed via invento robotics that's Bengaluru-based company. On the alternative hand "Candi" became advanvced to supplement human Resource however it turned to be quite smaller than Mitra.

19.6.10   Punjab National Bank

To enhance the audit system, it has implemented an AI primarily based technique in account reconciliation in addition to the usage of analytics; however, this move does not worked because of the fraud carried out by Nirav Modi and Mehul Chowksi of about 20,000 crores rupees which has paralyzed the banking operations for a short period.

19.6.11   IndusInd Bank

Alexa Skill and Indus Assist were the AI-based apps developed by the bank with the help of which consumers can operate their financial and non-financial banking transactions.

19.6.12   City Union Bank

Lakshmi, a banking robot which can interact with customers on more than 125 topics was launched by a City Union Bank. This robot also connects with core banking solutions apart from interacting and responding to the questions of the consumers.

19.7   Pros and Cons of Artificial Intelligence in Banking Sector

19.7.1   Pros

19.7.1.1   Tracking of Transactional and Other Data Sources

With the assistance of AI technology, the expenditure pattern of its customer can be easily understood by the banks and by using the data, and it can offer customized investment plans to its customers. By keeping a check on the data related to expenses and investment, it is easy to understand the behavior of the consumer and their preferences which can help in improving their experience by offering such customized products which can fulfill their needs and requirements [15].

19.7.1.2   Identification of Pattern Which May Be Eluded by Human Observers

AI can help in collection of massive data and identifying the pattern which might not be observed by a human observer. An AI and ML solution enables financial carrier companies in real-time fraud detection. AI allows bank to access customer data on the basis of widely used tolls such as online banking and mobile banking and can integrate and analyze these data for customer recommendations.

19.7.1.3   Risk Assessment

Accuracy and confidentiality are very important during risk assessment process while giving loans. With the assistance of AI, it becomes quite easier to handle this complex process as AI helps in collecting and analyzing the data related to prospective borrower. This data is then analyzed on market trends and most recent financial activity of the borrower to access the potential risk in giving loan.

19.7.1.4   Secure and Swift Transaction

On the basis of behaviors analysis, the suspicious activity in customers account can be detected through a mobile app. Bank must be able to provide secure and swift transactions and to detect fraud on the basis of pre-defined rules.

19.7.1.5   Protection of Personal Data

AI plays an important role in analyzing the cyber crimes and protecting the personal data of the consumers. AI-based fraud detection tools are used by the banking sector to keep its scope within the domain of cyber security.

19.7.1.6   Hedge Fund Trading and Management

AI-based mobile app solution for banking sector helps in hedge fund trading and management. It can access data from various markets across the world and can help the user in making quick and appropriate decision.

19.7.1.7   Quick Transaction

AI-based application helps in quicker and safer transaction with high security. Banks handle customer-oriented operations easily by reducing the cost of employing additional human resource.

19.7.1.8   Reduce Cost and Time

Shifting of task from human being to AI-based technology can speed up the process and thus can reduce cost. Computer programs can carry out the repeated activities through self-regulating programs to respond to data request from exterior auditors.

19.7.1.9   Upgraded Personnel Effectiveness and Customer Observation

From cash transfer to bill payment to card management, AI offers greater accuracy and precision. It improves customer experience and enhances employ effectiveness through targeted emails. It can improve the satisfaction level of the consumer because all the operations can be managed easily through desktop or smart phone or such devices.

19.7.1.10   Enhanced Banking Services

A new level of comfort ability is being provided to the customers of bank with exclusive use of AI. It meets the expectation the consumers by providing digital support to them. Varied banking services can be availed easily by the consumer anywhere and anytime with the help of desktops, smart phones, and mobile devices [13].

19.7.2   Cons

Traditional banking has been vanished with the extended use of AI. Some of the disadvantages of AI are as follows:

19.7.2.1   High Cost

Development of AI-based software involves huge investment since they are very complex machines. These softwares are required to get updated from time to time as per the needs of the changing environment and this updation also involves some cost. In case of failure, it requires huge time and cost to reinstate the system and recover the codes.

19.7.2.2   Bad Calls

AI may improve or learn but it is not able to make judgment calls. When we talk about manual banking, a human can understand individual circumstances and make judgments while taking decisions and this is what AI might never be able to do. Introduction of AI by replacing adaptive human behavior has resulted into irritational behavior within the eco-system of human and things.

19.7.2.3   Distribution of Power

AI carries the risk as it takes away the control system from the hands of human and results into dehumanization of actions in several ways. Thus, there is always a fear of AI super seeding human beings.

19.7.2.4   Unemployment

India being a highly populated country is facing a biggest problem of unemployment [14]. With the introduction of AI, machine has taken the place of human being and resulted into more increase in the problem of unemployment. This dependency on machines to perform any work has resulted into loss of creativity within the human. Whether it is banking sector or any other sector, AI has contributed a lot in increasing the unemployment rate.

19.8   Intelligent Mobile Applications Drive Growth in Banking

Mobile application usage in past few years has increased a lot. AI-powered applications have become a basic requirement of all the finance companies to improve the customer experience. Areas where artificial intelligence has been exclusively used in banking sector are as follows:

AI-based solutions used by the insurance companies help to improve the customer experience. Major advantages of AI-based insurance mobile applications are as follows [11]:

- Lead management
- Retention of customer
- Automated notification system
- Online payments

19.8.1   Investment

Investment-related mobile applications based on AI help the customer to collect the information related to the value of portfolio, detailed summary of their holdings, and a deep insight or knowledge related to their investments. Some of the benefits of using investment mobile applications are as follows:

- Advise on smart investment
- Management of portfolio
- Summary of holdings
- Regulatory compliance
- Performance reporting

19.8.2   Accounting

All the financial transactions can be handled smoothly by using this kind of applications.

AI applications related to accounting manage information such as cash, asset, liabilities, and fixed assets. Benefits from such accounting solutions are as follows:

- Automated invoicing
- Tax saving
- Tax preparation
- Bank reconciliation

19.8.3 Banking Apps

AI-based mobile application related to banking helps in expanding the market globally within short time duration. The advantages include the following:

- Personalized banking experience
- Customer involvement
- User friendly and secure
- Compliance safety apps

19.8.4 Digital Wallet Apps

This type of AI-based applications enables the user to make the payment from their smart phones only. It allows the user to pay with credit card, debit card, and net banking by using a secured payment gateway. The benefits include the following:

- Payment using NFC, QR, and mobile number
- Extreme security
- Avoids fraudulent practices
- Leading payment gateways
- Reduce response speed
- Improved user experience
- Quick transactions

19.9 Conclusion

Customer is the king of the market, and therefore, everything in the market revolves around the customer. When we talk about service sector, the area which first comes to the mind and plays a very important role is customer service. Rushed working hours, fixed business timings, lack of availability of human resource, and busy schedule have disrupted the customer service. All the above-mentioned things lead to dissatisfaction among the customers and thus affect banker customer relationship. To all these problems, AI has become the only solution. Banks are adopting new technologies for higher boon potentialities and to provide services to the young customers of the society. For each and every operations performed by the bank from sales to accounting to contracts and cyber security, AI plays an important role in transforming banking day by day.

Starting from the conventional brick and mortar branch banking to computerization to AI, Indian banking sector has undergone tremendous changes over the past few years. Now, the banking services are packed in the pocket of the customer, and we are managing all our operations and transactions independently. AI technology has very well revolutionized the banking industry and can further go on with the more new technologies in the near future.

"Artificial Intelligence related applications" became a reality of today's world. The use of Artificial intelligence in almost all aspects of life has changed our lives beyond imagination. its not wrong to say that it has became an dominant part of our lives. AI is actually nothing but the duplication of human intelligence into artificial machines and the main reason or goal behind the simulation is to speed up the tasks.

References

1. Tait, D. and Wang, R., *Artificial Intelligence in Banking Report*, IHS Markit, 2019.
2. Mangnani, D., *5 AI applications in Banking to look out for in next 5 years*, Analytics Vidhya, New Delhi, 2017, April 28, https://www.analyticsvidhya.com/blog/2017/04/5-ai-applications-in-banking-to-look-out-for-in-next-5-years/.
3. *Digital payments in India to reach $1 trillion by 2023: Credit Suisse*, The Economic Times, New Delhi, 2018, February 15, https://economictimes.indiatimes.com/smallbiz/startups/newsbuzz/digital-payments-in-india-to-reach-1-trillion-by-2023-credit-suisse/articleshow/62935890.cms.
4. Pandey, R., *Artificial Intelligence Impact on Banking Sector in INDIA*, Techiexpert.Com, Karnatak, 2019, May 21, https://www.techiexpert.com/artificial-intelligence-impact-on-banking-sector-in-India/.

5. Digalaki, E., *The impact of artificial intelligence in the banking sector & how AI is being used in 2020*, Business Insider, 2019, http://www.businessinsider.in/finance/news/the-impact-of-artificial-intelligence-in-the-banking-sector-how-ai-is-bieng-used-in-2020/articleshow/72860899.cms.

6. North, R., *Artificial intelligence- A boon to the banking industry*, Enterprise Edges, 2018, http://www.enterpriseedges.com/artificial-intelligence-banking-industry.

7. Mirjankar, R., *7 ways digital disruption is shaping the Indian banking sector*, Outlook Money, Delhi, 2020, http://www.outlookindia.com/outlookmoney/banking/7-ways-digital-disruption-is-shaping-the-indian-banking-sector-4214.

8. Padhi, U., *Future of artificial intelligence in the banking sector*, Youth ki Awaaz, New Delhi, 2019, https://www.youthkiawaaz.com/2019/07/future-of-artificial-intelligence-in-banks/.

9. Vijai, C., Artificial intelligence in Indian banking sector: challenges and opportunities. *Int. J. Adv. Res.*, 7, 1581–1587, 2019.

10. *The power of AI & ML technologies in banking & financial sector*, Usm Marketing, Chantilly, 2019, http://www.usmsystem.com/the-power-of-ai-ml-technologies-in-banking-financial-sector/.

11. Sloane, T., *The 18 top use cases of artificial intelligence in banks*, Payments Journal, 2016, https://www.paymentsjournal.com/the-18-top-use-cases-of-artificial-intelligence-in-banks/.

12. *Nick Bostrom: what happens when our computers get smarter than what we are?*, Singularity weblog, 2015, https://www.singularityweblog.com/nick-bostrom-ted/.

13. *Pros and cons of artificial intelligence- A threat or a blessing*, Data Flair, 2019, https://data-flair.training/blogs/artificial-intelligence-advantages-disadvantages/.

14. Mali, G., *Pros and cons of Artificial Intelligence (AI) in banking*, Small Business Bonfire, 2018, http://www.smallbusinessbonfire.com/artificial-intelligence-banking/.

15. Soffar, H., *Artificial Intelligence in banking advantages, disadvantages & mobile banking services*, Online Science, 2019, http://www.online-sciences.com/robotics/artificial-intelligence-in-banking-advantages-disadvantages-mobile-banking-services/.

16. Khurshid, A., *Why banks need artificial intelligence*, Wipro, http://1.http//www.wipro.com/en-IN/business-process/why-banks-need-artificial-intelligence/.

17. Baruah, A., *AI application in the top 4 Indian banks*, Emerj, 2020, http://emerj.com/ai-sector-overviews/ai-applications-in-the-top-4-indian-banks/.

18. Venkat, K., *Future of artificial intelligence in the banking sector*, Usm, 2019, https://medium.com/@venkat34.k/future-of-artificial-intelligence-in-the-banking-sector-8dc51c7b9f22.

19. *How AI is revolutionizing the banking sector*, Info security, 2019, http://
     www.infosecurity-magazine/com/opinions/ai-revolutionizing-banking/.
20. Agarwal, M., *How Artificial intelligence algorithms are changing India's
     banking industry*, Inc42, 2019, https://inc42.com/features/how-artificial-
     intelligence-algorithms-are-changing-India%E2%80%99s-banking-
     industry.
21. Guha, S., *Artificial intelligence in Indian banking scenario: practically
     possible*, Times of India, 2019, https://timesofindia.indiatimes.com/
     readersblog/smallscribbler/artificial-Intelligence-in-indian-banking-
     scenario-practically-possible-5312/.

20

The Potential of Artificial Intelligence in Public Healthcare Industry

Megha Shrivastava[1]* and Devendra Kumar[2]

[1]Department of Zoology, Govt. PG College, Guna, Madhya Pradesh, India
[2]Department of Zoology, Mohanlal Sukhadia University, Udaipur, Rajasthan, India

Abstract

Artificial intelligence (AI) is moving rapidly to revolve the whole healthcare system in the world and is driven by the collaboration of big data and powerful machine learning techniques. Many innovators have been initiated to develop several tools and techniques to improve the procedure of clinical healthcare, to advance medical research, and to improve efficacy. AI tools also depend on algorithms and programs fashioned from healthcare data that are able to make predictions or recommendations. Numerous types of AI are already being used by healthcare providers and scientific industries. The key categories of applications are involved in drug development, disease diagnosis, prevention, and also in treatment activities. A lot of examples are there in which AI technologies are able to execute healthcare jobs as well otherwise better compared to humans such as image recognition, speech analysis, and strategic game planning. There are many more AI also present which increases the efficacy of healthcare for peoples to understand the daily patterns and also wishes of the individuals they care for, along with that AI provides better direction, support, and response for their glowing life.

In this chapter, we have discussed briefly about different fields of public healthcare and various excepted AI applications or tools in the medical industry.

Keywords: Healthcare, disease, software, medical, drug, treatment

*Corresponding author: meghapatan@gmail.com

S. Balamurugan, Sonal Pathak, Anupriya Jain, Sachin Gupta, Sachin Sharma, Sonia Duggal (eds.)
Impact of Artificial Intelligence on Organizational Transformation, (349–360) © 2022 Scrivener
Publishing LLC

20.1   Introduction

Healthcare artificial intelligence (AI) predominantly uses computer-based methodology to carry out medical diagnoses and advocate treatment. AI has the ability to detect important relationships among a dataset of medical symptoms and also to delicacy and guess the results. In the following line of investigation and studies of clinical AI, we mainly focus on the possibility to incorporate various computer-based AI techniques in medical data modeling and clinical method placements. AI tools and techniques have been shown vast capabilities and capacities in detection of evocative data and then used extensively experimented as apparatus for clinical trials, particularly, to serve the result making in each phase for diagnoses and successive treatments, as well as prognoses.

AI tools and techniques have huge waves diagonally healthcare; it is a vigorous discussion of whether AI clinical doctors will ultimately replace individual physicians in the upcoming time. It is also believed that in the coming time, individual physicians cannot replace by machines, but in some specific fields of healthcare industry, the medical AI technology may take some important decisions to replace human judgement which may helpful for a physician. AI technology has made rapid advance in the methods of large data analysis that can lead to successful experiments in the healthcare department. In this article, we covered the current status of AI in medical system, as well as discussed its upcoming.

In this chapter, we have discussed following specific areas of healthcare that covers different software and tools of AI:

1. Drug Discovery
2. Medical Imaging
3. Disease Prevention
4. Disease Diagnosis
5. Robotic AI

20.1.1   Drug Discovery

A scientist, who is going to research in regard to drug discovery, uses hundreds of plans and well-designed experiments in excess of years of work and assesses in the laboratory where various chemicals are tested with other chemicals in the flask or test tube. Just the once those tests get succeeded, the experiments shift on to the next trial with rodents like swiss albino mice usually, then on to chimps and rabbit, and finally human trials [1].

20.1.1.1   *The Main Stages of Drug Discovery Might Take Several Years in Completion*

These procedures are laborious and time consuming and its expenses can acquire into the billions of Rupees, instead of this, there is a much more possibility of failure of experiment. A failure at any one stage sends the researcher reverse to zero level. It consumes hundreds of chemical combinations and hard work. Normal procedure of drug discovery comprised in four steps:

- First step is screening and hit identification: High screening of chemicals in libraries to test their ability to modify the goal positive hits that are selected for further confirmation.
- Hit to lead selection: Hits are confirmed and analog clusters are synthetized; three to six molecule bunches with better affinity and drug properties are selected.
- Lead optimization: Lead molecules are further modified and upgraded into a number of drugs candidates and select the most active one.
- Preclinical testing: *In vivo* assays are planned to test pharmacodynamics, pharmacokinetics, and toxicity of novel molecules, one drug candidate that is selected for clinical trial studies.

Patients or hospitalized persons in the human trials are every so often exposed to side effects at the end; it has to go in the course of regulatory authorization. It may or may not obtain this endorsement which authorized in the United States by the Food and Drugs Administration (FDA). AI provides the opportunity to avoid the uncertainties and inefficiencies that may arise in the process of classical drug development; it also minimizes bias and human intervention. Current medical AI is mainly effective where there is a particular set of data, and a set of repetitive actions makes drug discovery a major candidate. This technology has versatile tools that can be applied at various steps of drug development, such as drug identification and validation, drug designing, and improving the R&D potential. AI can aggregate and analyze biomedicine information and then refine the decision-making process to recruit patients for clinical trials.

20.1.1.2   *Companies or Startups Used AI Techniques for Drug Discovery*

A company named Atomwise (San Francisco, California) develops Convolutional Neural Networks (CNNs) to accomplish enormous experiment-based searches for definite drugs. Developing the correct drug for the correct application is a delicate balance of making somewhat that is both effective and safe devoid of side-effects. Usually, these require countless experiments, and still, we are not cent percent convinced that the drug will always be hundred percent safe and sound. The company (Atomwise) is moving effectively which works onto the computer and into an AI technology by training CNNs to perform the experiments automatically. These allow scientists to carry out further experiments, millions of them, to choose a more trustworthy subset of drugs that could be feasible.

Some other startups which are analogous to Atomwise are Deep Genomics, Schrodinger, Recursion AI [1], Amgen, Astellas, and Bayer.

20.1.2   Medical Imaging

Medical imaging data is an essential and most complex source for finding out the essential facts about patients in diagnosis. The outcomes from CAT scans, MRIs, X-rays, and other testing techniques, examining through very high resolution images, are often difficult even for the most practiced clinical process. It can diagnose commonly occurring abnormalities, such as chest x-ray imaging test by automating invention with fast and fewer diagnostic mistakes.

20.1.2.1   Areas of Medical Imaging

- **Fracture Analysis:** Usually, it is difficult to spot a sort of fracture by normal images, but this AI technics can ascertain slight differences with in the image that needs medical surgery. It allows trauma patients images to be review by unbiased algorithms so that necessary care is taken to archive positive results [2].
- **Cardiovascular Diseases:** Determining the different structures of a person's heart can tell the risk of heart disease which will get to be addressed through surgery. AI has already proven that it is becoming very valuable for radiologists as it is greatly improved productivity and their accuracy [2].
- **Neurological Diseases:** Amyotrophic Lateral Sclerosis (ALS) is a degenerative nervous disorder, its diagnosis is very challenging, but there is currently no treatment for this disease or other similar neurological problems, exact diagnosis of these diseases helps individuals to know about their outcomes for the treatment [2].

- **Diagnose Pneumonia:** Radiology images are frequently used to identify the different lung diseases like pneumonia and bronchitis. It differentiates the images of lungs among different diseases for potential diagnose and permit for quicker treatment [2].
- **Breast Cancer Detection:** In carcinoma disease like micro-calcification in tissues, it becomes difficult to identify while it is malignant or benign. In that condition, the wrong outcomes could lead unnecessary testing, treatment, delayed diagnoses, and worse outcomes. During the diagnosis of images, the interpretation of micro calcifications greatly varies in radiology. For more exact categorization of microcalcifications, AI technique can help and enhance the accuracy and use the quantitative imaging features, and it can potentially decreasing the speed of unnecessary benign biopsies [2].

20.1.2.2   Some Applications for AI in Medical Imaging Are at Present Applied in General Healthcare

Following medical imaging techniques or softwares are used generally for analyze the health problems:

- **CureMetrix:** This is a San Diego–based company, it helps radiologist in analysis of mammograms for cancer detection, and it uses machine learning, tongue understanding (NLU), and other computer vision technology.
- **Imagia:** It is a man-made intelligence in healthcare company, and its software analyzes radiological images so as to predict the event of a patient's disease and response to possible treatments.
- **GE Medical Imaging:** GE healthcare is an American company and has thousands of imaging devices that are used around the world. These devices are AI-based and used to hurry up the procedure of examining CT scans and X-ray with enhanced accuracy.
- **Siemens Medical Imaging:** Siemens Healthcare is German company, developed software named "AI Rad Companion Chest CT". This software can identify and measure lesions in CT scan, then automatically gives a report which help to increase efficacy and proper identification in radiology procedure.

- **Aidoc:** It is an Israeli company that develops computer-aided simple triage (CASIT) systems. CASIT is a computerized method or system that assists physicians in initial interpretation and classification of medical images. It helps the doctors to identify over a billion patients.

20.1.3 Disease Prevention

Epidemiological study can track the basis of any disease outbreak and examines which section or area of the people face the maximum risk. With the help of AI, it becomes very easy to identify the pattern of the course of the outbreak and then to guess possibly affected people [3]. For prevention of infection and its control, applications of AI suggest vast potential for implement the core components of WHO [4].

20.1.3.1 Areas of Disease Prevention, Supported by AI System

AI systems can discover patterns of the information, speed up the disease spreading in any area, and provide heavy datasets for succeeding study. AI can support in disease prevention by finding the speed of infection. It can help by simulating the behavior of varied types of agents in a posh system and support the modification by collecting data and creating analysis [5].

In the medical microbiology laboratory, from the genomic characters of *Staphylococcus epidermidis,* AI might detect the danger of infection and powerfully identify the high threat genotypes pre-operatively to focus on pre- and post-operative health AI preventative programs [6]. Gram staining for bacterial analysis is often time taking, this procedure is totally operator-based which needs a novel and advance technologies for prevention of infections and an expert laboratory scientist for its analysis. Microscopy based on AI opens abilities for those areas which lacking medical microbiologist expertise with the potential to for analysis and suitable clinical link about management of patient [7].

20.1.3.2 Some Recent Software Used for Disease Prevention

In present times, the use of AI in the COVID-19 pandemic condition has proved its efficacy for generation of real facts for community health. AI could enable to a decision when large numbers of infection data were emerging festally; these data analyzed by a range of sources like report of government, news reports, and social media reporting to create applications like health map. It also can accelerate contact tracing by pattern of AI identification within the data.

ArogyaSetu App of World Bank praises India, which is currently used for contact tracing and control COVID-19. It is another initiative toward controlling the pandemic. The Indian government had set up AarogyaSetu App to interrupt the spreading of COVID-19 to trace people's place and Bluetooth to affect the danger of getting the virus. This is often a crucial app to fight contrary to COVID-19. By leveraging technology, it offers useful information. Instead, it has been also observed that as more and more people will use it, its efficiency will increase [8].

20.1.4   Medical Diagnosis

The significance of medical diagnosis by AI is very clear now. The growing demand of AI for disease diagnosis shows well performance in this field. AI techniques containing the development for developing a computer-based decision system, it was done by a human being. Several AI tools are developed that supports doctors in diagnosing the patients more appropriately and accurately. It provides a very general method of approaching problems. Within the last few years, AI has become more exact in identifying disease diagnosis and has become a more feasible source of diagnostic information.

20.1.4.1   Categories of AI Tools for Disease Diagnosis

Today, a lot of machines learning diagnostic applications fall under the following medical areas:

- **Oncology:** Scientists are used deep learning tool to identify cancerous tissue up to expert physicians.
- **Pathology:** Pathology is a clinical field that is related with the diagnosis of disease; it is particularly based on the analysis of bodily fluids like blood and urine and body tissues. Machine vision and machine learning technics can develop the efforts usually left only to pathologist with microscope.
- **Rare Diseases:** Software for facial recognition is being united with another technique machine learning to help clinician's in diagnosis of rare diseases. With photos of patient, the facial analyses are performed in assistance of deep learning and for spotting the phenotype that link with the rare genetic diseases [9].

Beside them, many more applications of AI also are available. Here, we aimed to point out a brief descriptive area of current initiative based on the research.

20.1.4.2   Software Developed for Disease Diagnosis

Some softwares are developed for detection of disease for different proposes and they are used by many clinical laboratories:

- **Ada:** This type of clinical software talks to the patient and questions about its symptoms and complains and gives him reference of a good doctor or offers to contact an expert for consultation in replying.
- **Lunit:** During normal diagnosis process of cancer, several types of breast and lung are ignored. Lunit can help to identify some challenging diseases like Air Route Cancer with the help of deep learning and 3D visualization. This software increases the probability of identifying any cancer disease manifold.
- **Sensely:** Sensely is a program that is useful for those persons who have recently undergone long treatment or traveling through prolonged diseases. This application creates a data on the patient's condition; this software also gives information about when to take medicine and when a doctor's visit will be required.
- **PathAI (Boston):** This software helps doctors in timely diagnosis of some challenging diseases, like cancer, with the help of machine learning to rapidly and exactly analyze cell pictures.
- **Aira (San Diego):** It helps to blind and visually weakened persons to see the entire world by joining the competences of the human body and the abilities of AI by using different applications or smart glasses [10].
- **Chatbots:** Chatbot is a software which is used for online conversation in form of text or text to speech, and it provides a facility to directly interact with a live human being. Many companies use this AI technology to identify the disease symptoms of patients and its prevention and to recommend an appropriate course of action.

20.1.4.3   Making Smartphone as Powerful Diagnostic Tools

The feature of mobile phone camera is developing each year, and the created images are feasible for analysis by AI. This technology is very beneficiary in Ophthalmology and Dermatology [11].

In the United Kingdom, such type of tool has been developed which can recognize a disease in the progression, by analyzing face images of a child. This identification was done by AI to identify different types of facial features such as the child's jaw line, child's nose, and displacement and some other qualities, which point toward facial detection. This technique can help above 90 diseases by matching the ordinary images to provide medical support [11].

20.1.5   Robotic AI

AI, disruptive technologies such as robotics, is changing the whole healthcare system, medicine, and pharma, as well as the way we collect medical facts. The healthcare industry will be one of the largest beneficiaries for AI and robotics technology in the healthcare ecosystem. Robotic technology fulfills all technology demands originated by AI and robotics applications in healthcare fields, such as virtual nursing assistants, robot-assisted surgery, image analysis, and automated preliminary. With the start of AI and robotics in healthcare, some of the few job visions that will be shaped include the following:

- **Tele-surgery:** The demand for robot-supported surgeries will continue to grow. This is due to tele-surgeries that are probable to be well-timed, specific, and accurate as compared to entirely normal operations. Thus, to meet this novel requirement, medical institutes and many universities are going to offer specializations in conducting bot assisted surgeries.
- **Deep learning experts:** Experts of deep learning can help by evolving end to end sophisticated AI explanations that can provide the insights at each stage of the healthcare sector, from diagnostics level to care delivery and from health data analytics level to people health administration. Therefore, companies are looking for highly expert data scientists and deep learning specialists to understand this vision.
- **Robot-assisted diagnostics:** AI, robots, and machine learning are being joined within a real physical robotic model to

do diagnostics. Robots can handle the initial level of disease diagnosis and finding.

- **AI Chatbot Designers:** AI-based medical bots can examine symptoms; it identifies the problems and suggests the correct medicines and most probable details for symptoms.

- **Evidence-Based Treatment and AI Experts:** Bioinformatics is an area where abundant data needs to be analyzed to originate significant outcomes and discover new treatments. To accomplish this, healthcare companies are trying to find AI experts who have an honest grasp of AI tools and programming languages, like Prolog [12].

20.2   The Future of Artificial Intelligence in Healthcare

This transformative technology is going to change the medical sectors in different ways. AI has help out from drug development to medical research to increase patient outcomes at reduced costs. In addition, the utilization of that technique in healthcare promises easy access, affordability, and effectiveness.

The highest challenge to AI in this healthcare system is not whether the technologies will be capable enough to be useful but rather confirming their implementation in daily clinical practice. For widespread adoption to take place, these challenges will finally be overcome, but they will take much longer time to do so than it will take for the technologies themselves to complete. As a result, we are supposed to see more widespread use of AI within 10 years [3].

Recent developments in AI have driven discussion of whether AI doctors will substitute human doctors in the future. The idea of substituting human doctors may sound specious, but AI can assist human physicians to make superior decisions. In some areas of healthcare such as radiology, it can replace human finding completely. Speech and text recognition are now in employment for jobs like patient communication and capture of clinical notes and their application will increase.

Huge data has made powerful applications of AI in healthcare sector. There has been a quick progress in bulky data analytic procedures, and so much healthcare data is available. Using this data, a lot of clinically relevant info hidden in a large amount of data can be unlocked by potent AI techniques. This will support in taking better clinical decisions [13].

References

1. Seif, G., *How Artificial Intelligence is Accelerating Drug Discovery*, Towards data science, Canada, 25 Nov. 2019, https://towardsdatascience.com/how-artificial-intelligence-is-accelerating-drug-discovery-931047f6ea9a.
2. Bresnick, J., Top 5 Use Cases for Artificial Intelligence in Medical Imaging. *Tools & Strategies News*, Health It Analytics, Boston, 30 Oct. 2018, https://healthitanalytics.com/news/top-5-use-cases-for-artificial-intelligence-in-medical-imaging.
3. Davenport, T. and Kalakota, R., The potential for artificial intelligence in healthcare. *Future Healthc. J.*, 6, 2, 94–8, 2019, https://www.ncbi.nlm.nih.gov/pmc/articles/PMC6616181/.
4. Storr, J., Twyman, A., Zingg, W., Damani, N., Kilpatrick, C., Reilly, J. et al., Core components for effective infection prevention and control programmes: new WHO evidence-based recommendations. *Antimicrob. Resist. Infect. Control*, 6, 6, 2017, https://aricjournal.biomedcentral.com/articles/10.1186/s13756-016-0149-9.
5. Lopez-Garcia, M. and Kypraios, T., A unified stochastic modelling framework for the spread of nosocomial infections. *J. R. Soc. Interface*, 15, 143, 1–15, 2018, https://royalsocietypublishing.org/doi/10.1098/rsif.2018.0060.
6. Meric, G., Mageiros, L., Pensa, J., Laabei, M., Yahara, K., Pascoe, B. et al., Disease-associated genotypes of the commensal skin bacterium *Staphylococcus epidermidis. Nat. Commun.*, 9, 1, 5034, 2018, https://www.ncbi.nlm.nih.gov/pmc/articles/PMC6261936/.
7. Drew, R.J., Murphy, T., Broderick, D., O'Gorman, J., Eogan, M., An interpretation algorithm for molecular diagnosis of bacterial vaginosis in a maternity hospital using machine learning: proof-of-concept study. *Diagn. Microbiol. Infect. Dis.*, 96, 2, 114950, 2020, https://pubmed.ncbi.nlm.nih.gov/31836253/.
8. MYBRANDBOOK, *India leads the way in tracing for Covid-19: Aarogya Setu Tracking App*, Mybrandbook, New Delhi, 2020, https://www.mybrandbook.co.in/redirect.php?p=12994.
9. Faggella, D., *Machine Learning for Medical Diagnostics – 4 Current Applications*, Emerj, Boston, 14 March 2020, https://emerj.com/ai-sector-overviews/machine-learning-medical-diagnostics-4-current-applications/.
10. Kharkovyna, O., *Artificial Intelligence & Deep Learning for Medical Diagnosis On the road to better healthcare*, Towards data science, Canada, 2019, https://towardsdatascience.com/artificial-intelligence-deep-learning-for-medical-diagnosis-9561f7a4e5f.
11. Bresnick, J., Top 12 Ways Artificial Intelligence Will Impact Healthcare. *Tools & Strategies News*, Health It Analytics, Boston, 30 Apr. 2018, https://healthitanalytics.com/news/top-12-ways-artificial-intelligence-will-impact-healthcare.

12.   Verma, G. and Kapoor, M., *AI and robotics reshaping jobs in the healthcare sector*, Timesjobs, India, 26 May 2018, https://content.timesjobs.com/ai-and-robotics-reshaping-jobs-in-the-healthcare-sector/articleshow/64321707.cms.

13.   Deep, A., *How AI Is Transforming The Future Of Healthcare Industry*, Hackernoon, 04 Apr. 2019, https://hackernoon.com/how-ai-is-transforming-the-future-of-healthcare-industry-f6020cc18323.

21

Banks to Lead Digital Transformation With Artificial Intelligence

Lavika Jaroli[1], Sachin Gupta[2]* and Parul Dashora[3]

[1]Faculty of Commerce & Management, Mohanlal Sukhadia University, Udaipur (Raj.), India
[2]Department of Business Administration, Mohanlal Sukhadia University, Udaipur (Raj.), India
[3]Department of Accountancy and Statistics, Mohanlal Sukhadia University, Udaipur (Rajasthan), India

Abstract

Indian banking industry is growing rapidly with the help of Artificial Intelligence (AI), virtual assistant, and chatbots over a past few decades. The world has entered the fourth industrial revaluation. Technology is surging ahead and innovation is fast becoming the key indicator of country's growth and development. Nowadays, AI becomes a backbone of Indian banking system. The aim of banking industry in development of economy and in the financial life of human being is very important.

Banking industry is one of the growing sectors which seeing rapid adoption of AI. The AI technology ensures one-to-one customized interaction with the customers with the help of virtual assistants and chatbots and their services, available 24*7 to the customers. Today, we want everything automated from home to business to make our work easier. AI becomes the essential part of our lives. To leverage maximum profit, it is important to adopt new technology, AI mechanism encapsulating with automation robotic process, data analytics to enhance the customer experience, which business revolves around and different chatbots and virtual assistants will help their customers in financial decision-making process.

According to Shannon [1] AI is a branch of computer science, which is developing such type of machine which thinks and acts like human brain, such as voice recognition, solving a problem, planning, and learning. It is antithetical from natural intelligence to machine intelligence. Using these technologies, it is planning to make a robot or software, which thinks like a human mind by this computer

---

Corresponding author: sachinguptabusadm@gmail.com

S. Balamurugan, Sonal Pathak, Anupriya Jain, Sachin Gupta, Sachin Sharma, Sonia Duggal (eds.)
Impact of Artificial Intelligence on Organizational Transformation, (361–386) © 2022 Scrivener Publishing LLC

that can be trained to accomplish particular task by processing large amount of data and recognizing pattern in the data. According to Fintech India report spending by PWO in 2017, the worldwide AI application launched $5.1 billion up from $4 billion in 2015. This chapter starts with the meaning and definition of AI and also includes what are the different AI applications used by different banks of India and what are the benefits and risk faced by banks.

Keywords: Artificial Intelligence, technology, leverage, PwC FinTech, digital, banking, revaluation, innovation leveraging

21.1 Artificial Intelligence

It is a man-made computer-controlled machine, which can perform task like human being and which works on automatic process. It works on data science or data analytics. AI is the most dynamic and global field of computer science, which provide smarter solution by way of using comprehensive technology. According to the father of Artificial Intelligence (AI), John McCarthy, it is the science, engineering, or arts of making intelligent machines and quick computer program. In AI, there is no need to pre-program the machine to do some work. We have to create machine with program algorithm which can work with own intelligence. It is a man-made and thinking power AI which is for people who are in hurry.

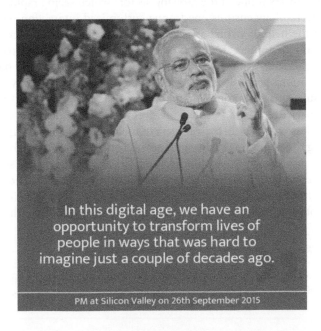

In this digital age, we have an opportunity to transform lives of people in ways that was hard to imagine just a couple of decades ago.

PM at Silicon Valley on 26th September 2015

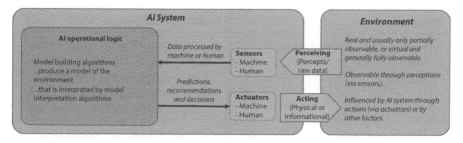

Source: AIGO in February 2019.

AI means the ability of computer control machine to perform tasks commonly associated with intelligent individuals. It is all about planning, controlling analyzing the data, and giving result within few second with accuracy. It has no brain and completely depends upon data analytics. The goal of AI includes planning, problem solving, reasoning, speech recognition, and ability to move object around. AI is based on deep learning and machine learning. By these technologies, computers are trained to accomplish particular task by processing huge amount of data or acknowledge pattern in the data.

There is no particular global definition of AI. In November 2018, the AI Group of specialists at the OECD (AIGO) developed a float chart to understand it in better way.

Its aim is to understand accurate and cognitive technology which is appropriate to short- and long-term time perspective. AI commonly used by the business, policies, and scientific body. As well, as per the OECD committee report [2] it informed the development of the OECD *recommendation of the committee on AI.*

It is in the reference with the human. Humans are the most intelligent creatures and AI is broad section of computer data science. The aim of AI is to make the system functions intelligently and independently.

21.1.1   Human Versus Artificial Intelligence

As humans have their own brain, memory and emotions which can think and understand on their own whereas AI is totally technology-based and depends on machines and work according to the given data.

21.1.2   Difference Between AI, NLP, NN, ML, or DL

- **Artificial Intelligence (AI):** This system can do intelligent things.
- **Nature Language Process (NLP):** This is a building system that can understand language by speech and text in natural

Human	Artificial Intelligence
• Human can rightly speak and listen and convey through language.	• Artificial Intelligence is an area of identification. Most of the speech identification is in the form of code or statistical based; thus, it is called codding statistical learning.
• Human can write and read text in their own language.	• It is the field of NLP (natural language process).
• Human can see with their eyes and observed things and tells about something.	• Virtual vision comes under symbolic way for computing process information; thus, it is a process of virtual vision.
• Human can notice image through their eyes which makes images of that world; in observation process, human can understand their surroundings.	• AI is an area of robotics and data science.
• Human have ability to see pattern such as grouping.	• AI is the field of pattern recognition.
• Human brain works on neurons. It is a network of neuron.	• AI is a system of Deep learning that is NN (Neural Network).
• Human brain can recall the images from top to bottom, left to right.	• AI works on computer vision that is object recognition that is Convolution Neural Network (CNN).

language; they are perfume to interact with human in a personalized natural way; it is used as chatbot and other similar application.

- **Machined Learning (ML):** This enables machine to lean by its own and learn from past data or experience, without being pre-programmed. ML works on algorithm.
- **Neural Network (NN):** This is biologically inspired network of artificial neurons.
- **Deep Learning (DL):** Deep learning is a constructed from of machine learning. These techniques focus on building Artificial Neural Network (ANN), where ANNs are algorithms inspired by human brain. Automatic car driving is a best example of deep learning.

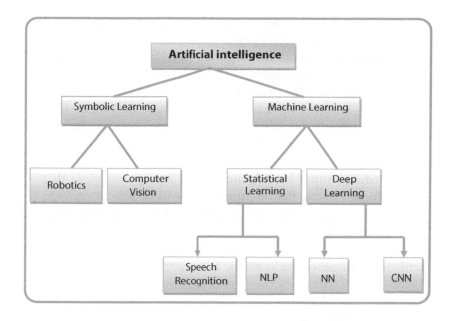

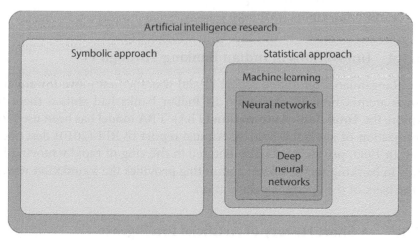

Source: Provided by the Massachusetts Institute of Technology (MIT)'s Internet Policy Research Initiative (IPRI).

21.1.3   Types of Artificial Intelligence

1. **Artificial Narrow Intelligence (ANI):** AI is also known as weak or narrow AI. It is focused on one narrow single task narrow; AI interacts with on a daily basis performance by Chatbots, Google Assistant, Google Translator, Siri, Cortana,

or Alexa. It is also used in medicine to diagnose cancer and other illness with accuracy.

2. **Artificial General Intelligence (AGI):** AGI is all about hypothetical intelligence. It understands work like a human being. The main objective of AGI is to understand future studies, for example, AI system diagnoses cancers with greater accuracy than human doctors. Tesla is working on driverless cars and makes the transportation automated.

3. **Artificial Super Intelligence (ASI):** ASI is a life of AI that is more capable than a human if it will be able to perform extraordinary, such as decision-making and emotional relationship

Artificial Intelligence works on the following:

- Supervised learning
- Unsupervised learning.
- Reinforcement learning.

21.1.4   Innovations in Indian Banking Through IT

The Rangarajan Committee report (1980) was the first move toward the bank's atomization. IT expansion in Indian banks had shifted them to explore the **Total Bank Automation** (TBA). TBA model has been used for atomization of any bank branch. Annual report of RBI (2010) described that, in 1980, private banks also entered in the ring of rapidly moving IT tools in banking sector. Cloud computing provides the foundation which is the bank of the upcoming generation.

21.1.5   A Short History of Artificial Intelligence

The term AI was introduced in the year 1956 by John McCarthy and along with Alan Turning, he was the first to define AI science and engineering of making intelligence machine. As per History of AI - project report of University of Washington [3] in 1956, computers were solving mathematical problems, providing thermos in geometry and learning to speak English. In 1974, computer became faster and affordable; 1980 is the year of Artificial intelligence; 2000 landmark of AI establishment achievement, 2011 deep learning, big data, and artificial general intelligence.

Automated Data Flow and Cloud Computing Trends in Banking Sector	
National Institute of Standards and Technology (NIST) publications report (2011) explained the various innovative, future-oriented, and WAP-enabled technological tools to be implement in banking sector, as given below:	
Automated Data Flow	**Cloud Computing Trends in Banking Sector**
RBI puts first initiative on ADF and focuses on banking operations analysis. RBI annual report (2013) directed the banks to implement Automated Data Flow (ADF) through CBS banking and achieve maximum returns. Banks have adopted various strategies to attain the suitable solutions.	**RBI annual report (2013) stated the** increased use of information technology (IT) in banking and suggested the requirement to examine the shared IT resources to optimize the cost and increases the efficiency and security with data integrity. The **NIST publications report (2011)** described cloud computing is a parallel, large, and distributed computing system. It connected and virtualized networking resources. National Institute of Standards and Technology NIST explained about cloud computing as "a pay-per-use mode" used for convenient and shared access of network banking application services.

Source: Report (2011) of National Institute of Standards and Technology (NIST).

21.2 Artificial Intelligence History Timeline

21.2.1 Objectives

1. The leading objective of this chapter to investigate the about the use of AI in banking sector.
2. To study about the self-learning capabilities of AI that are able to recognize customers' quarries and to solve their problems like human and how to make their customer happy.

21.2.2 Scope

The development of AI in financial sectors only.

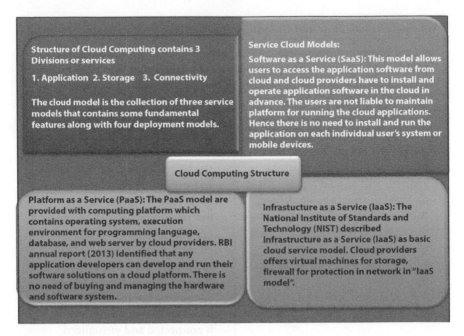

Source: National Institute of Standards and Technology (NIST) Report (2011).

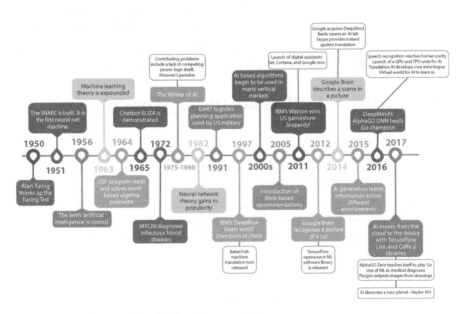

Source: A short history of artificial intelligence, 1956.

21.2.3   Methodology

The study is suited on secondary data like journals, new papers, various report or internet sources, and also based on descriptive in nature.

21.3   Why Artificial Intelligence in Banks

Fraud Detection: Banking and financial sector are growing day by day, and millions of transactions are done online irrespective of time anywhere. As AI is growing in the same way cybercrime is increasing, so banking industry must be secure to prevent such cyber-attack. Customer trust is foremost priority for banking. As per Turing [4] AI-based fraud detection is a helping hand in preventing frauds. The conjecturing analytics can manage the whole process softly.

Decision-Making: AI provides all the information of markets within the seconds, and chatbots can suggest their customer to manage their portfolio according so that it can help in taking better decision and also provide suggestion of investment in the market.

- **Robotics Banking:** Chatbots and personal assistant give the new shape to the banking industry. Thousands of customers query handle within a second. It became easy to make personal portfolio with the help of AI strategies, for example, if a customer wants to purchase new house, then the chatbots will help them according to their bank statement and financial status.
- **Customer Relationship Management:** Customers are the king of every business. CRM software helps in improve customer retentions, increase sales, better marketing efforts, and increase productivity. Banks provide personalized service to their client through AI in most efficient way. It not only generates new customers and but also helps in maintaining their old customers by providing better services. It ensures that their customer is happy with their services and it also provides well-organized front and back office and builds strong relationship with their customers.
- **New Technologies and Trends:** AI makes banking easier; it is only a click away. Customers need not to stand long in the queue. Money transfer and deposit become easier. AI helps to identify fraud detection and anti-money laundering through AI bank that can able to take necessary steps.

- **Comprehensive Process Automation:** Through automation, it become easier to handle large data, reduce human error, cost cut more accuracy, claim management, and fast processing of services in every step.

21.4   Goal of Artificial Intelligence

- The main goal of AI in banking sector is customer satisfaction, to know customer's need and to provide solution of their quarries.
- To reduce human error, AI help bankers to use data to be more productive, efficient way, and also save time to their customers and their employees.
- Another aim of AI is providing security to their customers, reducing payments fraud and anti-money laundering, and managing account and huge data with record speed and accuracy.
- To help focus on profitability and submissive to bring in effective decision-making.
- Finding new business, demand and opportunities, and performance evaluation.
- Replicate human intelligence through automation robotics process and building a machine which can perform task that requires human intelligence.
- Solve knowledge-intensive task, relating operational efficiencies.

21.4.1   Innovations in Indian Banking Through IT

Automation in banks through IT first mention in Rangrajan Committee Report in 1980. Afterwards many private banks also introduced IT tools in banks.

21.4.2   Innovation in Indian Banking Sectors

Year	Main Innovations
1980	Entrance of debit card–based payments

(Continued)

Year	Main Innovations
1983	Understand the scope and expediency of the computerization and automation
1981	Branch electronic communication through internet
1986	Existence of MICR technology, also setting up network of ATMs
1990	Arrivals of banking Clearing Services (ECS) and Credit Cards
1994	Introduction of an Electronic Funds Transfer (EFT) system and SWIFT
1998	Building up or enhance banking system or technology
1991	Exchange of memorandum by BANKNET
1999	Establishment of INFINET (The Indian Financial Network)
2000	Introduction of Information Technology (IT) ACT 2000 and Electronic Fund Transfer (EFT)
2004	Launched, Real-Time Gross Settlement system (RTGS)
2005	Installation of National Electronic Fund Transfer (NEFT) as a replacement of EFT
2006	Initiation Cheque Truncation System (CTS)
2009	Suggestions of Nationwide Electronic Financial Electronic Financial Inclusion System by Linking No-Frills account (NEFIS)
2011	Introduce of digital assistants Siri, Cortana, and Google assistance.
2016	**YES Bank** launched "YES mPower", YES Bank in partnership with PAYIO on Facebook messenger, is launching its wallet service through a chat-based financial assistant. YES, Pay Bot not only does financial transaction but also answers customer queries.
2016	**ICICI Bank** launched its Artificial Intelligence–based chatbot named iPal; it simply answers the customer queries; it can also be work on voice-based command.
2017	**SBI bank** launched SIA "code for bank"; it is a chat assistant that will help their clients on daily banking transaction just like a bank representative. SIA was developed by PAYIO; it handles nearly 10,000 enquires mini-second on 864 million per day.

(Continued)

Year	Main Innovations
2017	**Axis Bank:** Third largest private sector bank of India has a convectional interface for customers "Axis Aha" on basis of Artificial Intelligence and ML-powered chatbot.
2017	**HDFC Bank:** "Eva" built by HDFC bank by Tense forth Artificial Intelligence research answered more than five million user queries, instead of browsing, clicking buttons, or waiting on a call.
2017	**Punjab National Bank:** The bank announced its plan to improve its audit systems or to improve automated service by using analytics.
2017	**UMANG** (Unified Mobile Application for New-Age Governance) is providing a platform to all Indian people who need to interact with any government or semi government department at center, state, or local level in India. It offers them e-gov services, all-in-one single unified mobile app with multi-services in multi-language. It is the main component of digital India government which enables all offline services into online services.
2018	**Bank of Baroda:** Bank of Baroda is using technology to reduce cost of managing account focusing on improving customer services; it is also using AI application like Baroda Brainy and Digital Lab.
2019	**Andhra Bank:** Andhra Bank launched its chat assistant ABHi; through this, customer can ask detail of banking services, loan, insurance, payment mode, deposit/EMI, recharge, different government scheme, lodge complaints, etc., anytime. Floatbot gives answer to customer queries in milliseconds and also digitally engage and automate customer support for its 5 Cr customers.

21.5 Artificial Intelligences Used by Different Banks

- **State Bank of India:** The largest public sector bank of India, with 420 million customers, has embarked on using AI by launching "Code for Bank" for focusing on technologies such as predictive analytics, Fintech/block chain, digital payments, IoT, AI, machine learning, BOTS, and robotic process automation. SBI has also launched SIA, developed by Payjo, that addresses customer enquiries instantly and helps them their daily banking transaction just like a bank representative.
- **Allahabad Bank:** Its app "emPower" is scheduled to get major enhancements like robotic process and AI which

helps in internal banking process and customers e-commerce payments more efficient.

- **Bank of Baroda:** Bank of Baroda is extensively focusing on chatbots, both internally and externally. Bank launched "ADI" (Assisted Digital Interaction) that works on natural language processing, understands different queries, and contextually keeps guiding the customer to the endpoint.
- **Canara Bank:** It launched Mitra that was deployed in July and is supplementing the human resource. The other one is Candi, which is slightly compact than Mitra.
- **Andhra Bank:** Bengaluru-based AI startup; Andhra Bank has launched an AI Chatbot ABHi. Floatbot has launched AI Chatbot integrated with Core Banking Servers of Andhra Bank, to digitally engage and automate customer support for its 5 Crore customers.
- **Punjab National Bank:** PNB bank planned to improve its audit system, update its credit software system, and also reunite its customers' accounts, so that it reduces fraudulent activities in banking. Bank is updating its technology to enhance customer services and their faith. PNB focusing on

India's first banking robot

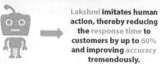

Lakshmi **imitates human action, thereby reducing the** response time **to customers by up to** 60% **and improving** accuracy **tremendously.**

Indian banks plan to use robots with artificial intelligence. Kumbakonam-based, City Union Bank became the first to deploy robots launched as Lakshmi. The robots can perform repetitive, high volume and time-consuming business tasks - raising productivity and efficiency.

procuring, assessment, action and subsidizing, documentation and disbursement, and recovery, so that they can aware any fraud activities. PNB uses AI to bolster fraud detection mechanisms.

- **IndusInd Bank:** It launched its AI which is based on voice-based commands generally named Alexa skill, "Indus Assist", which provides all information through voice command. All transaction and done through this mode which is completely secure.
- **City Union Bank:** City Union Bank has launched AI-based application CUB Lakshmi; it is the India's first bank who has launched first robot; it works on voice-based interaction and connects with core banking solution, giving current time updating regarding loan, interest rate, foreign exchange rate, current charges regarding any banking services, and many more.
- **YES Bank:** It launched YES ROBOT with Microsoft, advanced NLP engine LUIS (Language Understanding Intelligent Service), and other services. YES Bank launched its wallet service through a chat-based financial assistant. YES ROBOT is any time chat assistant. YES Pay Bot not only does financial transaction but also answers customer queries without the need for human intervention.
- **HDFC Bank:** HDFC bank launched AI-based application EVA, which gives answer of thousands of banking queries, tracks, and analyzes all the transaction. It was built with the aim of providing faster services. It reduces search browsing and answer within few seconds, and it helps not only its customer but also help non-bank customers. HDFC bank was the first bank in India to introduce IRA—a robot for branch assistance.
- **ICICI Bank:** India's second biggest private sector bank is rendering its services by giving automatic robotics software. ICICI Bank has launched its AI-based chatbot named iPal; it simply answers the customer queries; it can also works on voice-based command such as Cortana and Siri. It offers financial services like bill payment, micro transaction, find transfer, account operate, or more. It is also available anytime to answer the question, and iPal is also available on e-wallet.
- **AxisBank:** It is India's third immense private sector bank and has launched conversational interface for customers.

"Axis Aha" on the basis of AI- and ML-powered chatbot enables 24*7 works on chat and voice-enabled banking assistant who helps the customers in account transaction, bill payment, recharge manage debit, and other cards. Customer can simply speak or text axis aha and get a response.

21.6   Implementation of Artificial Intelligence in Banking

Today, banking and finance sectors are growing very fast. Millions of transactions occur online. There are some key applications of Artificial Intelligence in banking industry which shape the world of banking life. Some of these are based on pattern detection, data science, voice interaction, chat bots, fraud detection, or customer recommendation. Where such application is installed in banks, its benefits are better customer interaction using chatbots, fraud detections using machine learning algorithms, accurate recommendation, and quick information on financial service.

The following are some fields where Artificial Intelligence is being used in banking sector.

Areas Where Banks Are Adopting AI

1) **Individual Financial Services:** Artificial Intelligence gives powers to the smart chatbots that provide customer self-help solution for every problem and also provide automated financial advisers more suited and safer ways to obtain, spend, save, and infuse their money.

2) **Digital Wallets:** Digital money and its use has reached new height with support of digital wallets. This magical wallet can be operated through mobile, computer, etc. They made purchase easier and cashless too. This plays major role in the world of technology like Google, Apple, Paypal, and others that are developing their own payment gate ways.

3) **Underwriting:** This service is provided by insurance, bank, or investment industry. When there are any losses and damages on financial risk, they provide guarantee to pay when liability arises from them. It reduces the risk, and also machine learning models assess the credit worthiness of a customer. Remove duplicate line of text.

4) **Voice Assisted Banking:** Consumers can quickly get personalized information simply by asking their voice-assisted device or on-demand service by helping banks reduce costs. Voice command and touch screen have given new look to banking sector. This shows the physical presence is finding service like payment, loan, deposit, and transfer of payment done without personal interaction. This reduces human error and saves the tissue of both customer and employee.

5) **Improve Customer Interaction:** AI deals with personalized and intelligent customer services, and with new attributes, AI minimizes the errors and provides accurate analysis and solution and provides more interactions, for example, speech and advisory skills like personal financial management.

6) **Data-Driven:** Data has become the latest talk of the town which influence decision-making framework. Banks use the data-by-data analytics to give or informed better decision so that they serve their customer in better way; the financial institution is providing customized financial advice after analyzing a huge volume of data. Through data research, they can also provide customized investment plan, different types of loans, and other benefits.

7) **Customer Support:** All the services of banking depend open the customers. Customer support includes answering to customer's questions and complaints on time through

face-to-face meetings, telephone, fix, mail, SMS, or call. Today, existing or new customers require quick and error-free services. Banks have lots of competitors; banks encourage their staff members, pay attention toward staff, give customer relationship award, and also motivate staff members to improve the customer support.

8) **Digitalization:** Digital banking is also called internet banking or online banking. It means adoption of technology, which convert data in digital form. ICICI bank was the first bank in India who offer internet banking in the year 1956. Digitalization reduces human error and also saves the time of customer; then, it is builds customer loyalty. Through chatbots, virtual assistants, analytics tools, and recognition algorithms, digital wallet makes banking easier.

9) **Wealth Management for Masses:** Wealth management is basically dealing with customer's portfolio. Through portfolio investing plans, risk goals, and better opportunities, wealth management basically involves advises and execution of investments to be held for different clients and personal portfolio that can be managed by them.

21.7   Path Ahead Chatbots in Banking

Banks in India are acquiring latest technology in order to achieve proficiency in operational banking. New technology and trends make banking easier; it helps in trimming in cost of operation and finer financial control. Banks are accruing different chatbots and virtual assistants by these features chatbots that are serving in real-time communications and handling customer interrogations and other aspects of occupation to boost overall customer satisfaction.

Interactive Voice Response Systems (IVRS): It is a technology which is intact to their customer on telephone, limiting the role of the bank's representative and creating self-service opportunities for customers. It not only saves time of banking activities but also makes banking process more convenient, accurate, and error free. For the last few decade, IVRS system used a pre-recorded voice, and customers were required telephone keypads to record their voice which take caller to appropriate agent; nowadays, it is completely changed and it is now without any agent. It facilitates account summary/transaction status, service request, fraud notification/lost card, overdraft facilities, loan facilities, product information, payment processing, and many more.

Moving from mobile banking to conversational banking

Mobile Banking		Conversational Banking
Mobile App	Channel	Messaging APP* WhatsApp, Facebook Messenger, Telegram, WeChat...
Graphic User Interface (GUI) Based on icons, menus and click	User Interface	Conversational User Interface (CUI) Voice, or text-based
Digital Customers	Target Customers	Digital & Under-Digitalized Customers Heavy users of messaging apps e.g Millennials
Information and Transactions	Main Services In Scope	Information, Caring and Advisory (+ Transactions)
UX Designers Mobile App Developers	Kay Talents for Success	Language & Voice Interaction Experts, AI Experts
Appstore presence, Functional coverage, Compelling UI, Easy-to-use UX	Differentiation Factors Among Banks	Channel presence, Language understanding ability, Personalized CUI (tone of voice...)

SOURCE: Accenture © February 2018 The Financial Brand

*Subject to availability of branded channels and end2end privacy protection

Chatbots: A chatbot is a piece of software that can have a conversation with human being. They listen to their problems and respect with relevant information. It can be in farm of voice and text. It can also act on requests that require action such as sending payments and changing passwords; it also tells our account balance, fetches, or statements. Different chatbots are used by different bank; some of these are as follows:

> ➢ Erica-Bank of America
> ➢ Amen bot - American express
> ➢ Eva - HDFC BANK
> ➢ Amy - HSBC Bank (Hong Kong)
> ➢ Alexi - Siri by Google
> ➢ Abhi - Andhra Bank

➤ SIA - State bank of India and many others through chat bot banks are able to understand each customer.

- **Alexa, Siri, or Google Home Assistants:** Home assistants are uplifted slowly and will soon become a part of every house as much as anything else. The experience of having a Jarvis-like (from Iron Man) system in the house would really strike at the core of the conversational experience. Linking that to manage your bank accounts, fund transfers, etc., and availing banking services can literally be a walk in the park.
- **Blockchain:** Blockchain is basically used for money changing, record keeping, and other back function. According to Panagariya [5] it changes all the paper-intensive international trade in electronic decentralization, which enable to access a single source of information, reduce fraud in the financial market, and track all documentation. Banking system in the world works on centralized database system; if hackers attack, they can get all data, but blockchain would get rid of some of current cybercrimes.

21.8 Advantage of Artificial Intelligence in Banking Sector

Source: NetGuardians.

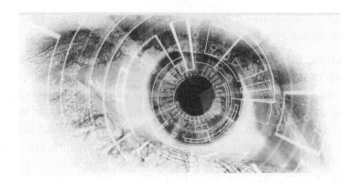

21.9 Types of Risks and Threats Associated With Banking

Technical committee has been constituted in August 2012 by the Reserve bank to study the issues of risk in e-banking and provide recommendations. The chairman **Mr. Vijay Chugh (August 2012)** examined the risk and threats in e-banking transactions. It is panic that with the expansion of e-commerce and net banking, the deceptive fund freaking through credit cards have been increased extremely. **Indumathi (2014)** studied that e-banking is a cost-effective and efficient delivery channel among traditional banking channels. The ITC proves to be a significant tool in online banking to control the risks.

21.10 Nature of Risks in Wireless Banking

1. Operational Risk	Operational risk is defined as transactional risk with online banking. **Indumathi (2014)** described that Operational risk captures the in accurate processing of transactions, unable to enforce legal contracts, redundant data, unauthorized access of bank's system. Operational risk has been found in banking due to the flaws in pattern, execution, and observed process of banks' management information system (MIS).

2. Security Risk Security Risk: I	SP provides flow of data with unrestricted access of online banks at high bandwidth. Banks must ensure security firewall and encryptions for all those financial transactions to frame a secured and user-friendly web-space for the customers. **Nadagoudar (2014)** illustrated that security is a key issue in online banking. Virtual banks are likely to offer the logical and physical security with data privacy to protect customer data from online risk. There is a rationalized and well-run risk control system which provides a preventive and corrective measures to maintain the integrity of banking management information system
3. Authentication and Non-repudiation	Authentication and non-repudiation is an additional issue in e-banking. Indian banking sector implemented the symmetric means private key and symmetric means public/private key with cognitive technology to secure messages and to authenticate parties. Asymmetric encryption has two keys. **1. Public key and 2. Private Key. Digital signature** is the most reliable techniques in banks to act as virtual banks.
E-Banking Threats	
The Basel Committee Electronic Banking Group (EBG) (2001) has explained various principles for fraud management in online banking. The Network Cyber Security threats in online banking are as follows:	
1. Phishing	**Kumbhar (2011)** identified Phishing as the center stage of Internet Scams. Several unauthorized organizations are in random practice of sending e-mails; claim as authorized can attempt to trick the customers through their false websites. The customers' valuable information can be captured by the false websites for their deceptive purposes.

2. Skimming	"Trend and Progress of Banking" report in India (2013) explained threats of SKIMMING in IT-enabled banking. It is a card swipe device which reads the details of a customer's ATM card. **Scammers** are usually trap into the ATM and can swipe the valuable information of the specific customers. Scammers encode the complete hack information on blank card with PIN by a tiny camera installed on the ATM machines.
3. Spoofing	**Chavan (2013)** identified that unauthorized individual usually misleads the customers to trick on them which are related to incompatible security decisions. **Spoofing** includes the setup of forged ATM machines by some hackers to get the customers PIN with entire information for erroneous transactions.
4. Credit Card	**Frauds Mohamed (2013)** illustrated in his research paper that credit card fraud is becoming extensive in current scenario; it means theft from banks and customers. RBI Report on Technological Up gradation in the Banking Sector (2013) explained that the credit card is made of three plastic sheets of polyvinylchloride. The central sheet is known as the core stock. The credit card contains valuable information of customers and has specific size. **The credit cards frauds:** 1. Authentic cards can be manipulated and altered. 2. Counterfeit cards can be created. 3. Fake mobile massaging, calls, and unauthorized use of credit cards are irregular practice. 4. Fraudulent tools are applied to get the genuine cards in the names of other persons.

Source: Network Cyber Security & E-Banking Threats.

21.11   Advent of Information Technology in Indian Banking Sector

PEST Analysis in Banking
Mckinsey research report (2013) described that banking sector in India has been constantly moving toward the development of emerging technological changes in banking operations and services. Banks play a pivotal role through improved e-banking technologies to reduce cost and time and enhance the customer satisfaction as well as customer retention. Information technology provides the flow of information for CBS bank branches and online transactions. Development in information technological tools for banking provides faster data leading with faster judgment and decision-making on customers and employees both.

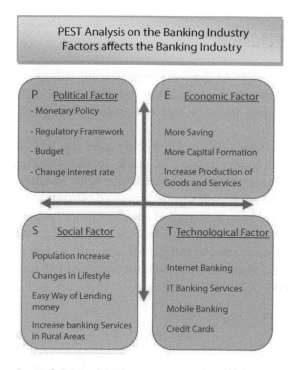

Source: Mckinsey Research Report (2013).

21.12   Future Scope of AI

There is no doubt that banking industry will be run by AI, but it is only feasible when banking sector is able to manage the security risk of AI system. Along with the growth of AI, hacker's growth is also increasing accordingly. To stay ahead from hackers, cyber security will be needed and become more advance in that. Banking and finance industry have a several benefits from AI like accuracy, costs cuts, reduction in human error, identifying irregularities or pattern in transaction, reducing money laundering, or making data analytics easy through AI.

AI is in the plans for the future of banking as it brings the power of advance coadding data analytics; highly advance digital assistants can help with all kinds of financial transactions; through global banking, every transaction can be dealt and tracked from any part of the world. AI focuses on building smart machine that behaves like human. As per Wright [6] the major future trends that control the financial sector will be "Customer Intelligence". It will be the main factor to generate revenue and growth.

21.13   Conclusion

To conclude, through AI, banking organization will be able to open up participants for new business models and then serves client better. It will reshape the banking industry and also freeing their employee's time for high level work.

Banking plays major role in the world's economy. AI helps in customer relationship management, helps in quick decision-making process, and also helps to enhance efficiency level. It also helps in understanding what the needs are and what needs to be improved. Through different applications, banks are able to understand each customer requirement and give them correct offers. It is necessary that each financial transaction must be appropriately documented to mitigate frauds, and AI has ability to reduce human errors and also minimize banking fraud. AI will give new height to banking industry in future.

References

1.   Shannon, C., XXII. Programming a computer for playing chess. *Philos. Mag.*, 41, 314, 256–275, 1950. https://vision.unipv.it/IA1/Programming aComputerforPlayingChess.pdf

2. OECD, *Recommendation of the Council on Artificial Intelligence*, OECD, Paris, pp. 1–11, 2019. https://legalinstruments.oecd.org/en/ instruments/ oecd-legal-0449

3. UW, *History of AI*, University of Washington, History of Computing Course (CSEP590A), University of Washington, Berkeley, https://courses. cs.washington.edu/courses/csep590/06au/projects/history-ai.pdf, 2006.

4. Turing, A. M., Computing machinery and intelligence, in: *Parsing the Turing Test*, pp. 23–65, Springer, Dordrecht, German, https://doi. org/10.1007/978-1-4020-6710-5_3, 1950.

5. Panagariya, A., E-commerce, WTO and Developing Countries, United Nations Conference on Trade and Development. *Policy Issues in International Trade and Commodities*; Study series; no. 2, pp. 1–24, United Nations Publication, Geneva, 2000.

6. Wright, S., Characterization of E-commerce Revenue: the Final OECD Report Revealed, vol. 22, no. 14, pp. 1671–1712, Tax Notes International, OECD Publications Service, Paris, France, April 2001.

22

Effectiveness of E-HRM Tools Using the Functionalities of Artificial Intelligence During Remote Working in Lockdown Period

Nidhi Saxena[1]* and Aditi R. Khandelwal[2]

[1]School of Business and Management, Jaipur, India
[2]IIS University, Jaipur, India

Abstract

The world's response to COVID-19 has changed how we work and the need for technology to link workers at all levels within an organization. It is also important that leadership listens to employees and acts to respond. The one way through which we can link a whole workforce and see what are their needs is through artificial intelligence (AI).

The incorporation of AI into human resource (HR) activities would strengthen companies because they can observe, forecast, and diagnose these technologies to help HR teams make better choices.

AI can be incorporated in such functions as hiring, training, onboarding, tracking performance, retention, etc. However, due to the cost constraints, most of the companies still lag behind in incorporating AI into their HR operations. Implementing AI should be looked as an opportunity, as AI improves lives, makes wok effective, and promotes optimized use of resources. AI pitches a better future prospect, if understood clearly, implemented effectively and used appropriately.

The evolution and upgrades in AI and machine learning are rapidly entering the mainstream. This has led to a major change around the world in how people communicate with technology and their teams.

The main aim of this study is to analyze different approaches and practices used by corporates and organization in the field of Electronic HRM with the integration of AI. How the organizations have used the tools of AI-enabled HR practices

*Corresponding author: nidssaxena00@gmail.com

S. Balamurugan, Sonal Pathak, Anupriya Jain, Sachin Gupta, Sachin Sharma, Sonia Duggal (eds.)
Impact of Artificial Intelligence on Organizational Transformation, (387–398) © 2022 Scrivener Publishing LLC

to engage, manage, and optimize employee performance during the "work from home scenario" and how did the above tools help in business continuity have been the major focus of this study.

Keywords: Artificial Intelligence (AI), COVID-19, Electronic HR management (EHRM), machine learning, business continuity, lockdown, employee engagement

22.1   Introduction

The lockdown situation in the nation due to COVID-19 pandemic has impacted lives and livelihood on many in the nation.

Although the lockdown measure seems important to control the spread of novel corona virus infection, the side effects of the same has spelled major problems for some people and industries.

The impacts have been huge due to disruption in business continuity small as well as large businesses. The major impacts have been witnessed in manufacturing, retail, real estate, etc., to even brick and mortar shops and small-time businesses.

The COVID-19 situation has largely bought miseries for many, but for many industries and sectors, it has also bought opportunities in many aspects.

Companies and corporates have evolved into alternative and innovative ways of doing business. Digital inclusion has been a thing since many years, but it has proven to be a winner and important aspect of driving business continuity in the tomes of lockdown when traditional ways of doing business were restricted.

In all these times, the employees of these organization have been relentlessly working and driving business continuity and minimizing disruptions. The organizations have mobilized the workforce with optimum and resourceful staffing practices and making enough facilitating the employees to work from home efficiently.

Remote working practice or popularly known as "work from home" was an ongoing practice for few sectors like IT and ITES, advertising, analytics, and rating agencies, but for majority of the industries like BPOs, automobile, retail, and finance, it was novel practice and new to their way of work.

More than the employees, it was a challenging task for the employers to arrange the IT infrastructure and other connectivity solutions for the employees working from home. But gradually people succeeded in doing so.

Work from home during lockdown had given companies and employees both the option to continue with their day-to-day activities and drive the business of the company much to the normal.

22.1.1   Artificial Intelligence in Electronic HR Management

Artificial intelligence (AI) tool will and have become the major drivers in managing the HR through Electronic HRM (E-HRM).

The major constituents of the E-HRM will have a lot of inclusion of AI and machine learning. Many aspects of HR are and will be driven by the AI tool and its usage will depend upon the sector or industry where it is used.

AI can have big impact in the way each business function operates. Since machine learning technologies are continuously evolving, and regular innovations are happening in the technology, the effectiveness and productivity of the HR function relies on the optimized and efficient mix of AI technologies with human resource (HR) function.

Job seekers and employees can enjoy a more intuitive, personal and simple HR experience through AI-powered automated systems. In the HR and the recruitment industry, there are various trends and applications for AI that respond to talent recruitment, candidate selection and recruiting growth, interviews and meetings, as well as contact with employees.

Below are major beneficiary processes of AI in HR:

22.1.1.1   Prospective Employee Engagement and Development

The intent procedure to hire a prospective candidate can be automated to provide a better and real time experience for the candidate. Keeping the candidate informed on the application status, stage of the application, which helps to maintain a contact with the candidate and thus helps reduce the ambiguity and anxiety of the prospect.

After recruitment also, such contact with the employee is very important for the onboarding process. AI tools can automate the updating of records, new information regarding the employee, employee profile, and other such tasks which needs minimal human intervention.

AI function can also be used for retrieving information, through bots and other digital virtual interfaces. Depending upon the degree of the employee query and problems, the system decides when to depute a manual intervention for the resolution of the employee issues and problems by scheduling required interactions.

AI can also maintain the timeline legacy and future scheduling of the tasks which requires the HR intervention and actions.

22.1.1.2 Employee Training

During their initial phase with the company, new hires would require training, orientation, and support. AI interfaces may use relevant procedures, protocols, rules, and resources to respond the new recruits in real time to common problems and queries. No matter how limited their question might be, AI may serve as a corporate knowledge pool for new employee to use at any time. When the process is overseen by a virtual AI instructor rather than a senior employee, many workers may also find training more relaxed and efficient. This can reduce the burden of productivity and improve personal confidence in asking questions without fear of judgment.

22.1.1.3 Candidate Selection for Recruitment

By asking preliminary questions, AI instruments will gather the information required by the employer. Initial screening procedures for prospective candidates will be carried out by bots and virtual interfaces. This makes sure that the basic requirements have already been met by the time the applicants come in for interviews. This saves HR representative's time in asking certain basic questions and covering these fundamental subjects, leaving them to deal with the more complex, individual screening areas.

22.1.1.4 Development Needs of Employees

AI tools can eventually identify the training and development needs of an existing employee and plan and assign training modules and arrange trainings for the employees. It can create a plethora of combinations for the employees and create novel courses basis identified gaps in the employee working life cycle.

22.2 Literature Review

Anupam Jauhari (2017): In the paper titled "How AI and Machine Learning will impact HR practices today", it shows that HR manager's greatest obstacle is performance appraisal, which ensures the performance review will be calculated on the basis of employee results. Machine learning tools can use Chat Bot to perform all recruitment tasks. AI-activated tools will screen applicants and send emails about acceptance or refusal.

Prasanna Tambe, Peter Cappeli, and Valery Yakubovish (2018): It is clarified in the paper titled "AI in HRM challenges and a way forward" that with its innovations such as decision making, AI mainly equips the human brain for productivity. Amazon used the AI in their company in the year 2018 to make major choices.

In AI, it uses algorithmic approaches which means that the criteria for selection, training, and growth are used based on different algorithms. If these algorithms are once incorporated in the program, then algorithms will run on incorporated base code so that AI can surely have outstanding benefits and is one of the best technologies to be used and hence improving results in sales and sales forecasting as well.

Prashant Srivastava (2018): In the paper titled "The Impact of AI on Strategic HR Decision making", its states that, in reality, determining the performance of an employee manually is very difficult, so that recruitment can be done automatically using AI. The cumulative recruiting time HR spends is primarily to assess the prospect skills. Hence, AI tools can help reduce this time by assessing the skills sets based on various algorithms and provide and optimum shortlist.

Dr. Surbhi Jain (2018): The paper "HRM and AI" demonstrates that HR used to focus on the management of organizational employees but has now gradually shifted its focus to create an organization that adapts to the ever-evolving environment. HR will educate the workers on the latest technology to a better future. HR experts should also be prepared to face threats such as unemployment, inequity, devices that discriminate, and security due to such changes.

Rajeev Bhardwaj (January 5, 2019): In this article titled "Artificial Intelligence is Revolutionizing Recruiting", it was clearly mentioned AI re-forms and revolutionizes all domains of life, including the management of human capital. It can be integrated into processes such as on-boarding, performance evaluation, reviews, training and development, and retention apart from acquiring talent. It helps HR managers to devote more time and resources to mentoring and inspiring employees. The AI support program helps the HR department greatly.

22.3   Objective of the Study

The main aim of this study is to analyze different approaches and practices used by corporates and organization in the field of E-HRM with the integration of AI. How the organizations have used the tools of AI-enabled HR practices to engage, manage, and optimize employee performance during the "work from home scenario" and how did the above tools help in business continuity have been the major focus of this study.

22.4 Research Methodology

Secondary research methods have been used in this chapter like Websites, Journals, Newspapers, Blogs, and Podcasts.

22.5 Impact and Efficiency of AI-Enabled EHRM Tools in Work From Home Scenario Under Lockdown

As India went into total shutdown to contain the spread of the novel coronavirus, businesses are opening up new ways of doing business.

The country has reported many thousands of cases of COVID-19 infection so far, although the number is expected to rise in other countries, given the situation. Indian companies and business leaders have been pulled in various directions in recent weeks as they try to maintain business continuity while keeping their employees secure.

Safety of the employee has been the primary motive of the companies.

Most of the corporates across the nation have taken special provisions for precautions and formed high level teams which has senior executives of the company to monitor and act according to the situation. All offices and factories throughout the country were closed with few exceptions after the nationwide lockout that began in March. Most of the companies moved to a work-from-home way of working, that has certain cons of its own.

To keep the employees focused and motivated is the man focus of the HR and companies in this situation.

AI-enabled E-HRM tools have contributed hugely into keeping the employees engaged, accountable, traceable, and having optimized work efficiency.

   a. **Online attendance system/portal:** Most of the organizations have created the remote and online attendance system to keep the employees connected and payroll running. It helps to track the employee's availability and effectiveness.
   b. **Health declaration system:** Companies have created online health declaration and health assessment system so as to

keep the track of employee health during the pandemic time. Employees are required to record their daily temperature and submit questions related to health on daily basis. Based on the answers, the online system assesses the need and measures for the employee and creates a response mechanism for the same.

c. **Contact tracing tool using Bluetooth and location features of phone:** Few organizations have created certain apps and online tools which could state the employee health status basis their categorized responses track their proximity to each other using the Bluetooth and location features of the phone. This app can help in alerting the employees if anyone around in their companies ecosystem is facing health issues, or have reported any symptoms or if someone is tested positive for COVID-19.

d. **Online reward and recognition system:** Companies have extensively used the online reward and recognition system to keep the employees engaged by recognizing their efforts basis certain work and tasks assigned to them. Managers have created an extensive system of creating assignment modules and to track the progress of the same. Based on the task achievement, the employees have been recognized ad appreciated on the reward and recognition portal and system and rewarded with online shopping vouchers, coupons, etc.

e. **Online engagement modules:** Organization have organized certain online engagement initiatives like family day, quiz contests, treasure hunts, and many other such innovative engagement ideas to engage with the employees and keep them motivated and energetic. All these activities have been carried out through online interactive tools.

f. **Online awareness and situation portal:** Companies have set up portals which are continuously updated with guidelines, guidance on how employees can stay healthy, answers to coronavirus FAQs, and the company's actions. Companies are still using other methods of contact, such as e-mails and webcasts, like doctor webcasts, to exchange details about how to defend against the virus and what to do if there are symptoms.

g. **Online learning portals:** Companies have created online learning portals where many courses and modules have been created and uploaded by the HR for employee up skill. Workshops and webinars have been conducted on internal portals to keep the workforce motivated and engaged. These webinars share tips on how to collaborate in a remote environment and be productive.

h. **Online performance management:** Employee performance management and appraisals have been conducted through online performance management tools. Employees have self-assessed their own performance and submitted the same for appraisal by the manager. Managers conducted one-to-one discussion with employees and submitted their view on employee performance and appraised their performance. Hence, the entire process has been contactless and yet extensive and productive.

i. **Online interaction modules:** Many companies have created online interaction modules and platforms wherein employees can interact, discuss, and keep themselves and others posted about the updates and can indulge in fun activates and social networking within company environment.

j. **Product training and development:** Online self-help modules have been created so that employees can get more knowledge about the products and processes of the companies. Formal trainings have also been included on such platforms wherein new development and updates regarding the product and processes have been trained.

When employees work from home, there is a sense of isolation, because we are all social beings. To prevent this, managers and companies are required to check in with staff frequently and look out for their well-being.

Focused HR leaders and EHRM activities will help companies handle the epidemic situation as the coronavirus is taking over the planet. Improved business management approaches pave the way for greater human and digital work force integration.

The HRM and e-processes therefore need to take into account the following factors:

- Bring new methods and practices on board for simulated work zones.
- Problems of demand-supply, competitiveness, or profitability.

- Devise community and quality improvement strategies in view of the latest disturbances.
- Willing to meet current management criteria and analytics.
- Improve e-learning as a primary method for organizational learning and growth activities.
- Through work from home remote working, managing time, and making employees to autonomously manage projects through an effective tool or mechanism.

The best thing is that companies reacted quickly and managed the unexpected fallout. Many organizations had implemented work from home, adopted travel restrictions, and formed crisis management teams, which enabled them to collaboratively continue their operations.

While this situation was complicated and unprecedented for everyone, those who were previously trained were able to move smoothly. Among these, the large technology firms were ahead of others and quickly turned to remote work for all of their employees. They worked around their pre-existing infrastructure such as cloud data, intra organization messenger groups, remote access to critical resources, and company CRM solutions and could easily be operating remotely. It was a convenient transition for company from physical to remote jobs which was planned well in advance.

22.6 Conclusion

Change is the only constant, and according to the global shift, the organizations that adapt to the new and innovative disruptive changes will survive and grow in the short and long term perspective.

HR and technology must interact deeply. The relationship between humans and machines is being reinvented at work, and there is no single standard approach to effectively handle this transition. Rather, companies need to collaborate with their HR department to adapt the approach to implementing AI at work to meet the evolving needs of their teams all over the world.

Business/HR managers will need to use next-generation human capital management methods in the current scenario to ensure that such disruptive innovations do not impact work and build processes and procedures to ensure that work performance is not affected while taking into account employee well-being. It is time for HR to consider what keeps people motivated, what drives successful organizations, and what makes it possible to completely integrate human ability with technology.

Reading List

1. Bohr, A. and Memarzadeh, K. (Eds.), *Artificial Intelligence in Healthcare*, 1st edition, Copyright Elsevier, Denmark, International, 2020.

2. Huang, M.-H. and Rust, R.T., Artificial Intelligence in Service. *J. Serv. Res.*, 21, 2, 5 February 2018, https://doi.org/10.1177/1094670517752459.

3. Khandelwal, A.R. and Saxena, N., Impact of Work Environment on Employee job Satisfaction. *Res. Rev. Int. J. Multidiscip.*, 4, 4, 37–41, 2019, https://rrjournals.com/past-issue/impact-of-work-environment-on-employee-job-satisfaction/.

4. Berhil, S., Benlahmar, H., Labani, N., A review paper on artificial intelligence at the service of human resources management. *Indones. J. Electr. Eng. Comput. Sci.*, 19, 1, 32–40, 2020, http://doi.org/10.11591/ijeecs.v18.i1.pp32-40.

5. Barani Kumari, P. and Hemalatha, A., Perception towards Artificial Intelligence in Human Resources Management Practices – with Reference to IT Companies in Chennai. *Int. J. Recent Technol. Eng.* 2019.

6. Khandelwal, A.R. and Saxena, N., A Comparative Study of Employee Satisfaction in Automobile Industry. *Our Herit.*, 2019, February-2020, http://archives.ourheritagejournal.com/index.php/oh/issue/archive.

7. Jia, Q., Guo, Y., Li, R., Li, Y., Chen, Y., A Conceptual Artificial Intelligence Application Framework in Human Resource Management. *International Conference on Electronic Business*, 2018, https://aisel.aisnet.org/iceb 2018/91.

8. Verma, R. and Bandi, S., Artificial Intelligence & Human Resource Management in Indian IT Sector. *Proceedings of 10th International Conference on Digital Strategies for Organizational Success*, January 6, 2019, http://dx.doi.org/10.2139/ssrn.3319897.

9. Kalyan Kumar, E.S., Divya, R., Uday Kumar, M., Artificial Intelligence And How It Is Reinventing The Hr –Practices In Making The Organizations More Visible And Competitive. *EPRA Int. J. Multidiscip. Res. (IJMR) - Peer Reviewed Journal*, 6, 6, June 2020.

10. Tambe, P., Cappelli, P., Yakubovich, V., Artificial Intelligence in Human Resources Management: Challenges and a Path Forward. *Calif. Manage. Rev.*, 2019.

11. Jatobáa, M., Santosa, J., Gutierriza, I., Mosconb, D., Odete, P., Evolution of Artificial Intelligence Research in Human Resources. *Proc. Comput. Sci.*, 164, 137–142, 2019, https://doi.org/10.1016/j.procs.2019.12.165.

12. Ashwini, N. and Patil, A., A Study on Artificial Intelligence its Opportunities and Challenges in Human Resource Management. *Int. J. Arts Sci. Humanit.*, 6, 1, August 2018, https://doi. org/10.5281/zenodo.1469459.

13. George, G. and Thomas, M.R., Integration of Artificial Intelligence in Human Resource. *Int. J. Innov. Technol. Exploring Eng. (IJITEE)*, 9, 2, December 2019.

14. Vrontis, D., Christofi, M., Pereira, V., Tarba, S., Makrides, A., Trichina, E., Artificial intelligence, robotics, advanced technologies and human resource management: a systematic review. *Int. J. Hum. Resour. Manag.*, 1–30, 2021.

15. Murgai, A., Role of Artificial Intelligence in Transforming Human Resource Management. Published *Int. J. Trend Sci. Res. Dev.*, 2, 3, 877–881, April 2018, https://doi.org/10.31142/ijtsrd11127.

16. Saxena, A., The Growing Role Of Artificial Intelligence In Human Resource. *EPRA Int. J. Multidiscip. Res. (IJMR) - Peer Reviewed Journal*, 6, 8, August 2020, https://doi.org/10.36713/epra4924.

17. www.hrkatha.com

18. www.thehindu.com

19. economictimes.indiatimes.com

20. www.hrtechnologist.com

21. Heromotocorp.com

Index

Also of Interest

Check out these published and forthcoming titles in the "Artificial Intelligence and Soft Computing for Industrial Transformation" series from Scrivener Publishing

The New Advanced Society
Artificial Intelligence and Industrial Internet of Things Paradigm
Edited by Sandeep Kumar Panda, Ramesh Kumar Mohapatra, Subhrakanta Panda and S. Balamurugan
Forthcoming 2022. ISBN 978-1-119-82447-3

Digitization of Healthcare Data using Blockchain
Edited by T. Poongodi, D. Sumathi, B. Balamurugan and K. S. Savita
Forthcoming 2022. ISBN 978-1-119-79185-0

Tele-Healthcare
Applications of Artificial Intelligence and Soft Computing Techniques
Edited by R. Nidhya, Manish Kumar and S. Balamurugan
Forthcoming 2020. ISBN 978-1-119-84176-0

Impact of Artificial Intelligence on Organizational Transformation
Edited by S. Balamurugan, Sonal Pathak, Anupriya Jain, Sachin Gupta, and Sachin Sharma and Sonia Duggal
Forthcoming 2022. ISBN 978-1-119-71017-2

Artificial Intelligence for Renewable Energy Systems
Edited by Ajay Kumar Vyas, S. Balamurugan, Kamal Kant Hiran Harsh S. Dhiman
Forthcoming 2022. ISBN 978-1-119-76169-3

Artificial Intelligence Techniques for Wireless Communication and Networking
Edited by Kanthavel R., K. Ananthajothi, S. Balamurugan and R. Karthik Ganesh
Forthcoming 2022. ISBN 978-1-119-82127 4

Advanced Healthcare Systems
Empowering Physicians with IoT-Enabled Technologies
Edited by Rohit Tanwar, S. Balamurugan, R. K. Saini, Vishal Bharti and
Premkumar Chithaluru
Forthcoming 2022. ISBN 978-1-119-76886-9

Smart Systems for Industrial Applications
Edited by C. Venkatesh, N. Rengarajan, P. Ponmurugan and S. Balamurugan
Published 2022. ISBN 978-1-119-76200-3

Human Technology Communication
Internet of Robotic Things and Ubiquitous Computing
Edited by R. Anandan. G. Suseendran, S. Balamurugan, Ashish Mishra and
D. Balaganesh
Published 2021. ISBN 978-1-119-75059-8

Nature-Inspired Algorithms Applications
Edited by S. Balamurugan, Anupriya Jain, Sachin Sharma, Dinesh Goyal,
Sonia Duggal and Seema Sharma
Published 2021. ISBN 978-1-119-68174-8

Computation in Bioinformatics
Multidisciplinary Applications
Edited by S. Balamurugan, Anand Krishnan, Dinesh Goyal, Balakumar
Chandrasekaran and Boomi Pandi
Published 2021. ISBN 978-1-119-65471-1

Fuzzy Intelligent Systems
Methodologies, Techniques, and Applications
Edited by E. Chandrasekaran, R. Anandan, G. Suseendran, S. Balamurugan
and Hanaa Hachimi
Published 2021. ISBN 978-1-119-76045-0

Biomedical Data Mining for Information Retrieval
Methodologies, Techniques and Applications
Edited by Sujata Dash, Subhendu Kumar Pani, S. Balamurugan and Ajith
Abraham
Published 2021. ISBN 978-1-119-71124-7

Design and Analysis of Security Protocols for Communication
Edited by Dinesh Goyal, S. Balamurugan, Sheng-Lung Peng and O.P. Verma
Published 2020. ISBN 978-1-119-55564-3

www.scrivenerpublishing.com